The Natural History of the Lewis and Clark Expedition

T0148834

MICHIGAN STATE UNIVERSITY PRESS
RED CEDAR CLASSICS

The Natural History of the Lewis and Clark Expedition

Raymond Darwin Burroughs, Editor

With a New Introduction
by Robert Carriker

Michigan State University Press
East Lansing
1995

All Michigan State University Press books are produced on paper which meets the requirements of American National Standard of Information Sciences—Permanence of paper for printed materials ANSI Z39.48-1984.

Michigan State University Press
East Lansing, Michigan 48823-5202

03 02 01 00 99   2 3 4 5 6 7 8 9

Library of Congress Cataloging-in-Publication Data

Cover art for the Paperback edition is a painting by Olaf Seltzer, "The Lolo Pass," oil on board, number 0137.797. From the Collection of Gilcrease Museum, Tulsa.

All maps were drawn by Antoinette C. Smith.

CONTENTS

FOREWORD

The journals of Meriwether Lewis and William Clark contain the first reliable descriptions of wildlife populations in the areas drained by the Missouri and Columbia rivers.

Dr. Elliott Coues, an eminent ornithologist, in 1876, wrote the following appraisal of the zoological results of the expedition:

"The contribution to zoology made by Lewis and Clarke, though not extensive, shares the interest which attaches to every result of this unprecedented expedition, and assumes, moreover, great importance in the fact that to it we owe our first acquaintance with a large number of species. It represented a decided advance upon the knowledge before possessed of this subject. Lewis and Clarke were the real discoverers, and actually the original describers, of many animals with which their names are seldom associated now in our acquired familiarity with the same species under names subsequently bestowed by others. They were not trained naturalists, nor naturalists at all, excepting in so far as good observers in any new field, keenly alive to the requirements of the case, become naturalists as a matter of course. Unfortunately for themselves, they imposed no scientific names, which throws them out of the case in questions of nomenclature. But their descriptions, characterized by a straightforward simplicity, and in general accurate, suffice for the identification of most of their species, and many of them are the whole basis of scientific terms afterward introduced into the system. These descriptions of physical characters are often accompanied by notices of habits, of geographical distribution, economic importance, etc."[1]

Lewis and Clark devoted much more space in their diaries to mammals and birds than to other classes of animals. They were primarily interested in game species and furbearers because, in the first instance, they were dependent on game for survival and, in the second, furs were a source of wealth. Yet, they did not neglect the small mammals and songbirds; and, among these lesser species, they made some notable discoveries. They must be credited with writing the first detailed descriptions of the grizzly bear, the mule deer, the pronghorn antelope, the Columbian whitetail deer, the Columbian blacktail deer, the kit fox, the Mountain beaver, the prairie dog, the Columbian ground squirrel, the bushytail woodrat, the eastern woodrat, the whitetail jackrabbit, the Oregon bobcat, and Douglas' squirrel. Moreover, it is an established fact that George Ord based his classifications of certain species of western birds and mammals solely upon descriptions contained in these diaries.

The explorers also discovered and wrote original descriptions of the whistling swan, the white-fronted goose, lesser Canada goose, ring-necked duck, the mountain quail, Oregon ruffed grouse, sage grouse, Franklin's grouse, prairie sharp-tailed grouse, Columbian sharp-tailed grouse, western grebe, least tern, great grey owl, American magpie, black-headed (Steller's) jay, Clark's nutcracker, Lewis' woodpecker, Nuttall's poor-will, western meadowlark, white-rumped shrike, western tanager, and the Pacific varied-thrush.

Among the hitherto unknown fishes described in technical detail by Lewis and Clark we find the king salmon, the blue-backed salmon which they called the *red char,* the Yellowstone cut-throat which they called the *mountain trout,* the steel-head trout which they referred to as the *salmon-trout,* the flounder, and the eulachon which was known among the coastal Indians as the *ulken.* In describing these fishes they noted the position of the fins, counted the finrays, and examined the mouth for evidence of vomerine teeth.

Their most notable discoveries among the reptiles include the prairie rattlesnake, the hog-nosed snake, two species of northwestern garter snakes, and the horned-lizard. In each instance cited above they wrote remarkably accurate descriptions based on such structures as, in case of snakes, the number of ventral scutae, the presence or absence of divided caudal scutae, and the shape of the pupil of the eye.

Among the amphibians they commented on the Pacific tree frog, the western cricket frog, the Columbian toad, and the warty salamander. The latter species, however, they referred to as a *water lizzard.*

Their references to insects, crustaceans, and mollusks were generally casual, and none of them was described in detail.

The explorers' journals clearly indicate that they were fully aware of the importance of supplementing their descriptions of plants and animals with specimens. Whenever possible they prepared bird and mammal skins and, in a few cases, preserved skulls of animals of unusual interest. Unfortunately they lacked adequate facilities for properly preserving their collections from insects and moisture. With the exception of the boxes of specimens consigned to President Jefferson from Fort Mandan, almost all of the material collected on the upper Missouri and west of the Rocky Mountains was lost.

The bird and mammal skins which they did succeed in bringing out of the wilderness were deposited, at Thomas Jefferson's suggestion, in Peale's Museum in Philadelphia. It was here that Alexander Wilson, who was then writing his famous book, *American Ornithology,*[2] examined them. Wilson evidently found only three birds in the collection which were new to science; namely, the western tanager, Clark's nutcracker, and Lewis' woodpecker. When the museum was disbanded after Peale's death in 1820, the specimens were scattered. According to Thwaites[3] in 1904, the only remnant of the Lewis and Clark collection which could be definitely identified was in the possession of Charles J. Maynard of Boston. It was Lewis' woodpecker.

Thwaites evidently was not well informed concerning the fate of the zoological specimens in Peale's Museum. However, we can thank Walter Faxon[4] for the following account of what happened to them.

Peale's Museum of Philadelphia, which was the repository of a number of bird specimens originally described by such authorities as Alexander Wilson, George Ord, C. L. Bonaparte, Richard Harlan and Thomas Say, was dissolved in 1846 and the zoological collection was sold at public auction[5] in 1850. One half of the specimens were purchased by Moses Kimball and the other half by P. T. Barnum for his American Museum in New York. Unfortunately, Barnum's acquisitions were destroyed when his Museum burned in 1865. Kimball, on the other hand, deposited his half of the Peale collection in the Boston Museum in 1850. Thereafter, in 1893 and 1899, the Boston Museum transferred these specimens to the Boston Society of Natural History. Then, in 1900 the Boston Society sold its collection of birds to C. J. Maynard who stored them for a time in his barn at Newtonville, Massachusetts.

This collection, which still included many of Wilson's type specimens, was subsequently redeemed by the Boston Society of Natural History. Shortly thereafter most of the birds, to the detriment of their legs and plumage, were wrenched from their stands and packed in tin cases. J. D. Sornborger was, at about this time, employed to examine the collection. Nothing resulted, however, except the loss of the original labels which, for unexplainable reasons, Sornborger removed from the specimens. Finally, in 1914, what remained of the collection was transferred to the Museum of Comparative Zoology.

Wilson, in his *American Ornithology*, usually refers to a Peale Museum specimen by its catalog number at the beginning of his description of each species. Thus, 71 out of 85 of the birds described and named by Wilson are definitely associated with specimens which, at that time, were in Peale's Museum.

Wilson's custom of drawing from mounted specimens affords a clue in some cases for determining whether he drew from a specimen in the Peale Collection, or from a specimen derived from some other source. This holds true only when Wilson drew a bird in an unusual posture for, in such cases, if the specimen and drawing are similar we can be fairly sure that there is a relation between specimen and the sketch. Conversely, nonconformity of specimens and drawings is not conclusive evidence that no relationship exists.

Faxon examined 53 species of birds, now in the collection of the Museum of Comparative Zoology, which were a part of the Boston Museum Collection. Presumably all of them were originally in the Peale Museum, and among them are many type specimens described by Wilson, Ord, Bonaparte, and others of that period. Some of the specimens were collected by the Major Long Expeditions between 1817 and 1823; several were collected by Wilson, himself; and only one, Lewis' Woodpecker, could definitely be attributed to the expedition.

It appears that almost all of the birds collected by the explorers and entrusted to Peale's Museum, must have been acquired by P. T. Barnum rather than Kimball. Otherwise their disappearance cannot be explained.

The Lewis and Clark journals are frequently overlooked as a source of information on primitive wildlife populations. Possibly this is because none of the early editions of the diaries included all of the zoological information contained in the original manuscripts.

Anyone interested in the scientific aspects of the expedition should consult Thwaites' *Original Journals of the Lewis and Clark Expedition* which contains the only complete and unaltered text of the diaries; but unfortunately this eight-volume edition of 1904 is out-of-print, and is not available in all libraries.

How it happened that one hundred years elapsed before the explorers journals and scientific notes were printed exactly as written is a curious but lengthy story. A few of the highlights relating to the history of the manuscript, and the publications which have been based upon them is, however, essential for reappraising the scientific results of the expedition.

In spite of Thomas Jefferson's prodding, it was 1814 before Lewis and Clark's diaries appeared in print. Clark was still looking for a publisher when Lewis met an untimely death in Kentucky in 1809; but, a few months later he persuaded Nicholas Biddle, a young Philadelphia attorney, to put their notes in shape for publication. It appears that Ordway's diary, which Clark had purchased, was included among the manuscripts handed to Biddle on this occasion.[6] Unfortunately, the pressure of business and politics was so great that this brilliant young man found it necessary to abandon the task before completing it. Accordingly, he turned his edited version of the Lewis and Clark journals over to Paul Allen who agreed to do the proof reading and to supervise the press work. This is why Allen's name appears as author of the publication even though he had little or nothing to do with editing the manuscript.

Biddle did a creditable and thorough piece of editing, but he improved the wording, spelling and punctuation to such an extent that the vigor, and sometimes the meaning, of both Lewis' and Clark's writing was lost. He cannot be criticized, however, for having omitted many of the descriptive accounts of plants and animals because he had been advised that Dr. Barton of Philadelphia, who had been given copies of the scientific notes, was authorized to edit and publish them. However, Barton failed to carry out his assignment, and a wealth of information concerning wildlife populations as seen by the explorers was lost to scholars for almost one hundred years.

Following the publication of Biddle's text of the journals by Paul Allen, other edited versions of the diaries were printed. Some of these books gave authentic accounts of the expedition, but others were spurious.[7]

In 1893, Elliott Coues published an annotated version of Paul Allen's *History of the Expedition* in which he attempted to identify and supply the technical names of all of the animals which the explorers had discussed in greater or lesser detail. Besides, he included much pertinent information dealing with the taxonomy and geographic distribution of many species. Coues was handicapped, however, by the incompleteness of the Biddle text. Nevertheless, his extensive knowledge of the habitat requirements and ranges of western birds and mammals enabled him to give the probable identity of species inadequately described. His *History of the Expedition Under the Command of Lewis and Clark*, four volumes, Francis P. Harper, New York, has served as an important reference in this study.

Sergeant Ordway's journal has been an important supplemental reference; but it omits most of the zoological data, particularly the detailed descriptions of most of the mammals and birds. On the other hand, Ordway sometimes mentions events that Lewis and Clark failed to record, or presents a somewhat different point of view regarding what was seen or done.

Sergeant Gass' diary[8] was not available to the writer; and those of Privates Floyd and Whitehouse, although included in Thwaites' *Original Journals*, added little of consequence concerning wildlife.

Sergeant Pryor's journal was never printed, and no one knows whether it was lost or destroyed.

Bernard DeVoto's book, *The Journals of Lewis and Clark* (published by Houghton Mifflin Company, 1953) was of little value as a reference. Faced with the necessity of cutting the journals to the limitations of a single volume, DeVoto was obliged to omit the entries dealing strictly with plants and animals. He did, however, include many of the passages dealing with game abundance or scarcity, and the most dramatic accounts of the explorer's hunting experiences.

Some of the material quoted will be found in DeVoto's text and some of it in Coues' *History of the Expedition*,[9] but all of it will be found only in Thwaites' *Original Journals of the Lewis and Clark Expedition*. In so far as practicable the explorers speak for themselves. This has been done in the belief that the reader will be more interested in what Lewis and Clark actually wrote than any edited version of what they saw and how they interpreted it.

ACKNOWLEDGMENTS

I am indebted to Dr. Warren W. Chase, Professor of Wildlife Management at the University of Michigan, for suggestions and criticisms concerning the organization and interpretation of the journal entries, and to Dr. William H. Burt of the University's Museum of Zoology for reviewing the chapters which relate to mammals.

I am particularly grateful to Dr. Ira N. Gabrielson of the Wildlife Management Institute and to Dr. Joseph P. Linduska of Remington Farm, Chestertown, Md., for reading the manuscript and making constructive criticisms. And I have valued the encouragement extended me by Professor Ralph T. King of New York State College of Forestry at Syracuse.

Among my associates in the Michigan Department of Conservation I must thank Dr. Donald W. Douglass for giving attention to the chapters which deal with birds; to Dr. George A. Ammann for assisting with the interpretation of descriptive data pertaining to certain gallinaceous species; and to Dr. Justin W. Leonard who provided both criticism and encouragement on numerous occasions. Mrs. Helen Wallin aided me materially in compiling the index and Miss Lillian Laviolette typed the manuscript.

The staff of the Michigan State Library was helpful in making books, periodicals, and reference works available for extended use. For these courtesies I thank Miss Gail Curtis, Mrs Althea Hogan, Miss Mary Armstrong and Mrs. Mary Ellen Marsh of the Library staff.

For the rest, friends and intimates, I do not name. My appreciation is between them and me.

INTRODUCTION TO THE PAPERBACK EDITION

[1995]

It has now been more than three decades since Raymond D. Burroughs edited *The Natural History of the Lewis and Clark Expedition*. The book, which sold for $7.50 on its publication date of May 10, 1961, now commands more than $100 from rare book dealers. When Burroughs researched the Lewis and Clark Expedition, collecting descriptions of the birds and animals encountered by the Corps of Discovery on its twenty-eight month journey to the source of the Missouri River and the mouth of the Columbia River, the only published edition available to scholars was Reuben Gold Thwaites's *Original Journals of the Lewis and Clark Expedition*.[1] Since then more than two dozen monographs have been published on various aspects of the expedition and Gary E. Moulton of the University of Nebraska is currently editing a completely new edition of the original journals, each volume meticulously annotated with the assistance of a cadre of distinguished consulting scholars.[2] It is worth noting that Moulton used *The Natural History of the Lewis and Clark Expedition* as a reference source in each of the eight volumes that record Lewis's and Clark's day-to-day entries for the entire journey.

Thomas Jefferson made it eminently clear to Meriwether Lewis that the exploring expedition for which he had recently petitioned $2,500 from Congress would include a scientific component as well as objectives in geography, commerce, and diplomacy. The president considered himself an amateur biologist and paleontologist and therefore included in his instructions to Lewis a request for information on "the animals of the [Western] country generally, & especially those not known in the U.S." If there were remains or accounts of any animals "which may be deemed rare or extinct," he wished to know that, too.[3] In order to prepare Lewis to make such observations, the president had him briefly tutored in the intricacies of natural history by Dr. Benjamin Smith Barton, Professor of Botany at the University of Pennsylvania and a luminary in the American Philosophical Society. Lewis almost certainly also visited Charles Willson Peale's Museum, a cluster of unexplained fossils, hundreds of miscellaneous "quadruped" skeletons, and approximately 1,800 stuffed birds. Later, Jefferson himself instructed Lewis in the techniques of taxidermy.

William Clark shared equal command of the Corps of Discovery with Lewis, and a congenial division of labor soon formed. Clark excelled at making maps, for example, and Lewis was the better naturalist. For the most part, each man took responsibility in the expedition for what he did best.

With quill pens and home-made ink, Lewis wrote wonderfully lucid descriptions of commonly known birds and animals. He could also be quite specific when cataloguing specimens he believed were new to science. In the interest of scholarship he once filled the bill of a pelican with five gallons of water in order to determine the capacity of its pouch. On other occasions he painstakingly counted the scuta on poisonous snakes and the gills on fish. He even speculated on the size of a grizzly bear's testicles! At Fort Clatsop on the Oregon coast, when dreary winter weather forced Lewis inside his cabin for long periods, he wrote lengthy "animal biographies" on thirty-seven mammals, fifty-six birds, four reptiles, and eleven fishes with which he had thus far come into contact during the exploration. Many scientists and historians credit Lewis with being the first explorer to describe western animals in a language sufficiently detailed and technical to benefit modern naturalists.

The untimely death of Lewis three years after the expedition's return to St. Louis, as Burroughs points out in his "Foreword," seriously altered both Clark's and Jefferson's timetable for the publication of the original journals. Worse, most of Lewis's botanical and zoological notes were left in the hands of Barton, his one-time tutor, and thus were virtually unavailable when Clark eventually persuaded Nicholas Biddle to write a history of the expedition using the original journals. The two-volume narrative that appeared in 1814 from Biddle's pen contained very little scientific material.[4]

Apparently, Lewis intended for Barton to edit a scientific volume on the results of the expedition, but the aging scientist died in December of 1815 with none of the work done. Hearing the news, Jefferson lamented that "the papers respecting natural history & geography of the country" might never be published.[5] Jefferson recovered several parcels of notes from Mrs. Barton, but, unfortunately, not as many as Lewis had given her husband. Eventually, Jefferson deposited all of the Lewis and Clark expedition material he could assemble in the vaults of the American Philosophical Society in Philadelphia for safekeeping.

For three-quarters of a century Biddle's narrative formed the only link between public curiosity and the Lewis and Clark expedition. A few select scientists made references to Lewis's contributions, but otherwise the natural history of the expedition remained little known. George Ord, for example, used Biddle's text to write the zoological section of William Guthrie's *A New Geographical, Historical, and Commercial Grammar*, but he did not specifically credit Lewis with discovering certain species.[6]

Sixty years passed before another naturalist developed an abiding interest in the expedition's scientific results. Dr. Elliott Coues, a respected ornithologist and army surgeon, appreciated Lewis's efforts, but, at the same time, he did not consider the explorer's description of flora and fauna adequate for true scientists.[7] In an attempt to correct that flaw Coues wrote "An Account of the Various Publications Relating to the Travels of Lewis and Clarke [sic] with a Commentary on the Zoological Results of the Expedition" for the *Bulletin* of the United States Geological and Geographical Survey of the Territories.[8] Coues not only gained respect for Lewis's scholarship during the course of this investigation, completely reversing his earlier opinion, his annotations also became the basis for an extensive set of footnotes he prepared for a new edition of Biddle's narrative in 1893.[9] Coues's lavish notes greatly enhanced Biddle's otherwise sparse references to topics of natural history and gave new life to a tired narrative. The extensive and often gregarious notes also extended Biddle's two-volume work into four volumes. Fortunately for readers, Coues indexed his 1,200-page work.

In 1901 the American Philosophical Society undertook to publish the original journals of the Lewis and Clark Expedition under the guidance of Reuben Gold Thwaites, an experienced and successful editor. With the publication in 1904-5 of this eight-volume edition, Lewis's notes on the flora and fauna of the Louisiana Purchase territory—the ones Mrs. Barton returned to Jefferson—came to light at last with all their original spelling, unique grammar, and, most important, their perceptive insights. Thwaites, however, annotated the original journals modestly, employing nether the enthusiasm nor the eloquence of Coues in his footnotes. As a result, it still required a great deal of searching for an individual researcher to establish a composite picture of specific mammals, birds, fishes, or reptiles identified by Meriwether Lewis during the course of his 8,000-mile journey. Moreover, it remained virtually impossible for either scientists or historians to distinguish which of the species and subspecies identified by Lewis and Clark had been previously unknown to nineteenth century scientists.

During the first half of the twentieth century only a few scholars investigated the zoological contributions of the Lewis and Clark expedition. Indeed, only two made genuine advancements: Walter Faxon and Elijah H. Criswell. Faxon, a Harvard zoologist, listed the birds noted during the Lewis and Clark expedition that had once been assigned to Charles Wilson Peale's Philadelphia museum and subsequently acquired by Harvard University's Museum of Comparative Zoology.[10] Elijah H. Criswell included in his 1940 book, *Lewis and Clark: Linguistic Pioneers*, a useful zoological index to discoveries made by the co-leaders.[11] All other academic inquirers in the field of zoology either limited themselves to birds in North Dakota and Idaho,[12] dismissed Lewis and Clark as scientific lightweights,[13] or merely repeated the research of Coues and Faxon.[14]

Raymond Darwin Burroughs (1899-1976), or "Dar" as his friends knew him, read Thwaites's edition of the journals in 1947 while working on some comparative research dealing with plants. Intrigued by the wealth of botanical and zoological data contained in the explorers' daily entries, he set about to learn all he could about the Corps of Discovery. In the process Burroughs became so learned about the expedition that in 1953 the Detroit Historical Society bestowed on him its highest honor, an invitation to deliver the Lewis Cass Lecture. Burroughs's presentation later appeared under the title *Exploration Unlimited: The Story of the Lewis and Clark Exploration.*[15] For the next several years Burroughs continued his research on the expedition, this time specifically targeting its zoological achievements. What began as a tabulation of game killed by the expedition eventually blossomed into *The Natural History of the Lewis and Clark Expedition.*

Burroughs was born in Iowa but spent most of his formative years on a farm in central Nebraska. A promising student, he took an undergraduate degree in biology from Nebraska Wesleyan University in 1924 and continued his education at Princeton University where he earned a master's degree in zoology. For eleven years Burroughs taught biology, first at Willamette University in Oregon, then at

Oklahoma City University, and, finally, at Macalester College in Minnesota. In 1937 Burroughs abandoned his college teaching career and joined the staff of the Game Division of the Michigan Department of Conservation. From 1949 until his retirement in 1965, Burroughs served as an administrator in the department's conservation education division. In this position he managed teacher training and education programs for the department. In addition, for fifteen years Burroughs wrote a delightful, popular column on the inside back page of the bimonthly magazine, *Michigan Conservation*.[16] His other articles appeared in *American Forests, Natural History, Nature Magazine, Michigan History*, and the *Journal of Wildlife Management*.

The Natural History of the Lewis and Clark Expedition consists of a fifty-one page introduction retracing the course of the expedition followed by eighteen topical chapters on the first faunal discoveries in the Louisiana Territory: mammals, birds, fishes, reptiles, and amphibians. As a trained scientist, Burroughs organized his chapters around the sequence of species generally accepted by zoologists for taxonomic works, interlacing his commentary with geographically localized quotations. The principal quotations come, of course, from Lewis and Clark, but there are also observations by frontier scientists John Bradbury, J. K. Townsend, and Prince Alexander Philip Maximilian.

The book was widely reviewed and immediately recommended by the scholarly communities of two disciplines, natural science and history. Writers in such publications as the *Quarterly Review of Biology*, the *Journal of Mammalogy*, the *Journal of Wildlife Management*, and *Atlantic Naturalist* praised the book for its taxonomic accuracy. One botanist called the volume a "card catalogue in book form of the vertebrate populations encountered from bears and buffaloes to *Bufo*." Historians appreciated Burroughs's painstaking research as he compiled large numbers of chronological references in Lewis and Clark's journals into succinct topical chapters. *Idaho Yesterdays* devoted four pages of its journal to a comprehensive review essay; the *Oregon Historical Quarterly*, the *William Mary Quarterly*, and other academic journals offered shorter, but no less approving, remarks.

This is not to say that Burroughs's volume is flawless. The title, for example, is misleading because the text contains material only on vertebrate zoology. Certainly, the reader would have benefited from some illustrations and several maps. Perhaps Burroughs should also have presented supporting material from other well-known pioneer naturalists, possibly adding quotes from the writings of Thomas Nuttall, Thomas Say, and George Ord. The only critical comment, however, that can be made with certainly about Raymond D. Burroughs's research is that he consistently misspelled the names of both Lewis's dog and Maximilian, Prince of Wied. When Burroughs readied *The Natural History of the Lewis and Clark Expedition* for press in 1961 the name of the Newfoundland dog that accompanied the expedition was variously represented as "Scannon" or "Scamon," but never "Scammon," as Burroughs has it. Since 1987 we know that the correct name is actually Seaman.[17] Similarly, Alexander Philip Maximilian, Prince of Wied-Neuwied, did not spell his last name "Maximillian." In addition,

Pierre Dorion is misspelled "Durion," the Clatsop leader Comowooll is more properly Chief Coboway, and modern scholars use Sacagawea rather than Sacajawea, though there is still controversy about the proper pronunciation and spelling—is it a Shoshone or Hidatsa word?—of Lewis's "Bird Woman." In a lapse of memory, Burroughs says in the "Foreword" that Lewis met his untimely death in Kentucky when, in fact, he died at Grinder's Mill in Tennessee.

After the publication of *The Natural History of the Lewis and Clark Expedition*, Burroughs turned briefly to an investigation of botanical items noted in the original journals. Apparently, however, he did not find as much to interest him as he did in the zoological references for he produced only one article, "The Lewis and Clark Expedition's Botanical Discoveries," which appeared in the January 1966 issue of *Natural History* magazine.[18]

Returning to the zoological elements of the expedition that he knew so well, Burroughs began work on a new book that he tentatively titled *Game Trails of Lewis and Clark*. A portion of this manuscript appeared as his final article, "Lewis and Clark in Buffalo Country," in *We Proceeded On*, the official publication of the Lewis and Clark Trail Heritage Foundation.[19] In 1974 "Dar" Burroughs received the Award of Meritorious Achievement from that organization at its annual meeting.

After his retirement from the Michigan Department of Conservation, Burroughs relocated to Fayetteville, New York, the home of his daughter, Mrs. William B. Norris. He died at the age of 77 on October 31, 1976. Mrs. Norris retains all of her father's research files and publications, a considerable body of material, and she has enthusiastically supported the writing of this introduction and the republication of *The Natural History of the Lewis and Clark Expedition*.[20]

The success of Burroughs's book encouraged other scholars to examine additional aspects of natural history in the Lewis and Clark expedition. The year after the publication of *The Natural History of the Lewis and Clark Expedition*, Donald Jackson edited his *Letters of the Lewis and Clark Expedition* and included in it a "trial list" of mammals and birds which Lewis and Clark identified that were new to science.[21] He counted twenty-five mammals and sixteen birds. Burroughs had not concentrated on such matters.

The next person to exhibit a sustained interest in the natural history of the expedition was another botanist, Dr. Paul R. Cutright, Professor of Botany at Beaver College in Pennsylvania. Early in his academic career Cutright wrote about Theodore Roosevelt's western experience, but, beginning in 1967, he devoted a considerable amount of his energy and talent to the field of Lewis and Clark scholarship.[22] His major research is contained in *Lewis and Clark: Pioneering Naturalists*, published in 1969 and reprinted twenty years later. Chronological in organization, rather than topical, *Pioneering Naturalists* recreated the journey across the continent and, at the end of each chapter, listed all plants and animals new to science.

Cutright viewed the natural history of the expedition in broader terms than Burroughs, including in his volume not only information on flora and fauna but also components of linguistics, geology, ethnography, and medicine. Chief among his goals was to identify the species and subspecies of animals discovered by the expedition. An appendix lists the locality and date where Lewis and Clark collected their information on 122 mammals, fishes, reptiles, and birds, each accompanied by a relevant quotation from Thwaites. It is particularly useful as a supplement to Burroughs's, *Natural History,* and Cutright credits Burroughs's *Natural History* with helping him to compile the list.

Used together, Burroughs's and Cutright's books answer almost every question about the natural history of the Lewis and Clark expedition. For specific animal encounters on specific dates it is also useful to consult the expertly constructed footnotes in Moulton's new edition of the journals inasmuch as his volumes summarize the latest scientific knowledge on every specimen noted by the explorers.

If Raymond Darwin Burroughs could have written his own introduction to the republication of this, his most famous work in the field of natural history, he probably would have included an updated bibliography. I hope it will not seem too presumptuous of me to satisfy that obligation on his behalf. The following is a list of publications relevant to the zoological aspects of the Lewis and Clark expedition that have been written since both Burroughs's and Cutright's books were issued in the 1960s.

Benson, Keith R. "Herpetology on the Lewis and Clark Expedition: 1804-1806." *Herpetological Review* 3 (1978): 87-91.

Christman, Gene M. "The Mountain Bison." *American West* 8 (1971):44-47.

Cutright, Paul Russell, and Michael J. Brodhead. *Elliott Coues: Naturalist and Frontier Historian.* Urbana: University of Illinois Press, 1981.

Hall, E. Raymond. *The Mammals of North America.* 2nd ed. 2 vols. New York: John Wiley and Sons, 1981.

Holmgren, Virginia C. "A Glossary of Bird Names Cited by Lewis and Clark." *We Proceed On* 10 (1984): 28-34

Jones, J. Knox, Jr., David H. Armstrong, Robert S. Hoffmann, and Clyde Jones. *Mammals of the Northern Great Plains.* Lincoln: University of Nebraska Press, 1983.

Kendall, Robert L. "Editorial: Taxonomic Changes in North American Trout Names." *Transactions of the American Fisheries Society* 117 (1988): 321.

Lee, David S., Carter R. Gilbert, Charles H. Hocutt, Robert E. Jenkins, Don E. McAllister, and Jay R. Stauffer, Jr. *Atlas of North American Freshwater Fishes.* Raleigh: North Carolina State Museum of Natural History, 1980.

Osgood, Ernest S. "A Prairie Dog for Mr. Jefferson." *Montana, the Magazine of Western History* 19 (1969): 54-56.

Robert C. Carriker
Gonzaga University
May 1995

INTRODUCTION (1995)

1. Reuben Gold Thwaites, *Original Journals of the Lewis and Clark Expedition,* 8 vols. (New York: Dodd, Mead & Co., 1904-1905).
2. Gary E. Moulton, ed., *The Journals of the Lewis & Clark Expedition,* 11 vols. (Lincoln: University of Nebraska Press, 1986-   ). Volume 1 is an atlas, volumes 2-8 are Lewis's and Clark's day-to-day travel record, and volumes 9-11 contain the journals of other expedition members and natural history material.
3. Thomas Jefferson to Meriwether Lewis, June 20, 1803, in Donald Jackson, ed., *Letters of the Lewis and Clark Expedition with Related Documents, 1783-1854,* 2nd ed., 2 vols. (Urbana: University of Illinois Press, 1978), 1:63.
4. Nicholas Biddle, ed., *History of the Expedition under the Command of Captains Lewis and Clark,* 2 vols. (Philadelphia: Bradford & Inskeep, 1814).
5. Thomas Jefferson to José Corrèa da Serra, January 1, 1816 in Jackson, *Letters,* 2:608.
6. William Guthrie, *A New Geographical, Historical, and Commercial Grammar,* 2 vols. (Philadelphia: Johnson and Warner, 1815).
7. Paul R. Cutright, *Lewis and Clark: Pioneering Naturalists* (Urbana: University of Illinois Press 1969; Lincoln: University of Nebraska Press, 1989), 397.
8. Elliott Coues, "An Account of the Various Publications Relating to the Travels of Lewis and Clarke [sic] with a Commentary on the Zoological Results of the Expedition," The United States Geological and Geographical Survey of the Territories *Bulletin,* ser. 2, no. 6 (Washington, February 6, 1876), 417-44.
9. Elliott Coues, ed., *History of the Expedition under the Command of Lewis and Clark,* 4 vols. (New York: Francis P. Harper, 1893).
10. Walter Faxon, "Relics of Peale's Museum," Museum of Comparative Zoology *Proceedings* 59 (1915): 18-32.
11. Elijah H. Criswell, *Lewis and Clark: Linguistic Pioneers* (Columbia: University of Missouri Studies, 1940).
12. Russell Reid and Clell G. Gannon, "Birds and Mammals Observed by Lewis and Clark in North Dakota," *North Dakota Historical Quarterly* 1 (1927): 14-36; M. Jollie, "The Birds Observed in Idaho by the Lewis and Clark Expedition, 1804-1806," *Murrelet* 34 (1953): 1-5.
13. Roland H. Alden and John D. Ifft, "Early Naturalists in the Far West," California Academy of Sciences *Occasional Papers* 20 (1943): 1-59.
14. Henry W. Setzer, "Zoological Contributions of the Lewis and Clark Expedition," Washington Academy of Sciences *Journal* 44 (1954): 356-57.
15. Raymond Darwin Burroughs, *Exploration Unlimited: The Story of the Lewis and Clark Exploration* (Detroit: Wayne University Press, 1953).
16. A collection of Burroughs's essays dealing with subjects related to conservation in *Michigan Conservation* was published as *Peninsular Country* (Grand Rapids, Michigan: William B. Eerdmans Publishing Company, 1965).
17. Donald Jackson, *Among the Sleeping Giants* (Urbana: University of Illinois Press, 1987), 43-54; Donald Jackson, "Call Him a Good Old Dog, but Don't Call Him Scannon," *We Proceeded On* 11 (1985): 5-8.
18. Raymond Darwin Burroughs, "The Lewis and Clark Expedition's Botanical Discoveries," *Natural History* 85 (1966): 56-62.
19. Raymond Darwin Burroughs, "Lewis and Clark in Buffalo Country," *We Proceeded On* (1976): 6-8.
20. The writing of this introduction also benefited from the expertise of Miss Sharon Prendergast at Foley Center Special Collections of Gonzaga University, Dr. Gary E.

Moulton of the Center for Great Plains Studies at the University of Nebraska, and George H. Tweney, Seattle, Washington.

21. Jackson, *Letters*, 2:293-98.

22. Paul R. Cutright, "The Odyssey of the Magpie and the Prairie Dog," Missouri Historical Society *Bulletin* 23 (1967): 215-28; Paul R. Cutright, "Meriwether Lewis: Zoologist," *Oregon Historical Quarterly* 69 (1968): 5-28; Paul R. Cutright, *Meriwether Lewis, Naturalist* (Portland: Oregon Historical Society, 1968).

The Natural History of the Lewis and Clark Expedition

1. **June 28, 1804,**
   The Corps of Discovery observed its first buffalo at the mouth of the Kansas River.

2. **August 23, 1804**
   Joseph Fields killed the expedition's first buffalo near the mouth of the Vermillion River.

3. **September 15 and October 18, 1804**
   "I do not think I exagerate when I estimate the number of Buffaloe which could be compreed at one view to amount to 3000," Lewis wrote near the mouth of the White River. A month later, after seeing herds almost daily, Clark said he could still count "in view at one time 52 gangues of Buffalow," at the Cannonball River.

4. **November 13, 1804 - April 7, 1805**
   Hunting was difficult and the expedition at Fort Mandan killed fewer than forty buffaloes

5. **April 22-25,1805**
   Buffalo calves, which the explorers likened to veal, were taken near the Yellowstone River; adult animals were too thin to provide anything more than scraps for sausage, marrow bones, or tongues.

6. **May 9, 1805**
   The buffalo were so numerous-and gentle- above the Milk River that "the men frequently throw sticks and stones at them to drive them out of their way."

7. **June 3-12, 1805**
   The expedition viewed numerous herds of buffalo at the mouth of the Marias River. For a year and 1,231 miles these animals had helped feed the expedition.

8. **July 16, 1805**
   The westward bound expedition shot its last buffalo on July 16, 1805, three days above Great Falls. Lewis breakfasted on the intestines: "here for the first time I ate of the small guts of the buffaloe cooked over a blazing fire in the Indian stile without any preperation of washing or other clensing and found them very good." Not until July 11,1806, will another buffalo be taken.

9. **July 25, 1806**
   Clark said the buffaloes near Pompey's Pillar made "Such a grunting nois which [was such a] very loud and disagreeable Sound that we are compelled to Scear them away before we can Sleep" by firing rifles in the air.

10. **August 29, 1806**
    Near the White River, Clark saw "a greater number of buffalow than I had ever Seen before at one time. I must have Seen near 20,000 of those animals feeding on this plain."

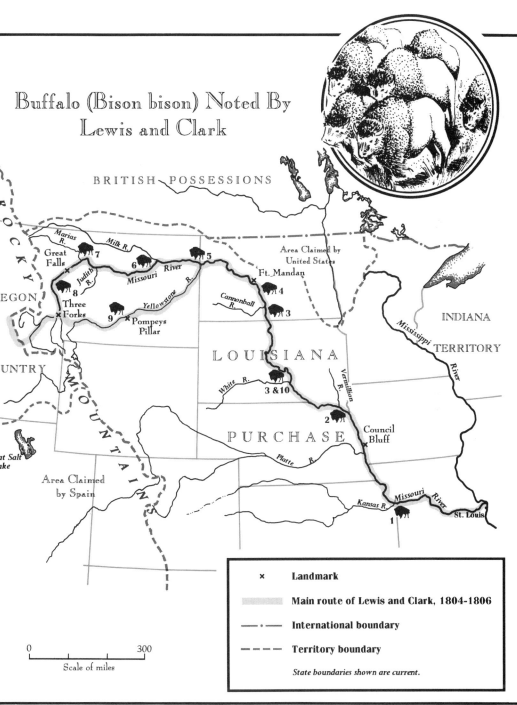

Buffalo (Bison bison) Noted By Lewis and Clark

BRITISH POSSESSIONS

ROCKY

Marias R.

Milk R.

Great Falls

7

6

5

Judith R.

Missouri River

Three Forks

8

Yellowstone R.

9

Pompeys Pillar

EGON

Area Claimed by United States

Ft. Mandan

Cannonball R.

4

3

INDIANA

TERRITORY

Mississippi River

L O U I S I A N A

UNTRY

White R.

3 & 10

Vermillion R.

MOUNTAIN

2

Council Bluff

at Salt ake

P U R C H A S E

Platte R.

Area Claimed by Spain

Kansas R.

Missouri River

St. Louis

1

✗	**Landmark**
	Main route of Lewis and Clark, 1804-1806
—·—	**International boundary**
- - -	**Territory boundary**
	State boundaries shown are current.

0   300

Scale of miles

Map by Toni Smith

CHAPTER I
Introduction

New France, before the English defeated Montcalm at Quebec in 1759, included all of the land drained by the Mississippi and St. Lawrence rivers. France held this vast territory by virtue of exploration and guarded it by a chain of fortifications located strategically from Montreal to New Orleans. Except for the settlements on the lower St. Lawrence and those near New Orleans the French made little attempt to conquer the wilderness. They showed almost no interest in agriculture, depending on the fur trade for livelihood. Excluding the Iroquois, who supported the British, the French made staunch friends of the Indians, and French voyageurs, trappers and traders traveled freely throughout the colonial territory.

The English colonies, however, on the basis of ill-defined land grants from the King, also claimed ownership of the lands lying west of the Appalachians. Sporadic fighting between the French and English colonists, supported by their respective Indian allies, occurred over a period of seventy years, and culminated in the French and Indian War (1754-63). In 1762 when the British blockade had cut off all aid to New France and defeat appeared imminent, Louis XV ceded all of his holdings west of the Mississippi River to Spain in order to keep them out of the hands of the English. Spanish troops moved into New Orleans and St. Louis, the two principal French settlements on the Mississippi, and Spain governed Louisiana for nearly four decades. She made no attempt to colonize the territory, wherefore the French inhabitants continued their trading and trapping as freely as though nothing had happened.

During the period of the Spanish rule over Louisiana, the United States was born. By 1800 the new nation had established its claim to all of the territory bounded on the north by the St. Lawrence River and the Great Lakes, on the west by the Mississippi, and on the south by the Gulf of Mexico and the Spanish colony of Florida.

France under Napoleon was a powerful, aggressive nation. Spain, her power declining, became apprehensive and in 1801 she secretly deeded Louisiana back to France, in the belief that under French rule the territory would serve as a buffer between the United States and Spain's possessions in Texas and California.

News of this transaction created a turmoil in Washington. President Thomas Jefferson, fearing that the United States would soon be at war with France, sent James Monroe to Paris with instructions to purchase Louisiana. Meanwhile, Congress hastily passed a war appropriation. Monroe, however, found a bargain awaiting him, and on April 30, 1803, the United States purchased Louisiana for $15,000,000.

Thomas Jefferson, a scientist as well as a statesman and philosopher, was keenly interested in botany, zoology, geography, and agriculture. Following the Revolutionary War, Jefferson's interest focused upon Louisiana. Although the territory belonged to Spain he felt a trade route from the United States to the Pacific should be opened. Such an expedition would also provide an opportunity for learning much about the geography and biology of the area west of the Mississippi.

Accordingly, in 1783 he attempted to interest General George Rogers Clark in leading an expedition to California, but the plan failed. Again, while in Paris as United States Minister in 1786, Jefferson persuaded John Ledyard, an American adventurer, to attempt to embark on a Russian vessel bound for Nootka Sound, British Columbia, find the headwaters of the Missouri River and descend it to St. Louis. This plan also failed when the Russians apprehended Ledyard and had him sent back to Paris.

Jefferson's next attempt to send an expedition into Louisiana was made in 1793 when he was serving as vice president of the American Philosophical Society. He arranged for Andrè Michaux, a French botanist working in the United States, to lead a party to the Pacific by way of the Missouri River. Michaux, however, became involved in a French scheme to enlist American frontiersmen for a military raid on New Orleans. Both the expedition and the raid were ultimately abandoned.

In spite of these failures and the uncertainty concerning the future of Louisiana under Napoleon, Jefferson did not waver in his determination to open a trade route to the mouth of the Columbia River. In 1803, after he became President of the United States, he sent a secret message to Congress in which he stressed the value of the Missouri River fur trade, and the importance of sending out a military expedition to explore the territory and make treaties with the Indians. Congress approved the project and authorized the expenditure of $2,500 to finance the undertaking. Jefferson immediately wrote to Meriwether Lewis asking him to organize and lead the expedition.

Meriwether Lewis was born and raised on a plantation near Monticello in Albemarle County, Virginia. At an early age he developed an interest in natural history, and gained a local reputation as a hunter. When he was thirteen he was sent to Latin school. After five years of study he came home and managed his mother's farm for two seasons. He gave strict attention to the problems of agriculture, but devoted his spare time to botany and zoology.

When the Whiskey Rebellion broke out in 1794, Lewis, now twenty years old, enlisted in the militia. After this disturbance was over, he transferred to the regular army and served under General Anthony Wayne, who was engaged in battling the Indians and certain die-hard British garrisons for the Ohio River country. By 1801, when Jefferson called him to Washington to serve as his private secretary, he had attained the rank of captain and was paymaster of his company. Although Lewis was not qualified by education or experience for this position, he accepted the appointment and for the next two years he handled the President's confidential business with dispatch and deftness.

It seems probable that Jefferson was primarily concerned with grooming Lewis for a job which he considered more important than being secretary to the President. The appointment gave the President a chance to test Lewis' character and ability; and it provided Lewis the opportunity to obtain additional training in the natural sciences and "readiness in astronomical observations." In any case, Jefferson spent many hours discussing the details of the proposed expedition with his secretary; and in July, 1802, Lewis was sent to Philadelphia to study with Dr. Benjamin S. Barton, an eminent naturalist and professor of medicine at the University of Pennsylvania. It was, then, no surprise to Lewis when in April, 1803, he received the President's letter advising him that Congress had approved the expedition and urging that he permit nothing to delay the final preparations for the journey.

Jefferson's confidence in Lewis is expressed in the following quotation from his "Life of Lewis," written subsequent to the untimely death of the explorer in 1809, and published in the Nicholas Biddle edition[1] of the history of the expedition:

> I had now had opportunity of knowing him intimately. Of courage undaunted; possessing a firmness and perseverance of purpose which nothing but impossibilities could divert from its direction; careful as a father of those committed to his charge, yet steady in the maintenance of order and discipline; intimate with Indian character, customs, and principles; habituated to the hunting life; guarded by exact observation of the vegetables and animals of his own country, against losing time in the description of objects already possessed; honest, disinterested, liberal, of sound understanding, and a fidelity to truth so scrupulous that whatever he should report would be as certain as if seen by ourselves—with all these qualifications, as if selected and implanted by nature in one body for this express purpose. I could have no hesitation in confiding the enterprise to him.

In his letter of instructions Jefferson clearly defined Lewis' responsibilities, and outlined the objectives of the expedition.[2] He pointed out the

3

necessity of dealing peaceably with the natives, and of keeping detailed, accurate records of all observations.

The scope of Lewis' assignment was almost beyond belief. It involved surveying and mapping the courses of the Missouri and Columbia Rivers; studying the mineralogy, climate, geography, botany, and zoology of the country to be explored; and making a detailed report on the ethnology of all of the Indian tribes to be encountered. Few, if any, scientists have ever undertaken a larger task, or one involving greater risk.

Lewis had made good use of his time in Philadelphia and the technical skills and knowledge he obtained there were to prove invaluable in reporting the results of the expedition. By the time he received Jefferson's letter announcing congressional approval of the expedition he was ready to give full attention to the details of assembling equipment and supplies for the journey. He conferred with members of the American Philosophical Society who had been asked by Jefferson to give him as much advice and assistance as possible. Dr. Benjamin Rush, a famous physician of Philadelphia, provided him with drugs and surgical instruments and instructed him in their use; Dr. Casper Wister, physician and vice president of the Society, listed items of scientific interest to which he should give attention, and Andrew Ellicott, Surveyor General of the United States, assisted him in selecting and obtaining astronomical instruments. He spent six weeks at Harpers Ferry in March and April overseeing the construction of the framework of an "iron" canoe which could be assembled and covered with bark or hides wherever the Missouri River became too shallow for heavy boats. The framework could be readily transported as it weighed only ninety-nine pounds, but when assembled the craft had an estimated buoyancy sufficient to support a load of one thousand, seven hundred and seventy pounds.

The President was urging Lewis to hasten his preparations because a month lost in the spring might delay the project for a full year. Lewis, accordingly, wrote to the Commandant of South West Point advising him of the need for volunteers with specific qualifications and experience in wilderness travel, "subject to my approval or otherwise." He dispatched similar letters to the commanding officers at Forts Massac and Kaskaskia to make certain of having a sufficient number of recruits from which to choose.

In view of the fact that Jefferson had emphasized the importance of a second in command in the event of the leader's death, Lewis proposed that a co-leader with equal rank and responsibility be appointed. Jefferson granted this request and authorized Lewis to select a companion. His first choice was Second Lieutenant William Clark, the youngest brother of General George Rogers Clark, under whom he had served for a brief period during the Indian Wars.

4

INTRODUCTION

William Clark was a leader of exceptional ability. During his period of military service he distinguished himself as an engineer in charge of the construction of fortifications. He was a skilled surveyor and cartographer. He was resourceful and fearless, and above all, he possessed an extraordinary knowledge of Indian psychology and customs. In ill health after five years of military life and Indian warfare, Clark had resigned his commission in the Corps of Engineers and assumed responsibility for the management of the family estate near Louisville, Kentucky. It was here he received Lewis' letter urging him to accompany the expedition as co-commander. He accepted immediately.

Lewis was by that time in Pittsburgh supervising the construction of a keelboat to move men and materials as far up the Missouri as practicable. Clark promised to wait for Lewis in Louisville, and in the meantime attempted to enlist recruits.

It was the end of August before Lewis had completed his preparations and started down the Ohio River. When he arrived at Louisville, Clark was ready with several Kentucky recruits. The trip to the mouth of the Ohio and up the Mississippi to St. Louis was slow. Lewis and Clark were obliged to spend a few days at Cape Girardeau and at Forts Kaskaskia and Cohokia to enlist additional military personnel for the journey. Finally in December they established winter headquarters at Riviére du Bois in United States territory opposite the mouth of the Missouri River.

During the winter Clark was kept busy drilling the recruits, building two pirogues to supplement the keelboat, and assembling supplies. Lewis, however, was frequently in St. Louis consulting with fur-traders and trappers who were more or less familiar with the Missouri River country as far north as Mandan Indian settlements situated near the present site of Bismarck, North Dakota. In St. Louis on March 9 and 10, 1804, he witnessed the formal transfer of Louisiana from Spain to France and from France to the United States. By late April preparations for the journey were near completion.

The quantity and variety of goods acquired for the expedition were surprising.[3] The gross weight of food alone exceeded seven tons. Equipment included such items as a blacksmith's forge, a mill for grinding corn, carpenter's tools and axes, instruments for surveying and navigation, medical supplies, cooking utensils, and the frame of the "iron" canoe. In addition there were fifty-two lead canisters weighing four hundred and twenty pounds for sealing one hundred and seventy-five pounds of gun powder, four hundred and twenty pounds of sheet lead, six kegs of brandy (thirty gallons), a few bundles of extra clothing, a few bolts of oiled linen for tents, canvas for tarpaulins, and several bales of Indian trade goods.

Some supplies and certain items of equipment were provided by the

War Department, but much of the material, including technical instruments, medical supplies, hand tools, food, and Indian trade goods, had to be purchased. However, total expenditures did not exceed the congressional appropriation of $2,500.00.

The personnel of the expedition included the following officers and men:

Commanding Officers
> Captain Meriwether Lewis—Commanding Officer
> Second Lieutenant William Clark—Co-Commander[4]

1st Squad
> Sergeant Nathaniel Pryor
> Privates: George Gibson
>> Thomas P. Howard
>> George Shannon
>> John Shields
>> John Collins
>> Joseph Whitehouse
>> Peter Wiser
>> Hugh Hall

2nd Squad
> Sergeant Charles Floyd (died of natural causes, August 18, 1804)
> Sergeant Patrick Gass (promoted to succeed Floyd)
> Privates: Hugh McNeal
>> Reuben Fields
>> Joseph Fields
>> John B. Thompson
>> Richard Windsor
>> Pierre Cruzatte
>> Robert Frazier
>> Francis Labiche
>> Richard Warvington[5]

3rd Squad
> Sergeant John Ordway
> Privates: John Robertson[5]
>> William Bratton
>> John Colter
>> Alexander Willard
>> William Werner
>> Silas Goodrich
>> John Potts
>> Baptiste Lepage (replaced Newman at Ft. Mandan)
>> John Newman[6]
>> Moses B. Reed[7]

6

Besides these men, the party included two interpreters, George Drouillard, hired because of his knowledge of Indian dialects and his familiarity with the sign language, and York, who was Clark's Negro slave. Toussaint Charbonneau and his wife, Sacajawea, the Shoshone Indian girl about whom so much truth and fiction have been written, joined the expedition at Fort Mandan. A few unnamed Frenchmen traveled with Lewis and Clark as far as Fort Mandan, but they had no official connection with the party. Thus the personnel which remained with the expedition and completed the journey from Fort Mandan to the Pacific and back to Fort Mandan and St. Louis consisted of the two captains, three sergeants, twenty-three privates, two interpreters, an Indian woman, who soon bore a son which survived the journey, and a Negro slave—thirty-three in all.

Preparations for the journey were finally completed on May 13, 1804. The last box, cask, and bale of equipment, foodstuffs, and trade goods had been stowed aboard the boats which consisted of one bateau, or keelboat, of twenty-two oars (fifty-five feet long, with a three foot draft), two pirogues of six and seven oars respectively, and six large canoes. The next day, May 14, Clark broke camp at Riviére du Bois, and the Corps of Discovery embarked on one of the most extraordinary adventures in American history.

Captain Lewis, who had been in St. Louis completing final arrangements for his departure, joined the party at St. Charles, a French village some twenty-one miles above the mouth of the Missouri. On May 21, with no fanfare whatever, the expedition moved out of St. Charles.

The journey upstream was slow and toilsome. The current was strong and the channel was obstructed by shifting sand bars and submerged timbers. The sail on the keelboat was of little use because of unfavorable winds. Oars alone were scarcely adequate for making progress in the swift waters and it was frequently necessary to employ tow ropes to drag the heavy boats forward. But the party moved resolutely ahead.

By July 4 the expedition was camped near the mouth of the Kansas River. In keeping with the date, the campsite was named Independence, which was fitting for its role as the home of a future President.

The party reached the mouth of the Platte River on July 21. A few miles above the Platte they established a camp on a high bluff overlooking the Missouri valley. Here they remained until August 4. This campsite was to become the city of Council Bluffs. Lewis' comments indicate how the city acquired its name: "The situation of our last Camp, *Councile Bluff,* or Handsom Prairie, appears to be a verry proper place for a Trading establishment and fortification. . . ."[3]

On August 14 they camped near the "Mahar Indian" villages, a few miles below the present site of Sioux City, Iowa, and spent a full week in council with the Mahar Chiefs (the Omaha Indians). During this period, Sergeant Floyd became violently ill "with a Biliose Chorlick," and died on August 20. He was buried on a high bluff on the east side of the river near a little stream which, in his honor, was named Floyd's River. Sergeant Floyd was the only man lost on the expedition although serious injury and sickness were not uncommon.

Patrick Gass was promoted to the rank of sergeant to replace Floyd, and the expedition moved on. Day after day the men took their turns at the oars and the tow ropes; they passed the mouths of the Vermillion, the James, the Niobrara, the White, and the Teton Rivers. Each day they discovered new plants and animals, which Lewis carefully described in his notes and, if possible, collected. Antelope, elk, and bison were seen in unbelievable numbers. Food was plentiful and the Indians were generally friendly.

However, at the mouth of the Teton River (now called the Bad River) they encountered a band of Tetons (Sioux). This meeting very nearly endangered the entire expedition. The Teton chiefs, under the leadership of Black Buffalo, feigned friendship with Lewis and Clark as they exchanged gifts. They then visited the boats on the river where each chief was treated to one-fourth of a glass of whiskey, but when the time came for departure they pretended drunkenness and demanded more gifts. When additional tobacco was withheld they became insolent and the second chief staggered against Clark who promptly drew his sword and signaled for his men to prepare for action. At this juncture Black Buffalo, the third chief, stepped forward and ordered his subordinates to leave the boats and permit the expedition to proceed unmolested. Black Buffalo and two braves then asked to be taken back on board the keelboat to make amends for the actions of the others. Gifts were again exchanged and the next day Lewis and Clark participated in another grand council which was followed by all night dancing. Fearing further trouble, however, the captains decided to move on as soon as practicable. Had it not been for the cool leadership of Lewis and Clark on this occasion the journey might have ended near the present site of Pierre, South Dakota.

Thereafter every possible precaution was taken to avoid being ambushed or detained by Indians. The party arrived at the Mandan Indian villages, about fifty miles above Bismarck, North Dakota, on October 24, and immediately set to work constructing log cabins and a stockade as shelter against the northern winter and the Indians. In general their relations with the Mandans, Minnetares, and Ricares were friendly. Perhaps too friendly for in addition to the usual fraternization through barter and councils, some members of the expedition party had to be treated for venereal diseases.

During the winter Lewis and Clark met Toussaint Charbonneau, the French Canadian who had spent many years among the Indians, and his young wife, Sacajawea. When Lewis learned that Sacajawea was a Shoshone girl who had been captured by the Mandans and sold to Charbonneau, he immediately hired the Frenchman as a cook in order to obtain Sacajawea as an interpreter. Although Charbonneau was more of a nuisance than an asset, Sacajawea proved to be a life-saver on many occasions. She was resourceful in emergencies; she collected native plants for food when the party was faced with starvation; and she persuaded her tribe to sell twenty-nine horses needed to carry equipment, supplies and men over the rugged Bitterroot Mountains.

On March 26 the ice in the river began to break up. The keelboat and the pirogues, which had suffered some damage from the ice, were repaired and the equipment and supplies were packed for loading. Because the keelboat could not be navigated in the swift, shallow water of the Missouri above Fort Mandan it was sent back to St. Louis under the command of Corporal Richard Warvington, whose term of enlistment had expired. He was accompanied by Private John Robertson whose period of service had also expired; by Moses B. Reed who had been court-martialed for attempted desertion; by John Newman who had been court-martialed for mutinous expression; and by a few French engagés.

On April 3, Lewis wrote in his diary, "we are all day engaged packing up sundry articles to be sent to the President of the United States."[9] These "articles" consisted of specimens of the fauna and flora, Indian weapons, pottery and articles of dress, reports and dispatches to the government and private letters.[10]

After Corporal Warvington and his party had departed for St. Louis on April 7, the personnel of the expedition was reduced to two captains, four sergeants, twenty-seven privates, one interpreter, a cook, Sacajawea and her infant son, and York, Clark's servant. York was a black giant, highly esteemed by the whole party for his strength and his dancing to the rollicking tunes of Private Cruzatte's violin. He was regarded as something of a god by Indian braves, and a favorite among their women.

Lewis and Clark left Fort Mandan "at the same moment that the Barge departed," and proceeded up river. Lewis described their leave-taking in his diary under the date of April 7, 1805. His notes reflect his reminiscences of the objectives of the expedition and, at the same time, his concern for the men and the mission. But most of all, his enthusiasm and confidence in success were evident:

Our vessels consisted of six small canoes, and two large perogues. This little fleet altho' not quite so rispectable as those of Columbus or Capt. Cook, were still viewed by us with as much pleasure as those deservedly famed adventurers ever beheld theirs; and I dare say with quite as much anxiety for their safety and preservation, we were now about to penetrate a country at least two thousand miles in width, on which the foot of civilized man had never trodden; the good or evil it had in store for us was for experiment yet to determine, and these little vessels contained every article by which we were expected to subsist or defend ourselves, however, as the state of mind in which we are, generally gives the coloring to events, when the imagination is suffered to wander into futurity, the picture which now presented itself to me was a most pleasing one, entertaining as I do, the most confident hope of succeeding in a voyage which had formed a darling project of mine for the last ten years, I could but esteem this moment of my departure as among the most happy of my life. The party are in most excellent health and sperits, zealously attached to the enterprise, and anxious to proceed; not a whisper of murmur or discontent to be heard among them, but all act in unison, and with the most perfect harmony. I took an early supper this evening and went to bed.[11]

The party set out early the next morning, but their progress was slow. The winds as well as the currents were against them. Lewis walked on shore to hunt and better observe the country. He paid a final visit to Black Cat, Chief of the Mandans, and then proceeded slowly for about four miles. The boats overtook him at noon. Naturally, the party's progress varied from day to day, but there was always something of interest and importance to record in the diaries. There were new plants and animals to describe in detail, minerals to analyze, soils to evaluate, unknown rivers and mountains to name and place on the maps in the making, and many strange tribes of Indians to deal with.

They camped for three days at the mouth of the Yellowstone River to chart its course. On April 28th they broke camp at the Yellowstone and moved forward averaging ten to twenty miles daily. On May 3rd they paused briefly at the mouth of a clear stream from the north which they called the Porcupine River[12] because of the unusual number of these animals in the vicinity. Lewis notes that "this stream discharges itself into the Missouri on the Stard. side 2,000 miles above the mouth of the latter,— $\frac{1}{4}$ of a mile above the entrance of this river a large creek falls in which we call 2,000 Mile Creek."[13]

Two thousand miles in a year, less ten days, from the date of departure with more than five months of this period spent in winter quarters at Fort Mandan! Clark's estimates of distance were surprisingly accurate. Every mile of travel was plotted on maps and each diary entry was followed by a table of courses and distances covered during the day's travel.

Courses & Distances of 3rd of May, 1805.[14]

N. 50° W ¾ mile to a point of high timber on the Std. Side in a bend

S. 65° W 2¼ " to a point of high timber on the Ld. side

N. 40° W 1 " to a point of wood on the Std. side

N. 55° W 2½ " to some dead timber in the Std. bend

South 3 " to the upper part of timber in a bend to Ld. side

N. 80° W ½ " to a point of wood on the Std. Side

S. 85° W 1¼ " to the commencement of a timber on the Ld. side in a bend

North 1½ " to the upper part of the high timber in a bend on the Std. side passing a sand point at ½ a mile

S. 65° W ½ " to a point of woodland on the Ld. side

S. 75° W 1¾ " to a point of woodland on the Std. side at the mouth of a large river on the Std. side

S. 45° W 3 " to a high timber on the Lard. Side—passed the mouth of 2,000 Mile Creek at ¼ of a mile on the Lrd. side

N. 40° W ½ " to some high timber on the S. side just above an old channel of the river on the Std. side. encamped

—————

18½ miles

Disaster was narrowly averted on May 14th when "a squall of wind struck our Sail broad side and turned the pirogue nearly over." The boat filled with water and did not right itself until the sail was cut down. The articles which floated out were nearly all salvaged by Sacajawea. Both Lewis and Clark were on shore, but the boatman, Cruzatte, allayed the confusion and brought the boat to shore. "This accident had like to have cost us deerly; for in this perogue were embarked our papers, Instruments, books, medicine, a great proportion of our merchandise, and in short almost every article indespensibly necessary to further the views, and insure the success of the enterprize in which, we are now launched to a distance of 2,200 miles."[15]

By four o'clock the next day all supplies and equipment had been dried. The losses were not as great as first believed, "our medicine sustained the greatest injury, several articles of which were entirely spoiled, and many others considerably injured."

On May 29th the party arrived at the mouth of the Musselshell River; and nine days later, they discovered the Judith River, so named by Clark for Julia Hancock of Virginia whom he married several years later. Then, on June 2nd they came to a major fork of the Missouri, the mouth of the

Marias River. The problem here was to determine which branch was the Missouri and which was a tributary. The Indians had told them about a great waterfall on the upper Missouri which would necessitate a long and difficult portage. Lewis was sure that he was nearing this landmark; but, facing the necessity of crossing the mountains before winter he could not afford to ascend the wrong stream. Accordingly, both Lewis and Clark selected five men to accompany them, and proceeded to explore the two rivers. Lewis, who investigated the north branch for a distance of sixty miles, returned to the main camp convinced that its source was too far north to be the Missouri. Every member of the expedition, with the exception of Clark, disagreed with him. Nevertheless, the Captains began making preparations to ascend the south branch.

Because of the need for haste and the labor involved in navigating the swift current of the river, it was decided to abandon one of the pirogues and hide as much equipment as could be spared. Cruzatte, familiar with devising underground caches which would escape detection by the Indians, took charge. Some of the provisions, gun-powder and lead, salt, and the heavier tools, such as the blacksmith's bellows, were wrapped in dry skins and deposited in brush-lined excavations; then the earth and sod were replaced with such care as to leave no sign that the ground had been disturbed.

Because the men were still of the opinion that they should have taken the north branch, it was agreed that Lewis should move ahead as rapidly as possible until he located the falls; or, until he could tell whether he had chosen the right course. Accordingly, he ordered Drewyer, Joseph Fields, Gibson and Goodrich to be ready to accompany him the next morning.

Although he had been ill on the previous day, Lewis and his small party shouldered their packs and departed at eight o'clock on June 11th. After only a few miles the party came upon a small herd of elk. They soon killed and dressed-out four of these animals and hung up the meat and skins where the main party would find them. They then prepared dinner, but Lewis again became violently ill so the party made camp for the night. Having no medicine for Lewis, a strong decoction was made of chokeberry bark. It evidently was an effective cure. "By 10 in the evening I was entirely relieved from pain and in fact every symptom of the disorder forsook me, my fever abated, a gentle perspiration was produced and I had a comfortable and refreshing night's rest."[16]

The next morning the party set out at sunrise. After walking fifteen miles across the plains, they cut back to the river for water. Here they discovered two large grizzly bears. Both were killed at first fire, "a circumstance which has never happened with the party in killing the brown bear before." They then had breakfast, rested for two hours, left a note for Clark and again took to the plains. In the afternoon they had their first view of the Rocky Mountains, which "appear to be formed of several ranges each succeeding range rising higher than the preceding one until the most distant appear to lose their snowey tops in the clouds; this was an august spectacle and still rendered more formidable by the recollection that we had them to pass."[17]

That evening camp was made before sunset. Lewis' diary indicates that he felt slightly concerned about not having made greater progress during the day. "We traveled about 12 miles when we agin struck the Missoury at a handsome little bottom of Cottonwood timber and altho' the sun had not yet set I felt myself somewhat weary being weakened I presume by late disorder; and therefore determined to remain here during the balance of the day and night, having marched about 27 miles today.—— This evening I ate very heartily and after penning the transactions of the day amused myself catching those white fish mentioned yesterday."[18]

By noon of June 13th Lewis could see the mist and hear the roar of the Great Falls of the Missouri. In a few minutes he was standing on a rocky promontory looking at what he considered the grandest falls, save one, in the world. They were three hundred yards wide with a sheer drop of eighty-seven feet according to Clark's measurements. Lewis described them in great detail and in superlative language, but he felt he had not done justice to "this majestically grand scenery."

> After writing this imperfect description I again viewed the falls and was so disgusted with the imperfect idea which it conveyed of the scene that I determined to draw my pen across it and begin again, but then reflected that I could not perhaps succeed better than penning the first impression of the mind; I wished for the pencil of Salvator Rosa (a Titian) or the pen of Thompson, that I might be enabled to give the enlightened world some just idea of this truly magnificent and sublimely grand object,— but this was fruitless and vain. I most sincerely regreted that I had not brought a crimee obscura (camera) with me by the assistance of which even I could have hoped to have done better.[19]

The next morning Lewis dispatched Joseph Fields with a letter to Clark. He suggested that Clark be on the lookout for a place to beach the canoes and start the portage since the falls were situated in a canyon with walls ranging from one hundred and fifty to two hundred feet.

Of the three men remaining with Lewis, one was directed to build a scaffold from driftwood for drying meat and the other two were sent to bring in the meat of a buffalo which had been killed on the previous evening; but they returned to report that wolves had devoured the greater part of it.

13

Lewis took his gun and espontoon and set out alone to explore the river. Fascinated by the wild beauty of the scenery he continued on charting the course of the river and noting its cascades and rapids. Late in the day he discovered a small herd of buffalo at a tributary which he recognized as the Medicine River. Pleased with the thought of fresh meat for dinner, he shot a cow from the herd, only to discover that he had disturbed a grizzly bear evidently intent on the same menu. His next discovery was equally alarming—he had neglected to reload his gun. The Medicine River was eighty yards behind him; the bear, only twenty. Lewis ran for the river and dived over the low bank. He thought he might have a fair chance to defend himself in the water, but when he faced about, his espontoon in hand, he was surprised to discover that the bear had stopped at the water's edge, and was retreating as rapidly as it had pursued him.

Having completed his examination of the river and being uncertain of the bear's intentions, Lewis decided to return to camp without delay. However, the day's adventures were not over. In the course of his homeward journey, three bull buffalo detached themselves from a herd and came charging toward him. He "prepared to give them some amusement," but they halted at a distance of one hundred yards and then retreated.

> It now seemed to me that all the beasts of the neighborhood had made league to destroy me—I thought it might be a dream, but the prickly pears which pierced my feet very severely once in a while, particularly after it grew dark, convinced me that I was really awake, and that it was necessary to make the rest of my way to camp.[20]

Clark had selected a camp site about five miles below the Great Falls near the mouth of Portage Creek. Lewis and his party joined Clark here. Immediately they set about making preparations for the portage. All supplies and materials were removed from the pirogue and canoes which were then lifted out of the water. The pirogue was hidden in a clump of willows and covered over with driftwood. All equipment and merchandise was inspected and sorted with a view to caching any items which could not be transported further. Some of the men were sent out to hunt in order to obtain a supply of jerked buffalo meat and some elk hides which were needed to cover the "iron" canoe. Others were assigned the task of constructing a cart on which it was hoped the heavy baggage and the canoes could be hauled. They sawed up the trunk of a large cottonwood tree to make wheels and used the mast of the pirogue for axletrees. Ill-suited as these materials were, nothing better was available. Clark in the meantime was charting a route well back from the river to avoid the ravines which were tributary to it.

On June 21st Lewis' personal baggage and that of three aides, the

INTRODUCTION

framework of the iron boat, and such tools as would be needed were transferred to a point on the plain three miles from the base camp on the Missouri.

Clark's report of the following day's experience is terse and graphic:

> A fine morning. Capt Lewis and myself and all the party except Sgt. Ordway, Guterich, and the Interpreter and his wife, Sar-car-gah-we-a (who are left at camp to take care of the baggage left) across the portage with one canoe on truck wheels and loaded with a part of our baggage. I piloted thro the plains to the camp I made at which place I intended the portage to end which is 3 miles above the medicine River, we had great dificuelty in getting on as the axeltree broke several times, and the cuppling tongus of the wheels, which was of cottonwood and willow, the only wood except Boxelder &——that grow in this quarter, we got within half a mile of our intended camp much fatigued at dark, our tongus broke and we took a load to the river on the mens back, where we found a number of wolves which had destroyed a great part of our meat which I had left at that place when I was up day before yesterday. soon we went to sleep & slept sound—we determine to employ every man cooks & all on the portage after today.[21]

All except Lewis and his three helpers returned to the base camp to move the rest of the baggage and canoes. It was July 1st before the last load was delivered to Lewis' camp above the rapids. The difficulties and physical discomforts incident to the portage were almost beyond credence:

> This evening the men repaired their mockersons, and put on double souls to protect their feet from the prickley pears. during the late rains the buffaloe have trodden up the praire very much which having now become dry the sharp points of earth as hard as frozen ground stand up in such abundance that there is no avoiding them. this is particularly severe on the feet of the men who have not only their own weight to bear in treading on those hacklelike points but have also the addition of the burthen which they draw and which in fact is as much as they can possibly move with. They are obliged to halt and rest frequently for a few minutes, at every halt these poor fellows tumble down and are so much fatigued that many of them are asleep in an instant; in short their fatigues are incredible; some are limping from the soreness of their feet, others faint and unable to stand for a few minutes, with the heat and fatigue, yet no one complains, all go with cheerfullness.[22]

On June 29th they were caught in a cloudburst accompanied by hail.

> The party dispatched for the baggage had returned in great confusion and consternation leaving their loads in the plains; the men who were all nearly naked and no covering on the head were sorely mawled with the hail which was so large and driven with such force by the wind that it nocked many of them down and one particularly three times. most of them were bleeding freely and complained of being much bruised.[23]

In the same storm Clark, Charbono (Charbonneau) and Sacajawea nar-

15

rowly escaped drowning. They had left the route of the portage to follow the course of the river so that Clark could make some additional notes on the falls and rapids. To escape the storm they had sought shelter in a deep ravine which merged with the canyon of the Missouri. Suddenly they heard and saw a wall of water descending upon them "with irrestible force driving rocks, mud, and everything before it." Clark seized his gun and shot pouch and climbed up the steep bluff pushing Sacajawea, who was carrying her child, before him. Charbono was endeavoring to pull her up, but he was too frightened to be of much assistance. The water was up to Clark's waist and "wet his watch" before he could ascend the bank. Everything they carried with them, except Clark's gun and shot pouch, was swept away. Charbono lost his gun, shot pouch, powder horn and tomahawk; Sacajawea lost the "bier" in which she carried her child; and Clark, his large surveyor's compass. Two men visited the scene of this accident the next day and found the compass in the mud near the mouth of the ravine. The other items were not recovered, but the loss of the compass would have been the most serious.

During the period in which Clark and his staff were moving the supplies and equipment, Lewis and his helpers were hard at work assembling the "iron" canoe. Sergeant Gass and Shields were detailed to scour the country for timber and bark suitable for making the ribs and lining. Joseph Fields and Drewyer were dispatched to hunt elk for skins to cover the frame. They found no elk but killed several buffalo, and so Lewis decided to piece out the elk skins with buffalo hides. Frazier was kept busy sewing hides together with rawhide thongs. Since it was impossible to shave the buffalo hides, they were singed quite closely with a torch. Twenty-seven elk skins and four buffalo hides were used in covering the boat which was then placed on a scaffold to facilitate drying. Lewis was dismayed to find that the holes made in sewing the skins pulled away from the thongs in drying rather than shrinking tightly around them. The need for pitch to pay the seams was acute, but no pine driftwood from which pitch could be made was available. As a last resort a mixture of tallow, beeswax, and charcoal, which was known to work fairly well in sealing the seams of ordinary canoes, was prepared and plastered liberally over the outer surface from bow to stern.

> The boat in every other respect completely answers my most sanguine expectation; she is not yet dry and eight men can carry her with the greatest ease; she is strong and will carry at least 8,000 lbs with her suit of hands.

Frequent showers kept the boat wet in spite of attempts to dry it over a slow fire. Finally, on July 9th, she was launched and "lay like a perfect cork on the water." While loading the canoes for departure a violent wind sprang up forcing further delay. By evening when the storm had abated Lewis discovered that the charcoal mixture had separated from the skins and the "iron" canoe was leaking badly. Obviously, for want of pitch, she was useless. Lewis' disappointment was doubly acute when he discovered that the section covered with the singed buffalo hides did not leak. It was, however, too late to experiment further.

The immediate problem was to find some other means of conveying the essential supplies and equipment. Clark and a few of the best craftsmen set out with axes and adzes to find timber large enough for dug-out canoes.

Lewis was occupied with reducing the baggage to the barest necessities and caching the surplus. By the time the dug-outs were completed all of the essential supplies had been moved up to Clark's camp.

The portage at Great Falls had delayed the expedition for a full month. It was now midsummer. Lewis, accompanied by three men, again moved out ahead of the main party. He collected and described a number of strange species of plants and animals, and made notes upon the occurrence of several with which he was familiar. He was impressed by the beauty and abundance of cacti: "the prickly-pear is now in full blume and forms one of the beauties as well as the greatest pests of the plains." He commented on the abundance of the sunflower and emphasized its importance in Indian economy. He discovered and described a species of currant with orange flowers and yellow fruits which he considered superior to any he ever had eaten.

While Lewis was thus engaged Clark and the main party were making good progress on the river. They overtook Lewis at the point where the Missouri River first enters the Rocky Mountains.

Before proceeding further Lewis and Clark discussed their situation. It was becoming increasingly important to locate the headquarters of the Shoshone Indians, make friends of them, and try to obtain horses to transport men and equipment over the Continental Divide. It seemed obvious that such a large party of white men would frighten any wandering band of Shoshones. Clark volunteered to move out ahead on the Indian trails which followed the course of the river. He was accompanied by four men including his servant, York.

Captain Lewis, now in command of the canoemen and hunters, found the swift water of the canyon difficult to stem. As he proceeded the current became stronger and it was necessary to use tow-ropes and setting-poles whenever the shore line and depth of the stream permitted. Every mile was won at the expense of prodigious labor: "The men complained of being much fortigued. Their labor is excessively great. I occasionally encourage them by assisting in the labour of navigating t. e canoes, and have learned to *push* a *tolerable good pole* in their fraize (phrase)."24

In spite of the fact that Lewis was responsible, in Clark's absence, for charting the courses and distances traversed on the river, and for handling all of the problems incident to the welfare of the expedition, he found time to collect and record scientific data on everything new or unusual. However, he did not permit these observations to delay his progress. The canoes averaged eighteen to twenty miles per day in spite of fatigue, insect pests, and the routine daily chores.

> Our trio of pests still invade and obstruct us on all occasions, these are Musquetoes, eye knats, and prickly pears, equal to any three curses that ever poor Egypt laboured under, except the Mohometant yoke.

Meanwhile, Clark was having his own difficulties. A part of his route lay over rough or mountainous country where sharp fragments of flint cut and bruised the feet. In the leveler country cactus was no less troublesome. The mosquitoes were a great annoyance and had it not been for the mosquito bars, sleep would have been impossible.

In spite of all efforts, Clark failed to overtake or surprise any Indians. He frequently found their abandoned camp sites, and occasionally observed the smoke of signal fires, but they were elusive.

Clark arrived at the three forks of the Missouri on July 25th. He set up a base camp and explored the north fork of the river for a distance of twenty-five miles. Charbono, who had been permitted to join Clark's party on the 23rd, was unable to stand the pace; one of his ankles failed him and Clark was obliged to assist him back to camp, and await Lewis.

The explorers were then again faced with the problem of deciding which of the three forks of the Missouri would lead them over the mountains to the headwaters of the Columbia River. Since they could not decide which of the three tributary streams was the Missouri they named the southwest branch, Jefferson's River in honor of the President, the middle stream, Madison's River in honor of James Madison, Secretary of State, and the tributary entering from the southeast, Gallatin's River in honor of Albert Gallatin, Secretary of the Treasury.

Preliminary surveys indicated that Jefferson's River had its source in the mountains to the west, and it was agreed that this would be the more practicable route to follow. The canoes were reloaded on July 30th and the expedition got under way. Lewis walked on shore accompanied by Charbono, Sacajawea, and two injured men. Sacajawea pointed out the place, about four miles above Three Forks, where she had been captured by the Minnetares after a battle in which a number of Shoshones had been killed.

I cannot discover that she shows any immotion of sorrow in recollecting this event, or of joy in again being restored to her country; if she had enough to eat and a few trinkets to wear I believe she would be perfectly content anywhere.[25]

Sacajawea, Charbono, and the two men boarded the canoes as soon as Captain Clark arrived, and Lewis moved out on the trail alone. He encountered many bayous and beaver ponds which necessitated wading waistdeep in mud and water, so he took to the highlands and did not return to the river until evening.

On August 4th Lewis, accompanied by Sergeant Gass, Drewyer, and Charbono, discovered another fork of the river. The right hand stream, which they named Wisdom River, appeared to arise in the high mountains to the west. Although it was fifty yards wide it looked to be too shallow to float the canoes. Nevertheless, Lewis decided to spend a day or two exploring this stream, but before setting out he wrote a note to Clark advising him to lead the party up the left branch of the river. However, an enterprising beaver cut the *green* pole and Clark elected to follow the right hand fork because it appeared to be the more direct route. He was turned back on the following day, however, by Drewyer who had been instructed to find Clark and hold the party in camp until Lewis returned.

The boatmen were discouraged and over-tired. The river above Three Forks had been characterized by shoals over which the heavily loaded canoes had to be dragged. Their discomfort and discouragement was intensified by having two canoes fill with water and one of them overturn. A large part of the baggage was completely saturated and a few items, including an opened canister of powder and one gun with all of its accessories, were lost. Since it was urgent to dry out the supplies and equipment the party was ordered to camp on a gravelly bar opposite the mouth of Wisdom River.

Lewis, accompanied by Drewyer, Shields, and McNeal, was proceeding as rapidly as possible on foot. They passed the mountainous landmark, Beaverhead, and from this point the river became "very crooked much divided by islands, shallow, rocky in many plases and very rapid"; so much so that Lewis doubted whether the canoes could "get on or not, or if they do it must be with great labour."

Some thirty miles beyond the Beaverhead the river lapped at the base of a high promontory which Lewis called Rattlesnake Cliff because these reptiles were more numerous than usual among the rocks. Fifteen miles beyond Rattlesnake Cliff they found a "handsome leavel vally where the river divided itself nearly into two equal branches."

Lewis concluded after examining both streams that it would be useless to try to navigate either of them with the canoes. At the forks of the river the trail divided also, and Lewis sent Drewyer up one branch and Shields up the other to determine by comparison which had been used most recently by the Indians. Meanwhile, he wrote a note to Clark advising him to proceed no farther. This time he took pains to place the note on a *dry* willow pole.

The trail which Lewis elected to follow soon gave out in the level plain so he directed his course toward the narrow pass to the west. He sent Drewyer to the right and Shields to his left with instructions to watch for the trail as they proceeded toward the pass. After walking about five miles Lewis saw an Indian mounted on a horse coming toward him.

> With my glass I discovered from his dress that he was of a different nation from any that we had yet seen, and was satisfyed of his being a Sosone; his arms were a bow and quiver of arrows, and was mounted on an eligant horse without a saddle, and a small string which was attached to the under jaw of the horse which answered as a bridle. I was overjoyed at the sight of this stranger and had no doubt of obtaining a friendly introduction to his nation provided I could get near enough to him to convince of our being white-men. I therefore proceeded towards him at my usual pace. When I had arrived within about a mile of he made a halt which I did also and unloosing my blanket from my pack, I made him the signal of friendship known to the Indians of the Rocky Mountains and those of the Missouri, which is by holding the mantle or robe in your hands at two corners and then throwing it up in the air higher than the head bringing it to the earth as if in the act of spreading it, thus repeating three times.[26]

This signal, however, did not produce the desired effect; the Indian gave no answering sign of recognition. Lewis removed a looking-glass, some beads, and other trinkets from his pack, turned his weapons over to McNeal, and continued his approach unarmed. It then became evident that the Indian was watching Drewyer and Shields who were also closing in from a distance on either side of him. Lewis signalled for them to halt, but Shields failed to observe his warning, and continued to move forward.

> I felt sorely chagrined at the conduct of the men particularly Shields to whom I principally attributed this failure in obtaining an introduction to the natives. I now called the men to me and could not forbare abraiding them a little for their want of attention and imprudence on this occasion. Aug. 11, 1805.[27]

They attempted to follow the tracks of the Indian but without success so they headed for the pass which they had seen from a considerable distance on the previous day. Here they found a much traveled road which followed the course of the stream in a south westerly direction. On August 12th they arrived at the headwaters of the Missouri.

Thus far I had accomplished one of those great objects on which my mind has been unalterably fixed for many years, judge then of the pleasure I felt in allaying my thirst with this pure and ice-cold water which issues from the base of a low mountain—McNeal had exultingly stood with a foot on each side of this little rivulet and thanked his god that he had lived to bestride the mighty and heretofore deemed endless Missouri. Aug. 12, 1805.[28]

Three quarters of a mile beyond the crest of the pass Lewis and his two companions discovered the Lemhi River, a "handsome, bold running creek, of cold, clear water." Here they camped for the night and, having killed no game for two days, prepared a scanty dinner from the last of their provisions.

They had not gone far on the following day before encountering two Indian women and a girl. The two parties were so close together that the elderly woman and girl made no attempt to escape, but seated themselves and lowered their heads "as if reconciled to die which they expected no doubt would be their fate." Lewis quieted their fears, however, and gave them some beads and other trinkets. The younger woman who had fled was induced by the old squaw to return. Lewis informed them by signs that he wished to be conducted to their encampment that he might become acquainted with their chiefs and warriors. This they agreed to do, and after traveling about two miles down the trail they were met by a party of sixty warriors mounted on fine horses. Lewis approached them unarmed making signs of friendship. Their chief spoke a few words to the women who explained that the white men were friendly and displayed their gifts. This satisfied the chief who then advanced and embraced Lewis.

"Bothe parties now advanced and we were all carressed and besmeared with their grease and paint till I was heartily tired of the national hug."[29]

After much ceremonial smoking of the pipe, and several speeches by the chief, Cameahwait, Lewis was escorted to the Indian encampment where a much more elaborate and prolonged ceremony was carried out.

Although the Shoshones were friendly, Lewis realized that his situation demanded diplomacy. It was obvious that Clark would need horses and additional manpower to transport the expedition's equipment and supplies over the crest of the mountains to the Indian encampment. The Indians had plenty of horses—three to four hundred of them according to Drewyer's estimate; but Lewis suspected that they would be reluctant to follow him over the pass into hostile territory. Even though he was able to persuade them to accompany him, timing would be an important factor; for, should Clark fail to be at the appointed rendezvous at the mouth of Prairie Creek when they arrived, the Shoshones would probably become suspicious and retreat. In this event his own life would be endangered and the success of the expedition would be jeopardized. Lewis decided to stall for time.

Food was scarce. The Indians were living on a diet of roots and berries because game was not plentiful and their hunting weapons were ineffectual. The salmon run in the Lemhi River had not yet started. So the morning after his ceremonious reception, Lewis sent Drewyer and Shields out to hunt, but to no avail.

Perhaps it was the lack of food in the encampment which led Lewis to broach the subject of the need for men and horses without further delay. He explained the situation to Chief Cameahwait, promising gifts to those who assisted him, and advising him of the advantages of friendly trade relations between the Shoshones and the United States.

"He complied with my request and made a lengthy harrangue to his village. He returned in about an hour and a half and informed me that they would be ready to accompany me in the morning."[30]

In spite of this promise, when morning came the Indians were reluctant to set forth. Lewis was informed that he was suspected of leading them into an ambush. Lewis asked him to explain to them that white men consider it a disgrace to lie, or to entrap an enemy by falsehood. Then, he taunted them by accusing them of being afraid to die. This strategy worked, and by noon the Chief and a handful of braves were ready to set forth. They had not proceeded far when they were joined by a dozen others and before nightfall nearly all of the men of the village and a few women had overtaken them. That night they camped high in the mountains and made the best of a poor supper on the last of the flour and berries.

The next morning (August 16) Lewis sent Drewyer and Shields out ahead of the party of Indians in the hope that they could kill some game. He asked Cameahwait to prevent the Indians from accompanying them because he feared they would alarm any deer in the vicinity with their whooping and noise. This immediately aroused suspicion among the Indians and two parties set out, one on each side of the valley to watch the hunters.

In about an hour one of the spies returned in great haste and reported that a deer had been killed. Immediately the whole party gave their horses the whip.

> When they arrived where the deer was which was in view of me they dismounted and ran in tumbling over each other like a parcel of famished dogs. . . . the seen was such when I arrived that had I not have had a pretty keen appetite myself I am confident I should not have taisted any part of the venison shortly. . . . I really did not until now think that human nature ever presented itself in a shape so nearly allyed to the brute creation. I viewed these poor starved divils with pity and compassion.[31]

Still, as the party proceeded, the Indians' suspicion grew. Lewis explained repeatedly to the Chief that Clark and the main party of white men might not yet have arrived at the forks of the river. Late in the day when they came within sight of the Forks, Lewis' premonition was validated. Clark had not arrived.

The situation was tense, but Lewis decided to restore confidence at any cost. He gave Chief Cameahwait his gun, and told him if he found any enemies hidden in the bushes he could use it as he saw fit. Drewyer, Shields, and McNeal also surrendered their arms. This appeared to satisfy the Indians and they moved forward and made camp at the forks of the river.

The next morning Drewyer, accompanied by a few of the braves, was sent out to find Clark and advise him to move forward as rapidly as possible lest the Indians decide to disperse. Within two hours one of the braves returned with a report that the white men were coming. The tension was immediately dissolved; the Shoshones "all appeared transported with joy, and the chief repeated his fraternal hug."

Captain Clark soon arrived with Charbono and Sacajawea. This meeting culminated one of the most remarkable coincidences in the entire history of the expedition. Sacajawea and Chief Cameahwait were brother and sister. "The meeting of those people was really affecting, particularly between Sacajawea and an Indian woman, who had been taken prisoner at the same time with her, and who, had afterwards escaped from the Minnetares and rejoined her nation."[32] The probability of being able to purchase horses from the Indians seemed assured.

When the excitement of Clark's arrival had died down and the Shoshones were satisfied that Lewis had not led them into an ambush, a long conference was held with Chief Cameahwait and two of his subchiefs. Now that Sacajawea was on hand to act as interpreter, Lewis was able to communicate with the Indians much more freely. He explained the expedition in considerable detail, and pointed out that future trade relations between the Shoshones and the United States might well depend upon the extent of their cooperation in the present emergency.

An Indian, as a rule, could not be hurried in making a decision, and Cameahwait was not an exception. However, he appeared to see the logic of Lewis' argument, and sent a message back to his village instructing his braves to return with as many additional horses as necessary to transport the baggage.

Since it was evident that several days might pass before the expected help could arrive, Lewis sent Clark forward with a small party of men to look for a route to some navigable tributary of the Columbia River. The Indians had mentioned that the Lemhi joined a much larger river a few miles below the site of their village, but they said it was impossible to descend this stream (the Salmon River) either by canoe or by trail. They maintained that it soon plunged into a deep, narrow canyon which penetrated a wild mountainous region totally devoid of wood and game. It seemed advisable for Clark to ascertain the truth of this report.

Lewis took advantage of this period to study the Shoshones.

> Notwithstanding their extreem poverty they are not only cheerful but even gay, fond of gaudy dress and amusements; like most other Indians they are great egotists and frequently boast of heroic acts which they never performed. They are also fond of games of wrisk. They are frank, communicative, fair in dealing, generous with the little they possess, extreemly honest, and by no means beggarly. Aug. 19, 1805.[33]

He noted that the Shoshone women were given a more prominent position in tribal affairs than was general among Indians in that they participated in tribal councils. However, in other respects their situation differed little from that generally occupied by women of other tribes.

Chastity was no more highly esteemed by the Shoshones than by other Indian nations. However, the clandestine behavior of a woman was regarded as a disgrace to her husband, and if apprehended she could expect to be killed, beaten, or driven out of the village. On the other hand, a brave might readily barter his squaw for a night, or longer, if he considered the reward adequate. Or, he might even insist upon a guest accepting her company as an act of courtesy, and would be grievously offended if refused. If his offer met with favor, he would sit all night at the entrance of his tepee to forestall any disturbance.

Captain Lewis repeatedly cautioned his men against violating any of these social customs, but he acknowledged the futility of forbidding all contact with the Indians: "to prevent this mutual exchange of good offices altogether I know it impossible to effect, particularly on the part of our young men whom some months abstanence have made very polite to those young damsels."

It was August 26 before the last bale of trade goods, and pack load of equipment was set down on the banks of the Lemhi beyond the ridge-pole of the continent. Clark had not yet returned from his reconnaissance of the Salmon River, but John Colter was waiting with a message from Clark which verified the Indian report that the Salmon River route was impassable. It was evident that the expedition would have to pursue the Indian trails leading far northward to find a less turbulent tributary of the Columbia. Lewis renewed his efforts to purchase horses. In spite of Sacajawea's influence the Indians were reluctant to part with them. A horse cost the equivalent of six dollars in trade goods, and a mule commanded twice that figure. The stock of trade goods was much depleted by the time Lewis had purchased twenty-nine animals including two colts and a mule.

The expedition set forth with their pack train on August 13. An elderly Indian who had accompanied Clark on his exploration of the Salmon River, volunteered to lead them over the trails commonly used by the Flatheads on their annual hunting excursions. They pursued the course of the Salmon River in a northwesterly direction for three days, and then deviated to the north following the course of Fish Creek, a tributary of the Salmon which flowed out of the Bitterroot Mountains.

The trail over which Lewis and Clark were being led passed over the Bitterroot Range in the vicinity of Lost Trail Pass and then dropped away sharply to the headwaters of Camp Creek, a tributary of the Bitterroot River. Several horses were injured on the steep and difficult route. The entire party was cold, tired, and hungry. Game had been scarce for three days. A band of big-horned sheep, quite beyond the range of their flint-lock rifles, contributed only to their discomfort; but, they surprised a deer on the bank of Camp Creek which provided them with venison for their evening meal.

Later in the evening while searching downstream for a good camp site, they encountered a band of four hundred Flathead Indians en route to the buffalo country. Lewis and Clark spent the next two days in their camp. Gifts were exchanged and Lewis explained at length the purpose of the expedition. Medals were conferred upon four of the principal chiefs in recognition of their avowed intention of maintaining friendly relations with the United States.

The Flatheads were well provided with horses for their journey and Lewis lost no time in starting negotiations for the replacement of some of his crippled animals. He succeeded in trading for seven, which were in better condition than those acquired from the Shoshones, and in purchasing eleven others.

The expedition moved on down the valley of the Bitterroot River at the rate of about twenty miles a day. The weather was rainy and the men were wet and cold most of the time, but deer and grouse were plentiful enough to keep them well fed. They camped for two days at the mouth of Lolo Creek, then crossing the Continental Divide by way of the Lolo Pass, took the Indian trails in the direction of Clearwater River. As they progressed the trail became more difficult. Snow made the footing slippery and dangerous. They killed only a few grouse, and were forced to sacrifice several colts to offset their hunger.

After seven days on the trail their situation was critical. The expedition seemed hopelessly lost in a mountainous wilderness which supported no game, and little accessible water. The horses, too, were in bad shape from

25

injuries, and a scarcity of feed. It was decided that Clark and six men should hurry ahead in the hope of finding more level country. Lewis followed at a much slower pace with the balance of the party and the pack train.

Clark made good progress. On September 20 he descended to a level open plain, where he made the expedition's first contact with the Nez Percé Indians.

While Clark feasted on dried salmon and camas roots in the Nez Perce village, Lewis and the main body of men were camped on the weary trail eating a scant dinner of the balance of the horse meat, a few pheasants, a prairie wolf, and some crayfish obtained from the stream. Their plight, however, was not as desperate as Lewis supposed. The party was encamped at a site located only ten miles above the Nez Percé village. Besides, Clark, anticipating that Lewis and his men might need some encouragement, had decided to send Reuben Fields out the next morning to find Lewis and lead him to the encampment. Fields proved to be a welcome envoy since he carried dried fish and roots enough to feed the entire party, but not enough to keep them from gorging themselves on the same fare upon arrival at the Indian village.

The Nez Perce supplied the party with a map of the Clearwater River and on September 24th the entire party set out. They set up a camp on the Clearwater River on the 26th and as many of the men as were able— most of them were suffering considerably from overeating—began felling trees. The small axes and hand tools were not calculated for shaping large dugouts, but they began hewing away on five logs as resolutely as their condition permitted.

In spite of having to resort again to a diet of fish and roots most of the men began to improve. Arrangements were made with two braves and a boy to look after the horses. Accordingly, thirty-eight horses were branded for later identification, and delivered to the Indians.

The canoes were beginning to take shape. Two were launched on the evening of October 5. One of them leaked a little, but the other was sound and buoyant. Two days later the rest of the dugouts were ready. The men were as glad to be back in canoes as they had been to leave them behind when they reached the headwaters of the Missouri.

The Clearwater River is a cold swift stream characterized by dangerous rapids which only the most daring and skilled boatmen would risk. Lewis and Clark ran most of these rapids without hesitation but not without accident. The main trouble was the canoes overturning as they hit large rocks. Neither men nor canoes were seriously injured, however.

The lack of game continued to be a serious problem. The men were forced to subsist mainly on dried fish and roots. Hunger and physiological necessity left little room for prejudice; so, any bird or beast which could be killed went into the cooking pot. They were driven by necessity to purchase Indian dogs; but Clark, at least, could not overcome a sense of revulsion at being obliged to eat them.

On October 16 the party arrived at the junction of the Snake and Columbia Rivers. Here they made camp for several days while small parties scouted the general area and the course of the Columbia River.

Indians of the Nez Percé nation were numerous on the Columbia above and below the mouth of the Snake River. The Chinookan tribes occupied some of this area, but were more numerous farther down the Columbia valley. It is sometimes claimed that these Nez Percé and Chinooks had a lower culture and mentality than those tribes of the mountains and the plains. Certainly it was a different culture, as determined by environment. These Indians were more friendly and peaceable than the tribes of the plains. However, the tribes dwelling close to the white tradesmen on the lower Columbia were more temperamental and less trustworthy than the tribes on the upper Columbia and its tributaries. The Indians living below the great rapids and falls of the river were cunning thieves; Lewis and Clark had a great deal of trouble in preventing them from walking away with material and equipment.

In a sense the expedition fiddled and danced its way down the river. They stopped frequently to visit the Indian villages along the banks of the Columbia and Cruzatte's violin combined with York's colorful dancing always delighted the Indians. And in spite of the delays of these visits the expedition was making excellent progress. The current of this section of the Columbia was swift, but comparatively free of rapids, and they were able to cover thirty to forty miles a day without over-exertion.

They made the portage around Celilo Falls on October 22, assisted by the Indians who provided horses for transporting the baggage over a one thousand, two hundred yard trail on the north bank of the river. The canoes were led down a narrow channel on the opposite side of the stream after a short portage around the falls. The Indians paid themselves adroitly, through theft, for their services.

The trip down the Columbia was accomplished without serious accident. In spite of warnings to the contrary the Indians encountered were friendly. Lewis and Clark were welcome in their lodges. Clark's diary is filled with information concerning their numbers, possessions, intertribal relations, and social and economic standards. The problem of food became much less acute as the party approached the heavily forested lowlands west of the Cascades. This was, indeed, a lush and provident country abounding in game, fish, fowl, and palatable roots for the taking. The taking, however, was not always easy. The rains of winter had started in earnest, and the party was ill prepared to cope with the problems of shelter and food under such conditions. However, they felt they were nearing their objective; the river was widening, and its tidal fluctuations were increasingly evident.

On November 7 they camped on a narrow beach on the north side of the river not far from Pillar Rock. It was dark and foggy, but they could hear the roar of breakers in the distance and assumed that they were in view of the ocean. "Great joy in camp. We are in view of the ocian . . . and the roreing or noise made by the waves brakeing on the rockey shores (as I suppose) may be heard distinctly." They were wrong, however. That which they mistook for the ocean was only the broad expanse of the river which widens to fifteen and more miles before discharging its waters into the Pacific.

The next day they pushed on for eight miles, rounded the point of Cape Swells and paddled across Gray's Bay, a shallow basin on the north side of the estuary of the Columbia. They landed near Gray's Point, which guards the Bay to seaward, and camped on a narrow beach barely above tidewater. Steep bluffs prevented them from moving to higher ground, and the waves were running so high opposite the point that they could not go forward. They were obliged to unload all of the canoes and stack the baggage on drift logs. When the tide came in, the waves washed over the beach, and the explorers were hard pressed to save their equipment.

> At 2 o'clock P.M. the flood tide came in accompanied with emense waves and heavy winds, floated the trees and Drift which was on the point on which we camped and tossed them about in such a manner as to endanger the canoes verry much, with every exertion and the Strictest attention by every individual of the party was scarcely sufficient to save our canoes from being crushed by those monsterous trees many of them nearly 200 feet long and from 4 to 7 feet through, our camp entirely under water dureing the hight of the tide, every man as wet as water could make them all the last night and today all day as the rain continued all day, at 5 o'clock P.M. the wind Shifted about to the S.W. and blew with great violence immediately from the Ocean for about two hours, notwithstanding the disagreeable Situation of our party all wet and cold (and one which they have experienced for Several days past) they are chearfull and anxious to see further into the Ocean. The water of the river being too Salt to use we are obliged to make use of rain water. . . . At this dismal point we must Spend another night as the wind and waves are too high to proceed.[34]

On the morning of November 10, the wind having subsided, the explorers reloaded the canoes, and continued down river. The lull in the storm, however, was of short duration, and by the time they were nearing Point Ellice, the waves were so high that they were obliged to put into a cove on the lee side of the point, and again establish a camp on a raft of drift-logs which were afloat at every flood tide.

It was November 15 before Clark succeeded in floating the canoes around Point Ellice, and in establishing a base camp near the head of Baker's Bay. From here Clark led as many of the men as wished to accompany him on foot to the tip of Cape Disappointment for an unobstructed view of the Pacific.

Lewis, impatient to get on with his explorations, had set out a couple of days ahead of Clark to discover whether a white settlement existed at the mouth of the river. In this he was disappointed, but not in his biological observations. It was here that he wrote the original descriptions of the Columbia blacktailed deer, and the California condor. Lewis and Clark spent a full week at the mouth of the Columbia exploring and mapping the adjacent area.

A combination of factors made the base camp on the north bank of the Columbia untenable as a winter headquarters. A band of Chinook Indians caused no end of trouble. They were friendly but also crafty and given to stealing. Deer and elk were plentiful but difficult to hunt in the dense tangle of brush and down-timber. And the camp site was too easily flooded. The party set out to locate a favorable camp site on the south shore.

The explorers spent several days in the vicinity of Tongue Point near Astoria, Oregon. The waves were so high off Tongue Point that the boats had to be beached pending a lull in the storm. Nevertheless, Lewis and five men, employing an Indian canoe designed for rough water, managed to paddle around the Point and continue their search for a permanent camp site. Meanwhile, Clark kept the rest of the men busy drying out their duffle, and dressing skins which were badly needed to repair their torn and rotten garments.

Discomfort and frustration were beginning to affect the morale of the party. Even Clark's spirit was sagging under the impact of the elements.

"Wind shifted about the S.W. and blew hard accompanied with hard rain all last night, we are all wet bedding and stores, haveing nothing to keep ourselves or our stores dry, our Lodge nearly worn out, and the pieces of sales and tents so full of holes and rotten that they will not keep anything dry, we sent out the most of the men to drive the point for deer, they scattered through the point some stood on the (peninsula), we could find no deer, several hunters attempted to penetrate the thick woods to the main South Side without suckcess the swan & gees wild and cannot be approached, and wind to high to go either back or forward, and we have nothing to eate but a little Pounded fish which we purchased at the Great falls. This is our present situation! truly disagreeable. aded to this the robes of our selves and men are all rotten from being continually wet, and we cannot procure others,

29

or blankets in these places. about 12 o'clock the wind shifted about to the N.W. and blew with great violence for the remainder of the day at many times it blew for 15 or 20 minutes with such violence that I expected every moment to see trees taken up by the roots, some were blown down. These squalls were suckceeded by rain O! how Tremendious is the day. This dreadful wind and rain continued with intervals of fair weather, the greater part of the evening and night."[35]

Lewis had been gone for a full week, and Clark was worried. His apprehension proved to be unwarranted, however, for Lewis returned on December 6 as casually as he had departed. Everyone was elated by his report of having found a suitable place for a fortification a few miles southwest of the present site of Astoria in an area where elk and deer were plentiful. Work began immediately on a stockade and cabins and "Fort Clatsop" (so named for a nearby Indian tribe) began to take shape. On December 24 most of the men moved into one of the cabins and by December 31 the last post of the stockades was in place, and the last crevice was daubed with clay. Rude though it was, Fort Clatsop was a dry, warm haven in comparison to the brush shelters and rotten tents which the men had been occupying.

But the party was not to have a winter's rest without some problems. Game was not terribly difficult to track and kill, but the humidity and temperature of the coastal climate made it impossible to store any reserve of meat without its spoiling. The salt supply was exhausted. So the search for salt, or a source of salt, became the particular plague of the expedition at Fort Clatsop. Boiling salt water was the final solution and a permanent "salt maker's" camp was established on the coast.

The Clatsop Indians were permitted free access to the Fort during the day, but were ushered out at sundown and the gate was closed. These daily contacts with Indians ranged from frustrating to profitable in trading and from entertaining to annoying in personal contact. They were helpful, however, in the information they were able to supply as to the extent of their trade with white men at the mouth of the Columbia. Specifically, they supplied Lewis and Clark with the names of thirteen British and American ship captains, described their vessels, and suggested the approximate date on which each of them might be expected to return. This information was of utmost importance to the explorers as President Jefferson had advised them to return to the United States by sea if at all possible. In any case the arrival of a ship would provide an opportunity to replenish their meagre stock of Indian trade goods.

Ignoring their hardships, the men attempted to celebrate Christmas.

At daylight this morning we were awake by the discharge of fire arms of all our party & a Selute, Shouts, and a Song which the whole party joined in under our windows, after which they retired to their rooms, were chearfull all the morning. After breakfast we divided our Tobacco which amounted to 12 carrots, one half of which we gave to the men of the party who used tobacco, and to those who doe not use it we make a present of a handkerchief. The Indians leave us in the evening all the party snugly fixed in their huts. I recvd a present of Capt. L. of a fleece hosiery Shirt, Draws and Socks, a pr. Mockersons of Whitehouse, a Small Indian basket of Guterich, two Dozen white Weazil tails of the Indian woman and some black root of the Indians before their departure. Drewyer informs me that he saw a snake pass across the path today. The day proved Showery wet and disagreeable.

We would have Spent this day the nativity of Christ in feasting, had we anything either to raise our Spirits or even gratify our appetites, our Diner concisted of pore Elk, so much Spoiled that we ate it thro' mear necessity, Some spoiled pounded fish and a fiew roots.[36]

With the approach of spring preparations for departure were going forward. During the winter the men had outfitted themselves with new elkskin clothing, especially extra moccasins. John Shields, the gunsmith, had repaired all firearms. The canoes were patched as effectively as possible though they had never dried completely. In spite of this, and the fact that several of the men were in ill health, Lewis and Clark decided to abandon Fort Clatsop as soon as the weather permitted.

Lewis appraised the winter's experience in the following words:

Alho' we have not fared sumptuously this winter and spring at Fort Clatsop, we have lived quite as comfortably as we had any reason to expect we should; and have accomplished every object which induced our remaining at this place except that of meeting the Traders who visit the entrance of this river, our salt will be very sufficient to last us to the Missouri where we have a stock in store. It would have been fortunate for us had some of those Traders arrived previous to our departure from hence, as we should then have had it in our power to obtain an addition to our stock of merchandize which would have made our homward bound journey much more comfortable.[37]

Actually, the brig "Lydia," out of Boston under the command of Captain Hill, had visited the Columbia River in November, probably while Lewis and Clark were encamped in Gray's Bay or on Point Ellice. It had remained on the Northwest Coast until August, 1806, possibly spending the winter at Nootka Sound, but the explorers were unaware that a ship was in the vicinity.

Since, to their knowledge, no ships had appeared, and it seemed unlikely that any would visit the harbor before late spring or summer, Lewis and Clark could not afford to wait; if, after waiting, passage could not be secured they would be obliged to spend another winter in the wilderness.

By March 20 all was in readiness for departure. However, there was further delay. The rain and wind continued with such force that it seemed improbable that the canoes could be taken around Point William after leaving Meriweather Bay. While waiting for the wind to subside Lewis and Clark bid farewell to Co-mo-wooll, Chief of Clatsops and to De-la-shel-wilt, Chief of the Cuthlahmahs. To the former they turned over Fort Clatsop, and the latter a certificate of good conduct. Lewis also gave them copies of a document certifying that he and his men, all of whose names were listed, had spent the winter of 1805-6 at Fort Clatsop; and that they had departed in March for their return journey across the continent. The Indians were advised to give this document to any "civilized person" who visited the mouth of the Columbia.[38] This was done in the hope that some knowledge of their success would find its way back to the United States even though none of the party survived the homeward journey.

The weather cleared on March 23: the time for departure had arrived.

> The rain seased and it became fair about Meridian, at which time we loaded the canoes and at 1 p m left Fort Clatsop on our homeward journey.—Soon after we had set out from Fort Clatsop we were met by Dela-shewilt, and 8 men of the Chinnook and Dashelwilt's wife the old baud and his six girls, they had a canoe, a see otter skin, dried fish and hats for sale, we purchased a sea otter skin, and proceeded on thro' Meriwether's Bay, there was a stiff breese from the S. W. which raised considerable swells around Meriwether's point which was as much as our canoes could ride.[39]

The high seas off Tongue Point also caused some anxiety; but the wind and waves did not deter the boatmen, and by nightfall they were safe in camp beyond the blustery point which had delayed them so long on their outward journey.

Despite their haste, Lewis and Clark took advantage of the opportunity to visit several Indian villages while proceeding up the river. It was essential to purchase food, and desirable to make further studies of the various tribes situated on the lower Columbia. Whenever possible their campsites were located near permanent, or temporary, Indian encampments. Generally they were welcomed, but they did not always find the association agreeable. Clark recorded his appraisal of a Cathlamah village in his usual forthright language: "the dirtiest and stinkingest place I ever saw in any shape whatever, and the inhabitants partake of the characteristics of the village."

The Skillutes, who occupied villages on both sides of the Columbia near the mouth of the Cowlitz River, invited Lewis and Clark to spend a day with them to hunt deer and elk which were reported to be plentiful in that locality. This invitation was declined, however, because the weather was still too wet for repairing the canoes, and Lewis did not feel that he could afford to lay-over in camp unless something more tangible than hunting could be accomplished; besides, he had sent Drewyer, and six of the best hunters on ahead with orders to proceed to Deer Island to hunt until overtaken. By the time the main party put in at Deer Island on March 26, the hunters who had arrived the night before, had killed seven deer. However, condors and eagles devoured four of them, but the three other deer, a goose, and a few ducks were salvaged. Late in the day the hunters went out again and returned with three additional deer, a duck, four eagles, and a lynx. While the hunters had been thus engaged Lewis had supervised drying-out the leaky canoes, and sealing them with pitch. The day being fair the men also succeeded in drying their clothes and blankets which had been wet since leaving Fort Clatsop.

By March 29 the expedition was back on Sauvies Island. Here they met the Cathlacumup, Multnomah, and the Quathlahphotle Indians from whom they obtained twelve dogs and some wappato in exchange for the hides of the deer which they had recently killed. The dogs were to supplement the venison which was "too poor for the men to subsist on and work as hard as they do."

Lewis and Clark concluded rightly that the Indians of Sauvies Island were allied to the Chinookan tribes in culture and language, but they described the men as being "stouter and much better formed than those of the seacoast." They learned that these tribes rarely, if ever, visited the lower river, but rather made seasonal journeys upstream to fish for salmon below the falls and rapids. When not fishing and hunting these Indians carried on a brisk trade with the coastal tribes, who always stopped at their villages to exchange beads and other trade goods for literally tons of wappato.

Oddly enough, in going downstream and in returning, Lewis and Clark had skirted the northern shores of the islands opposite the mouth of the Willamette River. Thus, in both instances, they missed seeing the Willamette, and assumed that the Sandy River drained the broad valley between the Cascade and Coast Range Mountains. They did not discover their error until a band of Indians who visited their camp at the mouth of the Sandy pointed out that this stream had its source near the base of Mount Hood. If such was the case it was evident that the broad valley to the south must be drained by some other river which they had overlooked. The Indians supported this assumption. "We readily prevailed on them to give us a sketch of this river which they drew on a Mat with a coal, . . ."

Clark hired a native guide for the price of a burning-glass and set forth with six men to look for the elusive Willamette. With the assistance of the current, they made good time and before nightfall they located the mouth of the Willamette which had been screened from view by three small islands. Clark ascended the river for a distance of ten miles, according to his estimate, taking survey notes as he proceeded. Here, probably within the limits of the city of Portland, in attempting to ascertain the depth of the river he failed to find bottom with a five fathom sounding cord, and concluded that it was deep enough "for a Man of War, or ship of any burden."

> The mist was so thick that I could see but a short distance up this river. When I left it, it was bending to the East of S.E. Being perfectly satisfied of the size and magnitude of this great river which must water that vast tract of country between the western range of mountains and those on the seacoast and as far S. as the waters of California about Lat^d· 37 North, I determined to return.[40]

While searching for the Willamette, Clark again demonstrated his resourcefulness in dealing with Indians. Being in need of food he stopped at a village of the Shahala nation to trade for fish and roots. Upon entering a large overcrowded hut, he quickly sensed the hostility of his hosts, but he averted trouble by employing tactics as mystifying as those of the native Medicine Man.

> I entered one of the rooms of this house and offered several articles to the natives in exchange for wappato. They were sulky and positively refused to sell any. I had a small piece of port fire match in my pocket, off which I cut a piece one inch in length and put it into the fire and took out my pocket compas and set myself down on a mat on one side of the fire, and also showed a magnet which was in the top of my ink stand. The port fire caught and burned vehemently, which changed the color of the fire; with the magnet I turned the needle of the compas about very briskly; which astonished and alarmed these natives and they laid several parsles of wappato at my feet, and begged me to take out the bad fire; to this I consented; at this moment the match being exhausted was of course extinguished and I put up the magnet, etc. This measure alarmed them so much that the women and children took shelter in their beads and behind the men, all this time a very old man was speaking with great vehemunce, appearently imploring his god. I lit my pipe and gave them smoke, and gave the women full value of the goods which they had put at my feet. They appeared somewhat passified and I left them and proceeded on.[41]

The trip back to the base camp on the Sandy River was uneventful. Clark stopped again at the Shahala village; but, finding the women and children still frightened and the braves resentful, he departed hurriedly and avoided further contacts with the Indians until he arrived at the village of his guide, a member of the Cashook tribe. Many of their bark huts were deserted and in ill repair. Upon inquiry Clark was told that smallpox had virtually wiped out this tribe about thirty years earlier. The elderly father of his guide produced a pock-marked woman as evidence of this malady, which had taken a heavy toll among the Clatsops, and probably among other northwestern tribes, during the same epidemic.

Clark prevailed upon the old man to draw a map of the Multnomah and its tributaries, and to give him the names and locations of the Indian tribes dwelling thereon. Thus, he obtained much information about the Clackamas, Charcowah, Kalapuya, and Cashook nations. He found them differing in language, dress, and manners from the Chinookan tribes, being more closely allied to the Quathlahpohtles in these particulars. Their women wore only a narrow, close fitting breechclout and a short jacket, the latter being discarded in warm weather. Clark considered this costume "more indasent" than the ogle-inducing, shredded-cedarbark skirts worn by the Chinook and Clatsop women.

During Clark's absence Lewis had entertained several parties of Indians who were returning from the falls of the Columbia. Invariably they reported a serious food shortage on the upper river. Salmon were not yet running and game was said to be scarce. With this prospect in view the hunters redoubled their efforts to kill enough big game to fulfill their needs until they reached the more productive game-lands of the Chopunnish nation on the Clearwater River. It was April 7th before they had killed and dried a sufficient quantity of elk, deer, and bear meat to risk moving forward.

Taking the canoes through the cascades below the Dalles was a major problem. The water was twenty feet higher than it had been during the previous November, and it was necessary to use a towrope in hauling the canoes through a succession of rapids, and then carry them over a two thousand, eight hundred yard portage. It was unfortunate but also a little remarkable that only one canoe was lost in the process.

The troublesome Clahclellahs had established a village above the rapids to await the return of the salmon. These people seemed bent on making as much trouble as possible short of open warfare:

> Many of the natives crowded about the bank of the river where the men were engaged in taking up the canoes; one of them had the insolence to cast stones down the bank at two of the men who happened to be a little detached from the party at the time. On the return of the party in the evening from the head of the rapids they met with many of the natives on the road, who seemed but illy disposed; two of these fellows met John Shields who had delayed some time in purchasing a dog and was a considerable distance behind the party on their return with Capt. Clark. They attempted to take the dog from him and pushed him out of the road. He had nothing to defend himself with except a large knife which he drew with the intention of putting one or both of them to death before they could get themselves in readiness to use their arrows, but discovering his design they declined the combat and instantly fled through the woods.

Three of this same tribe of villains, the Wahclellars, stole my dog (Scammon) this evening, and took him towards their village; I was shortly afterwards informed of this transaction by an Indian who spoke the Clapsop language (some of which we had learnt from them during the winter) and sent three men in pursuit of the thieves with orders if they made any resistance or difficulty in surrendering the dog to fire on them; they overtook these fellows at a distance of about 2 miles; the Indians discovering the party in pursuit of them left the dog and fled. They also stole an ax from us, but scarcely had it in their possession before Thompson detected them and wrested it from them. We ordered the sentinel to keep them out of camp, and informed them by signs that if they made any further attempts to steel our property or insulted our men we should put them to instant death.[42]

The attempt to steal Lewis' dog, Scammon, for their cooking pots was sufficient provocation for blood-letting. If the dog had not been recovered a battle surely would have ensued for Lewis' staunch Newfoundland companion was as much a member of the expedition as any of the men.

After passing the Memaloose Islands it became apparent to Lewis and Clark that horses would be needed to portage around the long chute below Celilo Falls. It would also be easier to follow the Indian trails to the Nez Percé villages on the Clearwater River than to stem the swift currents of the upper Columbia and the Snake. They displayed their merchandise at Sepulchre Island, but the Indians refused to trade. They had no better success at several other villages between Sepulchre Rock and the Dalles, where Lewis made camp while Clark, accompanied by Drewyer, Charbono, Sacajawea and nine men set out to trade with Indians on the north side of the river. They spent several days here with the Skillute Indians in which bargaining seemed to have reached an impasse. However, by April 18 when Lewis moved his party to the cove below the Long Narrows, Clark was able to send four horses to him before leaving the Skillutes to try his luck with the Eneshers.

It was noon of April 21 when Lewis and his party joined Clark at the Enesher village below Celilo Falls. Between them they had managed to secure ten horses and the portage of the falls and rapids of the Columbia was accomplished without mishap. From here the party proceeded as rapidly as circumstances would permit, following the trail along the course of the Columbia and gradually acquiring an additional horse here and there from wandering bands of Indians. By April 24 they had acquired a sufficient number of pack animals to enable them to sell the two remaining canoes for a few strands of beads.

With the assistance of the friendly Wallah-wallah tribe, the party crossed the Columbia on April 30. They then followed the course of the Walla Walla River as far as the mouth of Touchet Creek, ascending this stream for several miles, and then crossing the plains to the junction of the Snake and Clearwater Rivers. Lewis observed that the creek bottom was fertile and sparsely wooded. The country reminded him of the upper Missouri, except that the "herds of buffalo, Elk, etc." were missing. The hunters saw a few deer, but succeeded in killing only one of them. The last of the jerked elk meat was eaten on May 1, and, thereafter, because game was scarce the expedition was dependent for food on the Indians.

In order to conserve trade goods, now nearly exhausted, Clark resumed his medical practice in the Indian villages. He had treated some of the Indians during the previous autumn and his fame as a "medicine man" had assumed such proportions that he was overburdened with requests for assistance. He realized that many of his "cures" had been psychological, or merely lucky, but he felt justified in keeping up the deception in order to obtain food for himself and his companions. In one instance he was given a horse for draining an abscess; and in another, an "eligant horse" for a vial of eyewater. Dogs and roots, however, were more readily obtainable than horses, possibly because the Chopunnish were averse to eating dog.

It was an irritating experience for Lewis and Clark to find themselves the butt of raillery because they were obliged to eat meat which these Indians disdained:

> an Indian fellow verry impertinently threw a poor half starved puppy nearly into my plait by way of derision of our eating dogs and laughed very heartily at his own impertinence; I was so provoked at his insolence that I caught the puppy and threw it with great violence at him and struck him in the breast and face, siezed my tomahawk and showed him by signs if he repeated his insolence, I would tomahawk him, and the fellow withdrew apparently much mortifyed and I continued my repast *on dog* without further molestation.[43]

On May 8 they were surprised to meet the Chopunnish Chief, The Twisted Hair, on the trail. He had been friendly in November when they had arranged for him to care for their horses during the winter, but now he was decidedly cool. To compound their confusion, a violent quarrel between Twisted Hair and a rival chief, The Cutnose, immediately ensued. The captains could neither account for this dispute, nor for Twisted Hair's lack of cordiality. Being anxious to terminate the quarrel, Lewis tried to persuade his Shoshone guide to explain; but this circumspect individual insisted that it was a private matter concerning which he preferred to remain silent. Disappointed and somewhat alarmed, Lewis and his companions withdrew and prepared to camp for the night. Thereon, the rival chiefs established separate camps nearby.

Being anxious to placate Twisted Hair, Lewis dispatched Drewyer with

37

an invitation for the chief to come and smoke with him. Evidently, the warmth of the campfire and the fragrance of the tobacco were sufficient to warm his spirit and loosen his tongue. He explained how his acceptance of responsibility for the captain's horses had resulted in trouble with Cut-nose and other subordinate chiefs of his nation. Eventually, he had been obliged to concede to them. In short, he had granted permission for Cut-nose and one or two subchiefs to use the horses during the winter. As a result they were scattered, and it would be difficult to round them up. Moreover, the cache of pack saddles had been exposed during the spring floods, and some of them were lost in spite of the fact that he himself had supervised the depositing of them. He thought most of the horses could be recovered, but it would take time to find them.

Lewis was disturbed by this news, but he thanked the chief and assured him that when the horses were delivered the fee originally agreed upon, two guns and a supply of ammunition, would be paid in full. Twisted Hair was now entirely satisfied, and promised to do everything possible to recover the horses. Cutnose, who was then brought into the council, agreed rather grudgingly to cooperate.

The next day, Lewis and Clark proceeded to Twisted Hair's village, which was six miles distant. The hunters were sent out, but they soon returned with nothing more tangible than a few grouse. During the afternoon the saddle cache was opened. About half of the pack saddles, and some powder and lead were recovered. Late in the day the Indians delivered twenty-one of the horses; three of them had saddle sores, and a few showed evidence of hard riding, but the majority were in good condition.

At Lawyer's Creek Lewis and Clark were surprised to find another friendly chief, Broken Arm, waiting to welcome them back to his village. After the ceremonial pipe had been smoked and put aside, Lewis pointed out that he was destitute of provisions and that his men were hungry. Two bushels of dried roots and some smoked salmon were brought forth immediately. However, fearing that this diet would induce the usual discomfort if not supplemented by meat, Lewis offered to trade two good horses which were rather thin for two fat ones. The chief declined to barter, but said he would be glad to give his guests as many horses as they might require, and two fine animals were promptly delivered. Lewis was deeply moved by this act of hospitality and ordered his men to treat the Indians with more than ordinary respect.

News of the white men's return spread rapidly, and two neighboring chiefs with their respective retinues appeared the next morning to pay their respects. Finding four important chiefs assembled Lewis concluded that a grand council was in order. He took advantage of the opportunity to address them at length concerning the objectives of the journey, and the good intentions of the United States government. He urged them to make peace with their neighbors and ended by inviting them to send a representative to visit the Great White Father in Washington.

Broken Arm then spoke for his people saying that he was now convinced of the sincerity of the white men; that he agreed in principle with what had been proposed but could not make any commitments until the issues had been considered by all of the chiefs assembled.

Because of the difficulty of communication such councils generally lasted for several hours. In this instance Lewis' words were translated into French, repeated in Minnetare by Charbono, then in Shoshone by Saca-jawea, and, finally, converted into the Chopunnish dialect by a Shoshone prisoner.

While waiting for the Indians to reach an agreement, Lewis and Clark resumed their medical practice administering to all who consulted them. Scrofula, rheumatism, and sore eyes were familiar afflictions, but one case had them baffled. It involved a middle aged chieftain who had been totally helpless for three years. Unable to move his legs or arms, he was brought to them on a litter. Otherwise, he appeared healthy. This certainly was a case that might ruin Clark's reputation. Fortunately, however, Bratton, who had been unable to walk since January, had recently been relieved con-siderably by a few sweat-baths. It seemed likely that the Indian might be helped by similar treatments. Accordingly, Clark supervised the digging of a deep pit, in the bottom of which hot stones were placed. A stool was pro-vided for the convenience of the patient; but, because he could not sit up alone, one of the braves entered the pit with him. Water was then poured over the stones, and hides were draped over the mouth of the pit to retain the steam. After an hour in the sweat-chamber the Indian was dunked in cold water and wrapped in blankets. After two treatments he could move his hands and feet, and in a few days he was able to stand and walk about with some assistance. Clark's reputation was not impaired.

A view of the snow covered heights of the Bitterroot Mountains ap-peared to support the Indians' contention that the mountain passes would not be open before mid-June. It was evident to Lewis and Clark that they would have to establish a base-camp where grass was plentiful for the horses, and where game was more abundant. Broken Arm recommended a site at the edge of an extensive meadow bordering the Clearwater River.[44]

Occasionally, the hunters brought in a bear or a deer, but more often they returned empty-handed. On May 21 Lewis divided his meagre stock of merchandise among the men so that each of them could take advantage of any chance that presented itself to buy food. Each man's share consisted of one awl, one knitting pin, two needles, a few skeins of thread, a yard of ribbon, and a half ounce of vermillion. The results were not wholly successful. Two of the men lost their allotments, and two blankets and a coat besides, when they overturned a canoe in crossing the river; two others lost their trading stock when a horse slipped off a cliff and fell into the river; and another lost a supply of roots and "bread" when some Indians capsized a raft in attempting to deliver it.

> This failure completely exhausted our stock of merchandise; . . . . We therefore created a new fund by cutting off the buttons from our clothes, preparing some eye water and basilicon, to which were added some vials, and small tin boxes, in which we once kept phosphorus.[45]

During the month spent with the Chopunnish Indians the Clearwater River had fallen about six feet. This seemed to indicate that the snow in the mountains was receding. On June 10 it was decided to move northward to Weippe Prairie and tackle the rugged trail to Lolo Pass. They made the attempt, but were forced to turn back because the snow was still twelve to fifteen feet deep at high elevations. The trail was obscure and there was no grass for the horses. Finally, on June 24, they moved out of the Quamash Flats, near Weippe, for a second attack on the western slope of the Bitterroots. This time they were successful. By July 1, they were back at Traveler's Rest on the Bitterroot River.

Lewis had learned from the Nez Percé the previous year that he might have avoided several hundred miles of exhausting travel if he had led his party westward from Great Falls to Lolo Pass instead of pursuing the Missouri to its headwaters and then going over the Beaverhead Mountains via Lemhi Pass.

Since it was obviously desirable to explore as much territory as possible, Lewis and Clark decided to divide the party and take separate routes. Lewis agreed to pursue the reported shortcut to Great Falls and explore the Marias River; meanwhile Clark would return to the headwaters of the Missouri in order to recover the canoes and other materials that had been cached at the mouth of Prairie Creek, and then descend the Yellowstone River.

Accordingly, Lewis selected nine men and one or more Indian guides to accompany him. The trail which he followed passed through the present site of Missoula, Montana, thence eastward by way of the Blackfoot River Valley, over the Rockies in the vicinity of Roger's Pass. By July 11, 1806, he was back at the old campsite on the Missouri opposite Whitebear Island.

As soon as possible the cache of supplies and specimens was opened, but Lewis was disappointed to find that water had seeped into the pit during the spring floods and ruined all of the animal skins and pressed plants. However, several other articles that had been packed in trunks were damaged but little, and Clark's carefully drafted maps of the Missouri were in good condition.

Having completed all arrangements for transporting the equipment and supplies over the long portage around the Great Falls, Lewis set out with three men and six horses to explore the headwaters of the Marias River. They rode northward across the plains and on the second day after leaving the falls of the Missouri they arrived at the Marias. They travelled upstream at a leisurely pace for four days. It is difficult to ascertain just how far they ascended the Marias because cloudy weather prevented Lewis from making astronomical observations at his furthermost campsite.

Although Lewis waited three days for the sky to clear, it did not do so. On September 26 he decided to turn back, being somewhat apprehensive of being discovered by a band of Indian hunters. Evidently there was reason to be alarmed. He had not proceeded far down river when he saw a small party of Indians, with more than two dozen ponies, on the bluff about a mile ahead. They were evidently watching Drewyer who was hunting on the opposite side of the stream. Lewis and his two companions, the Fields brothers, were tempted to flee; but they concluded that to do so would mean sacrificing Drewyer. Instead they rode forward resolutely in the hope of establishing friendly relations. They were relieved to see only eight braves approaching. The Indians halted at a distance of one hundred yards, and one of them came forward alone. Lewis, likewise, stopped his companions, and met the Indian unattended. They exchanged a few words of greeting, and it appeared that hostilities had been averted.

The two parties exchanged gifts, smoked together, spent the evening in conversation, and retired for the night before the same campfire. Lewis' apprehension appeared to have been groundless. Nevertheless, Joseph and Reuben Fields were ordered to share the watch throughout the night.

Sunday, July 27, 1806.

This morning at daylight the indians got up and crouded around the fire, J. Fields who was on post had carelessly laid his gun down behind him near where his brother was sleeping, one of the indians the fellow to whom I had given the medal last evening sliped behind him and took his gun and that of his brother unperceived by him, at the same instant two others advanced and seized the guns of Drewyer and myself, J. Fields seeing this turned about to look for his gun and saw the fellow just runing off with her and his brother's he called to his brother who instantly jumped up and pursued the indian with him whom they overtook at the distance of 50 or 60 paces from the camp seized their guns and rested them from him and R. Fields as he seized his gun sťabed the indian to the heart with his knife, the fellow ran about 15 steps and fell dead; of this I did not know untill afterwards,[46] having recovered their guns they ran back instantly to the camp; Drewyer who was awake saw the indian take hold of his gun and instantly jumped up and seized her and rested her from him but the indian still retained his pouch, his jumping up and crying damn you let go my gun awakened me, I jumped up and asked what was the matter which I quickly learned when I saw Drewyer in a scuffle with the indian for his gun. I reached to seize my gun but found her gone, I then drew a pistol from my holster and terning myself about saw the indian making off with my gun. I ran at him with my pistol and bid him lay down my gun which he was in the act of doing when the Fieldses returned and drew up their guns to shoot him which I forbid as he did not appear to be about to make any resistance or commit any offensive act, he droped the gun and walked slowly off, I picked her up instantly, Drewyer having about this time recovered his gun and pouch asked me if he might not kill the fellow which I also forbid as the indian did not appear to wish to kill us, as soon as they found us all in possession of our arms they ran and indeavored to drive off all the horses. I now hollowed to the men and told them to fire on them if they attempted to drive off our horses, they accordingly pursued the main party who were driving the horses up the river and I pursued the man who had taken my gun who with another was driving off a part of the horses which were to the left of the camp. I pursued them so closely that they could not take twelve of their own horses but continued to drive one of mine with some others; at the distance of three hundred paces they entered one of those steep nitches in the bluff with the horses before them being out of breath I could pursue no further, I called to them as I had done several times before that I would shoot them if they did not give me my horse and raised my gun, one of them jumped behind a rock and spoke to the other who turned arround and stoped at the distance of 30 steps from me and I shot him through the belly, he fell to his knees and on his wright elbow from which position he partly raised himself up and fired at me, and turning himself about crawled in behind a rock which was a few feet from him. he overshot me, being bearheaded I felt the wind of his bullet very distinctly. not having my shotpouch I could not reload my piece and as there were two of them behind good shelters from me I did not think it prudent to rush on them with my pistol which had I discharged I had not the means of reloading untill I reached camp; I therefore returned leasurely towards camp, on my way I met with Drewyer who having heard the report of the guns had returned in surch of me and left the Fieldes to pursue the indians, I desired him to haisten to the camp with me and assist in catching as many of the indian horses as were necessary and to call to the Fieldes if he could make them hear to come back that we still had a sufficient number of horses, this he did but they were too far to hear him. we reached the camp and began to catch the horses and saddle them and put on the packs. the reason I had not my pouch with me was that I had not time to return about 50 yards to camp after geting my gun before I was obliged to pursue the indians or suffer them to collect and drive off the horses. we had caught and saddled the horses and began to arrange the packs when the Fieldes returned with four of our horses; we left one of our horses and took four of the best of those of the indian's; while the men were preparing the horses I put four sheilds and two bows and quivers of arrows which had been left on the fire, with sundry other articles; they left all their baggage at our mercy. they had but 2 guns and one of them they left the others were armed with bows and arrows and eyedaggs. the gun we took with us. I also retook the flagg but left the medal about the neck of the dead man that they might be informed who we were. we took some of their buffaloe meat and set out ascending the bluffs by the same rout we had decended last evening leaving the ballance of nine of their horses which we did not want. the Fieldses told me that three of the indians whom they pursued swam the river one of them on my horse. and that two others ascended the hill and escaped from them with a part of their horses, two I had pursued into the nitch one lay dead near the camp and the eighth we could not account for but suppose that he ran off early in the contest. having ascended the hill we took our course through a beautifull level plain a little to the S. of East. my design was to hasten to the entrance of Maria's river as quick as possible in the hope of meeting with the canoes and party at that place having no doubt but that they (the Indians) would pursue us with a large party and as there was a band near the broken mountains or probably between them and the mouth of the river we might expect them to receive inteligence from us and arrive at that place nearly as soon as we could, no time was therefore to be lost and we pushed our horses as hard as they would bear. at 8 miles we passed a large branch 40 yds wide which I called battle river.[47] At 3 P. M. we arrived at rose river about 5 miles above where we had passed it as we went out, having traveled by my estimate compared with our former distances and courses about 63 ms. here we halted an hour and a half took some refreshment and suffered our horses to graize; the day proved warm but the late rains had supplyed the little reservoirs in the plains with water and had put them in fine order for traveling, our whole rout so far was as level as a bowling green with but little stone and few prickly pears. after dinner we pursued the bottoms of rose river but finding it inconvenient to pass the river so often we again ascended the hills on the S. W. side and took the open plains; by dark we had traveled about 17 miles further, we now halted to rest ourselves and horses about 2 hours, we killed a buffaloe cow and took a small quantity of meat. after refreshing ourselves we again set out by moonlight and traveled leasurely, heavy thunderclouds lowered arround us on every quarter but that from which the moon gave us light. we continued to pass immence herds of buffaloe all night as we had done in the latter part of the day. we traveled untill 2 OCk in the morning having come by my estimate after dark about 20 m⁵· we now turned out our horses and laid ourselves down to rest in the plain very much fatiegued as may be readily conceived.[48] my indian horse carried me very well in short much better than my own would have done and leaves me with but little reason to complain of the robery.[49]

Monday, July 28, 1806.

The morning proved fair, I slept sound but fortunately awoke as day appeared, I awaked the men and directed the horses to be saddled, I was so soar from my ride yesterday that I could scarcely stand, and the men complained of being in a similar situation however I encouraged them by telling them that our own lives as well as those of our friends and fellow travellers depended on our exertions at this moment; they were allert soon prepared the horses and we again resumed our march; the men proposed to pass the missouri at the grog spring where rose river approaches it so nearly and pass down on the S. W. side, to this I objected as it would

43

delay us almost all day to reach the point[50] by this circuetous rout and would give the enemy time to surprise and cut off the party at the point if they had arrived there, I told them that we owed much to the safety of our friends and that we must wrisk our lives on this occasion, that I should proceed immediately to the point and if the party had not arrived that I would raft the missouri a small distance above, hide our baggage and march on foot up the river through the timber untill I met the canoes or joined them at the falls; I now told them that it was my determination that if we were attacked in the plains on our way to the point that the bridles of the horses should be tied together and we would stand and defend them, or sell our lives as dear as we could. we had proceeded about 12 miles on an East course when we found ourselves near the missouri; we heard a report which we took to be that of a gun but were not certain; still continuing down the N. E. bank of the missouri about 8 miles further, being then within five miles of the grog spring we heard the report of several rifles very distinctly on the river to our right, we quickly repared to this joyfull sound and on arriving at the bank of the river had the unspeakable satisfaction to see our canoes coming down. . . . having now nothing to detain us we passed over immediately to the island in the entrance of Maria's river . . . and reimbarked on board the white perogue and five small canoes. . . .[51]

It was July 29 when Lewis and his enlarged party started down river. They made rapid progress with the aid of the current. By August 7 they reached the mouth of the Yellowstone where they found a note from Clark informing them that he had moved down stream to look for a more comfortable place to camp. According to Clark's diary the mosquitoes were so numerous in the river bottom near the Yellowstone that it was impossible to rest or sleep.

Lewis had not yet overtaken Clark three days later. On August 11 he stopped opposite the "birnt hills," in the vicinity of the Little Knife River, to determine the latitude at high noon. He arrived at this geographic landmark, however, twenty minutes too late to take the meridian altitude. Instead, Lewis and a few hunters set off to kill some elk. Unfortunately, during the excitement of the hunt, occurred one of the earliest, and probably the first recorded, instance of a type of accident too common today.

Aug. 11, 1806

Just opposite to the birnt hills there happened to be a herd of Elk on a thick willow bar and finding that my observation was lost for the present I determined to land and kill some of them accordingly we put too and I went out with Cruzatte only. we fired on the Elk I killed one and he wounded another, we reloaded our guns and took different routs through the thick willows in pursuit of Elk; I was in the act of firing on the Elk a second time when a ball struck my left thye about an inch below my hip joint, missing the bone it passed through the left thye and cut the thickness of the bullet across the hinder part of the right thye; the stroke was very severe; I instantly supposed that Cruzatte had shot me in mistake for an

Elk as I was dressed in brown leather and he cannot see very well; under this impression I called out to him damn you, you have shot me, and looked towards the place from whence the ball had come, seeing nothing I called Cruzatte several times as loud as I could but received no answer; I was now preswaded that it was an indian that had shot me as the report of the gun did not appear to be more than 40 paces from me and Cruzatte appeared to be out of hearing of me; in this situation not knowing how many indians there might be concealed in the bushes I thought best to make good my retreat to the perogue, calling out as I ran for the first hundred paces as I could to Cruzatte to retreat that there were indians hoping to allarm him in time to make his escape also; I still retained the charge in my gun which I was about to discharge at the moment the ball struck me. when I arrived in sight of the perogue I called the men to their arms to which they flew in an instant, I told them that I was wounded but I hope not mortally, by an indian I believed and directed them follow me that I would return & give them battle and releive Cruzatte if possible who I feared had fallen into their hands; the men followed me as they were bid and I returned about a hundred paces when my wounds became so painfull and my thys so stiff that I could scarcely get on; in short, I was compelled to halt and ordered the men to proceed and if they found themselves overpowered by numbers to retreat in order keeping up a fire. I now got back to the perogue as well as I could and prepared myself with a pistol, my rifle and air-gun being determined, as a retreat was impracticable, to sell my life as deerly as possible. in this state of anxiety and suspense I remained about 20 minutes when the party returned with Cruzatte and reported that there were no indians nor the appearance of any; Cruzatte seemed much allarmed and declared if he had shot me it was not his intention, that he had shot an Elk in the willows after he left or separated from me. I asked him whether he did not hear me when I called to him so frequently which he absolutely denied. I do not believe that the fellow did it intentionally but after finding that he had shot me was anxious to conceal his knowledge of having done so. the ball had lodged in my breeches which I knew to be the ball of the short rifles such as that he had, and there being no person out with me but him and no indians that we could discover I have no doubt in my own mind of his having shot me. with the assistance of Sergt. Gass I took off my clothes and dressed my wounds myself as well as I could, introducing tents of patent lint into the ball holes, the wounds blead considerably but I was hapy to find that it had touched neither bone nor artery. I sent the men to dress the two Elk which Cruzatte and myself had killed which they did in a few minutes and brought the meat to the river. the small canoes came up shortly after with the flexh of one Elk. my wounds being so situated that I could not without infinite pain make an observation I determined to relinquish it and proceeded on.[52]

After taking leave of Lewis at Traveler's Rest, Clark with fifteen men and about fifty horses proceeded southward to the head of the Bitterroot Valley. Sacajawea guided them over the mountains, probably by way of

Gibbon's Pass, to the valley of the Big Hole River, thence, southward to the mouth of Prairie Creek.

The canoes which had been sunk in the stream at this, the head of navigation, before Lewis and Clark had gone over Lemhi Pass on the outward journey, were raised and the cache of surplus supplies was opened. Everything was recovered intact except one canoe which was staved in at the bow.

After the canoes had been dried out, and everything made ready for departure on July 10, some of the men were put in charge of the horses, and others manned the canoes for the trip down the Beaverhead and Jefferson Rivers. At Three Forks Clark divided his party. Sergeant Ordway and nine men set off down the Missouri in six canoes to join Lewis' party at the Great Falls; whereas, Sacajawea led Clark and six of his men across the plains to the Yellowstone River.[53]

Clark's immediate problem was to find timber on the banks of the Yellowstone that was large enough for making dugout canoes, and with this in mind he continued downstream. They were detained by the necessity of rounding up the herd of horses every morning. Besides, their favorite mounts had become footsore, and Clark resorted to making moccasins for them out of raw buffalo hide. After marching down the Yellowstone for three days, they saw smoke in the distant hills which they interpreted as being a signal of the Crow Indians, but could not afford the time to make certain. Their situation was further aggravated by an accident. Private Gibson fell in attempting to mount his horse after shooting a deer and drove the sharp stump of a sapling into the muscular part of his thigh. The wound was deep and painful; and, as a result, it was necessary to rig a horse-borne litter that permitted him to ride in a semiprone position. After a few miles, however, his injury became so painful that he could not proceed, so he was left with two men in the shade of a small tree. Clark went on to look for timber, and made camp in a grove several miles downstream. The two men carried Gibson into camp late in the evening. None of the trees comprising the grove were as large as desirable, but under the circumstances, Clark decided they would have to serve and the men were instructed to chop down two of the largest. Since the horses were much fatigued they were turned loose to graze in the valley. The next morning twenty-four of them were missing, probably stolen by the Indians whose signal fires had been seen at a distance. Men were sent out to search for the horses, or for signs that they had been stolen, but they could not be found.

The rest of the men were kept busy at hunting, dressing skins for clothing, and working on two canoes which were described as being twenty-eight feet long, sixteen to eighteen inches deep, and sixteen to twenty-four inches

46

wide. When completed, they were lashed together for greater stability and loaded for departure on July 24. Before leaving, Sergeant Pryor and Privates Shannon and Windsor were ordered to round up the remaining horses and take them over the plains to Fort Mandan. Clark then wrote a letter to Mr. Haney, of the Hudson Bay Company, asking him to prevail on some of the important Sioux chiefs to accompany him to Washington. Since it was expected that Sergeant Pryor could make much better time with the horses than Clark could with the canoes, the letter was entrusted to him for delivery.

On the second day of canoe travel, Clark landed to examine a notable feature of the landscape which he named Pompey's Pillar. This was, and is, a towering column of rock four hundred paces in circumference and two hundred feet in height. He scrambled up the northeast slope of this tower for a look at the countryside, and carved his name and the date on the face of the rock.[54]

Clark's notes on the topographic and physiographic features of the Yellowstone were extensive. His reports on the abundance and distribution of game birds and mammals were equally detailed. Bison and elk were plentiful, but deer and antelope were less numerous. Near Glendive, Montana, he was delayed by buffalo which were crossing the river. A herd of forty bighorns was seen in the vicinity of Pompey's Pillar. Beaver, especially on some of the tributaries of the Yellowstone, were considered to be as abundant as on the upper Missouri.

When Clark arrived at the mouth of the Yellowstone on August 3, the canoes were unloaded and the baggage exposed to dry. The mosquitoes were so numerous, however, that the camp was uninhabitable. The men could neither work nor rest. Accordingly, Clark left a note for Lewis advising that he was continuing down the Missouri until he found a more favorable campsite. On the night of August 7 he camped on a sandbar where a violent wind temporarily solved the mosquito problem.

Sergeant Pryor and his companions arrived the next day, but without the horses. He reported that a band of Indians had stolen them on the second night after he had left Clark on the upper Yellowstone. After trailing the Indians for a few miles on foot they gave up the chase and returned to their camp on a tributary stream. Then they carried their baggage to the Yellowstone, near Pompey's Pillar, where they killed a couple of bison and utilized their hides in constructing two bullboats which had served admirably for floating down the river.

Clark did not wait for Lewis, but continued down the Missouri at a leisurely rate. On August 11 he observed a canoe near the shore and landed to investigate. He was surprised at finding two trappers, Dickson and Hancock, of Illinois, who were bound for the upper Missouri in quest of

47

beaver. Instead of continuing, however, they decided to return to the Mandans with Clark's party.

Lewis' party finally overtook Clark a few miles above the mouth of the Little Missouri on August 12. Clark was much disturbed at finding Lewis wounded, but there was much rejoicing over the fact that everyone was accounted for, and that Fort Mandan was only a few miles ahead.

Back among the Minnetarees and Mandans, Lewis and Clark were well received. Blackcat, chief of the Mandans, was particularly hospitable; and Le Borgne, the grand chief of the Minnetarees, accepted a personal invitation to visit Lewis and Clark's camp for a council meeting. Clark addressed the chiefs assembled, both individually and collectively. He advised them to make peace with their neighbors and their traditional enemies. He reminded them of the advantages of trade with the United States, and again invited them to send one or more of their influential chiefs to Washington for a visit with President Jefferson. Both Blackcat and Le Borgne expressed fear that the Sioux would ambush the expedition. Eventually, however, Big White, a subchief of the Mandans, agreed to go with Lewis and Clark provided his wife and son could accompany him.[55]

During these councils which occupied the better part of two days John Colter was persuaded by Dickson and Hancock, the trappers from Illinois, to accompany them back up the Missouri to trap beaver. Accordingly, he asked for his discharge from the Army; and Clark, upon being assured by all other enlisted men that none of them would make similar requests, approved Colter's request and paid him off.

On August 16, all business having been concluded, Lewis and Clark bid the Mandans and Minnetarees farewell, and got under way. Clark's description of their leave-taking illustrates the high level of diplomacy that was characteristic of their dealings with most of the Indians which they encountered.

> The principal chiefs of the Minnetarees came down to bid us farewell, as none of them could be prevailed on to go with us. This circumstance induced our interpreter, Chaboneau, with his wife and child, to remain here, as he could be no longer useful; and notwithstanding our offers of taking him with us to the United States, he said that he had there no acquaintance and no chance of making a livlihood, and preferred remaining among the Indians. This man has been very serviceable to us, and his wife particularly useful among the Shoshonees. Indeed, she has borne with a patience truly admirable the fatigues of so long a route incumbered with the charge of an infant, who is even now only nineteen months old. We therefore paid him his wages, amounting to five hundred dollars and thirty-three cents, including the price of a horse and a lodge purchased of him; and soon afterwards dropped down to the village of the Bigwhite, attended on shore by all the Indian chiefs who went to take leave of

48

him. We found him surrounded by his friends, who sat in a circle smoking, while the women were crying. He immediately sent his wife and son, with their baggage, on board, accompanied by the interpreter and his wife, and two children; and then after distributing among his friends some powder and ball, which we had given to him, and smoking a pipe with us, went with us to the river side. The whole village crowded about us, and many of the people wept aloud at the departure of the chief. As Captain Clark was shaking hands with the principal chiefs of all the villages, they requested that he would sit with them one moment longer. Being willing to gratify them he stopped and ordered a pipe, after smoking which they informed him that when they first saw us they did not believe all that we then told them; but having now seen that our words were all true, they would carefully remember them, and follow our advice; that he might tell their great father that the young men should remain at home and not make war on any people except in defence of themselves. They requested him to tell the Ricaras to come and visit them without fear, as they meant that nation no harm, but were desirous of peace with them. On the Sioux, however, they had no dependence, and must kill them whenever they made war parties against their country. Captain Clark, in reply, informed them that we had never insisted on their not defending themselves, but requested only that they would not strike those whom we had taken by the hand; that we would apprise the Ricaras of their friendly intentions, and that, although we had not seen those of the Sioux with whom they were at war, we should relate their conduct to their great father, who would take measures for producing a general peace among all his red children.

The Borgne now requested that we would take good care of this chief, who would report whatever their great father should say; and the council being then broken up, we took leave with a salute from a gun, and then proceeded. On reaching fort Mandan, we found a few pickets standing on the river side, but all the houses except one had been burnt by an accidental fire. At the distance of eighteen miles we reached the old Ricara village, where we encamped on the southwest side, the wind being too violent and the waves too high to permit us to go any further. The same cause prevented us from setting out before eight o'clock the next day.[56]

A few miles below the Mandan villages, Clark landed to pay his respects to the Arikaras, and the Cheyennes who were camped nearby. In spite of this delay and others necessitated by unfavorable weather, or the want of meat and specimens, the party made good progress.

Below the mouth of the White River in South Dakota, a large band of Indians was seen on the bluffs of the river; and suspecting them to be Tetons, Clark ordered the boats to the opposite shore. Then, to ascertain their identity and intentions, Clark, with three men, crossed over to a sandbar. He was met by eight young men who affirmed that they belonged to the Teton nation. Their leader was Black-buffalo, the same chief who had attempted to stop the explorers on the trip upstream, two years earlier. Clark reminded them of this incident, and of their reported raids on the

Mandans and Arikaras. He also advised them that if they attempted to cross the river to his camp they would be killed. Both parties then withdrew, and Clark prepared for an attack. The Indians, however, declined the challenge and departed.

No other hostile tribes were encountered below the Dakotas, and the boatmen, with the aid of the current, averaged fifty miles per day. They passed the mouth of the Platte River on September 9. Below the Nodawa they met a small party of traders headed for the Arikara villages. With them were Mr. Gravelines and old Pierre Durion, both of whom had served Lewis and Clark previously as interpreters when they were dealing with the tribes encountered below Fort Mandan. Since last seen Mr. Gravelines had visited Washington with an Arikara chief who had died in that city. He was now returning to Arikaras with presents which had been given to the unfortunate Indian. Lewis and Clark spent the evening with Gravelines and McClellan, the leader of the party, getting their first news of happenings in the United States in more than two years.

The expedition arrived safely in St. Louis on September 23, 1806. All members of the party were paid for their services and discharged. Lewis and Clark purchased new clothing, attended a dinner and a dance on the evening of their arrival, and the next morning began the task of transcribing their journals. Thus ended one of the most adventurous expeditions in American history.

And, what was accomplished?

Certainly, much more was achieved than might have been expected. Not all, but many of the objectives delineated by Jefferson in his letter of instructions were accomplished.

Most obvious, of course, was the journey itself which opened a trail to the Pacific; a trail over which the vast wealth of the Rocky Mountain fur trade, for more than forty years, poured into St. Louis, Missouri.

Every mile of the route up the Missouri, across the mountains, and down the Columbia was surveyed and measured. Compass bearings and distances, from landmark to landmark, were faithfully recorded as Lewis and Clark followed the courses of the meandering rivers. This data, combined with their determinations of the latitude and longitude of all of the principal topographic features, enabled Clark to prepare maps of the territory— maps which were not improved upon until government surveys were made forty to fifty years later.

Lewis and Clark listed all of the Indian tribes which they encountered and located their villages on the maps. They estimated the population and designated the principal chiefs of each tribe. They described the intertribal relations, the economic status, the customs and ceremonies and, insofar as practicable, recorded the languages of the tribes. In addition, they determined the boundaries of the lands claimed by the different tribes, and assayed the trade potential of the more important Indian nations in terms of United States money.

The expedition's leaders diligently studied the strange plants and animals which they discovered. Nevertheless, Lewis and Clark got little, if any, scientific credit for their discoveries because in most instances they could not produce specimens to verify their descriptions. Most of the animals and plants which they collected were damaged or lost for lack of adequate means of preserving and transporting them. Only a few mammal and bird skins and only one hundred and fifty-five pressed plants were brought out of the wilderness.

I have been able to recount only the highlights of the Lewis and Clark Expedition, but I have attempted to include sufficient detail to enable one to envision the magnitude and significance of the undertaking. Louisiana Territory was paid for with substance other than money; it was won through the hardship and perseverance of Lewis and Clark, and the trappers, fur traders, and pioneer settlers who succeeded them.

June, 1960   Raymond Darwin Burroughs

CHAPTER II
Bears and Raccoons

No significant reports dealing with wildlife populations in the Missouri valley and westward to the Pacific were available to zoologists prior to those made by Lewis and Clark. With respect to the black bear, they added to our knowledge of its geographic range and color variations; and, in case of the grizzly bear, their description of the species led to its recognition as a species and their records relating to its abundance, distribution, and habits are remarkable in scope and detail. Besides, their graphic accounts of encounters with the grizzly are as exciting as any fictional experience.

THE BLACK BEAR

The black bear, *Ursus americanus* Pallas, was one of the most widely distributed big game mammals on the North American continent in primitive times. It occupied an area extending from the Atlantic to the Pacific coasts and from the tundras of Canada to the Gulf of Mexico. There was, however, a wide gap in their range which included southeastern Oregon, southwestern Idaho, all of Nevada, western Utah, western Arizona, southern California and western Mexico.

The Lewis and Clark party killed their first black bear near the mouth of Good Woman's River in Missouri on June 7, 1804. Thereafter they reported killing bear in the vicinity of the Chariton River, the Grand River, and Malta Bend of the Missouri which was evidently located near the town of Carrollton, Missouri. On June 24, 1804, in the vicinity of Little Blue River, Jackson County, Missouri, they "Observed great quantities of Bear Signs, where they had passed in all Directions thro' the bottoms in Search of Mulberries, which were in great numbers in all the bottoms thro' which our party passed."

Black bears were not mentioned again until April 15, 1805, when one of them was seen in North Dakota near the mouth of the Little Missouri. However, in a letter to his mother, written at Fort Mandan, Lewis listed "some bear" among the big game animals inhabiting the Missouri valley between Kansas and Big Sioux Rivers (Appendix).

While encamped above the mouth of the Musselshell River in Montana, Lewis commented on the scarcity of black bear on the upper Missouri:

May 22, 1805.

"I do not believe that the Black Bear, common to the Lower part of this river and the Atlantic States, exists in this quarter; we have neither seen one of them nor their tracks, which would be easily distinguished by its shortness of tallons when compared with the brown, grizly or white bear."

Lewis, of course, was not beyond the range of the black bear, and it seems odd that he did not kill any of them on the Missouri above the Kansas River. John Bradbury,[1] a reputable naturalist who accompanied an expedition to Fort Mandan in 1809, had a similar experience. He made note of the killing of a female bear and the capture of three cubs near Fort Osage, Jackson County, Missouri, but he made no further reference to the black bear above that point on the river. During his journey to the Yellowstone River by steamboat in 1833 Maximillian[2] likewise mentioned the killing of only one black bear and the capture of her three cubs, at the mouth of the James River near Yankton, South Dakota.

On the other hand, Alexander Henry[3] found no scarcity of black bears in the valley of the Red River in the vicinity of his Park River and Pembina River posts.[4] According to Henry, his trappers collected 746 black bear skins in a five year period, 1800-1805. It is interesting to note that 195 of these hides were of the brown phase.

Some idea of the abundance of black bear on the Red River may be gained from Henry's diary:

Sept. 20, 1800 (Post at Mouth of Park River)

"At noon two Indians came from above to ask me to send a large canoe for what they had collected at their tents. They informed me they had killed 40 bears, some red deer, moose, and a few beavers and raccoons."—Henry.

Sept. 22, 1800 (Park River Post)

"Bears make prodigious ravages in the brush and willows; the plum trees are torn to pieces, and every tree that bears fruit has shared the same fate; the tops of the oaks are also roughly handled, broken and torn down to get the acorns. The havoc they commit is astonishing; their dung lies about in the woods as plentiful as that of the buffalo in the meadow."
—Henry

We cannot account for the apparent scarcity of black bears in the Missouri River bottoms above the lush woodlands and intermittent prairies of the lower river; we can only suggest that some factor in the habitat of the more sparsely wooded valley of the upper river limited their numbers. Not a single specimen of the black bear was seen or taken by the Lewis and Clark party between the Little Missouri River and the Bitterroot Mountains of Montana. Grizzly bear, however, were encountered and killed frequently between the mouth of the Yellowstone and Three Forks,

Montana. Thereafter, on the outward journey, no bear of any description were reported until the Expedition had settled at Fort Clatsop for the winter of 1805-06.

Feb. 9, 1806 (Fort Clatsop)

"In the evening Drewyer returned; he had killed nothing but one beaver. He saw one black bear, which was the only one which has been seen in this neighborhood since our arrival; the Indians inform us that they are aboudant but now in their holes."—Lewis

Possibly Lewis and Clark abandoned Fort Clatsop before the bears became active in the Spring; they started back up the Columbia on March 23, 1806. The only black bear reported in the kill records of the Expedition, west of the Cascade Mountains, was taken near the mouth of the Sandy River.

April 4, 1806 (Sandy River camp site)

"Serg't. Gass and party brought the flesh of a Bear and some venison . . . Collins who had killed the Bear found the Bed of another in which there was three young ones, and requested to be permitted to return in order to waylay the bed and kill the female bear; we permitted him to do so; . . ."—Lewis

April 5, 1806 (Sandy River camp site)

"This morning at 10 o'clock Serg't. Gass returned with Collins and Windsor . . . they had not succeeded in killing the female bear tho' they brought the three cubs with them. The Indians who visited us today fancyed these petts, and gave us wappetoe in exchange for them."—Lewis.

Several bears were killed during May and June while Lewis and Clark were camped on the Clearwater River in the neighborhood of Kamiah and Weippe, Idaho. Ten of these were listed as cinnamon bear, three were adult grizzlies, and two were grizzly cubs.

The various color phases of the black bear were not well understood by the pioneer settlers and hunters of the 17th and 18th centuries. The brown, or cinnamon phase of the black bear was not unknown, but it was generally regarded as a distinct species except, perhaps, by some of the early fur traders and trappers of Northwest. Alexander Henry reported an incident which indicates he was familiar with the fact that black bears produce both blond and brunette cubs in the same litter.

Aug. 11, 1808 (Pembina River Post).

"Late this evening, while the Indians were still drinking, there arrived a party of young men who had been hunting *en canot* up the Dead River;

54

they brought some fresh meat, including that of a large black bear, and her two cubs, one of which was brown, and the other perfectly black."— Henry.

Lewis and Clark were confused for a time by the color phases of both the black and grizzly bears. Eventually, they arrived at the correct conclusion with respect to the grizzly bear, and at a partial solution to the problem of color phases of black bear. As a result of their own observations and supplemental information obtained from the Indians they concluded that the black, black with white hairs intermixed, black with a white breast, uniform "bey", brown, and light reddish brown color phases of the so-called "cinnamon bear" of the intermountain states of the Northwest were all of one species, but they still regarded the "common black bear" as a separate species.

Lewis, while camped in the Clearwater River valley near Weippe Prairie on May 31, 1806, summarized his observations and conclusions relating to this problem:

"Goodrich and Willard visited the Indian Villages this morning and returned in the evening. Willard brought with him the dressed skin of a bear which he had purchased for Capt. C. this skin was an uniform pale redish brown colour, the indians informed us that it was not the Hoh-host or white bear, that it was the Yack-kah. this distinction of the indians induced us to make further inquiry relative to their opinions of the several speceis of bear in this country. we produced the several skins of the bear which we had killed at this place and one very nearly white which I had purchased. The white, the deep and pale red grizzle, the dark brown grizzle, and all those which had the extremities of the hair of a white or frosty colour without regard to the colour of the ground of the poil, they designated Hoh-host and assured us that they were the same with the white bear, that they associated together, were very vicisious, never climbed trees, and had much longer nails than the others. the black skins, those which were black with a number of entire white hairs intermixed, the black with a white breast, the uniform bey, brown and light redish brown, they designated the *Yack-kah;* said that they climbed trees, had short nails and were not vicious, that they could pursue them and kill them with safety, they also affirmed that they were much smaller than the white bear. I am disposed to adopt the Indian distinction with respect to these bear and consider them two distinct speceis. the white and the grizzly of this neighbourhood are the same of those found on the upper portion of the Missouri where the other speceis are not, and the uniform redish brown black etc. of this neighbourhood are a speceis distinct from our black bear and from the black bear of the Pacific coast which I believe to be the same with those of the Atlantic coast, and that the common black bear do not exist here. I had previously observed that the claws of some of the bear which we had killed here had much shorter tallons than the varigated or white bear usually have but supposed that they had woarn them out by scratching up roots, and these were those which the Indians called Yak-kah. on inquiry I found also that a cub of an uniform redish brown colour, pup to a female black bear intermixed with entire white hair had climbed a tree. I think this is a distinct speceis from the common black bear, because we never find the latter of any other colour than an uniform black, and also that the poil of this bear is much finer thicker and longer with a greater proportion of the fur mixed with the hair, in other rispects they are much the same."—Lewis

May 15, 1806 (Camp Chopunnish)

"at 11 A.M. the men returned with the bear that Labuich had killed. These bear gave me stronger evidence of the various coloured bear of this country being one species only, than I have heretofore had. The female was black with a considerable proportion of white hairs intermixed and a white spot in the breast, one of the young bear was jut black and the other a light redish brown or bey colour. the poil of these bear were infinitely longer, finer and thicker than the black bear. their tallons also longer and more blont as if woarn by diging roots."—Lewis

June 3, 1806 (Vic. of Weippe prairie in Idaho)

"Colter, Jos. Fields and Willard returned this evening with five deer and one bear of the brown species; the hair of this was black with a large white spot on the breast containing a small circular black spot. (This species of bear is smaller than our common black bear.) This was a female bear and as our hunters informed us had cubs last year, this they judged from the length and size of her tits, etc. This bear I am confident is not larger than the yearling cubs of our country."—Clark

Lewis and Clark cannot be criticized for concluding that the black and cinnamon bears were distinct species. Reputable zoologists still disagree about the scientific status of the cinnamon bear which has at various times during the past one hundred years been shifted from a subspecies to a distinct species: from a subspecies to a mere color phase of the black bear: and recently again has been restored to the status of a subspecies. In 1854 Audubon and Bachman named the cinnamon bear *Ursus americanus cinnamomum,* thus establishing it as a subspecies of the black bear. In 1893 Brown[5] raised it to the status of a separate species, *Ursus cinnamomeus.* In 1923 G. S. Miller[6] listed it as a subspecies in his *List of North American Recent Mammals.* By 1928 H. E. Anthony[7] described it as merely a color phase of the black bear, thus removing it from scientific status except as that of the black bear, *Ursus americanus;* and since that time many zoologists have regarded it as such. However, in 1955, Miller and Kellogg[8] again raised it to the status of a subspecies, *Euarctos americanus cinnamomum* (Audubon and Bachman); and most recently (1959) Hall and Kelson[9] also list it as a subspecies, *Ursus americanus cinnamomum* (Audubon and Bachman).

Although the record indicates that only one black bear was seen by Lewis and Clark in the neighborhood of Fort Clatsop during the winter of 1805-06, and only one was killed west of the Cascades (at the mouth of the Sandy River in April, 1806), Lewis concluded that the black bear of the Northwest was identical with that of the East.

THE GRIZZLY BEAR

Lewis and Clark were not the first of the explorer-naturalists to report the occurrence of this species *Ursus horribilis* Ord, in western North America. Seton calls our attention to the fact that Edward Umfreville,[10] who spent three years (1784-87) on the Saskatchewan River as an agent of the Hudson's Bay Company, made the first unquestionable report on the occurrence of grizzly bears in the Rocky Mountains. Five years later, Samuel Hearne[11] reported their occurrence in the vicinity of the Coppermine River northeast of Great Bear Lake. Alexander Mackenzie[12] reported seeing the tracks and dens of the grizzly bear, as well as two individuals belonging to this species, on the Peace River in 1793.

These earlier reports do not detract appreciably from Lewis and Clark's contributions to knowledge of the natural history of the grizzly bear. They were the first to contribute factual data concerning its primitive range, habits, and physical characteristics. George Ord, who supplied its scientific name in 1815, relied mainly on their notes for his technical description of the species.[13]

Clark's first reference to the grizzly bear is contained in his diary entry for Sept. 1, 1804, when he was in the vicinity of Bon Homme Island.[14]

"Above the Isd. the high land approach and form a clift to the river on the south side. This clift is called White Bear Clift. one of those animals haveing been killed in a whole in it."

Tracks of a "white" bear were seen at the mouth of the Moreau River, in South Dakota, on Oct. 7, 1804, but no grizzlies were encountered until the party reached the mouth of the Heart River near Bismarck, North Dakota. Clark's diary for Oct. 20, 1804, includes the following statement:

"Our hunters killed 10 deer and a goat today and wounded a white bear, I saw several fresh tracks of those animals which is 3 times as large as a man's track."

No other bears were seen during the fall of 1804. If any others were to

57

be found in the vicinity of Bismarck and Fort Mandan, they undoubtedly retired to their dens with the advent of winter. Bear sign was not reported again until the expedition reached the mouth of Little Missouri River on April 13, 1805:

"we found a number of carcasses of the Buffaloe lying along the shore, which had been drowned by falling through the ice in winter and lodged on shore by the high water when the river broke up about the first of this month. we saw also many tracks of the white bear of enormous size, along the river shore and about the carcases of the Buffaloe, on which I presume they feed. we have not as yet seen one of these anamals, tho' their tracks are so aboundant and recent. the men as well as ourselves are anxious to meet one of these bear. the Indians give a very formidable account of the strength and ferocity of this anamal, which they never dare to attack but in parties of six, eight or ten persons; and are even then frequently defeated with the loss of one or more of their party. the savages attack this anamal with their bows and arrows and the indiferent guns with which the traders furnish them, with these they shoot with such uncertainty and at so short a distance, that (unless shot thro' head or heart would not mortal) they frequently mis their aim and fell sacrefice to the bear. two Minetaries were killed during the last winter in an attack on a white bear. this anamall is said more frequently to attack a man on meeting with him, than to flee from him. When the Indians are about to go in quest of the white bear, previous to their departure, they paint themselves and perform all of those supersticious rights commonly observed when they are about to make war upon a neighboring nation."—Lewis

Before the end of the summer the collective tastes of the explorers for bear, and bear hunting, were surfeited. Lewis' comment of May 6, 1805, when the party was approaching the junction of the Missouri and Milk Rivers, indicates that his men were disturbed at the prospect of facing the grizzly:

"saw a brown bear swim the river above us, he disappeared before we can get in reach of him; I find that the curiossity of our party is pretty well satisfied with rispect to this anamal, for formidable appearance of the male bear killed on the 5th added to the difficulty with which they die when even shot through the vital parts, has staggered the resolution of several of them, others however seem keen for action with the bear; I expect these gentlemen will give us some amusement shortly as they (the bears—Ed.) soon begin now to coppolate."

The explorers killed their first grizzly bear at the mouth of the Yellowstone River, but thereafter this species was encountered frequently on the upper Missouri. Bears were particularly troublesome in the vicinity of the Great Falls of the Missouri and several of the hunters, including Lewis, had narrow escapes from them. Between the mouth of the Yellowstone River and Three Forks, Montana, in 1805, twenty-three grizzly bears were killed, and several escaped the hunters. None were reported, however, between Three Forks and the mouth of the Columbia River during the outward journey; but, on the return trip, six grizzly bears were taken west of the Continental Divide on the Clearwater River in Idaho, and fourteen more were killed east of the Rockies in the valleys of the Yellowstone and the Missouri.

Lewis' summary statement, written at Fort Clatsop on Feb. 16, 1806, concerning the distribution of these bears is significant:

"The brown, white or grizly bear[15] are found in the rocky mountains in the timbered parts of it or Westerly side but rarely; they are more common below the rocky Mountain on the borders of the plains where there are copses of brush and underwood near the water courses. they are by no means as plenty on this side of the rocky mountains as on the other, nor do I believe that they are found at all in the woody country, which borders this coast as far in the interior as the range of mountains which, pass the Columbia between the Great Falls and rapids of that river."

Reference to the diaries of other naturalists and fur traders who traveled through the Louisiana Territory, and the North West has provided supplemental data on the distribution and abundance of the grizzly bear in the early years of the nineteenth century.

Robert Stuart[16] who led a small party of men on an overland trip from Astoria to St. Louis in 1812-13, killed a grizzly bear on Oct. 5, 1812, in the neighborhood of Driggs, Idaho, a few miles west of Grand Teton National Park.

Alexander Henry[17] found the grizzly bear inhabiting the valley of the Red River, and the neighboring Hair Hills in North Dakota.

Oct. 17, 1800 (Park River Post)

"During my absence the hunter had killed a large grizzly bear about a mile from the fort. He had seen two males and a female, but the latter escaped. My people having cooked and eaten some of the flesh were taken very ill, and most of them threw it up. This bear had been wounded in the fore leg some time before by an arrow, the iron head of which stuck fast in the one, and was beginning to rust. Grizzly bears are not numerous along the Red River, but more abundant in the Hair Hills. At Lac du Diable, which is about 30 leagues west they are very common—I am told as common as the black bear is here—, and very malicious. Near that lake runs a principal branch of the Schian (Sheyenne River), which is partially wooded. On the banks of the river I am informed they are also very numerous, and seldom molested by hunters, it being the frontier of the Sioux, where none can hunt in safety; so there they breed and multiply in security."—Henry

Grizzly bears were still plentiful in the Missouri valley above the mouth of the Little Missouri River in 1833. Maximillian[18] found them plentiful when he visted Manuel Lisa's trading post at the mouth of the Yellowstone in that year.

June 22, 1833.

"In the afternoon we saw in the prairie of the north bank a large grizzly bear, and immediately sent Ortubize and another hunter in pursuit of him, but to no purpose . . . Soon after we saw two other bears, one of a whitish, the other of a dark color, and our hunters when they returned, affirmed that they had wounded the largest . . . From this place upward the grey bear became more and more common, further down the river it is still rare. Brackenridge says it is not found below the Mandan Village, but this is not quite correct. Near the prairie where we saw the bears is the mouth of the White Earth river, called by Lewis and Clark the Goat-pen[19] river."

The first detailed description of the grizzly bear was written by Lewis after killing his first specimen near the mouth of the Yellowstone River on April 29, 1805. His account of the incident, and his description of this bear is of more than average interest:

"I walked on shore with one man. About 8 A.M. we fell in with two brown or yellow (White) bear; both of which we wounded; one of them made his escape, the other after my firing on him pursued me seventy or eighty yards, but fortunately had been so badly wounded that he was unable to pursue so closely as to prevent my recharging my gun; we again repeated our fire and killed him. It was a male not fully grown, we estimated his wt at 300 lb not having means of ascertaining it precisely.

"The legs of this bear are somewhat longer than those of the black, as are it's tallons and tusks in comparably larger and longer. the testicles, which in the black bear are placed pretty well back between the thyes and contained in one pouch like those of the dog and most quadrupeds, are in the yellow or brown bear placed much further forward, and are suspended in separate pouches[20] from two to four inches asunder; it's color is yellowish brown, the eyes small black and piercing; the front of the fore legs near the feet is usually black; the fur is finer, thicker and depper than that of the black bear; it is a much more ferocious and formidable anamal, and will frequently pursue the hunter when wounded. it is astonishing to see the wounds they will bear before they can be put to death."

May 5, 1805 (50 miles below Mouth of Milk River)
"Capt. Clark & Drewyer killed the largest brown bear this evening which we have yet seen. It was a most tremendous looking animal, and extremely hard to kill notwithstanding he had five balls through his lungs and five others in various parts he swam more than half the distance across the river to a sand bar, and it was at least twenty minutes before he died; he did not attempt to attack, but fled and made the most tremendous roaring from the moment he was shot. We had no means of weighing this monster; Capt. Clark thought he would weigh 500 lbs; for my own part I think the estimate to small by 100 lbs. He measured 8 ft. 7½ in. from nose to extremity of hind feet; 5½ ft. 10 in. around the breast, 1 ft. 11 in. around the middle of the arm; 3 ft. 11 in. around the neck. His talons five in number on each foot were 4⅜ in. in length."—Lewis

Aug. 5, 1806 (Near mouth of Milk River, Montana)
"the Fieldses killed 2 large bear this evening one of them measured nine feet from the extremity of the nose to that of his tail, this is the largest bear except one that I have seen. we saw several bear today but did not kill any of them."—Lewis

June 13, 1805 (Great Falls of the Missouri)
"I am induced to believe that the Brown, the white and the Grizly bear of this country are the same species only differing in color from age or more properly from the same natural cause that many other anamals of the same family differ in colour, one of those which we killed yesterday was of a cream colored white while the other in company with it was of the common bey or redish brown, which seems to be the most usual colour of them. the white one appeared from it's tallons and teeth to be the youngest; it was smaller than the other, and although a monstrous beast we supposed that it had not yet attained it's growth and that it was a little upwards of two years old. the young cubs which we have killed have always been of a brownish white, but none of them as white as that we killed yesterday. one other that we killed sometime since which I mentioned sunk under some drift-wood and was lost, had a white stripe or list of about eleven inches wide entirely around his body just behind the shoalders, and was much darker than these bear usually are. the grizly bear we have never yet seen. I have seen their tallons in possession of the Indians and from their form I am preswaded if there is any difference between this species and the brown or white bear it is very inconsiderable.

There is no such anamal as a black bear in this open country or of that species generally denominated the black bear."—Lewis

May 14, 1806 (Vic. of Kamiah, Idaho)

"Collins killed two bear this morning . . .; the mail bear was large and fat the female was of moderate size and reather meagre, we had the fat bear fleaced in order to reserve the oil for the mountains. both these bear were of the species common to the upper part of the Missouri They may be called the white black grizly brown or red bear for they are found in all those colours. perhaps it would not be unappropriate to designate them the variagated bear."—Lewis

May 15, 1806 (Camp Chopunnish)

"The white and redish brown or bey coloured bear I saw together on the Missouri; the bey and grizzly have been seen and killed together here for these were the colours of those which Collins killed yesterday. in short it is not common to find two bear here of this species precisely of the same colour, and if we were to attempt to distinguish them by their collours and to denominate each colour a distinct species we should soon find at least twenty. some bear nearly white have also been seen by our hunters at this place. the most striking differences between this species of bear and the common black bear are that the former are larger, have longer tallons and tusks, prey more on other animals, do not lie so long nor so closely in winter quarters, and will not climb a tree tho' ever so heardly pressed. the variagated bear I believe to be the same here with those on the missouri, but these are not so ferocious as those perhaps from the circumstance of their being compelled from scarcity of game in this quarter to live more on roots and of course not so much in the habit of seizeing and devouring living animals. the bear here are far from being passive as the common black bear they have attacked and fought our hunters already but not so fiercely as those in the Missouri. there are also some of the common black bear in this neighbourhood."—Lewis

May 16, 1806 (Vic. of Kamiah, Idaho)

"Drewyer had wounded three bear which he said were as white as sheep, but had obtained neither of them."—Lewis

May 25, 1806 (Vic. of Kamiah, Idaho)

"They had wounded a female bear and a deer but got neither of them. Gibson informed me that the bear had two cubbs one of which was white and the other black as jett."—Lewis

Lewis and Clark, before encountering the grizzly bear, were inclined to discount the Indian reports of their ferocity and toughness, but after a few encounters with charging bears they learned to approach them with as much caution as circumstances permitted. Obviously, muzzle loading, flint-lock rifles lacked sufficient shocking power to stop a grizzly bear, except in case of an extremely lucky shot.

The explorers had some thrilling encounters with these bears, and one is forced to conclude that they were, indeed, lucky that none of the hunters were killed. There is no reason to believe that the details of these experiences are exaggerated.

May 11, 1805 (Above mouth of Milk River)

"About 5 p m my attention was struck by one of the party running at a distance toward us and making signs & hollowing as if in distress, I ordered the perogues to put too, and waited until he arrived; I found that it was Bratton, the man with the sore hand whom I had permitted to walk on shore; . . .; at length he informed me that . . . he had shot a brown bear which immediately turned on him and pursued him a considerable distance but he had wounded it so badly that it could not over take him, I immediately turned out with 7 of the party in quest of this monster, we at length found his trail and pursued him about a mile by the blood through a very thick brush of rose-bushes and the large leaved willow; we finally found him concealed in some very thick brush an shot him through the skull with two balls; we proceeded to dress him and found him in good order; it was a monsterous beast, . . .; we now found that Bratton had shot him through the center of the lungs, not with standing which he had pursued him near half a mile and had returned more than double that distance and with his tallons had prepared himself a bed in the earth about 2 ft. deep and 5 long and was perfectly alive when we found him which could not have been less than 2 hours after he received the wound; these bear being so hard to die reather intimidates us all, I must confess that I do not like the gentlemen and had reather fight 2 Indians than one bear; there is no chance to conquer them with a single ball but by shooting them through the brains, and this becomes difficult in consequence of two large muscles which cover the sides of the forehead and the sharp projection of the frontal, which is also of pretty good thickness. The fleece and skin were as much as two men could possibly carry . . . directed the two cooks to render the bear's oil, and put it in the kegs, which was done. There was about eight gallons of it."—Lewis

May 14, 1805 (Between Milk and Musselshell Rivers)

"One of the party wounded a brown bear very badly, but being alone did not think proper to pursue him. In the evening the men in two of the rear canoes descovered a large brown bear lying in the open grounds about 300 yds. from the river, and six of them went out to attack him, all good

63

hunters; they took the advantage of a small emminince which concealed them and got within 40 paces of him unperceived; two of them reserved their fires as had been previously concerted, and the four others fired nearly at the same time and each put his bullet through him, two of the balls passed through the bulk of both lobes of his lungs. in an instand the monster ran at them with open mouth, and the two who had reserved their fires discharged their pieces at him as he came towards them, both of them struck him, one only slightly and the other fortunately broke his shoulder, this however retarted his motion for a moment only, the men unable to reload their guns took flight, the bear pursued and had very nearly over taken them before they reached the river; two of the party betook themselves to a canoe and the others separated and concealed themselves among the willows, reloaded their pieces, each discharged his piece at him as they had an opportunity. They struck him several times again but the guns served only to direct the bear to them. In this manner he pursued two of them separately so close that they were obliged to throw aside their guns and pouches and throw themselves into the river although the bank was nearly 20 ft. perpendicular; so enraged was this animal that he plunged into the river only a few feet behind the second man . . .; when one of those remaining on shore shot him through the head and finally killed him; they then took him on shore and butchered him when they found eight balls had passed through him in different directions."—Lewis

June 2, 1805 (Between Judith and Marias Rivers)
"The bear was very near catching Drewyer; it also pursued Charbono who fired his gun in the air as he ran, but fortunately eluded the vigilence of the bear by secreting himself very securely in the bushes until Drewyer finally killed it with a shot in the head; the (only) shot indeed that will conquer the farocity of those tremendious anamals."—Lewis

June 4, 1805 (Vicinity of Marias River)
"At the river near our camp we saw two white Bear, one of them was nearly catching Joseph Fields. Jos. Fields could not fire as his gun was wet, the bear was so near that it struck his foot, and we were not in a position to give him assistance, a clift of rocks separated us. The bear got alarmed at our shot and yells and took to the river."—Clark

June 14, 1805 (Vic. of Great Falls of the Missouri)
"I descended the hill and directed my course toward the Missouri near which there was a herd of at least 1000 buffalo; here I thought it would be well to kill a buffalo and leave him until my return from the river— (and if too late to return to camp I would have food & could make a shelter). Under this impression I selected a fat buffalo and shot him very

well, through the lungs. While I was gazing attentively at the poor animal discharging blood in streams from his mouth and nostrils, expecting him to fall every instant, and having entirely forgotten to reload my rifle, a large white, or rather brown bear, had perceived and crept up on me within 20 steps before I discovered him; in the first moment I drew up my gun to shoot, but at the same instant recollected that she was not loaded and that he was too near for me to hope to perform this operation before he reached me, as he was then briskly advancing on me; It was an open level plain, not a bush within miles or a tree within 300 yards of me, the river bank was sloping and not more than three feet above the level of the water; in short there was no place by means of which I could conceal myself from this monster until I could charge my rifle; in this situation I thought of retreating in a brisk walk as fast as he was advancing until I could reach a tree about 300 yds. below me, but I had no sooner turned myself about but he pitched at me, open mouthed and full speed. I ran about 80 yds and found he gained on me fast. I then ran into the water. The idea struck me to get into the water to such a depth that I could stand and he would be obliged to swim, and that I could in that situation defend myself with my espontoon; accordingly I ran hastily into the water about waste deep, & faced about and presented the point of my espontoon, at this instant he arrived at the edge of the water within 20 ft. of me; the moment I put myself in this attitude of defence he suddenly wheeled about as if frightened, declined the combat on such unequal grounds, and retreated with quite as great precipitation as he had just before pursued me. As soon as I saw him run off in that manner I returned to shore and charged my gun, which I had still retained in my hand through out this curious adventure. I saw him run through the level plain about 3 miles, till he disappeared in the woods on medicine river."—Lewis

June 25, 1805 (Vic. of Great Falls)

"About noon Fields returned and informed me that he had seen two white bear near the river a few miles above and in attempting to get a shot at them had stumbled uppon a third which immediately made at him being only a few steps distant; that in running in order to escape from the bear he had leaped down a steep bank of the river on a stony bar where he fell, cut his hand, bruised his knees, and bent his gun, that fortunately for him the bank hid him from the bear when he fell and that by that means he had escaped. This man is truly unfortunate with these bear, this is the second time he has narrowly escaped from them."—Lewis

June 26, 1805 (Great Falls of the Missouri)

"Soon after this storm was over Drewyer and J. Fields returned . . . They had killed 9 Elk and three bear during their absence; one of the bear

65

was the largest by far that we have yet seen; the skin appeared to me to be as large as a common ox. while hunting they saw a thick brushy bottom on the bank of the river where from the tracks along shore they suspected that there were bear concealed, they therefore landed without making any nois and climbed a leaning tree and placed themselves on its branches about 20 feet above the ground, when thus securely fixed they gave a whoop and this large bear instantly rushed forward to the place from whence he had heard the human voice issue, when he arrived at the tree he made a short paus and Drewyer shot him in the head. It is worthy to remark that these bears never climb—the fore feet of this bear measured nine inches across and the hind feet eleven and ¾ in length exclusive of the tallons and seven inches in width."—Clark

June 28, 1805 (Great Falls of the Missouri)

"The White bear have become so troublesome to us that I do not think it prudent to send one man alone on an errand of any kind, particularly where he has to pass through the brush. we have seen two of them on the large Island opposite to us today but are so much engaged that we could not spare the time to hunt them, but will make a frolick of it when the party return and drive them from these islands, they come close arround our camp every night but have never yet ventured to attack us and our dog gives us timely notice of their visits, he keeps constantly padroling all night. I have made the men sleep with their arms by them as usual for fear of accidents."—Lewis

July 15, 1806 (White Bear Island above Great Falls of Missouri)

"a little before dark McNeal returned with his musquet broken off at the breach, and informed me that on his arrival at willow run (on the portage) he had approached a white bear within ten feet without discovering him the bear being in the thick brush. the horse took the allarm and turning short threw him immediately under the bear; this animal raised himself on his hinder feet for battle, and gave him time to recover from his fall which he did in an instant and with his clubbed musquet he struck the bear over the head and cut him with the guard of the gun and broke off the breach, the bear stunned with the stroke fell to the ground and began to stratch his head with his feet; this gave McNeal time to climb a willow tree which was near at hand and thus fortunately made his escape. the bear waited at the foot of the tree until late in the evening before he left him, when Mc-Neal ventured down and caught his horse which had by this time strayed off to the distance of 2 Ms. and returned to camp. these bear are a most tremendous animal; it seems that the hand of providence has been most wonderfully in our favor with respect to them; or some of us would long since have fallen a sacrifice to their farosity. there seems to be a sertain fatality attached to the neighbourhood of these falls, for there is always a chapter of accidents prepared for us during our residence at them. the mosquetoes continue to infect us in such a manner that we can scarcely exist; for my own part I am confined by them to my bier at least ¾th of my time. my dog even howls with the torture he experiences from them. they are almost insupportable, they are so numerous that we frequently get them in our throats as we breath."—Lewis

Aug. 2, 1806 (On Yellowstone River, near Glendive)

"about 8 A.M. this morning a Bear of the large vicious species being on a Sand bar raised himself up on his hind feet and looked at us as we passed down near the middle of the river. he plunged into the water and swam towards us, either from a disposition to attack't or from the cent of the meat which was in the canoes. we Shot him with three balls and he returned to shore badly wounded. in the evening I saw a very large Bear take the water above us. I ordered the boat to land on the opposite side with a view to attack't him when he came within shot of the shore. when the bear was in a fiew paces of the Shore I shot it in the head. the men hauled her on Shore and proved to be an old Shee which was so old that her tusks had worn smooth, and Much the largest feemale bear I ever saw. after taking off her Skin, I proceeded on and encamp^d."—Clark

There is but little data in the Lewis and Clark diaries which refers specifically to the food habits of the grizzly bear. There are a few references, such as the following, to the fact that the bears fed to a considerable extent on the carcasses of dead buffalo and other carrion.

June 17, 1805 (Vic. of the Great Falls)

"Their mangled carcases (drowned buffalo) lie along the shores below the falls in considerable quantities and afford fine amusement for the bear, wolves and birds of prey; this may be one reason, and I think not a bad one either, that the bear are so tenatious of their right of soil in this neighborhood."—Lewis

Aug. 1, 1806 (Missouri River near mouth of Musselshell River)

"a white bear came within 50 paces of our camp before we perceived; it stood erect on its hinder feet and looked at us with much apparent unconsern, we seized our guns which are always by us and several of us fired at it and killed it, it was a female in fine order, we fleesed it and extracted several gallons of oil. this species of bear are nearly as poor at this season of the year as the common black bear nor are they ever as fat as the black bear is found in winter; as the feed principally on flesh, like the wolf, they are most fatt when they can procure a sufficiencty of food without rispect to the season of the year. the oil of this bear is much harder than that of the black bear, or Yahkah or party coloured bear of the West side of the mountains."—Lewis

It is well established that the Grizzly bear is a formidable predator. Although he was not above eating carrion he was equipped to kill any animal within reach, from bison to insects. Lewis and Clark did not record an actual observation of the killing of buffalo, elk, or deer by grizzly bears, but he must have had good reason for alluding to their habit of killing them.

Aug. 7, 1806.

"We overtook the Fieldses at noon. they had killed 2 bear and seen 6 others. we saw and fired on two from our perogue but killed neither of them. these bears resort to the river where they lie in water at the crossing places of the game for Elk and weak cattle (buffaloe); when they procure a subject of they lie by the carcase and keep the wolves off until they devour it. the bear appear to be very abundant on this part of the river."—Lewis

We have one reference, also, to this bear's habit of feeding on roots.

May 8, 1805 (Vic. of the Milk River)

"The white or brown bear feed very much on this root[21] which their tallons assist them to procure very readily."—Lewis

Seton quotes John Muir[22] on the food habits of the grizzly bear:

"To him almost everything is food, except granite. Every tree helps to feed him, every bush and herb, with fruits and flowers, leaves and bark; and all the animals he can catch—badgers, gophers, ground-squirrels, lizards, snakes, etc., and ants, bees, wasps, old and young, together with their eggs and larvae and nests. Craunched and hashed, down all go to his marvellous stomach, and vanish as if cast into a fire. What digestion! A Sheep or a wounded deer or a pig he eats warm, about as quickly as a boy eats a buttered muffin; or should the meat be a month old, it still is welcomed with tremendous relish. After so gross a meal as this, perhaps the next will be strawberries and clover, or raspberries with mushrooms and nuts, or puckery acorns and chokecherries."—Muir

After the buffalo, elk, and deer herds had been destroyed, and replaced by sheep and cattle throughout their range, the grizzly bears, at least those that managed to survive in the more remote mountains of the West, frequently resorted to the killing of sheep and cattle.

THE RACCOON

The raccoon, *Procyon lotor* (Linnaeus) had been named and described by Linnaeus in the 10th edition of Systema Naturae in 1758. Recognizing its affinity to the bears Linnaeus had classified it as a species of *Ursus;* however, in 1819, Desmarest, for sound taxonomic reasons, assigned it to the genus *Procyon,* and his classification has persisted to the present time.

Since Lewis and Clark were thoroughly familiar with the raccoon of Eastern United States, they gave it only slight attention:

June 13, 1804 (Vic. of Chariton River in Missouri)
"in the open prarie we caught a raccoon."—Clark

Oct. 21, 1805 (Above the John Day River on the Columbia)
"We saw among them (Indians) some small robes . . . some raccoon skins."—Lewis

Jan. 2, 1806 (At Fort Clatsop)
"The fur of both the beaver and otter as also the raccoon in this country are extreemly good."—Clark

Feb. 25, 1806 (Fort Clatsop)
"The Raccoon is found in the woody country on this coast in considerable quantities—the natives take a few of them in snares and dead falls, tho' appear not to vallue their skins much, and but seldom prepare them for robes."—Lewis

Mar. 21, 1806 (Fort Clatsop)
Serg't Gass in calculating the game killed by the Expedition which at Fort Clatsop during the winter of 1805-06 reported as follows:
"There were a few smaller quadrupeds killed, such as otter and beaver, and *one* raccoon."

CHAPTER III
The Weasel Family

The weasel family is comprised of carnivorous fur bearing mammals. None of them were as important in the fur trade as beaver, but they were of sufficient value to warrant attention by Lewis and Clark in estimating the fur potential of the Louisiana Territory and the Northwest.

Proof that the badger was indigenous to North America was of particular interest to Thomas Jefferson, and the discovery of the sea otter in the Columbia River below Celilo Falls is still a point of interest. However, because of the nocturnal and secretive habits of weasel, mink, marten and fisher, the explorers were obliged to base their remarks concerning the abundance and distribution of these animals mainly on signs which they observed and on information, as well as pelts, which they obtained from the Indians.

THE BADGER

Prior to Lewis and Clark's journey, Thomas Jefferson and other American naturalists who were associated with him in the American Philosophical Society were not aware that the badger, *Taxidea taxus* (Schreber), was native to this country. As evidence of this we may quote Jefferson's letter, dated Feb. 11, 1806, to Constantin Francois de Chasse Boeuf, Comte de Volney.[1]

"With his map he (Meriwether Lewis) sent us specimens of the following animals not before known to the northern continent of America. #4, the badger, not before known out of Europe." (Appendix)

However, Joseph Whitehouse's diary[2] indicates that the fur traders of the British North West Company were familiar with the badger even though American zoologists were not aware of its presence:

Jan. 18, 1805, (Fort Mandan)

"2 of our hunters came in—had killed 4 Deer, 4 wolves, and one brarow. 2 men who belonged to the N.W. Company that trades with the grossvanntares[3] villages came to our fort this day—they told us that these animals we called Brarows are a Specie of Badgers, which are common in Europe."—Whitehouse

Clark's description of the badger is amateurish and brief, but that of Lewis is remarkably complete:

July 30, 1804 (Near Council Bluffs)

"Joseph Fields Killed and brought in an Anamale Called by the French Brarow, and by the Panies, Cho-car-tooch. this Anamale Burrows in the ground and feeds on Flesh, (Prarie Dogs) Bugs & Vigatables "his Shape and Size is like that of a Beaver, his head, mouth etc. is like a Dogs with Short Ears, his Tail and Hair like that of a Ground Hog, and longer; and lighter. his Internals like the internals of a Hog, his skin thick and loose, his Belly is White and the Hair Short, a white Streek from his nose to his Sholders. The toe nails of his fore feet is one Inch and ¾ long, & feet large; the nails of his hind feet ¾ of an Inch long, the hind feet Small and toes Crooked, his legs are short and when he moves Just sufficient to raise his body above Ground He is of the Bear Species. We have his skin stuffed."—Clark

Feb. 26, 1806 (Fort Clatsop)

"The *Braro* so called by the French engages is an animal of the civit genus and much resembles the common badger. this is an inhabitant of the open plains of the Columbia as they are of those of the Missouri but are sometimes also found in the woody country. they burrow in the hard grounds of the plains with surprising ease and dexterity and will cover themselves in the ground in a very few minutes. they have five long fixed nails on each foot: those of the forefeet are much the longest; and one of those on each hind foot is double like those of the beaver. they weigh from 14 to 18 lbs. the body is reather long in proportion to it's thickness. the forelegs remarkably large and muscular and are formed like the temspit dog. they are short as are also the hind legs. they are broad across the sholders, and brest; the neck short. the head is formed much like the common fist dog only that the skull is more convex the mouth is wide and furnished with sharp streight teeth both above and below, with four sharp streight pointed tusks, two in the upper and two in the lower jaw. the eyes are black and small. whiskers are plased in four points on each side near the nose and on the jaws near the opening of the mouth. the ears are very short wide and oppressed as if they had been cut off. the apperture through them to the head is remarkably small. the tail is about 4 inches long; the hair longest on it at it's junction with the body and becoming shorter towards it's extremity where it ends in an accute point. the hairs of the body are much longer on the side and rump than any other part, which gives the body an apparent flatness, particularly when the animal rests on it's belley. this hair is upwards of 3 inches in length particularly on the rump where it extends so far towards the point of the tail that it almost conceals the shape of that part and gives to the whole of the hinder part of the body the figure of an accute angled triangle of which the point of the tail forms the accute angle. the

71

small quantity of coarse fur which is intermixed with the hair is of a redish pale yellow. the hair, of the back, sides, upper part of the neck and tail, are of a redish light or pale yellow for about 2/3 rds. of their length from the skin, next black, and then tiped with white; forming a curious mixture of grey and fox coloured red with a yellowish hue. the belley flanks and breast are of the fox coloured redish yellow. the legs black. the nails white. the head on which the hair is short, is variagated with black and white. a narrow strip of white commences on the top of the nose about ½ an inch from its extremity and extends back along the center of the forehead and neck nearly to the sholders. two stripes of black succeed the white on either side imbracing the nose, the eyes, and extends back as far as the ears. two other spots of black of a ramboidal figure are placed on the side of the head near the ears and between it (them) and the opening of the mouth. two black spots also immediately behind the ears. the other parts of the head white. This animal feeds on flesh, roots, bugs, and wild fruits. it is very clumsy and runs very slow. I have in two instances out run this animal and caught it. in this rispect they are not much more fleet than the porcupine."—Lewis

The diaries of the Explorers give us little information on the distribution and abundance of the badger. No badgers were observed below the site of Council Bluffs, Iowa. Above this point on the Missouri, badgers were encountered infrequently as far to the northwest as the Cascade Mountains. A tame specimen seen at the Indian village on Sauvies Island in the Columbia River (at the mouth of the Willamette) must have been captured above the Dalles of the Columbia by some party of Indians on one of their seasonal fishing trips to Celilo Falls.

July 29, 1804 (Ten miles above mouth of Platte River)

"Joseph fields Shot a Brareowe, he is the form of a dog. His colour is Gray. his talents on the four feet is 1½ Inch long his picture never was seen by any of the Party before."—Whitehouse

Oct. 7, 1804 (Near mouth of Moreau River)
"one of the men killed a Shee Brarow."—Clark

Sept. 5, 1805 (Camp Creek, upper tributary of Bitterroot River)
"the women brought us a few berries and roots to eate and the Principal chief a Dressed Brarow, Otter & two Goats & Antelope Skins."—Clark

Sept. 5, 1805 (Camp Creek)
"our hunters all came to camp towards evening. one of them had killed 2 young Deer and one brarow."—Whitehouse

Nov. 4, 1805 (Sauvies Island in the Columbia River)
"I saw a Brarow tamed at the 1st village today."—Clark

Among the specimens sent back to Thomas Jefferson from Fort Mandan on April 3, 1805 was a "female Braro or burrowing dog of the Prarie and the females Skeliton."

THE FISHER

According to Seton this fur-bearer, *Martes pennanti* (Erxleben), is known by a variety of common names, such as "pekan," "pekane," "we jack," etc. All of these with the exception of "fisher," are derived directly from Indian dialects.

Clark used the term, *pekan,* in referring to the fisher when he listed the animals involved in the Sioux-British fur trade.

Lewis, on the other hand, called this mammal a "black fox" because he considered the name, fisher, inappropriate.

Feb. 21, 1806 (Fort Clatsop)

"Drewyer saw a *fisher,* black fox, but it escaped from him among the fallen timber . . ."

"the Black-fox, or as they are most frequently called in the neighborhood of Detroit, *Fisher* is found in the woody country on this coast. how this animal obtained the name of fisher I know not, but certain it is, that the name is not appropriate, as it dose not pray on fish or seek it as a prey. they are extreemly active strong and prepared for climbing, which they do with great agility, and bound from tree to tree in pursuit of the squirrel or Rakoon their natural and most usual food. their colour is jut (jet) black except a small spot of white in the breast. the body is long, legs short and formed something like the ter-spit dog, with a remarkable long tail. it dose not differ here from those of the United States."—Lewis

Evidently Lewis was unaware of the fact that the fisher is as much at home in the northern bogs and swamps as it is in the upland. Seton quotes a number of observers, presumably reliable, who maintain that the fisher is wont to prowl along the borders of shallow lakes and streams "preying on reptiles, shell-fish, and fish which it catches with its paws in the water." If this is true the name, fisher, is not inappropriate.

THE MARTEN

Turton's original description of the American marten, *Martes americana* (Turton), appeared in the 1806 edition of Linnaeus' Systema Naturae, Vol. 1, page 60. The marten, however, was familiar to the French, British and American fur traders prior to the date of its official recognition by science.

Alexander Henry[4] in reporting the returns from the Red River Department of the North West Company, reported marten pelts regularly in the

73

fur harvest from the lower Red River, the Assiniboin and neighboring fur-trading posts under his jurisdiction. His records indicate that 5,647 martens were pelted between 1800 and 1808.

Lewis and Clark, following the course of the Missouri River, were south of the coniferous forest habitat of the marten until they approached the mountains in western Montana. Although there is no evidence in their diaries that they saw a single living specimen of this species, they did suc-ceed in obtaining a marten pelt from the Indians at Fort Mandan who probably had acquired it from the Assiniboins of Canada. This specimen was included in the shipment of bird and mammal skins consigned to Presi-dent Jefferson in the spring of 1805.

Reference has been made to the number of martens taken from the Red River Department of the North West Company between 1800 and 1808. The Marten did not appear among the furs bought down the Missouri until the American trappers penetrated the Rocky Mountains at a later date.

After returning to St. Louis in the fall of 1806 Lewis addressed a letter to President Jefferson in which he attempted to summarize some of the findings of the expedition. In this letter, dated Sept. 23, 1806, he discussed the problems incident to the establishment of an American fur-trading post at the mouth of the Columbia River so that furs taken on the headwaters of the Missouri and Columbia Rivers might be shipped from such a post direct to China.[5] In support of this, he reported as follows on the fur po-tential of the West:

"altho' the Columbia dose not as much as the Missouri abound in beaver and Otter yet it is by no means despicable in this respect and would furnish a profitable fur trade, in addition to the otter and beaver considerable quantities of the finest bear of three species affording a great variety of colours, the Tyger cat, several species of fox, the *Martin* and Sea Otter might be procured besides the rackoon and some other animals of an in-ferior class of furs." (Appendix)

THE MINK

The mink, *Mustela vison* Schreber, is one of the most widely distributed furbearers in the United States and Canada. It ranges from the barren tundras of the north to the Gulf of Mexico, and from the Atlantic to the Pacific. It does not occur, however, in the desert areas of the southwest.

Lewis and Clark gave little attention to the mink in their diaries; but in listing the quadrupeds of the Northwest, Lewis included the mink:

Feb. 23, 1806 (Fort Clatsop)

"The mink is found in the woody country on this coast, and does not differ in any particular from those of the Atlantic coast."—Lewis

He also noted that the mink pelt was used by the Indians as an item of ornament and dress:

April 3, 1806 (Vic. of Sandy River, Oregon)

"I observe some of the men among them who wear a girdle arround the waist between which and the body in front they confine a small skin of the mink or pole cat which in some measure conceals the parts of generation."
—Lewis

THE OTTER

The otter, *Lutra canadensis* (Schreber), was important in the fur trade long before it was given scientific status by Schreber in 1776. Lewis and Clark's records provided additional information concerning its distribution and abundance on the upper Missouri and lower Columbia Rivers, but beyond this they contributed nothing new or important. It was mentioned for the first time by Clark on Oct. 22, 1804, when the party arrived at the mouth of the Heart River, near the present site of Bismarck, North Dakota. His comment on this occasion is succinct: "one orter killed." We find no further reference to the species until April 14, 1805, when Lewis reported that "one of our hunters saw an Otter last evening and shot at it but missed it." This occurred in the vicinity of the Little Missouri River in North Dakota.

The following entries provide further evidence that otter were plentiful even though few of them were taken by the explorers:

June 12, 1805 (Between mouth of Marias River and Great Falls)

"Saw some sign of the Otter as well as beaver near our camp."—Lewis

July 3, 1805 (Vic. of Great Falls of the Missouri)

"six beaver and 2 otter have been killed within the last three days."—Lewis

July 12, 1805 (Above mouth of Sun River, on the Missouri)

"the otter are now plenty since the water has become sufficiently clear for them to take fish."—Lewis

July 19, 1805 (Vic. of Gates of the Rocky Mountains)

"the latter (otter) are now very plenty—one of the men killed one of them today with a setting pole (punt pole)."—Lewis

July 22, 1805 (Vic. of Beaver Creek above Canyon Ferry, Mont.)

"I killed an otter which sank to the bottom on being shot, a circumstance unusual with that animal—the water was about eight feet deep yet so clear that I could see it at the bottom; I swam in and obtained it by diving."—Lewis

75

July 26, 1805 (Approaching Three Forks of the Missouri)

"emence number of Beaver and orter in this little river which forks in the bottom."—Clark

July 31, 1805 (Near Mouth of Philosophy River)

"it has some timber in its bottoms and vast numbers of beaver and Otter."—Lewis

Aug. 7, 1805 (Above Wisdom River)

"emence number of Beaver, orter, Musk-rats, etc."—Clark

Aug. 11, 1805 (Vic. of Beaver's Head)

"our hunters . . . Tomahawked Several Orter today—killed one Beaver with a Setting pole."—Clark

Jan. 2, 1806 (Fort Clatsop)

"Drewyer visited his traps and took an otter, the fur of both the beaver and otter in this country are extreemly good; those animals are tolerably plenty near the sea coast, and on the small Creeks and rivers as high as the grand rappids (Celilo Falls), but are by no means as much so as on the upper part of the Missouri."—Lewis

The Indians on the Missouri and on the Columbia River and its tributaries regularly used otter pelts for robes, head bands, and in ceremonial dress. Lewis referred to this custom in describing the dress of the Arikaras, Shoshones, and the Clatsops. The Columbia River tribes frequently dressed otter skins with the head, feet and tail attached, and wore them draped over the shoulders as a neck piece. The Snake Indians combined an otter skin neck piece with a fringe of weasel tails "making the most eligant piece of Indian dress I ever saw." This "tippet" will be described in detail under the discussion of the weasel.

The Nez Percé and Shoshone Indians of eastern Oregon and Washington made use of the meat as well as the fur of the otter, probably because game and fish were scarce during certain periods of the year:

April 30, 1806 (Vic. of Walla Walla River)

"these people will not eat the dog but feast on the otter which is vastly inferior in my estimation."—Lewis

THE SEA-OTTER

Seton has reviewed the history relating to the discovery of the sea-otter, *Enhydra lutris* (Linnaeus), by white men. Padre Taraval reported finding them in large numbers on Cedros Island off the shore of Lower California in 1737; his account of this animal, however, was not published until 1757. In the meantime, Dr. G. W. Steller, who accompanied Vitus Bering on his ill-fated voyage of discovery, found a large colony of sea-otters on Bering

Island in 1741. The animals were so tame that 700 were killed without difficulty, and their pelts taken back to Kamchatka in 1742. Steller's description of the sea-otter provided the basis for its classification by Linnaeus, who perceiving that it was related to the weasels, named it *Mustela lutris*.[6]

Soon after the return of Bering's ship to Kamchatka, the Russian harvest of sea-otters from the Commander Islands began. In 1745, 1600 pelts were collected from Bering Island; but ten years later sea-otter were so scarce in this locality that only five of them were taken. Of necessity the Russian hunters moved into the Aleutian Islands and the Pribilofs. It has been reported that 5,000 sea-otters were taken in the neighborhood of the Pribilof Islands in 1786, and 2,000 during the following season. Under such heavy hunting pressure, by 1792, not a single sea-otter could be found in the vicinity of these Islands.

Despite the persistently heavy drain on the breeding populations of sea-otters from California to Unalaska, they persisted in sufficient numbers to permit annual harvests, ranging from a few hundred to a few thousand individuals, until late in the Nineteenth century. In 1885 through intensive hunting 4,152 sea-otters were harvested from Alaskan waters, but in 1896 only 724 pelts were collected from the same areas. By 1912 sea otters had become so scarce throughout their range that it was feared they were approaching extinction. So, in that year they were given complete protection through International Treaty. As a result of vigilance by the Governments concerned these animals have reappeared in certain sections of their former range. In 1937, O. J. Murie, on the basis of a summer survey of the Aleutian Islands, estimated the sea-otter population at about 2,000. In 1953 Richard E. Griffith, of the U. S. Fish and Wildlife Service, told the North American Wildlife Conference that the sea-otter population of the North Pacific area was in excess of 2,000 individuals, and that it might be as high as 5,000.[7]

When Lewis and Clark were descending the Columbia River in the fall of 1805 they reported finding sea-otter just below Celilo Falls.

Oct. 23, 1805 (Narrows below Celilo Falls)
"Great numbers of sea-Otters in the river below the falls, I shot one in the narrow chanel today which I could not get."—Lewis

Nov. 1, 1805 (Cascades of the Columbia River)
"Great numbers of Sea-Otters, they are so cautious that I with dificuelty got a shute at one today which I must have killed, but could not get him as he sunk."—Clark

Feb. 23, 1806 (Fort Clatsop)
"The Sea Otter is found on the sea coast and in the salt water. this anamal when fully grown is as large as a common mastive dog. the ears and eyes are remarkably small, particularly the former which is not an inch in

77

length thick fleshey and pointed covered with short hair. the tail is about 10 inches in length thick where it joins the body and tapering to a very sharp point; in common with the body it is covered with a deep fur particularly on the upper side, on the under part the fur is not so long. the legs are remarkably short and the feet which have five toes each are broad large and webbed. the legs are covered with fur and the feet with short hair. the body of this animal is long and nearly of the same thickness throughout. from the extremity of the tail to that of the nose they will measure 5 feet or upwards. the colour is a uniform dark brown and when in good order and season perfectly black and glossey. it is the richest and I think most delicious fur in the world at least I cannot form an idea of any more so. it is deep thick silkey in the extreem and strong. the inner part of the fur when opened is lighter than the surface in it's natural position. there are some fine black and shining hairs intermixed with the fur which are reather longer and add much to it's beauty. the nose, about the eyes ears and forehead in some of these otter is of a lighter colour. sometimes of a light brown. those parts in the young sucking Otter of this species is sometimes of a cream coloured white, but always much lighter than the other parts. the fur of the infant otter is much inferior in point of colour and texture to that of the full grown otter, or even after it has been weaned. there is so great a difference that I have for some time supposed it a different animal; the Indians called the infant Otter *Spuck,* and the full grown or such as had obtained a coat of good fur, *E-luck-ke.* This still further confirmed the opinion of their being a distinct species; but I have since learned that Spuck is the young otter. the colour of the neck, body, legs, and tail is a dark lead brown."—Lewis

During the winter at Fort Clatsop Lewis and Clark had plenty of time to appraise the Clatsop and Chinnook Indians who visited them frequently. They studied almost every aspect of their social, cultural, and economic life; they were particularly interested in their trade relations with the white seamen who brought ships to the mouth of the Columbia River each season to obtain furs from the natives.[8]

Jan. 9, 1806 (Written at Fort Clatsop)

"This Traffic on the part of the whites consists of vending guns, (principally old British or American musquits), powder, balls and shot, Copper and brass kettles, brass teakettles and coffee pots, blankets from two to three point, scarlet and blue Cloth (coarse), plates and strips of sheet copper and brass, large brass wire, knives, beads and tobacco with fishinghooks, buttons and some other small articles; also a considerable quantity of Sailor's cloaths, as hats, coats, trowsers and shirts. For these they receive in return from the natives, dressed and undressed Elk-skins, skins of the Sea Otter, common Otter, beaver, common fox, spuck (juvenile sea-otter), and tiger cat; also dryed and pounded sammon in baskets, and a kind of bisquit which the natives make of roots called by them, shappelell. The natives are most extravegantly fond of the most common, cheap blue and white beads, of moderate size, or such that from 50 to 70 will weigh one penneyweight. the blue is usually preferred to the white; these beads constitue the principal circulating medium with all the Indian tribes on this river; for these beads they will dispose of any article they possess. The beads are strung on strans of a fathom in length and in that manner sold by the breadth or yard."—Lewis

Nov. 20, 1805 (Camp on Gray's Bay, near Mouth of Columbia River)
"Many Indians about one of which had a robe made of 2 sea otters skins. Capt. Lewis offered him many things for his skins, with others a blanket, a coat, all of which he refused—at length we purchased it for a belt of Blue Beeds which the Squar had."—Clark

Nov. 23, 1805 (Gray's Bay, near Mouth of Columbia River)
"in the evening Seven indians of the Clat-sop Nation came over in a Canoe, they brought with them 2 Sea-otter Skins for which they asked blue beads, etc., and Such high prices that we were unable to purchase them without reducing our Small Stock of Merchandize, on which we depended for Subsistence on our return up this river. mearly to try the Indian who had one of those Skins, I offered him my Watch, handkerchief, a bunch of red beads and a dollar of the American coin, all which he refused and demanded ti-a-co-mo-Shack which is Chief beads and the most common blue beads, but fiew of which we have at this time."—Clark

Nov. 24, 1805 (Gray's Bay)
One of the men (Chinook Indians) brought a Small Sea-otter Skin for Which we gave Some blue beads."—Clark

Dec. 10, 1805 (Clatsop Village on Pacific Coast, west of Fort Clatsop)
"I attempted to purchase a Small Sea otter Skin for red beeds which I had in my pockets, they would not trade for those beeds not priseing any other Colour than Blue or White, I purchased a little of the berry bread and a fiew of their roots for which I gave Small fish hooks, which they appeared fond of."—Clark

Dec. 14, 1805 (Fort Clatsop)
"The Indians leave us today after selling a small sea otter skin and a roabe."—Clark

Jan. 19, 1806 (Fort Clatsop)
"we were visited today by two Clatsop men and a woman who brought

79

for sale some Sea Otter skins of which we purchased one, giving in exchange the remainder of our blue beads consisting of 6 fathoms and about the same quantity of small white beads and a knife."—Lewis

Feb. 18, 1806 (Fort Clatsop)

"in the forenoon we were visited by eight Clatsops and Chinnooks from whom we purchased a Sea Otter's skin and two hats made of way tape (slender roots of white spruce) and white cedar bark."—Lewis

Feb. 24, 1806 (Fort Clatsop)

"Capt. Lewis gave an old Coat and vest for a sea-otter skin, ..." —Clark

March 23, 1806 (Day of departure from Fort Clatsop)

"I obtained one Sea Otter skin from this party (Chinnooks)."—Lewis

March 25, 1806 (Near mouth of Clatskanie Creek)

"one of the men purchased a Sea Otter skin at this lodge, for which he gave a dressed Elk skin and a handkerchief."—Lewis

March 29, 1806 (Vic. of Sauvies Island)

"we purchased a considerable quantity of wappetoes 12 dogs, and 2 Sea otter skins of these people."—Lewis

Lewis, in a letter written to Pres. Jefferson from St. Louis, Missouri on Sept. 23, 1806, states:

"I have brought with me several skins of the Sea Otter."

THE STRIPED SKUNK

The explorers, probably because it was a familiar animal, gave the skunk, *Mephitis mephitis* (Schreber), scant attention.

Lewis made one reference to this species in listing the animals seen near the mouth of the White River in South Dakota, but he did not mention it again during the outward journey. However, in listing and describing the quadrupeds that he had seen west of the Rocky Mountains, he again referred to the "pole-cat."

Feb. 28, 1806 (Written at Fort Clatsop)

"The pole-cat is found in every part of the country. They are very abundant on some parts of the Columbia, particularly in the neighbourhood of the Great falls & Narrows of the river, where they live in the clifts along the river and feed on the offal of the Indians fishing shores. They are the same as those of other parts of North America."—Lewis

It appears that Lewis was referring to the striped skunk. We found nothing to suggest that he encountered the small spotted variety despite the fact that it is common in the Missouri valley.

The diaries contain nothing concerning the habits of skunks, but John Bradbury, in 1810, described an unusual experience with this species near the mouth of the Grand River in Missouri.

April 1, 1810

"In the evening I descended into the valley, and on my way to find the boat, observed a skunk, (Viverra mephitis) and being desirous of procuring the skin, fired at it, but with shot only, having this day taken out my fowling-piece instead of my rifle. It appeared that I had either missed entirely, or only slightly wounded it, as it turned around instantly, and ran towards me. Being well aware of the consequence, if over taken, I fled but was so closely pursued, that I was under the necessity of re-loading whilst in the act of running. At the next discharge I killed it; but as it had ejected its offensive liquor on its tail, I could not touch it, but cut a slender vine, of which I made a noose, and dragged my prize to the boat. I found that the Canadians considered it a delicacy, and were desirous of procuring it to eat; this enabled me to procure the skin without having to perform the disgusting operation of taking it off myself.

"On relating to the hunters that I had been pursued by a skunk, they laughed heartily, and said it was no uncommon thing, having often been in the same predicament themselves."—Bradbury

THE LONG-TAILED WEASEL

On November 9, 1804, Clark purchased a weasel, *Mustela frenata* Lichtenstein, from a Mandan Indian. It appears, however, that the Indian retained the animal's tail to adorn an article of clothing:

"We got a white weasel (taile excepted, which was black at the end) of an Indian."—Clark

Possibly this was the same skin that Lewis listed among the specimens packed in April, 1805, for shipment from Fort Mandan to the President. In any case, no other weasel, or weasel skin, was mentioned prior to the time this shipment was made.

The weasel was not referred to again except in connection with Lewis' description of a fur "tippet" worn as a ceremonial neck-piece by the Shoshone Indians.

Aug. 20, 1805 (Camp on the Lemhi River)

"The tippet of the Snake Indians is the most eligant piece of Indian dress I ever saw. The neck or collar of this is formed of a strip of dressed otter skin with the fur, it is about four or five inches wide and is cut out of the back of the skin, the nose and eyes forming one extremity and the tail the other. beginning a little behind the ear of the animal at one edge of this collar and proceeding towards the tail, they attach from one to twe hundred and fifty little roles of Ermin skin formed in the following manner. the skin is first dressed with the fur on it and a narrow strip is cut out of the back of the skin reaching from the nose and embracing the tail. this is sewed arround a small cord of the silk-grass twisted for the purpose and regularly tapering in such a manner as to give it a just proportion to the tail which is to form the lower extremity of the strand. thus arranged they are confined at the upper point in little bundles of two, three or more as the disign may be to make them more full; these are then attatched to the collars as before mentioned, and to conceal the connection of this part which would otherwise have a course appearance they attach a broad fringe of Ermin skin to the collar overlaying that part. little bundles of fine fringe of the same materials is fastened to the extremity of the tails in order to show their black extremities to greater advantage. the center of the otter skin collar is also ornamented with the shells of the perl oister, the collar is confined around the neck and the little roles of Ermin skin about the size of a large quill covers the (shoulders) and body nearly to the waist and has the appearance of a short cloak and is really handsome. these they esteem very highly, and give or dispose of only on important occasions. the ermin which is known to the traders of the N. W. by the name of white weasel is the genuine ermine, and might no doubt be turned to great advantage by those people if they would encourage the Indians to take them. they are no doubt extreemly plenty, and readily taken, from the number of these tippets which I have seen among these people and the great number of skins employed in the construction of each tippet. scarcely any of them have employed less than one hundred of these skins in their formation."—Lewis

THE WOLVERINE

The range of the wolverine is confined to the boreal life zone of North America, Europe and Asia. Lewis and Clark obviously had no opportunity to observe the wolverine until they reached the headwaters of the Missouri River at high elevations in the Rocky Mountains.

There is no conclusive evidence that the expedition encountered a wolverine, *Gulo lustris* (Linnaeus), anywhere within the western range of this species. Lewis' diary contains one entry in which he describes an animal that may, or may not, have been a wolverine.

Aug. 12, 1805 (Vic. of Lemhi Pass)

"We saw an animal which we took to be of the fox kind, as large or reather larger than the small wolf of the plains—its colours were a curious mixture of black, redish brown and yellow. Drewyer shot at him about 130 yards and knocked him down, but he recovered and got out of our reach— it is certainly a different animal from any that we have yet seen."—Lewis

While in the vicinity of the Great Falls of the Missouri he wounded another strange animal which Thwaites says in a footnote was possibly a wolverine or a cougar. Lewis' description of the animal is inadequate for identification:

June 14, 1805 (Vic. of Great Falls, Mont.)

"my direction led me directly to an animal that I at first supposed was a wolf; but on nearer approach, or about 60 paces distant, I discovered that it was not; its colour was a brownish yellow; it was standing near its burrow; and when I approached it thus nearly, it crouched itself down like a cat looking immediately at me as if it desired to spring on me. I took aim and fired, it instantly disappeared in its burrow; I loaded my gun and examined the place which was dusty and saw the track from which I am still further convinced that it was of the tiger kind."—Lewis

CHAPTER IV
The Wild Dogs and Cats

The western subspecies of wolves, foxes and wildcats were unknown in 1804. Lewis and Clark were the first naturalists to describe the coyote, the wolf of the plains, the kit fox, and the Oregon bobcat. Their observations and descriptions, however, were overlooked by scientists. Thomas Say, who classified the plain's wolf, coyote and kit fox almost twenty years later, based his descriptions on specimens collected by Major Long's expedition of 1819-20. On the contrary, Rafinesque, who named the Oregon bobcat in 1817, based his classification directly on Lewis and Clark's description.

THE GRAY WOLF

Thomas Say, in 1823, classified the gray wolf of the plains, *Canis lupus nobilis* Say, on the basis of a specimen taken near Blair, Nebraska by members of Major Long's Expedition to the Rocky Mountains. This was eighteen years after Lewis and Clark made their notations on the appearance and behavior of the gray wolves which inhabited the plains of Montana, and nine years after the publication of their diaries.

It may be assumed that failure to bring back a specimen of this wolf precluded Say, or any other zoologist of the period, from basing a technical description on the observations of the explorers.

May 5, 1805 (On the Missouri, above the Yellowstone River)

"The large woolf found here is not as large as those of the Atlantic states. They are lower and thicker made, shorter leged.—their color, which is not effected by the seasons, is gray or blackish brown and every intermediate shade from that to cream colored white; these wolves resort to the woodlands and are also found in the plains, but never take refuge in the ground or burrow so far as I have been able to inform myself. We scarcely see a gang of buffaloe without observing a parsel of those faithfull shepherds on their skirts in readiness to take care of the maimed wounded. The large wolf never barks, but howls as those of the atlantic states do."
—Lewis

Sept. 21, 1804 (Near Big Bend of the Missouri)

"At the mouth of this river the two hunters ahead left a Deer & its Skin, also the Skin of a White wolf."—Clark

May 14, 1805 (Between Milk and Musselshell Rivers)

"walked on shore and killed a very fine buffalow calf and a large wolf, much the whitest I had seen, it was quite as white as the wool of the common sheep."—Lewis

84

In 1804, wolves were plentiful on the lower Missouri River and abundant throughout the plains of the Upper Missouri basin. Seton estimates that there were, during primitive times, at least two million gray wolves in Canada, Alaska and the United States, exclusive of California and Nevada. They were most numerous where game was most abundant; that is, in the buffalo range and in the forested deer range of the Lake States and the Ohio valley. They were an important factor in the ecologic complex of the continent before the white man took over. They eliminated the weak, diseased, and hapless individuals among prey species ranging from bison to rodents; they helped to prevent over-population from developing within the ranks of many species. But, when farms and cities replaced the forests and livestock pre-empted the plains, wolves came into direct conflict with human activities. As a result, their numbers, in the settled sections of their range, have declined until only a few hundred remain in forested areas east of the Mississippi, and a few thousand, at most, in the remote wilderness areas of the West.

Lewis and Clark reported seeing wolves and coyotes from the mouth of Weeping Water Creek in southeastern Nebraska to the Pacific Ocean. The explorers were impressed with the abundance and persistence of the wolf in his attendance on the buffalo and other big game mammals; and, they were put to no end of trouble because the wolves almost invariably devoured any dressed meat left on the plains for want of man power or conveyance until it could be brought into camp.

June 3, 1805 (Near mouth of Marias River)
"The country in every direction around us was one vast plain in which innumerable herds of Buffalo were seen attended by their shepherds the wolves."—Lewis

Feb. 20, 1806 (Written at Fort Clatsop)
"The large brown wolf is like that of the Atlantic States[1] and are found only in the woody country on the Pacific Ocean imbracing the mountains which pass the Columbia between the Great falls and rapids of the same."
—Lewis

July 10, 1806 (Sun River, below Big Muddy Creek)
"vast assemblages of wolves"—Lewis

July 14, 1806 (White Bear Island, at mouth of Sun River)
"the wolves are in greatest numbers howling arround us and loling about in the plains in view at the distance of two or three hundred yards."—Lewis

July 24, 1806 (On the Yellowstone River, near Billings, Montana)
"for me to mention or give and estimate of the different Species of wild animals on this river particularly Buffalow, Elk, Antelopes and Wolves

85

would be incredible. I shall therefore be silent on the subject further."—Clark

August 20, 1806 (Vic. of the Big Beaver Creek, below Cannonball River)
"Saw a great number of wolves on the bank, some Buffalw & Elk, tho' not so abundant as near the River Rochejhone."—Clark

Oct. 20, 1804 (Near mouth of the Cannonball River)
"I observe near all the large gangues of Buffalw, wolves; and when the buffalo move those animals follow and feed on those that are killed by accident or those that are too pore to keep up with the gangue."—Clark

May 5, 1805
"a great number of these goats (antelopes) are devoured by the wolves and bear at this season when they are poor and passing the river from SW to NE."—Lewis

Other more specific instances of wolves preying upon buffalo and antelope are cited in the sections dealing specifically with those species.

May 29, 1805 (Vic. of Judith River)
"we saw a great many wolves in the neighborhood of these mangled carcases (buffalo), they were fat and extreemly gentle, Capt. C., who was on shore, killed one of them with his espontoon."—Lewis

July 14, 1806 (Near White Bear Island, mouth of Sun River)
"I counted twenty seven (wolves) about the carcase of a buffaloe which lies in the water at the point of the large island. These are generally the large kind."—Lewis

July 17, 1806 (Near Teton River, a tributary of the Marias River)
"immense and numerous herds of buffaloe were seen feeding attended by their scarcely less numerous sheepherds, the wolves."—Lewis

Dec. 7, 1804 (Vic. of Cannonball River)
"all meat which is left out all night falls to the Wolves which are in great numbers always in the neighborhood of the Buffalows."—Clark

Feb. 13, 1805 (Near mouth of Heart River)
"5th Day (of hunting trip) Dispatched one of the party, our interpreter, and 2 french men with 3 horses loaded with the best of the meat to the fort, 44 miles Distant, the remaining meat I had packed on 2 Slays and drawn down to the next point about 3 miles below, at this place I had all the meat collected which was killed yesterday & had escaped the Wolves, Ravin & mag pie (which are very numerous about this place) and put into a close pen made of logs to secure it from the wolves & birds & proceeded on to a large bottom nearly opposite the (heart) River, in this bottom we

found but little game, Great No. of Wolves in the hills, Saw Several parsels of Buffalows. Camped. I killed a Buck."—Clark

April 25, 1805 (Near mouth of Yellowstone River)

"I then proceeded to the place of our encampment with two of the men, taking with us the Calf (buffalo) and marrow bones, while the other two remained with orders to dress the cow that was in tolerable order, and hang the meat out of reach of the wolves, a precaution indespensible to its safe keeping, even for a night."—Lewis

June 14, 1805 (Vic. of Great Falls, Mont.)

"Sent the others to bring in the ballance of the buffalow meat, or at least that part whch the wolves had left us, for those fellows are ever at hand and ready to partake with us the moment we kill a buffaloe; and there is no means of putting the meat out of reach in those plains; the two men shortly after returned with the meat and informed me that the wolves had devoured the greater part of the meat."—Lewis

Despite the abundance of wolves that followed the buffalo herds and prowled about the campsites we find little or no support for their legendary viciousness with respect to man. On the contrary the explorers found them to be only moderately wary and comparatively docile. Only on one occasion was a member of the party attacked by a wolf.

Aug. 8, 1806 (Yellowstone River in southwestern Montana)

"the night after the horses had been stolen a Wolf bit Sgt. Pryor through his hand when asleep, and this animal was so vicious as to make an attempt to seize Winsor, when Shannon fortunately Shot him."—Clark

The British fur traders of both the Hudson's Bay Company and the North West Company had been maintaining fur trading posts on Rainy Lake, Lake Winnepeg, the Assiniboin River and the Red River of the North for several years prior to 1804. The Mandan and Hidatsa Indian tribes of North Dakota had been carrying on a listless trade with the British companies before Lewis and Clark visited them. Factors in charge of these trading posts occasionally visited the Indians[2] to obtain what furs they could in exchange for indifferent guns and trinkets, wolf hides, although of little value, were occasionally exchanged in this traffic. Lewis mentions one of two instances of such transactions.

Alexander Henry, reporting on the animal fur take in the Red River District, accounted for a total of 3,661 wolf pelts during the years 1800-1808. Seton estimates that these pelts came from an area of 2,500 square miles surrounding the Pembina Post. It should be understood that wolves constituted only a minor segment of the total fur catch considering all species.

No such volume of fur trade existed on the Missouri in 1804-06. Manuel Lisa, and a few other venturesome traders from St. Louis, were operating on the Missouri as far north as the Mandan villages, and the British companies occasionally visited the Mandans; but the boom period of the Missouri and Rocky Mountain fur trade arrived twenty years later.

THE COYOTE

We have been unable to determine whether or not Lewis and Clark were the first explorer-naturalists to call attention to the coyote, *Canis latrans* Say, but certainly they were among the first to report on its general appearance, habits and distribution. Yet, their reporting in case of the coyote is not as detailed or comprehensive as in case of the wolf or of the big game species. At times they did not indicate specifically whether they were referring to the coyote or the wolf in recording their observations.

Nearly twenty years elapsed after Lewis and Clark returned before Thomas Say[3] published the first technical description of the coyote and named it *Canis latrans*. Say based his classification on material collected near Council Bluffs, Iowa, during Major Long's Expedition in 1819-20.

Assuming that Thomas Say was familiar with Biddle's text of the diaries, he nevertheless would not have been able to write a technical description of the coyote on the basis of the explorers' sketchy descriptions.

Sept. 18, 1804 (Near mouth of White River in South Dakota)

"I killed a Prarie Wolf, about the Size of a Gray fox, bushy tail, head and ears like a Wolf, Some fur, Burrows in the ground and barks like a Small Dog. What has been taken heretofore for a Fox was those Wolves, and no Foxes has been seen; . . ."—Clark

May 5, 1805 (On the Missouri between Poplar and Porcupine Rivers)

"Capt. Clark found a den of young wolves in the course of his walk today and also a great number of those animals; they are very abundant in this quarter, and are of two species the small wolf or burrowing dog of the praries are inhabitants almost invariably of the open plains; they are usually ascociate in bands of ten or twelve sometimes more and burrow near some pass or place much frequented by game; not being able alone to take a deer or goat they are rarely ever found alone but hunt in bands; they frequently watch and seize their prey near their burrows; in these burrows they raise their young and to them they also resort when pursued; when a person approaches them they frequently bark, their note being precisely that of a small dog. they are of an intermediate size between that of the fox and dog, very active fleet and delicately formed; the ears large erect and pointed the head long and pointed more like that of the fox; tale long and bushey; the hair and fur also resembles the fox tho' is much coarser and inferior. they are of a pale redish brown colour. The eye of a deep sea green colour small and piercing. their talons are reather longer than those of the ordinary wolf or that common to the atlantic States; none of which are found in this quarter, nor I believe above the river Plat."—Lewis

Earlier references, in Clark's diary, to the "prairie wolf" would appear to refer to the coyote, viz.:

Aug. 12, 1804 (On the Missouri River, Monona County, Iowa)
"A Prarie Wolf came near the bank and Barked at us this evening, we made an attempt but could not get him, the animale Barkes like a large ferce dog."—Clark

Aug. 23, 1804 (Union County, South Dakota)
"Several Prarie Wolves seen today."—Clark

Sept. 17, 1804 (On the Missouri above the White River)
"a great number of wolves of the small kind, hawks, and some pole-cats were seen."—Lewis

July 24, 1806 (Marias River Plains)
"Several wolves visited our camp today, I fired on and wounded one of them very badly, the small species of wolf barks like a dog, they frequently salute us with this note as we pass through the plains."—Lewis

Sept. 11, 1806 (Nodaway River, western Missouri)
"Wolves were howling in different directions this evening after we had encamped, and the barking of the little prarie wolves so resembled those of out Common small Dogs that 2/3 of the party believed them to be dogs of Some boat assending whch was yet below us. The Barking of those little wolves I have frequently taken notice of on this, as well as the other Side of the Rocky mountains, and their bark so much resembles or Sounds to me like our common Small cur dogs that I have frequently mistaken them for that species of dog."—Clark

Feb. 20, 1806 (Fort Clatsop)
"the large and small wolves of the plains are the inhabitants principally of the open country and the woodlands on their borders, and resemble in their habits and appearance those of the plains of the Missouri precisely. They are not abundant in the plains of the Columbia because there is but little game on which for them to subsist."—Lewis

Lewis included "the bones and Skeleton of a small burrowing wolf of the Prairie, the Skin being lost by accident" among the specimens sent to President Jefferson from Fort Mandan.

THE KIT FOX

The kit fox, *Vulpes velox* Say, was seen for the first time in the neighbor-hood of Great Falls, Montana. It was described as a small fox that lived in communities and burrowed in the ground. Lewis' diary entry for July 8, 1805, suggests that the name "kit fox" was already in common use by the fur traders of that period.

Alexander Henry, in reporting the furs shipped from the Pembina Post of the Red River District for the 1800-01 season, reported the take of kit foxes separately from that of red foxes. This is substantial proof that the species, *Vulpes velox,* was well known to the British fur trade prior to Lewis and Clark's exploration.

Nevertheless the kit fox was not given scientific status until Thomas Say described and named a specimen, in 1823, which had been taken by Major Long's expedition to the Rocky Mountains.[4]

Lewis' observations:

July 6, 1805 (Vic. of Great Falls of the Missouri)

"There is a remarkable small fox which associate in large communities and burrow in the praries something like the small wolf, but we have not as yet been able to obtain one of them; they are extreemly watchful and take reffuge in their burrows which are very deep; we have seen them no where except near these falls."—Lewis

July 8, 1805 (Vic. of Great Falls)

"The party who were down with Capt. Clark also killed a small fox which they brought with them. it was a female appeared to give suck, other-wise it was so much like the common small fox of this country commonly called the, kit fox that I should have taken it for a young one of that species; however, on closer examination it did apear to differ somewhat; its colour was of a light brown, its (y)ears proportionably larger, and the tale not so large or the hair not so long which formed it. They are very delicately formed, exceedingly fleet, and not as large as the common do-mestic cat. Their tallons appear longer than any species of fox I ever saw and seem therefore prepared more amply by nature for the purpose of burrowing. There is sufficient difference for descrimination between it and the kit fox, and to satisfy men perfectly it is a distinct[5] species."—Lewis

July 26, 1806 (On the Two Medicine River, a tributary of the Marias River)

"we saw . . . 2 of the smallest species of fox of a redish brown colour with the extremity of the tail black. It is about the size of the domestic cat and burrows in the ground."—Lewis

90

The diaries contain one reference to the kit fox in the British fur trade. On April 14, 1805, Lewis alluded to the fact that the Assiniboin Indians exchanged "the large and small wolves and the smallfox" for "spirituous liquor."

Some idea of the extent of this traffic with respect to the kit fox may be gained by examining the records of Alexander Henry[6] who listed 117 kit foxes among the furs shipped from the Red River Department of the North West Company during the years 1801-1805.

THE RED FOX

It is evident from the following quotations that Lewis and Clark did not recognize the different subspecies of the red fox, *Vulpes fulva* Desmarest. They were confused, too, by the color phases of the red fox. Both the cross fox and the silver fox were regarded as distinct species.

Feb. 19, 1806 (Written at Fort Clatsop)

"The large red fox of the plains, and the Kit fox are the same which we met with on the Missouri and are the inhabitants almost exclusively of the open plains, or of the copse of bushes within the plain country. The common red fox or grey fox of the United States is also found in the woody country on this coast nor does it appear to be altered in respect to its fur colour or any other particular. We have seen none of the large red fox." —Lewis

May 31, 1805 (On the Missouri, between the Musselshell and Marias Rivers)

"I saw near those bluffs the most beautiful fox that I ever beheld, the colours appeared to me to be a fine orrange, yellow, white and black; I endeavored to kill this anamal but he discovered me at a considerable distance, and finding that I could get no nearer, I fired on him as he ran and missed him; he concealed himself under the rocks of the clift; it appeared to me to be about the size of the common red fox of the Atlantic States, or reather smaller than the large fox common to this country; convinced I am that it is a distinct[7] species."—Lewis

Feb. 21, 1806 (Fort Clatsop)

"The Silver fox—this animal is very rare even in the country where it exists; I have never seen more than the Skins of this anamal, and those were in the possession of the natives of the woody Country below the great falls of the Columbia from which I think that it is most probably the inhabitant of the woody country exclusively. from the skin it appeared to be about the size of the large red fox of the plains and much of its form with a large tail. The legs I think somewhat longer—it has a fine long deep fur poil (pile) the poil is of a dark lead colour and the long hairs intermixed with it are either white, or black at the lower part and white at the top, the whole mixture forming a beautiful silver grey."—Lewis

Fourteen red fox skins were placed in a large trunk for shipment from Fort Mandan to President Jefferson when the big bateau headed down river in the Spring of 1805.

THE CANADA LYNX

Only a few references to the Canada lynx, *Lynx canadensis* Kerr, can be found in the diaries. The course of the Missouri River through the Dakotas and eastern Montana is generally regarded as being south of the range of this animal.[8] In the Rocky Mountains, however, they occurred as far south as central Colorado, and in the Cascades as far south as central Oregon.

It is not surprising, then, that Lewis and Clark did not encounter the Canadian lynx east of the Rockies, but we cannot account for their failure to find it in western Montana or Idaho. We must assume that the lynx pelts acquired at Fort Mandan were purchased from the Indians because they make no reference to having killed a single specimen.

Dec. 12, 1804 (Fort Mandan)

"I line my Gloves and have a cap made of the Skin of the Louservia of (the wild Cat of the North) the fur near 3 inch long."—Clark

According to Thwaites, "Louservia" was a corruption of *loup cervier*, the French name of the Canada lynx.

There is also the possibility that the "louservia" skins purchased from the Mandan Indians, may have been from the northern bobcat, *Lynx rufus pallescens* Merriam rather than the Canada lynx.

Regardless of which species they represented, Lewis sent a "louservia" pelt to President Jefferson.

April 3, 1805

"The large Trunk contains . . . a Mandan robe containing two burrowing Squirrels, a white weasel, and the Skin of a Louservia."

THE OREGON BOBCAT

Lewis and Clark can be credited for the discovery, if not the naming, of the Oregon Bobcat, *Lynx rufus fasciatus* Rafinesque. The remarks of Elliott Coues[9] in this connection are of interest:

"Under the misleading name, Tiger-cat, but with minute accuracy, is thus described the lynx of the Columbia, discovered by our authors (Lewis and Clark). This is quite distinct from the Canadian lynx, *Lynx canadensis*, and has often been considered also a different species from the bay lynx, *Lynx rufus*, of which, however, it appears to be a local race. It was first named *Lynx fasciatus* by C. S. Rafinesque, in 1817, through a misunderstanding of Lewis and Clark."

Clark wrote the description to which Coues referred:

Feb. 18, 1806 (Fort Clatsop)
"Whitehouse brought me a roab which he purchased of the Indians formed of three skins of the *Tiger Cat*. this Cat differs from any which I have ever seen. it is found on the borders of the plains and the woody Country lying along the Pacific Ocean. this animale is about the size or reather larger than the wild cat of our country and is much the same in form, agility and ferosity. the colour of the back, neck and sides, is a redish brown irregular varigated with small spots of dark brown the tail is about two inches long nearly white except the extremity which is black; it termonates abruptly as if it had been cut off. the belly is white with small black spots, butifully varigated. the legs are of the same colour with the sides and back marked with transvers stripes of black the ears are black on the outer side covered with fine black hair, short except at the upper point which is furnished with a pencil of verry fine streight black hair, ¾ of an inch in length, the fur of this animale is long and fine, much more so than the wild cat of the U. States but less so than the Louserva of the N West. the native of this Country make great use of the skins of this cat, to form the robes which they wear; three whole skins is the complement usually employed and sometimes four in each roab. Those cats are not marked alike many of them have but fiew spots of a darker colour, particularly on the back."—Clark

The explorers saw more skins than specimens of the Oregon bobcat. Only one of these wild cats was killed by a member of the Expedition during the winter and spring of 1805-06.

March 28, 1806 (Deer Island, below the mouth of the Willamette River)
"Drewyer also killed a tiger-cat."—Lewis

Failure to kill more than one specimen was probably due more to its nocturnal and elusive habits than to a scarcity of this species.

According to Vernon Bailey[10] the Oregon bobcat is exclusively an inhabitant of the dense, humid coastal forests west of the Cascade Mountains, from northwest California to southern British Columbia.

Lewis does not indicate whether or not the specimen killed by Drewyer on March 28, 1806 was preserved and added to his collection of western animals.

THE MOUNTAIN LION

The mountain lion, *Felis concolor couguar* Kerr, was undoubtedly a familiar species to the men who fought for the Northwest Territory under George Rogers Clark and Anthony Wayne. Records indicate that hundreds of them were killed by the pioneers who pushed over the Appalachians in the late years of the eighteenth and early years of the nineteenth centuries to establish settlements in Pennsylvania, West Virginia, Kentucky and Tennessee. Thus, we can assume that the men who accompanied Lewis and Clark were well acquainted with this species; and, yet, we find surprisingly few references to the mountain lion in their diaries.

May 16, 1805 (On the Missouri, between Milk and Musselshell Rivers)

"In the early part of the day two of our men fired on a panther, a little below our encampment, and wounded it; they informed us that it was very large, had just killed a deer, partly devoured it, and in the act of concealing the balance as they discovered him."—Clark

Aug. 3, 1805 (On Jefferson's River, near Pipestone Creek)

"This morning they passed a small creek on the Star'd side at the entrance of which Reubin Fields killed a large Panther . . . the Panther which Fields killed measured seven and ½ feet from the nose to the extremity of the tail—it is precisely the same animal common to the western part of our country."—Lewis

A somewhat different version of this incident was given by Private Joseph Whitehouse:

Aug. 3, 1805 (Vic. of Pipestone Creek)

"Saw two deer a little ahead, one of the hunters went after them and killed a panther on an Island. it differed Some from those in the States— it was 7½ feet long, & of a redish colour—the turshes (tusks) long—the tallants (talons) large but not very long."

Aug. 6, 1805 (Near mouth of the Big Hole River)

"We found that the three deer skins which we had left at a considerable hight on a tree were Taken off, which we supposed had been done by a panther."—Lewis

Dec. 7, 1805 (Fort Clatsop)

"We proceeded on around the point into the bay and landed to take breakfast on 2 Deer which had been killed and hung up, one of which we found and the other had been taken off by some wild animal probably Panthors or the Wild (cat)."—Clark

Dec. 23, 1805 (Fort Clatsop)

"I also purchased a panthor Skin 7½ feet long including the tail, for all of which I gave 6 Small fish hooks, a Small worn out file & Some pounded fish which we could not use as it was So long wet that it was Soft and molded."—Clark

Feb. 26, 1806 (Fort Clatsop)

"The Panther is found indifferently either in the Great Plains of the Columbia the Western side of the Rocky Mountains or on this coast in the timbered country—it is precisely the same animal common to the Atlantic States, and most commonly met with on our frontiers or un-settled parts of the country—this animal is scerce in the country where they exist and are so remarkably shye and watchfull that it is extreamly difficult to kill them."—Clark

CHAPTER V
Rodents, Hares and Rabbits

The scope of Lewis and Clark's interest in wildlife was remarkable considering their background of education and experience. No rodent was too small to warrant attention.

In some instances their descriptions are so incomplete that positive identification of the species or subspecies to which they referred is impossible. In other cases their descriptions are remarkably detailed and accurate. There is no question about their discovery of the western gray squirrel, the chickaree, the Columbian ground squirrel, the prairie dog, the bushy-tailed woodrat, and the mountain beaver.

They can be credited also with the discovery and the first description of the white-tailed jackrabbit of the northern plains.

Their experiences with the prairie dog, which they called the "barking squirrel," were informative and, in some instances, amusing.

TOWNSEND'S CHIPMUNK

In describing the mammals inhabiting the area between the Rocky Mountains and the Pacific Coast, Lewis included a reference to the "ground squirrel." Coues,[1] after considering various possibilities, concluded that Lewis habitually referred to the chipmunk as a ground squirrel, and that in the following reference he was comparing Townsend's chipmunk, *Eutamias Townsendi* (Bachman), with the eastern chipmunk.

Feb. 25, 1806 (Written at Fort Clatsop)

"the ground squirrel is found in every part of the country, as well the praries as woodlands, and is one of the few animals which we have seen in every part of our voyage, it differs not at all from those of the U' States."—Lewis

THE EASTERN FOX SQUIRREL AND THE GRAY SQUIRREL

The only significant references to these species[2] relate to the northern limits of their ranges on the Missouri River.

Aug. 31, 1806 (About 20 miles above the mouth of the Niobrara River, 1030 miles above St. Louis.)

"This is also the highest up the river where I observe the fox Squirrel, in the bottom above the doome of the N.E. side I killed 2 fox Squirrels."—Clark

"Gray squirrels are found as high up as the little Sioux R." (733 miles above St. Louis.)—Clark

THE WESTERN GRAY SQUIRREL

Lewis and Clark can be credited with writing the earliest description of the western gray squirrel because George Ord, in 1818, based his classification of this species, *Sciurus griseus* Ord, on their description. Coues evidently overlooked Ord's classification of this squirrel when he gave Peale credit for originally naming it *Sciurus fossor* in 1848. In this connection, Coues remarked that it was odd that Ord, who named so many of the mammals described by the explorers should have overlooked this one.

Feb. 25, 1806 (Written at Fort Clatsop)

"The large grey squirrel appears to be a native of a narrow tract of country on the upper side of the mountains just below the grand falls of the Columbia which is pretty well covered in many parts with a species of white oak. in short I believe this squirrel to be co-extensive with timber only, as we have not seen them in any part of the country where pine forms the majority of the timber, or in which the oak does not appear. this animal is much larger than the grey squirrel of our country. it resembles it much in form and coulours. it is as ᴌᴂrge as the fox squirrel of the southern Atlantic States. the tail is reather longer than the whole length of the body and head, the hair of which is long and tho' inserted on all sides, reispect the horizontal ones only. the eyes are black, whiskers black and long. the back, sides, head, tail and outer part of the legs are of a blue, lead-coloured grey. the breast, belley, and inner part of the legs are of a pure white. the hair is short as that of the fox-squirrel, but is much finer and intermixed with a proportion of fur. the natives made great use of these skins in forming their robes. This squirrel subsists principally on the acorn and filbird (filbert) which last grows abundantly in the oak country."—Lewis

Oct. 26, 1805 (Vic. of Celilo Falls on Columbia River)

"hunters killed . . . 4 verry large grey squirrels . . ."—Lewis

April 16, 1806 (Vic. of Sepulchre Island, Columbia River)

"Reubin Fields returned in the evening and brought with him a large grey squirrel, and two others of a kind I had never before seen. they are a size less than the gray squirrel common to the middle Atlantic States and of a pided grey and yellowish brown colour, in form it resembles our grey squirrel precisely. I had them skinned[3] leaving the head, feet and tail to them and placed in the sun to dry."—Lewis

THE CHICKAREE

In many respects, other than appearance, the chickaree *Tamiasciurus douglasi* (Bachman), is the western counterpart of the red squirrel.

97

Seton credits David Douglas with the discovery of this species in 1824; moreover, John Bachman, in 1838, named it in honor of Douglas.[4]

Seton apparently overlooked Lewis' description of the chickaree; and if Bachman considered his description at all, he probably disregarded it for want of a specimen.

Coues, however, specifically identified this "small brown squirrel" as *Sciurus douglasi* Bachman. Lewis' description of the species leaves little or no reason for questioning Coues' conclusion. The fact that he failed to mention the black lines which mark the sides of the chickaree is understandable considering the fact that this feature of the summer pelage becomes indistinct during the winter months.

Feb. 25, 1806 (Written at Fort Clatsop)

"The small brown squirrel is a beautiful little animal about the size and form of the red squirrel of the Eastern Atlantic states and western lakes. the tail is as long as the body and neck, formed like that of the red squirrel, or somewhat flat. the eyes are black, whiskers long and black but not abundant, the back, sides, head, neck and out part of the legs are of a redish dark brown. the throat, breast, belley, and inner part of the legs are of a pale brick red, the tail is a mixture of black and fox coloured red in which the black predominates in the middle and the other on the edge and extremity. the hair of the body is about ½ inch long and so fine and soft that it has the appearance of fur. the hair of the tail is coarser and doubly as long. this animal subsists principally on the seeds of various species of pine, and are always found in the piney country. They are common to the tract of woody country on this coast. they lodge in clifts of rocks, holes in the ground, old stumps of trees and the hollow trunks of fallen timber. in this respect they resemble the rat always having their habitation in or near the earth."—Lewis

RICHARDSON'S RED SQUIRREL

There has been some confusion concerning the identity of a squirrel which Lewis referred to as "a small grey squirrel common to every part of the rocky mountain which is timbered."

Coues[5] suggested that the squirrel described by Lewis might be either Richardson's red squirrel, *Tamiasciurus hudsonicus richardsoni* (Bachman), or Fremont's squirrel, *Tamiasciurus hudsonicus fremonti* (Audubon and Bachman). However, the former seems more probable because the range of Fremont's squirrel is now, and probably was in 1806, confined to the Rocky Mountains of Utah, Colorado, New Mexico and Arizona. Richardson's red squirrel, on the other hand, is common in the northern Rockies to which Lewis and Clark confined their explorations.

Feb. 25, 1806 (Written at Fort Clatsop)

"the small gray squirrel common to every part of the rocky mountain which is timbered, difirs from the dark brown squirrel just described only in its colour. its back, sides, neck, head, tail, and outer sides of the legs are of a brown lead-coloured grey; the tail has a slight touch of fox colour near the extremity of some of the hairs. The throat, breast, belly and inner parts of the legs are of the colour of tanner's ooze, and have a narrow stripe of black, commencing just behind each shoulder and extending longitudinally for about 3 inches between the colours of the sides and belley. their habits are also the same of the dark brown squirrel of this neighborhood, and like them are extreemly nimble and active."—Lewis

COLUMBIAN GROUND SQUIRREL

Arthur H. Howell[6] credited Lewis and Clark with the first description of the Columbian ground squirrel; and Ord[7] named the species *Arctomys columbianus* in 1815, on the basis of their description of specimens collected on a camas prairie near Kamiah, Idaho.

They referred to this species first as a "whistling squirrel," and subsequently as a "burrowing squirrel." This obviously leads to confusion because other ground squirrels of similar habits occur along the route of their travels. It seems possible that some of their later reports of burrowing squirrels in Montana and the Dakotas may have related either to Richardson's ground squirrel or to the pocket gopher. However, this doubt does not seem to pertain in case of the following entries:

May 23, 1806, (Vic. of Kamiah, Idaho)

"Labiech also brought a whistling squirel which he had killed on it's hole in the high plains. this squirel differs from those on the Missouri in their colour, size, food and the length of tail and from those found near the falls of the Columbia."—Clark

May 27, 1806 (Vic. of Kamiah, Idaho)

"There is a species of Burrowing squirel common to these plains which in their habits somewhat resemble those of the Missouri but are a distinct species. this little animal measures one foot five and ½ inches from the nose to the extremity of the tail, of which the tail occupys 2¼ inches only; in the girth it is 11 In. the body is proportionately long, the neck and legs short; the ears are short obtusely pointed, and lie close to the head; the aperture of the ear is larger proportionably than most animals which burrow. The eyes are of moderate size, the puple black and iris of a dark sooty brown. the teeth are like those of the squirel as is it's whole contour. the whiskers are full, long and black; it also has some long black hairs above the eyes. it has five toes on each foot; the two inner toes of the fore feet are remarkably short, and have short blont nails. the remaining toes on those feet are long, black, slightly curved and sharply pointed, the outer and inner toes of the hind feet are not short yet they are by no means as long as the three toes in the center of the foot which are remarkably long but the nails are not as long as those of the fore feet tho' of the same form and colour, the hair of the tail tho' thickly inserted on every part rispects the two sides only. this gives it a flat appearance and a long oval form. the tips of the hair which form the outer edges of the tail are white. the base of the hairs are either black or a fox red. the under disk of the tail is an iron gray, the upper a redish brown. The lower part of the jaws, under part of the neck, legs and feet from the body down and belly are of a light brick red. The nose as high as the eyes is of a darker brick red. the upper part of the head, neck and body are of a curious brownish grey colour with a cast of the brick red. the longer hair of these parts being of a redish white colour at their extremities, fall together in such a manner as to give it the appearance of being speckled at a distance. these animals form large associations as those of the Missouri, occupying with their burroughs one or sometimes 200 acres of land. the burrows are separate and are each occupied by ten or 12 of those animals. There is a little mound in front of the hole formed of the earth out of the burrow and frequently there are three or four distinct holes forming what I term one burrow with their mouths arround the base of this little mound which seems to be occupied as a watch-tower in common by the inhabitants of those several holes. these mounds are sometimes as much as 2 feet high and 4 feet in diameter, and are irregularly distributed over the tract they occupy at the distance of from ten to thirty or 40 yds. when you approach the burrow the squirrels, one or more, usually set erect on these mounds and make a kind of shrill whistleing nois, something like *tweet, tweet, tweet,* etc. they do not live on grass as those of the Missouri but on roots. one which I examined had in its mouth two small bulbs of a species of grass, which resemble very much what is sometimes called the grass-nut. the intestines of those little animals are remarkably large for its size. fur short and very fine. the grass in their villages is not cut down as in those of the plains of the missouri. I preserved the skins of several of these animals with the heads feet and legs entire."—Lewis

June 10, 1806 (Vic. of Weippe Prairie, Idaho)

"We find a great number of the burrowing squirels about our camp of which we killed several; I eat of them and found them quite as tender and well flavoured as our grey squirel."—Lewis

July 3, 1806 (Clark in the Bitterroot valley)

"I also observed the burrowing Squirel of the Species common about the quawmarsh flats West of the Rocky Mountains."—Clark

July 6, 1806 (Vic. of Ross' Hole; headwaters of Bitterroot River)

"I observe great numbers of the whistling squirrel which burrows, their holes scattered on each side of the glades through which we passed."—Clark

July 6, 1806 (Lewis & his party on Salmon Trout Creek, east of Missoula)

"Great Number of burrowing squirrels in this prarie of the species common to the plains of the Columbia."—Lewis

July 23, 1806 (On Cut Bank branch of Marias River)[8]

"near this place I observe a number of the whistling squirrel of the species common to the plains and country watered by the Columbia river, this is the first instance in which I have found this squirrel in the plains of the Missouri."—Lewis

PALE-STRIPED GROUND SQUIRREL

During the period that the explorers were encamped opposite White Bear Island above the Great Falls of the Missouri, one of their men brought in a specimen of the thirteen-lined ground squirrel, *Citellus tridecemlineatus pallidus* (Allen). On the basis of Lewis' description of this animal and the locality from which it was taken, Coues[9] concluded that it probably belonged to the subspecies, *pallidus*, which in 1874 had been given technical status by Allen in his Monographs of the North American Rodentia.[10]

It seems odd that Lewis and Clark failed to observe or to mention the thirteen-lined ground squirrel at some earlier time and place on their outward journey since they entered the range of this species before reaching the western boundary of Missouri. In fact they were nearing the western limits of its range in Montana when they recorded the brief description which follows:

July 8, 1805 (Vic. of Great Falls, Mont.)

"the men also brought me a living ground squirrel which is something larger than those of the U' States or those of that kind which are also common here. this is a much handsomer anamal. like the other it's principal colour is a redish brown but is marked longitudinally with a much greater number of black or dark brown stripes; the spaces between which is marked by ranges of pure white circular spots, about the size of a brister blue shot. these colours embrace the head neck back and sides; the tail is flat, or the long hair projecting horizontally from two sides of it only gives it that appearance. The belly and breast are of much lighter brown or nearly white! this is an inhabitant of the open plain altogether, where it burrows and resides; nor is it like the other found among clifts of rocks or in the woodlands. their burrows sometimes like those of the mole run horizontally near the surface of the ground for a considerable distance, but those in which they reside or take refuge strike much deeper in the earth."—Lewis

RICHARDSON'S GROUND SQUIRREL

We have no conclusive evidence that Lewis and Clark observed this species, *Citellus richardsoni* (Sabine), of ground squirrel, but it is probable that Lewis referred to it in his journal when he wrote:

April 9, 1805 (Vic. of present Garrison Dam)

"Capt. Clark walked on shore to-day and informed me on his return, that passing through the prarie he had seen an anamal that precisely resembled the burrowing squrril, accept in point of size, it being only about one third as large as the squirrel, and that it also burrows."

Clark's version of the same incident is as follows:

"I saw in the prarie an animal resembling the Prarie dog or Barking Squirel & burrow in the same way, this animal was about 1/3 as large as the barking Squirel."

Reid and Gannon[11] have pointed out that Coues seemed to think that Lewis and Clark applied the name "burrowing squirrel" to any of the spermophiles of the plains, especially to the Richardson ground squirrel and less frequently to the prairie dog.

In the foregoing quotations it is evident that Lewis was referring to the prairie dog when he wrote "burrowing squrril," because Clark leaves no room for doubt in saying that the animal he saw resembled a "Prarie dog or barking Squirel."

However, the quotation from Lewis' diary is immediately followed by a description of the workings of the pocket gopher, and the Biddle version of the diaries implies that the mammal Clark observed was a pocket gopher rather than Richardson's ground squirrel.

Reid and Gannon point out that "It is evident, however, that the animal seen by Clark was Richardson Ground Squirrel, as the prairie dog is much larger and the pocket gopher is more nearly of the same size. The animal they compared it with is the prairie dog. Thus we find the prairie dog referred to as the barking and also as the burrowing squirrel."

BLACK-TAILED PRAIRIE DOG

Lewis and Clark first observed the prairie dog, *Cynomys ludovicianus* (Ord), in the fall of 1804, shortly after entering South Dakota. This

RODENTS, HARES AND RABBITS

remarkable rodent appears to have challenged their interest and curiosity to a greater degree than any other ground squirrel that inhabited the plains of the Missouri. Ord named the species, in 1815, solely on the basis of their description.

Sept. 7, 1804 (Approx. 25 miles above the Niobrara River)

"in decending this Cupola, discovered a Village of Small animals that burrow in the grown (those animals are called by the French, Petite Chien) Killed one and Caught one a live by poreing a great quantity of Water in his hole. we attempted to dig to the beds of one of those animals, after diging 6 feet found by running a pole down that we were not half way to his Lodge, we found two frogs in the hole, and Killed a Dark rattle Snake near with a Ground rat (or prarie dog) in him, (those rats are noumerous) the Village of those animals Covered about 4 acres of Ground on a gradual decent of a hill and Contains great numbers of holes on the top of which those little animals Set erect, make a Whistling noise and whin allarmed Step into their hole. we por'd into one of the holes 5 barrels of Water without filling it. Those Animals are about the Size of a Small Squirel Shorter (or longer) and thicker; the head much resembling a Squirel in every respect, except the ears which is Shorter, his tail like a ground squirel which they shake & whistle when allarm'd. the toe nails long, they have fine fur and the longer hairs is gray, it is Said that a kind of Lizard also a Snake[12] reside with those animals (did not find this correct.)"—Clark

July 1, 1806 (Vic. of Lolo, Montana)

"The little animal found in the plains of the Missouri which I have called the *barking squirrel* weighs from 3 to 3½ pounds, it's form is that of the squirrel. it's colour is an uniform light brick red grey, the red reather predominating. the under side of the neck and belley are lighter coloured than the other parts of the body. The legs are short, and it is wide across the breast and sholders in propotion to it's size, appears strongly formed in that part; the head is also bony muscular and stout, reather more blontly terminated wider and flatter than the common squirrel. the upper lip is split or divided to the nose. the ears are short and lie close to the head, having the appearance of being cut off, in this particular they resemble the guinea pig. the teeth are like those of the squirrel rat etc. they have a false jaw or pocket between the skin and the mustle of the jaw like that of the common ground squirrel but not so large in proportion to their size. they have large and full whiskers on each side of the nose, a few long hairs of the same kind on each jaw and over the eyes. the eye is small and black, they have five toes on each foot of which the two outer toes on each foot are much shorter than those in the center particularly the two inner toes of the forefeet, the toes of the forefeet are

remarkably long and sharp and seem well adopted to scratching or burrowing those of the hind feet are neither as long or sharp as the former;
the nails are black, the hair of this animal is about as long and equally as
course as that of the common grey squirrel of our country, and the hair
of the tail is not longer than that of the body except immediately at the
extremity where it is somewhat longer and frequently of a dark brown
colour. the part of generation in the female is placed on the lower region
of the belley between the hinder legs so far forward that she must lie on
her back to copolate. the whole length of this animal is one foot five inches
from the extremity of the nose to that of the tail of which the tail
occupyes 4 inches. it is nearly double the size of the whistleing squirrel of
the Columbia. it is much more quick active and fleet than it's form would
indicate. these squirrels burrow in the ground in the open plains usually
at a considerable distance from water yet are never seen at any distance
from their burrows. six or eight usually reside in one burrow to which
there is never more than one entrance. these burrows are of great debth.
I once dug and pursued a burrow to the debth of ten feet and did not
reach it's greatest debth. they generally associate in large societies placing
their burrows near each other and frequently occupy in this manner
several hundred acres of land. when at rest above ground their position
is generally erect on their hinder feet and rump; thus they will generally
set and bark at you as you approach them. their note being much that
of the little toy dogs, their yelps are in quick succession and at each they
give a motion to their tails upwards. they feed on the grass and weeds
within the limits of their village which they never appear to exceed on
any occasion. as they are usually numerous they keep the grass and weeds
within their district very closely graized and as clean as if it had been
swept. the earth which they throw out of their burrows is usually formed
into a conic mound around the entrance. this little animal is frequently very
fat and it's flesh is not unpleasant. as soon as the hard frosts commence
it shuts up it's burrow and continues until spring. it will eat neither grain
or meat."—Lewis

At the time these descriptions were written the prairie dog was unknown to scientists, and Coues credited Lewis and Clark with being the
first to write anything approaching a technical description of this species.
Oddly enough, Seton, who cited their pioneer work in connection with
the discovery of other mammals and birds that were new to science,
failed to mention their contributions to our knowledge of the prairie dog.

Ord, who originally named this mammal *Arctomys ludoviciana* in 1815,
based his description on a specimen taken on the upper Missouri River.
Whether he had access to the two cased skins shipped to President Jefferson from Fort Mandan is not known.

Coues,[13] in a footnote to Clark's diary entry of Sept. 7, 1804, made some interesting comments concerning the taxonomic history of the prairie dog:

"This is an early description of the prairie dog *Cynomys ludoviciana*, then unknown to science, and not technically named until 1815, when it was called *Arctomys ludoviciana* by George Ord, in *Gutherie's Geog.*, 2nd ed., Vol. II, pp. 292-302. . . . The earliest notice I have ever seen of the prairie dog occurs in a letter from Capt. Clark to Gov. Harrison, dated Fort Mandan, Apr. 2, 1805, and, I think, published in 1806—if so, before the appearance of Lt. Z. M. Pike's Travels, 1810, . . . Pike is usually cited in this connection before Lewis and Clark, but he must yield to Clark and Gass in priority."

During both their outbound and return trips the explorers recorded the location and extent of some of the more conspicuous prairie dog villages seen on the upper Missouri.

Sept. 11, 1804 (Vic. of Scalp Creek, Gregory Co., S. Dakota)
"We saw a Village of Barking Squirel 970 yards long and 800 yards Wide Situated on a jentle Slope of a hill, those animals are noumerous. I killed 4 with a View to have their Skins Stufed."—Clark

Sept. 16, 1804 (Near the Mouth of the White River)
Two men who were sent up the White River for a few miles reported seeing "the Barking Squirels Villages."

Sept. 17, 1804 (Crow Creek, above the mouth of the White River)
Here Lewis described a plain, one mile wide and about three miles long, which was "intirely occupyed by the burrows of the barking squiril heretofore described; this anamal appears here in infinite numbers."

June 5, 1805 (Few miles below Marias River mouth)
"In this plain and from one to nine miles from the river or any water, we saw the largest collection of the burrowing or barking squirrels that we had ever yet seen; we passed through a skirt of the territory of this community for about 7 miles."—Lewis

Feb. 25, 1806 (Written at Fort Clatsop)
"the barking squirrel and handsome ground squirrel[14] of the plains or the East side of the rocky mountains are not found in the plains of Columbia."—Lewis

Aug. 31, 1806 (Few miles above Niobrara River)
"passed the doome and lowest village of Barking Squirels."—Clark

Lewis' observations and conclusions concerning the habits of prairie dogs were remarkably accurate:

May 23, 1805 (Several miles west of the Musselshell River)

"just above the entrance of Teapot creek on the star'd side there is a large assemblage of the burrows of the Barking Squirrel. they generally select a south or south Easterly exposure for their residence, and never visit the brooks or river for water; I am astonished at how this anamal exists as it dose without water, pariculary in a country like this where there is scarcely any rain during ¾ of the year and more rarely any due (dew) yet we have sometimes found their villages at a distance of five or six miles from any water, and they are never found out of the limits which their burrows occupy; in the autumn when the hard frosts commence they close their burrows and do not venture out again untill spring, indeed some of them appear to be yet in winter quarters."—Lewis

Prairie dogs are not ordinarily regarded as game animals, but the explorers were not above testing the edibility of any species that wore feathers or fur.

June 5, 1805 (Few miles below Marias River)

"as we had not killed or eat anything today we each killed a burrowing squirrel as we passed them in order to make sure of our suppers . . . I had the burrowing squirrels roasted by way of experiment and found the flesh well flavoured and tender; some of them were very fat."—Lewis

Maximilian, in 1833, made some pertinent comments on the prairie dog-rattlesnake relationship as a result of his observations in North Dakota.

"In this neighborhood are many villages of the prairie dogs (Arctomys ludoviciana Ord) in the abandoned burrows of which rattlesnakes abound. It has been affirmed that these two species live peaceably together in these burrows; but observers of nature have proved that the snakes take possession of abandoned burrows only, which is in the usual course of things."

THE WOODCHUCKS

The woodchuck or groundhog, *Marmota monax* (Linnaeus), was mentioned only in the Lewis and Clark journals; and in this instance Clark merely compared the tail and hair of the badger to that of the woodchuck.

The yellow-bellied marmot, *Marmota monax flaviventris* (Audubon and Bachman), of the west is mentioned only twice by Lewis and Clark. On one occasion Lewis mentioned seeing robes worn by the Shoshone Indians on the Lemhi River that were made from the skins of the "moonox"; and on the second occasion he reported seeing "a moonox which the natives had petted" in a Salishan Indian village on the lower Columbia River. Coues identified these western marmots as *Marmota flaviventris*.

DAKOTA POCKET GOPHER

Although Lewis and Clark did not actually see the Dakota pocket gopher, *Thomomys talpoides* (Richardson), Lewis described the mounds of earth thrown up by this rodent:

April 9, 1805 (Above Fort Mandan)

"I have observed in many parts of the plains and praries, the work of an anamal of which I could never obtain a view. Their work resembles that of the salamender[15] common to the sand hills of the States of South Carolina and Georgia, and like that animal also it never appears above ground. the little hillocks which are thrown up by these anamals have much the appearance of ten or twelve pounds of loose earth poured out of a vessel on the surface of the plain. in the state they leave them you can discover no whole (hole) through which they throw out this earth; but my removing the loose earth gently you may discover that the soil has been broken in a circle manner for about an inch and a half in diameter; where it appears looser than the adjacent surface, and is certainly the place through which the earth has been thrown out, tho' the operation is performed without leaving any visible aperture."—Lewis

Reid and Gannon upheld Coues' conclusion that the mound and den building activity described above was that of the pocket gopher. Their comments in this regard are as follows:

"The description of its methods of mound building given in the journals for April 9, 1805 (Thwaites, Vol. I, page 289) leaves no doubt as to the identity of this species."[16]

THE BEAVER

The beaver of North America was important in the fur trade before it was established as a distinct species. The type specimen was collected in the Hudson Bay area and named *Castor canadensis* by Kuhl in 1820. Prior to that time it evidently was thought to be the same as the Old World beaver, *Castor fiber*.

Since one of the objectives of the Expedition was to ascertain the possibility of diverting some of the fur trade with the western Indians from the British companies, Lewis and Clark were careful to record their observations on the distribution and abundance of beaver. They noted the occurrence of dams and lodges, tree cutting activities, and the availability and distribution of tree species commonly utilized by these mammals. These records indicate that beaver were once abundant on streams that have not known them for so many years that it is hard to believe they were ever present.

Beaver and beaver signs were first seen on the outward journey in the neighborhood of Leavenworth, Kansas, and again near Council Bluffs. Thereafter they were mentioned frequently in the diaries as the party ascended the Missouri. A few were taken at Fort Mandan before winter interrupted trapping.

Above Fort Mandan beaver were plentiful wherever cottonwood and willow were sufficiently abundant to insure an adequate food supply. They were taken in traps at almost every campsite.

April 10, 1805 (Approx. 50 miles above Fort Mandan)

"At 1 P.M. we overtook three french hunters who had set out a few days before us with a view of trapping beaver; they had taken 12 since they left Fort Mandan. These people avail themselves of the protection which our numbers will enable us to give them against the Assiniboin who sometimes hunt on the Missouri, and intend ascending with us as far as the mouth of the Yellowstone river and continue there hunt up that river —This is the first essay of a beaver hunter of any description on this river—the beaver these people have already taken is by far the best I have ever seen."—Lewis

April 12, 1805 (Vic. of Little Missouri River)

"George Drewyer shot a Beaver this morning which we found swimming in the river a small distance below the entrance of the little Missouri. the beaver being seen in the day is a proof that they have been but little hunted, as they always keep themselves closely concealed during the day where they are so."—Lewis

April 13, 1805 (Vic. of Little Missouri River)

"our party cought three beaver last evening; and the French hunters 7. —as there was much appearance of beaver just above the entrance of the little Missouri these hunters concluded to remain some days, we therefore left them without expectation of seeing them again."—Lewis

April 16, 1805 (Approx. 70 miles above the Little Missouri River)

"there was a remarkably large beaver caught by one of the party last night. These animals are now very abundant. I have met with several trees which have been felled by them 20 Inches in diameter. bark is their only food; and they appear to prefer that of cotton wood and willow as we have never met with any other species of timber on the Missouri which had the appearance of being cut by them."—Lewis

April 17, 1805 (90 miles above mouth of the Little Missouri River)

"there were three beaver taken this morning by the party. the men prefer the flesh of this animal, to that of any other which we have, or are able to procure at this moment. I eat very heartily of the beaver myself, and think it excellent; particularly the tale, and liver."—Lewis

April 19, 1805 (Vic. of Little Knife River)

"The beaver of this part of the Missouri are larger, fatter, more abundant and better clad with fur than those of any part of the country that I have yet seen; I have remarked also that their fur is much darker." —Lewis

April 22, 1805 (Vic. of mouth of White Earth River)

"Saw an emence number of beaver feeding on the waters edge & swimming, killed several"—Clark

"We saw a number of bever feeding on the bark of trees alonge the verge of the river, several of which we shot, found them large and fat." —Lewis

April 26, 1805 (Mouth of Yellowstone River)

"beaver is in every bend"—Clark

April 27, 1805 (Mouth of Yellowstone River)

"I saw several beaver and much sign, I shot one in the head which immediately sunk."—Clark

April 28, 1805 (Mouth of Yellowstone River)

"the beaver have cut great quantities of timber, saw a tree nearly 3 feet in diameter that had been felled by them."—Lewis

May 2, 1805 (Approx. 35 miles above Yellowstone)

"on our way this evening we also shot three beaver along the shore; these anamals in consequence of not being hunted are extreemly gentle, where they are hunted they never leave their lodges in the day, . . . the flesh of the beaver is esteemed a delicacy among us; I think the tale a most delicious morsal, when boiled it resembles the fresh tongues and sounds of the codfish, and is usually sufficiently large to afford a plentifull meal for two men."—Lewis

May 6, 1805 (Few miles above the mouth of the Poplar River)

"two beaver were taken in traps this morning and one since shot by one of the party. saw numbers of these anamals peeping at us as we passed, out of their wholes which they form of a cilindrical shape by burrowing in the face of the abbrupt banks of the river"—Lewis

May 8, 1805 (Vic. of mouth of Milk River)

"great appearance of beaver on this river, and I have no doubt but what they continue abundant, there being plenty of cotton wood and willow, the timber on which they subsist."—Lewis

May 9, 1805 (Mouth of the Milk River)

"we also saw this evening emence quantities of timber cut by the beaver which appeared to have been done the preceeding year, in one place particularly they had cut all the timber down for three acres in front and nearly one back from the river and had removed a considerable proportion of it, the timber grew very thick and some of it was as large as a man's body."—Lewis

May 18, 1805 (Vic. of mouth of Fourchette Creek)

"some of the party shoot and catch beaver every day and night."—Clark

May 19, 1805

"one of the party wounded a beaver, and my dog as usual swam in to catch it; the beaver bit him through the hind leg and cut the artery; it was with great difficulty that I could stop the blood; I fear it will yet prove fatal[17] to him."—Lewis

May 24, 1805 (Above mouth of the Musselshell River)

"Game is becoming more scarce, particularly beaver, of which we have seen but few for several days. the beaver appears to keep pace with the timber, as it declines in quantity they also become more scarce."—Lewis

June 30, 1805 (Vic. of the Great Falls of the Missouri)

"wherever we find timber there is also beaver."—Lewis

July 3, 1805 (Mouth of Sun River)

"Six beaver and 2 orters has been killed at this camp within a fiew days."—Clark

July 15, 1805 (Between Great Falls and the Gates of the Mountains)

"we camped on the Star'd Side at which place I saw many beaver, the timber on the edge of the river more Common than below the falls."—Clark

July 18, 1805 (Vic. of Ordway's Creek, above Great Falls, Montana)

"Capt. Clark ascended the river on the Star'd side . . . in the evening he passed over a mountain by which means he cut off many miles of the rivers circuitous rout . . . he passed two streams of water, the branches of Ordway's Creek, on which he saw a number of beaver dams succeeding each other in close order and extending as far up those streams as he could discover them in their course towards the mountains."—Lewis

July 24, 1805 (Vic. of Townsend, Montana)

"we saw many beaver and some otter today; the former dam up the small channels of the river between the islands and compell the river in these parts to make other channels, which soon as it has effected that which was stoped by the beaver, becomes dry and is filled up with mud,

sand, gravel and driftwood. the beaver is then compelled to seek another spot for his habitation where he again erects his dam. Thus the river in many places among the clusters of islands is constantly changing the direction of such sluices as the beavers are capable of stoping, or of 20 yards in width. This animal in that way I believe to be very instrumental in adding to the number of islands with which we find the river crouded."
—Lewis

July 27, 1805 (Three Forks, Montana)

"Our hunters returned this evening with 6 deer, 3 otter and a Muskrat. they inform me that they had seen great numbers of Antelopes, and much sign of beaver, otter, deer, Elk, etc."—Lewis

July 30, 1805 (Jefferson River, a few miles above Three Forks)

"saw a vast number of beaver in many large dams which they had maid in various bayoes of the river which are distributed to a distance of three or four miles on this side of the river over an extensive bottom of timbered and meadow lands intermixed. in order to avoid these bayoes and beaver dams which I found difficult to pass, I directed my course to the high plain to the right which I gained after some time with much difficulty and waiding many beaver dams to my waist in mud and water."—Lewis

July 31, 1805 (Mouth of Philosophy River; 15 miles above Three Forks)

"it has some timber in its bottoms and vast numbers of beaver and otter."—Lewis

Aug. 2, 1805 (Jefferson River, near White Tail Deer Creek)

"we saw some very large beaver dams today in the bottoms of the river, several of which were five feet high and over flowed several acres of land; these dams are formed of willow brush, mud, gravel and are so closely interwoven that they resist the water perfectly. the base of this work is thick and rises nearly perpendicularly on the lower side, while the upper side or that within the dam is gently sloped. the brush appear to be laid in no regular order yet acquires a strength by the irregularity with which they are placed by the beaver that it would puzzle the ingenuity of man to give them."—Lewis

Aug. 5, 1805 (Mouth of Big Hole River)

"at 4 P M they (Clark and main party) arrived at the confluence of the two rivers where I left the note. This note had unfortunately been placed on a green pole which the beaver had cut and carried off together with the note . . . this accident deprived Capt. Clark of any information with respect to the country and supposing that the rapid fork was most in the direction which it was proper we should pursue, or West, he took that stream and ascended it with much difficulty about a mile and encamped on an island that had been lately over flown and was yet damp; they were compelled therefore to make beds of brush to keep themselves out of the mud."—Lewis

Aug. 7, 1805 (Ascending Beaverhead River)
"All those streams (tributaries of Jefferson and Big Hole Rivers) Contain emence numbers of Beaver, otter, Musk-rats, etc."—Clark

Aug. 11, 1805 (Prairie Creek, vic. of Horse Prairie)
"I passed the river which was about 12 yards wide and barred in several places entirely across by beaver dams, and proceeded through the level plain directly to the pass."—Lewis
"the men (Clark's party dragging canoes up Jefferson River between the Beaver Head and Dillon, Mont.) killed a beaver with a setting pole and tomahawked several otter."—Clark

Aug. 20, 1805 (Mouth of Prairie Creek; vic. of Grayling, Mont.)
"Drewyer went in search of his trap which a beaver had taken off last night; he found the beaver dead with the trap to his foot about 2 miles below the place he had set it. this beaver constituted the whole of the game taken today. the fur of this animal is as good as I ever saw any, and I believe that they are never out of season on the upper part of the Missouri and its branches within the mountains."—Lewis

Sept. 13, 1805 (Lolo Creek)
"This Creek is verry much damed up with the beaver, but we can see none."—Clark

Nov. 7, 1805 (Vic. of Pillar Rock, approaching Gray's Bay)
"An Indian village on one of those Islands. they came and Traded 2 beaver skins for fishing hooks and a fiew Wapto roots. The beaver skins I wish for to make a robe as the one I have is worn out."—Clark

Nov. 21, 1805 (Vic. of Astoria, Oregon)
"They (Clatsop Indians) also have robes of Sea Otter, *Beaver*, Elk, Deer, fox and cat common to this Countrey. . . ."—Clark

Jan. 9, 1806 (Fort Clatsop)
Lewis lists *beaver* along with otter, Sea otter, among other furs sought by American, British, and Russian sea captains who visited the mouth of the Columbia each summer to trade with the Indians.

Jan. 15, 1806 (Fort Clatsop)
"The spear or gig is used to take the sea otter, the common otter, spuck, and *beaver*."—Lewis

Feb. 15, 1806 (Fort Clatsop)

Lewis listed the beaver among the native wild animals of the Northwest, but he failed to discuss this species along with others that were "severally noticed" in his diary during the next few weeks. However, on Feb. 22, 1806 he added the following comment:

"The Beaver and common Otter have before been mentioned in treating of the occupations of the natives in hunting, fishing, etc. these do not differ from those of other parts of the continent."—Lewis

April 30, 1806 (Touchet River, a tributary of the Walla Walla River)

"Drewyer killed a beaver and an otter; a part of the former we reserved for ourselves and gave the indians the ballance."—Lewis

July 7, 1806 (Lewis and Clark Pass, approx. 45 miles N.N.W of Helena)

"After we encamped Drewyer killed two beaver and shot a third which bit his knee very badly and escaped."—Lewis

July 20, 1806 (Lewis & party on the Marias River)

"there is much appearance of beaver on this river, but not any of otter."
—Lewis

July 10, 1806 (Clark and his party on the Beaverhead River)

"McNeals Creek, Track Creek, Phelanthropy river, Wisdom (Big Hole) river, Fields river and Frazier's creek each throw in a considerable quantity of water and have innoumerable beaver and otter on them."—Clark

July 14, 1806 (Vic. of Three Forks and Gallatin River)

"Sent Shields ahead to kill a deer for our breakfast, and at an early hour set out with the party. Crossed Gallitines river which makes a considerable bend to the N. E. and proceeded on nearly S. 78° E. through an open Leavel plain. at 6 miles I struck the river and crossed a part of it and attempted to proceed on through the river bottoms which was several miles wide at this place. I crossed several chanels of the river running through the bottom in different directions. I proceeded on about two miles crossing those different chanels all of which was damed with beaver in such a manner as to render the passage impracticable and after being swamped as I may say in this bottom of beaver, I was compelled to turn short about to the right and after some difficuelty made my way good to an open low but firm plain. . . .

"emence quantities of beaver on this Fork (of the Gallatin River) quite down, and their dams very much impeed the navigation of it from the 3 forks down, tho' I believe it practicable for small canoes by unloading at a fiew of the worst of those dams."—Clark

113

July 26, 1806 (Bighorn River, a tributary of the Yellowstone)
"it is very long and contains a great perportion of timber on which there is a variety of wild animals . . . , and the river is said to abound in beaver." —Clark

July 27, 1806 (On Yellowstone River)
"much more beaver sign than above the big horn. I saw several of those animals on the bank today."—Clark

"Beaver is plenty on this part of the Rochejhone."—Clark

Aug. 3, 1806 (Evidently written at a later date from information supplied by Clark)
"like all other branches of the Missouri which penetrate the Rocky Mountains, all that portion of it (Yellowstone River) lying within those mountains abound in fine beaver and Otter, its streams also which issuing from the rocky mountain and discharg themselves above Clark's fork inclusive also furnish an abundance of beaver and Otter and possess considerable proportions of timber in their vallies."—Lewis
July 29, 1806 (On the Yellowstone near mouth of Tongue River)

In checking through the kill records of the expedition, it was noted that the first beaver taken by the hunters and trappers were obtained near the mouth of the Platte River on July 26, 1804. Thereafter beaver were killed every few days as the party moved up the Missouri to Fort Mandan. Between July 26th and November 3rd inclusive, twenty beaver were accounted for. None was taken during the cold winter months; but after the journey was resumed in April, 1805, beaver were again killed frequently between the mouth of the Little Missouri River and Great Falls. The records indicate that at least 71 beaver were taken on this stretch of the Missouri between April 11th and July 5, 1805. However, between Great Falls and Three Forks only one beaver was killed; and, even though their dams and cuttings were much in evidence on the Jefferson River and its tributaries only one beaver was accounted for between Three Forks and Lemhi Pass. Four were taken on the Lemhi River during August; and one was killed on Lolo Creek on Sept. 10, 1805. Thereafter, none was reported between the Bitterroot Mountains and the mouth of the Columbia, and only three were recorded during the winter of 1805-06 at Fort Clatsop.

Few beaver were taken on the return journey; two were killed by Drewyer on Touchet River in eastern Washington, but none was recorded thereafter until the explorers had again made their way over Lolo Pass and were descending the Bitterroot Mountains in Montana. Although Lewis reported on the occurrence of beaver on the Marias River and on the Missouri, and Clark frequently reported on their abundance on the Jefferson River, the Gallatin River, and on the Yellowstone and its tributaries, neither of them could afford to permit time being spent in trapping or hunting beaver on the return journey. As a result only eleven were killed between July 3rd and Sept. 23rd, when they arrived at St. Louis.

In all, 107 beaver were recorded as killed, but in a few instances an exact figure was omitted in favor of an indefinite "several." Thus, the recorded kill is somewhat lower than the number actually taken.

During the winter at Fort Clatsop Lewis described in detail his method of preparing bait from the castors of the beaver. His recipe should be of considerable interest to modern trappers and wildlife managers.

Jan. 7, 1806 (Fort Clatsop)

"this bate when properly prepared will intice the beaver to visit it as far as he can smell it, and this I think may be safely stated at a mile, their sense of smell being very acute. To prepare the beaver bate, the castor or bark stone is taken as the base, this is gently pressed out of the bladderlike bag which contains it, into a phial of 4 ounces with a wide mouth; if you have them you will put four to six stone in a phial of that capacity, to this you will add half a nutmeg, a douzen or 15 grains of cloves and thirty grains of cinimon finely pulverized, stu them well together and then add as much ardent sperits to the composition as will reduce it the consistency of mustard prepared for the table; when thus prepared it resembles mustard precisely to all appearance. when you cannot procure a phial a bottle made of horn or a tight earthen vessel will answer, in all cases it must be excluded from the air or it will soon loose it's virtue; it is fit for uce immediately it is prepared but becomes much stronger and better in about four or five days and will keep for months provided it be perfectly secluded from the air. when cloves are not to be had use double the quantity of Allspice, and when no spice can be obtained use the bark of the root of Sassafras; when spirits can not be had use oil stone of the beaver adding mearly a sufficient quantity to moisten the other materials, or reduce it to a stif paste. it appears to me that the principal uce of the spices is only to give a variety to the scent of the bark stone and if so the mace vineller (vanilla) and other sweet smelling spices might be employed with equal advantage."

Jan. 10, 1806 (Fort Clatsop)

"The bate is put on the point of a stick and stuck in the ground so as the bait will be over the trap which is under the water Set for the beaver."— Clark

Robert Stuart,[18] who led a small company of men from Astoria to St. Louis in 1812-13, reported on the abundance of beaver on the Walla Walla River and on several tributaries of the Snake River.

Alexander Henry[19] kept an accurate account of all furs collected at his Pembina Post of the North West Company, located on the Red River a few miles south of the Canadian boundary. His reports on beaver and muskrats taken largely by Indian and French trappers on the tributaries of the lower Red and Assiniboin Rivers are of interest.

Year	Number of beaver	Weight of beaver pelts	Number of muskrats
1801	1,475	1,904 lbs.	27
1802	1,369	1,805 "	13
1803	1,801	2,825 "	144
1804	1,866	2,868 "	—
1805	2,763	4,000 "	6,712
1806	1,621	2,625 "	12,470
1807	1,184	1,750 "	544
1808	696	908 "	—
	12,775	18,685 lbs.	19,910

It will be noticed that the annual catch of beaver increased through the 1804-05 season, and then declined rapidly during the next three years.

The record for muskrats shows a parallel trend, except that there was evidently little interest in, or demand for, muskrat pelts until 1805 and 1806, when 6,712 and 12,470 respectively, were trapped. In 1807 the catch dropped to 544, and in 1808 none was taken.

At the end of the 1808 season the Pembina Post was closed, and the Company moved westward to virgin territory.

The great harvest of beaver and other fur bearers did not begin on the headwaters of the Missouri and Snake Rivers until 1822, after William H. Ashley and Jedediah Smith had opened the overland route and explored the northern Rocky Mountains. It was Ashley's lieutenants, Jed Smith, William Sublette, and David Jackson who reaped the first harvest of fur in Wyoming, Montana and Idaho. These masters of the wilderness sold out to Jim Bridger, Milton Sublette, Tom Fitzpatrick, Henry Fraeb, and John Baptiste Gervais, who organized the Rocky Mountain Fur Company. But in 1832, the powerful American Fur Company, supported by the wealth of Astor in New York and Chouteau of St. Louis, set out to take over the Rocky Mountain trade and crush the "Opposition" company, headed by Jim Bridger and his "Mountain Men." The history of this struggle for wealth and power, which virtually wiped out the beaver in a decade, and thousands of Indians as well. has been described in detail by Bernard De-Voto.[20] By 1838 beaver were so reduced in numbers that buffalo robes were supplanting them in the fur trade.

BUSHY-TAILED WOODRAT

There is no question about Lewis and Clark being the first field naturalists to describe the packrat *Neotoma cinerea* (Ord); nor is there any question about the identity of the animal Lewis describes below:

July 2, 1805 (Vic. of Great Falls, Montana)

"after our return in moving some of the baggage we caught a large rat[21] (copy for Dr. Barton) it was somewhat larger than the common European rat, of lighter colour; the body and outer part of the legs and head of a light lead colour, the belley and inner side of the legs white as were also the feet and (y)ears. the toes were longer and the ears much larger than the common rat; the ears uncovered with hair. the eyes were black and prominent. the whiskers very long and full. the tail was reather longer than the body covered with fine fur or poil of the same length and colour of the back. the fur was very silkey, close and short. I have frequently seen the nests of these rats in clifts of rocks and hollow trees but never before saw one of them. They feed very much on the fruit and seed of the prickly pear; or at least I have seen greater quantities of the hulls of that fruit lying about their holes and in their nests."—Lewis

Feb. 26, 1806 (Written at Fort Clatsop)

"The Rat in the rocky mountains on its west side are like those on the upper part of the Missouri in and near those mountains, and have the distinguishing trait of possessing a tail covered with hair like other parts of the body; one of these we cought at the white bear Islands in the beginning of July last, and then partially described."—Clark

Ord,[22] who named this rodent in 1815, based his classification on a specimen from the vicinity of Great Falls, Montana. Possibly he had access to the specimen collected by Lewis and Clark; certainly he was familiar with their journals, as edited by Biddle and Allen and printed in 1814, for he relied on Lewis and Clark's descriptions of certain other species which he classified and named.

EASTERN WOODRAT

Following his brief description of the packrat, Clark continued with a short paragraph on the eastern woodrat, *Neotoma floridana* (Ord).

Feb. 26, 1806 (Written at Fort Clatsop)

"There is rats in this neighbourhood, but I have not seen them. it is most probable that they are like those of the Atlantic States, or at least the native rat of our country which have no hair on their tail. this species we have found on the Missouri as far up as the woody country extended. it is as large as the common European house rat or reather larger, is of a lighter colour, bordering more on the lead or drab colour, the hair longer; and the female has only four tits which are placed far back near the hinder legs. this rat I have seen in the southern parts of the state of Kentucky and west of the Miami."—Lewis

In this instance Lewis' intuition led him astray. The woodrat of the Oregon coast is a bushy-tailed rat rather than the smooth-tailed woodrat, *Neotoma floridana,* of the eastern States. He was also careless in stating that the eastern woodrat has a hairless tail; undoubtedly he used this extreme term to emphasize the contrast between the bushy (long-haired) tail of the packrat and the smooth (short-haired) tail of the eastern woodrat.

Coues[23] credited Lewis and Clark with the discovery of the woodrat:

"It was unknown to science when thus discovered by Lewis and Clark. It was rediscovered by Thomas Say of Major Long's party on the Mississippi, a little below St. Louis, . . . on June 7, 1819. In 1825 Mess'rs Ord and Say made this the type of their new genus, Neotoma."

Clark probably saw the eastern woodrat for the first time in the vicinity of Independence, Missouri. On July 7, 1804 he mentioned seeing "a large rat on the bank." Obviously this statement gives no clue to the animal's identity; but Sergeant Gass, who kept an independent diary, described the rat seen on this date as having hair on its tail.[24]

MEADOW MOUSE

The meadow mouse, *Microtus pennsylvanicus* (Ord), being a familiar rodent, is mentioned only incidentally in the Lewis and Clark journals. There is, however, one interesting incident reported wherein the meadow mouse contributed to the larder of the explorers.

April 9, 1805

"When we stopped for dinner the squaw[25] busied herself in searching for the wild artichokes which the mice[26] collect and deposit in large hoards. this operation she performed by penetrating the earth with a sharp stick about some small collections of drift wood. her labour soon proved successful, and she procured a good quantity of these roots. the flavor of this root resembles that of the Jerusalem Artichoke, and the stalk of the weed which produces it is also similar, tho' the root and the stalk are much smaller than the Jerusalem Artichoke. the root is white and of an ovate form, from one to three inches in length and usually about the size of a man's finger. one stalk produces from two to four, and sometimes six of these roots."—Lewis

MOUNTAIN BEAVER

The mountain beaver, *Aplodontia rufa* (Rafinesque), was unquestionably discovered and first described by Lewis and Clark, while at Fort Clatsop, during the winter of 1805-06. The explorers did not see or collect a living specimen of this animal, but based their description on dressed skins and information obtained from the Indians.

Rafinesque, who is credited with naming the species, based his classification solely on Lewis and Clark's account of it. His generic designation, *Anisonyx*, was subsequently found to be taxonomically untenable; and, in 1829, John Richardson assigned the mountain beaver to a new genus, *Aplodontia*.

Lewis' principal account of the mountain beaver follows:

Feb. 26, 1806 (Fort Clatsop)

"*Sewelel* is the Chinnook and Clatsop name for a small animal found in the timbered country on this coast. it is more abundant in the neighbourhood of the great falls and rapids of the Columbia than immediately on the coast. the natives make great use of the skins of this animal in forming their robes, which they dress with the fur on them and attatch together with sinews of the Elk or deer. I have never seen the animal and can therefore discribe it only from the skin and a slight view which some of our hunters have obtained of the living animal. the skin when dressed is from 14 to 18 inches in length and from 7 to 9 in width; the tail is always severed from the skin in forming their robes I cannot therefore say what form or length it is. one of the men informed me that he thought it reather short and flat. that he saw one of them run up a tree like a squirrel and that it returned and ran into a hole in the ground. the ears are short thin pointed and covered with short fine hair. they are of a uniform colour, a redish brown; tho' the base of the long hairs, which exceed the fur but little in length, as well as the fur itself is of a dark colour for at least two thirds of its length next to the skin. the fur and hair are very fine, short, thickly set and silkey. the ends of the fur and tips of the hair being of the redish brown that colour predominates in the ordinary appearance of the animal. I take this animal to be about the size of the barking squirrel of the Missouri, and believe most probably that it is of the Mustela genus, or perhaps the brown mungo itself. I have indeavored in many instances to make the indians sensible how anxious I was to obtain one of these animals entire, without being skined, and offered them considerable rewards to furnish me with one, but have not been able to make them comprehend me. I have purchased several of the robes made of these skins to line a coat which I have had made of the skins of the tiger cat. they make a very pleasant light lining."

THE YELLOW-HAIRED PORCUPINE

According to Reid and Gannon the porcupines which were seen by the explorers in the Dakotas and Montana were of the subspecies commonly known as the yellow-haired porcupine, *Erethizon dorsatum epixanthum* Brandt.[27]

Sept. 13, 1804 (Near Brule City, S. Dak.)

"Capt. Lewis killed a Porcupine on a Cotton tree feeding on the leaves and bowers of said tree."—Clark

May 3, 1805 (Vic. of Poplar, Montana)

"I walked out a little distance and met with 2 porcupines which were feeding on the young willow which grow in great abundance on all the sandbars; this animal is exceedingly clumsy and not very watchful. I approached so near one of them, before it perceived me that I touched it with my espontoon.

"near the entrance of the river mentioned in the 10th course of this day, we saw an unusual number of Porcupines from which we determined to call the river after this anamal, and accordingly denominated it Porcupine River."[28]—Lewis

THE WHITE-TAILED JACKRABBIT

The white-tailed jackrabbit was officially described and named *Lepus townsendi* by John Bachman in 1837, in honor of J. K. Townsend, who collected the type specimen near Walla Walla, Washington. Evidently the 19th century zoologists either overlooked or disregarded Lewis and Clark's description of this hare.

The white-tailed jackrabbit was first observed by the explorers in South Dakota.

Sept. 14, 1804 (In the Missouri valley, several miles below the mouth of the White River)

"Shield's killed a Hare like the mountain hare of Europe, weighing 6¼ pounds (altho pore) his head narrow, its ears large, i.e. 6 Inches long & 3 Inches Wide, one half of each White, the other and out part a lead gray, from the toe of the hind foot to toe of the fore foot is 2 feet 11 Inches. the hith (height) is 1 foot 1 Inch and ¾. his tail long thick and white."—Clark

While at Fort Clatsop, Lewis wrote a much more detailed description of the white-tailed jackrabbit. It will be noted that the specimen described was larger than average, but that the measurements and other details of the description are remarkably accurate, even to the fact that the white tail is held straight out behind when the animal is running.

Feb. 28, 1806 (Fort Clatsop)

"The *Hare* on this side of the Rocky Mountains is exclusively the inhabitents of the Great Plains of the Columbia, as they are of those of the Missouri East of the Mountains. they weigh from 7 to 12 pounds. the measure of one which weighed 10 pounds, was as follows. from the extremity of the hinder, to that of the fore feet when extended is 3 Feet.

length from nose to the extremity of the tail 2 feet, 2 inches. Hight when standing erect 1 foot, 3 inches. Girth of the body 1 foot, 4 inches. length of tail 6½ inches. length of ear 5½ inches. width of ear 3 inches and ⅛. from hip to the extremity of toe of the hind foot 1 foot 4¼ inches. the eye is large and prominent. the pupil is circular, of a deep sea green and occupies one third of the diameter of the eye, the iris is of a bright yellowish silver colour. The ears are placed far back on the head and very near each other, they are flexable and the animal moves them with great ease and quickness and can dilate and throw them forward, or contract and fold them back at pleasure. the fold at the front of the ear is of a redish brown colour. the inner folds are those which lie together when the ears are thrown back, and which occupies 2/3 ds. of the width of the ears of a pure white except the tips of the ears for about one inch. the hinder folds of those which lie on the back are of a light grey; the sides as they approach the belly become gradually more white, the belly brest, and inner part of the legs and thyes are white, with a slight shade of lead colour. the Head, neck, back sholders, sides, outer part of legs and thyes are of a Lead coloured Grey. the tail is bluntly pointed and round covered with fine soft white fur not quite as long as on other parts of the body. the body is covered with a deep fine soft close fur. the colours here described are those which the animale assumes from the middle of April to the middle of November, the ballance of the year they are of a pure white except the black and redish brown of the ears which never changes. a fiew redish brown spots are sometimes seen intermixed with the white, at this season on the heads and upper parts of the neck and sholders, the body of this animal is smaller and longer in proportion to it's hight than the Rabbit. when it runs it carries its tail streight behind the direction of it's body. they appear to run with more ease and bound with greater agility than any animal I ever saw. they are extreemly fleet and never burrow or take shelter in the ground when pursued. It's teeth are like those of the rabit, as is also its upper lip which is divided as high as the nose. it's food is grass, herbs, and in winter feeds much on the bark of several arematic shrubs which grow in the plains and the young willows along the rivers and other water courses. I have measured the leaps of this animal and find them commonly from 18 to 22 feet. they are generally found separate and never seen to associate in any number or more than two or three."—Clark

April 12, 1805 (Missouri valley, about 75 miles above Ft. Mandan)

"I killed a Hare changeing its colours. some parts retaining its long white fur & other parts assuming the short grey."—Clark

Unquestionably the foregoing quotation refers to the white-tailed jackrabbit, since the observation was made in an area lying considerably south of the range of the snowshoe hare at the same longitude.

April 26, 1805 (Near mouth of Yellowstone River)
"the willow of the sandbars also furnish winter food to . . . the hare and rabbit."—Lewis

May 12, 1805 (Between the mouths of the Milk and Musselshell Rivers)
"the wild hysop sage,[29] flesh leaf thorn[30] and some other herbs also grow on the plains and hills, particularly the arromatic herb on which the Antelope and large hare feed."—Lewis

The following records probably refer to the white-tailed jackrabbit, since the range of the black-tailed jackrabbit lies to the west or south of the Missouri valley from Pierre, South Dakota, to the Beaverhead Mountains of southwestern Montana.

Sept. 17, 1804 (Vic. of White River)
"Capt. Lewis saw a hare & killed a Rattle snake in a village of the Barking Squarels."—Clark

Sept. 20, 1804 (Vic. of the Big Bend of the Missouri River)
"I saw a Hare & believe he run into a hole in the side of a hill, he run up this hill which is Small & has several holes on the Side & I could not see him after."—Clark

Sept. 24, 1804 (Vic. of Bad River, near Pierre, S. Dak.)
"we Saw one Hare today."—Clark

Jan. 3, 1805 (Fort Mandan)
"8 men go to hunt buffalow, killed a hare & wolf."—Clark
"one of the men killed a butifull white hair which is common in this country."—Whitehouse

May 26, 1805 (Between the Musselshell and Judith Rivers)
"he (Clark) also saw . . . the large hare."—Lewis
"one of our hunters killed a hare which weighed 8½ pounds."—Whitehouse

Aug. 25, 1805 (Lemhi River, near Tendoy, Idaho)
"I also saw several large hares. . . ."—Lewis

Aug. 26, 1805 (Lemhi River valley)
"Some hares which were very wild."—Clark

The records for Aug. 25 and 26, may have referred to either the white-tailed or the black-tailed jackrabbit, as the explorers were then within the range of both species.

On Feb. 15, 1806, Lewis listed the hare and the rabbit among other mammals inhabiting the area between the Rocky Mountains and the Pacific coast.

Specimens of the white hare were included among the specimens packed in a large trunk for shipment to President Jefferson by the keelboat returning to St. Louis from Fort Mandan.

THE COTTONTAIL RABBIT

Rabbits are mentioned among the mammals seen or killed in Missouri, in the Dakotas, and west of the Rocky Mountains. Presumably those observed east of the Rocky Mountains were cottontails, *Sylvilagus floridanus* (Allen).

June 25, 1804 (Vic. of Mill Creek, Jackson Co., Mo.)
"Capt. Lewis killed a Rabit."—Sgt. Floyd

Sept. 11, 1804 (About midway between Niobrara & White Rivers)
"here the man who left us with the horses 22 (16) days ago, George Shannon,[31] *He started 26 Augt* and has been ahead ever since joined us nearly Starved to Death, he had been 12 days without anything to eate but Grapes & one *Rabit*, which he killed by shooting a piece of hard stick in place of a ball . . thus a man had like to have Starved to death in a land of Plenty for want of Bullitts or Something to kill his meat."—Clark

Sept. 15, 1804 (Near south of the White River in S. Dak.)
"We proceeded on passed a Small Island Covered with Ceedars . . . I saw great numbers of Rabits & Grapes."—Clark

Sept. 18, 1804 (Nearing Big Bend of the Missouri River)
"many . . . rabits . . . in this quarter."—Clark

Feb. 28, 1806 (Written at Fort Clatsop)
"the rabbit are the same of our country and are found indifferently either in the praries or woodlands. they are not very abundant in this country."—Lewis

MOUNTAIN COTTONTAIL

There is no evidence of a substantial nature on which to conclude that Lewis and Clark saw the Mountain cottontail, *Sylvilagus Nuttalli* (Bachman). Only one reference that might be interpreted as referring to this rabbit can be found in their diaries. This observation and the locality in which it occurred, led Coues to conclude that the species referred to is the Mountain cottontail. The diary entry alluded to is as follows:

July 6, 1806 (Headwaters of the Big Hole River)
"Shields killed a hare of the large Mountain Species."—Clark

CHAPTER VI
Deer, Elk, and Antelope

Among Lewis and Clark's most notable contributions to zoology was their discovery of the mule deer. They not only wrote the first accurate description of this species, but they coined the name "mule deer" to designate it.

They recognized that the white-tailed deer of the plains differed somewhat in appearance from the typical Virginia deer of the East, and to emphasize this difference they usually referred to the western whitetails as "fallow deer" or "long-tailed fallow deer."

They can be credited also with the discovery of the Columbian black-tailed deer, which they described as a distinct species.

Although both the American elk and the pronghorn antelope had been described briefly by French and Spanish explorers in the 16th century, the elk was not classified as a distinct species until 1777, and the antelope was not recognized by science until 1815 when George Ord described and named it on the basis of specimens furnished by the explorers. Moreover, little was known about the distribution or habits of these species in the West until Lewis and Clark's diaries were published.

WHITE-TAILED DEER

The first identifiable description of the white-tailed deer, *Odocoileus virginianus* (Boddaert),[1] appears to have been written by Thomas Hariot who, while in the service of Sir Walter Raleigh, visited Virginia in 1584. Two hundred years later (1784) Boddaert wrote the first technical description of the Virginia deer, and named it *Cervus virginianus*.

Little is known about the geographic distribution of the different races of white-tailed deer in 1804-6, or about possible shifts in their ranges since that time. It becomes difficult, therefore, to correlate either Lewis or Clark's specific reference to the white-tailed deer with any particular subspecies. However, the reader may draw his own conclusion on the basis of the localities in which their observations were made.

Obviously, both Lewis and Clark were familiar with the white-tailed deer in Virginia and in the Ohio valley, but there is nothing in their diaries to indicate that they noted any distinction between the Virginia deer and the northern subspecies which is characteristic of Maine and the states bordering the Great Lakes. They consistently referred to the white-tailed deer of the lower Missouri valley as the "common deer of our country."

It was not until they had ascended the Missouri as far as the Dakotas that they began to notice that the white-tailed deer of the west differed in any respect from those which had been killed on the lower Missouri. On September 16, 1804, in referring to the observations of his hunters who had made a short exploratory excursion in the vicinity of the White River in South Dakota, Clark mentioned seeing a fallow deer, *Odocoileous virginianus dacotensis* Goldman and Kellogg.

"They Saw a great Number of Goats such as I killed, also Wolves near the Buffalow, *falling (fallow) Deer,* and the Barking Squirls Villages."

And on Sept. 17, 1804, he wrote: "8 fallow deer, 5 Common and 3 Buffalow killed today."

Although the first quotation leaves doubt as to his meaning, the second indicates clearly that he recognized the "fallow deer" as distinct from the "common" Virginia deer.

Subsequently both Lewis and Clark made repeated references to the "fallow or red deer," to the "common deer," and to the "mule deer" in reporting on the game seen or killed by different members of the party.

Both the white-tailed deer and the mule deer were seen at the mouth of the Yellowstone River on April 28, 1805, and in the vicinity of the Poplar River a few days later. White-tailed deer were rarely mentioned thereafter until the explorers reached the Three Forks of the Missouri, but while encamped there on July 29, 1805, Lewis made the following notation:

"This morning some of the hunters turned out and returned in a few hours with four fat bucks, the venison is now very fine. We have killed no mule deer since we lay here, they are all of the long-tailed red deer which appear quite as large as those of the United States."

Deer were plentiful on the eastern slopes of the Beaverhead and Bitterroot Mountains, and approximately one hundred were killed between Three Forks and Lolo Pass, west of Missoula, Montana. A few deer were killed near the Shoshone Indian camp on the Lemhi River, west of the Beaverhead Range. What proportion of them were whitetails is not indicated. However, we might be justified in inferring that those killed in the Lemhi valley were whitetails for, in discussing the food and hunting problems of the Shoshones in this area, Lewis made the following comment:

"they have but few Elk or black-tailed deer, and the common red deer they cannot take as they secrete themselves in the brush when pursued, and they have only the bow and arrow which is a very slender dependence for killing any game except such as they can run down with their horses."

Few deer were seen or killed by the hunters after the expedition passed over the Bitterroot Mountains and started down the Lolo trail to the Clearwater River; none were killed while the party was floating down the Clearwater, Snake and Columbia Rivers to Celilo Falls. Below The Dalles of the

Columbia, deer were common, but the combination of incessant rain and dense cover made hunting them difficult.

The white-tailed deer of western Oregon have long been regarded as a distinct subspecies. David Douglas, in 1829, recognized them as such and can be credited with establishing them as a new subspecies, *leucrurus*. Lewis and Clark apparently did not distinguish these Columbian whitetails from the other races of white-tailed deer which they had seen on the Upper Missouri and in the inter-mountain valleys of Idaho.

March 28, 1806 (Near the mouth of the Willamette River)

"This morning we set out very early and at 9 A.M. arrived at the old Indian village on the Lar'd side of Deer Island (opposite the mouth of the Willamette) where we found our hunters had halted and left one man with the two canoes at their camp; they had arrived last evening at this place and six of them had turned out to hunt very early this morning; by 10 A.M. they had all returned to camp having killed seven deer. these were all of the *common fallow deer with the long tail*. I measured the tail of one of these bucks which was upwards of 17 Inches long; they are very poor, tho' better than the black-tailed fallow deer of the coast. these are two very distinct species of deer."

Bailey,[2] in referring to this entry in the Lewis' diary, concluded that the "common fallow deer with the long tail" belonged to the subspecies *O. virginianus leucrurus* (Douglas) even though the tail measurement as given by Lewis is much too long. Evidently Lewis included the long terminal hairs of the tail in his measurement. It is interesting to note that David Douglas (1829) made the same error in his original description of the Columbian white-tailed deer in giving the tail measurement as 12-15 inches. According to Bailey (1936) the correct tail measurement for this subspecies is about 7 inches, exclusive of terminal hair.

The Columbian whitetail was a deer of the river bottoms, where it ranged through the willow thickets and wet meadows. However, occasionally it wandered into the foothills of the mountains. According to David Douglas, in 1826, it was the most common deer found in the Columbia valley below the Sandy River, and in the valleys of the Willamette and the Umpqua Rivers. In Washington it was abundant along the Cowlitz River.

Lewis' diary for April 15, 1806, records the killing of a Columbian whitetail above the Cascades of the Columbia:

"Drewyer and some others took a hunt and killed a deer of the long-tailed kind, it was a buck, and the young horns had shot forth about 2 inches."

A week previously, April 8, 1806, when in the neighborhood of Beacon Rock on the Columbia he pointed out that the "common long-tailed fallow deer" were more abundant in that vicinity than "the black-tailed jumping or fallow deer, such as are found around Fort Clatsop."

According to Bailey (1936), old residents of the Willamette valley claimed that this deer was plentiful from 1847 to 1875, but by 1898 it had been reduced to a mere remnant of its former population. Fortunately, this subspecies still survives in the more remote sections of its original range.

Bailey (1932), as a result of his systematic studies of the deer of the West, concluded that the whitetails of the intermountain areas of Idaho and northwestern Montana were sufficiently different from those east of the Rockies and west of the Cascades to warrant giving them status as a distinct subspecies. He, accordingly, named them *Odocoileus virginianus ochrourus*, the yellow-tailed deer.

Neither Lewis and Clark nor David Douglas (1825) indicated in their writing that they noted the distinctions described by Bailey, although they observed and killed many white-tailed deer while exploring the country drained by the Clearwater River and its tributaries. It is reasonable to assume that some of the deer taken by these explorers belonged to Bailey's race of yellowtails.

COLUMBIAN BLACK-TAILED DEER

Elliott Coues (1893) credits Lewis and Clark with writing the original description of the Columbian black-tailed deer, *Odocoileus hemionus columbianus* (Richardson). Clark mentioned this species for the first time while the party was encamped at an abandoned Chinook village on Baker's Bay some 15 to 18 miles east of Cape Disappointment.

Nov. 19, 1805 (Fort Mandan)

"The Deer of this coast differ materially from our Common deer in as much as they are much darker, deeper bodied, shorter legged, horns equally branched from the beam, the top of the tail black from the rute (root) to the end. Eyes larger, and do not lope but jump."

During the winter of 1805-6 while at Fort Clatsop, Lewis wrote a more detailed description of these deer:

Feb. 19, 1806 (Fort Clatsop)

"The Black-tailed fallow deer are peculiar to this coast and are a distinct species of deer partaking equally of peculiarities of the mule deer and the common deer. Their ears are reather larger and their winter coat darker than the common deer; the recepticle of the eye or drane is more conspicuous; their legs shorter and body thicker and larger than the common deer; their tail is about the length of our deer or from 8 to 10 inches the hair on the underside of which is white, and that of its sides and top quite black. the horns resemble in form and colour those of the mule deer which

127

it also resembles in its gate; that is, bounding with all four feet off the ground at the same time when running at full speed and not loping as the common deer or antelope do. they are sometimes found in the woodlands but most frequently in the prairies and open grounds. They may be said generally to be a size larger than the common deer and less than the mule deer. They are verry seldom found in good order, or fat, even in the season which the common deer are so, and their flesh is inferior to any species of deer which I have seen."

This description of the Columbian blacktail, though not complete, is fairly accurate except with respect to its habitat preferences. The Columbian blacktail definitely is a deer of the dense forests and brushlands; and this habitat preference has enabled it to evade its natural enemies, as well as to withstand excessive hunting.

Richardson (1829) wrote the first technical description of this species, and thereby established the Columbian black-tailed deer as a separate subspecies, *Cervus macrotis* var. *columbiana*. During subsequent years several different technical names for this race of deer appeared in zoological literature. In 1898, C. Hart Merriam classified this deer as *Odocoileus columbianus* Merriam. Cowan (1936) in his exhaustive report on the "Distribution and Variation in Deer (Genus Odocoileus) of the Pacific Coast Region of North America" reviewed the synonomy of the Columbian black-tailed deer, and evidently came to the conclusion that this race of deer may properly be classified as *Odocoileus hemionus columbianus* (Richardson).

Originally this species occupied an area extending from the western slopes of the Cascade and northern Sierra Nevada Mountains to the Pacific coast; and it is still the most plentiful deer in western Oregon.

THE MULE DEER

Rafinesque (1817) described and named the mule deer, *Cervus hemionus*. His work was based on the typical mule deer of the plains and badlands of Dakota (type locality, Sioux River, South Dakota). In 1898, C. Hart Merriam assigned this species to the genus, *Odocoileus,* thus establishing the scientific name in use today.

Most authorities, including Coues and Seton, credit Lewis and Clark with having written the first accurate descriptions of the mule deer. Seton, however, suggests that Rafinesque (1817) was responsible for the popular name, mule deer, when he designated the species, *hemionus*. However, Lewis applied the name "mule" to this species when he described it in detail on May 10, 1805.

Clark wrote a brief preliminary description of a mule deer killed in the vicinity of the mouth of the White River, near Chamberlain, South Dakota, on Sept. 17, 1804.

"Colter killed . . . a curious kind of Deer of a Dark gray colour—or more so than common, hair long and fine, the ears large and long, a Small recepticle under the eyes like the Elk, the taile about the length of the Common Deer, round (like a cow) a tuft of black hair about the end, this Species of Deer jumps like a goat or Sheep."

Lewis' description of May 10, 1805 is more detailed:

"There are several essential differences between the Mule deer and the common deer as well in form as in habits. They are fully a third larger in general, and the male is particularly large; I think there is somewhat greater disparity of size between the male and the female of this species than there is between the male and female fallow deer; I am convinced I have seen a buck of this species twice the volume of a buck of any other species. The ears are peculiarly large, I measured those of a large buck which I found to be eleven inches long, and 3½ in width at the widest part; they are not so delicately formed, their hair is thicker, longer and of a much darker gray; in summer the hair is still coarser, longer and of a paler red, more like that of the Elk; in winter also have a considerable quantity of very fine wool intermixed with the hair and lying next to the skin as the Antelope has. The long hair which grows on the outer sides of the 1st joint of the hinder legs and which in the common deer do not usually occupy more than 2 inches in them occupyes from 6 to eight; their horns also differ, these in the common deer consist of two main beams from which one or more points project, the beam gradually diminishing as the points proceed from it; with the mule deer the horns consist of two beams which at the distance of 4 or 6 inches from the head divide themselves each into two equal branches which again either divide into two other equal branches, or terminate in a smaller, and two equal ones, having either 2, 4 or 6 points on a beam; the horn is not so rough about the base as the common deer and are invariably of a much darker colour. The most striking difference of all is the white rump and tale. From the root of the tail as a center there is a circular spot, perfectly white, of about 3 inches radius, which occupys a part of the rump and extremitys of the buttocks and joins the white of the belley underneath; the tail which is usually from 8 to 9 inches long, for the first 4 or 5 inches from its upper extremity is covered with short white hairs, much shorter indeed than the hairs of the body; from thence for about one inch further the hair is still white but gradually be- comes longer, the tail then terminates in a tissue of black hair of about 3 inches long. From this black hair of the tail they have obtained among the French engages the appelation of the black-tailed deer, but this I conceive by no means characteristic of the anamal as much the larger portion of the tail is white. The ear and tail of this anamal when compared with those of the common deer, so well comported with those of the mule when compared with the horse, that we have by way of distinction *adapted the appellation of the mule deer,* which I think much more appropriate. On the inner corner of each eye there is a drane, or large recepticle which seems to answer as a drane to the eye, which gives it the appearance of weeping, this in the common deer of the Atlantic states is scarcely perceptible, but becomes more conspicuous in the fallow deer, and still more so in the Elk; this recepticle in the Elk is larger than in any of the pecora order with which I am acquainted."

Lewis' comments dealing specifically with the habits and habitat of the mule deer are brief. His direct references to mule deer, seen or killed, when taken out of their context, shed little light on this question; however, by correlating these data with his remarks about the topography and vegetation of the country through which they were traveling at the time the observations were made, we can gain a fair idea of the type of country the mule deer inhabited. For example, on April 28, 1805, when a few miles above the mouth of the Yellowstone River, Lewis made the following notation:

"we saw great quantities of game today; consisting of the common and mule deer, Elk, Buffaloe and Antelopes; also four brown bear, one of which was wounded by one of the party but we did not get it; the beaver have cut great quantities of timber; saw a tree nearly 3 feet in diameter that had been felled by them. Capt. Clark in the course of his walk killed a deer and a goose, and saw three black bear; . . . ."

This passage provides a fair idea of game abundance, but it means nothing in terms of habitat. However, Lewis preceded this quotation with a brief description of the country in which these observations were made:

"the country through which we passed today is open as usual and very broken on both sides near the river hills, the bottoms are level, fertile and partially covered with timber."

Considered together these two statements provide us with a clue, at least, as to the type of habitat in which the mule deer, as well as the other species mentioned, were found at that particular time.

The infrequency of direct references to the habits and habitats of the animals which Lewis observed, does not indicate that he was unaware of the importance of such data. Actually he devoted much space to descriptions of the topography and vegetation of the territory which he traversed, but he had neither time nor energy to make careful ecologic studies of any species. His only direct reference to the habits of the mule deer was written on May 10, 1805 as a prelude to his description of the animal:

"we saw several deer of the Mule kind of immence size and also three of the Big-horned anamals, from the appearance of the mule deer and the big-horned anamals we believe ourselves fast approaching a hilly or mountainous country; we have rarely found the mule deer in any except rough country; they prefer the open grounds and are seldom found in woodlands or river bottoms, and are pursued, they invariably run to the hills or open country as the Elk do. The contrary happens with the common deer."

The Lewis and Clark diaries do not provide a complete picture of the geographic range of the mule deer, or any other species of animal, because the urgency of making headway and the hardships and hazards of wilderness travel precluded many side-trips into the back-country or up the tributary streams. Nevertheless, the recorded observations of game seen and killed constitute substantial data on distribution of numerous species along the direct routes of travel.

Clark's diary indicates that mule deer were first seen near the junction of the Missouri and Niobrara Rivers, approximately 30 miles west of Yankton, South Dakota.

Sept. 5, 1804 (Vic. of Niobrara River)

"One of our hunters, Shields, informed that he Saw Several black-tailed Deer."

Sept. 19, 1804 (Near Big Bend of the Missouri)

"The Hunters on Shore Killed 4 Deer with black tails one of which was a Buck with two main Prongs on each Side forked equally, which I never before Seen."

Oct. 7, 1804 (Vic. of Moreau River)

"another man Killed a Black-tailed Deer, the largest Doe I ever Saw, black under her breast."

Lewis and Clark did not mention the "mule or black tail deer" again until April 23, when they were nearing the Yellowstone River, although they reported seeing and killing many "deer."

April 23, 1805 (Vic. of Painted Wood Creek)

"I killed 3 mule or black tail Deer, which was in tolerable order, Saw several others."

It seems doubtful that mule deer were as scarce in North Dakota as the Lewis and Clark records indicate. Reid and Gannon (1927) writing in the North Dakota Historical Quarterly, support this opinion:

"As this deer inhabits the rougher and higher land back from the river bottoms not many were seen by the explorers, and it was probably much more common than the number killed would indicate."

Lewis and Clark's recorded observations suggest the mule deer were more abundant in Montana, east of the Rocky Mountains, than in North Dakota. The mere fact, however, that they observed more of these deer in

131

central and eastern Montana does not necessarily prove that they were actually more numerous. Possibly a larger percentage of favorable mule deer habitat occurred within hunting distance of the Missouri and its tributaries above the mouth of the Yellowstone River. In any case, mule deer were killed in the vicinity of the Milk River, above the mouth of Judith River, on the Marias River above Willow Creek, and in the neighborhood of Great Falls. None were recorded above the "gate of the Mountains" nor in the vicinity of Three Forks.

On July 29, 1805, while encamped at Three Forks, Lewis commented:

"We have killed no mule deer since we lay here, they are all of the long tailed red deer."

No further mention is made of the mule deer until after the expedition entered Idaho via Lemhi Pass and encamped near the Shoshone Indian village not far from the present site of Tendoy:

Aug. 23, 1805 (Camp at mouth of Prairie Creek, Montana)

"The Indians pursued a mule buck near our camp. I saw this chase for about 4 miles; it was really entertaining, there were about twelve of them in pursuit of it on horseback, they finally rode it down and killed it."

Lewis summarized his observations on the distribution of mule deer west of the Rocky Mountains during the winter at Fort Clatsop. On February 20, 1806, he wrote as follows:

"The Mule deer are the same with those of the plains of the Missouri so frequently mentioned. We met with them under the Rocky Mountains in the Neighborhood of the Chopunnish nation on the Kooskooske river,[3] but have not seen them since nor do we know whether they exist in the interior of the great plains of the Columbia or on their lower border near the mountains[4] which pass the river near the great falls."

While on their return journey in 1806, Lewis and Clark supplemented some of their earlier observations on the distribution of several species of animals. Concerning the mule deer the following diary entries may be cited:

July 20, 1806 (On the Marias River, near Shelby, Montana)

"also some mule deer; this species of deer seems most prevalent in this quarter."

Aug. 24, 1806 (Vicinity of Cheyenne River in S. Dakota)

"the deer on this part of the river is mostly the mule or black tail species."

Aug. 29, 1806 (Vic. of White River in S. Dakota)

"Drewyer . . . informed me that he saw some antelopes and Mule deer but could kill none of them. Jo Fields informed that he wounded a female of the Mule deer a little below our camp late this evening. . . ."

Aug. 30, 1806 (Same general locality)

"Jo Fields had killed 3 black tail or mule deer." This was Lewis' last reference to the mule deer, and presumably no others were seen below this point on the homeward journey.

THE AMERICAN ELK

By 1804 the elk population in the Appalachian Mountains and in the old Northwest Territory had been much reduced in the vicinity of the pioneer settlements and along the principal routes of travel. The Lewis and Clark diaries did not mention the elk, *Cervus canadensis* Erxleben, until the expedition was nearing the western boundary of Missouri.

July 5, 1804 (Vic. of Independence Creek)

"Deer is not so plenty as usual, great deal of Elk sign."—Clark

No elk were seen until the explorers had ascended the Missouri as far as Nishnabotna Creek, about 70 miles above the site of St. Joseph, Missouri. The first elk taken by the hunters was killed near Fort Calhoun, a few miles north of Omaha, the second, at the mouth of the Little Sioux River, and the third, in the neighborhood of Yankton, South Dakota. Thereafter, elk were seen and killed frequently in the Dakotas, Montana, and in western Oregon. During the winter of 1804-5 in the Fort Mandan area north of Bismarck, North Dakota, the expedition killed 50 elk, 120 deer, and 38 bison.

During the spring and summer of 1805 in ascending the Missouri, elk were seen and killed frequently between Fort Mandan and Three Forks, Montana. However, Lewis was unable to procure enough elk skins in the vicinity of Great Falls, Montana, during July to cover the frame of his "iron canoe," and was obliged to supplement them with buffalo hides. A few elk were killed on the Jefferson and Beaverhead Rivers west of Three Forks, but they were by no means plentiful. This scarcity may have been due to the fact that most of the elk in this region had migrated to the high mountain meadows earlier in the season.

Lewis and Clark saw no elk between Lolo Pass and the mouth of the Columbia River during their outward journey in the fall of 1805. Elk tracks were seen on November 13, 1805, at Point Ellice on the north shore of the Columbia's estuary, but the combination of dense cover and continuous rain made hunting unrewarding. Late in November, on the advice of a band of Chinook Indians, Lewis and Clark moved to the South side of the river where elk were reported to be numerous. During the winter at Fort Clatsop, between November 27, 1805 and March 23, 1806, the hunters killed 128 elk and 18 deer.[5]

On the return journey, 18 elk were killed at the mouth of the Sandy

River, a few miles below Bonneville, Oregon. None was seen or killed thereafter until the expedition had again surmounted Lolo Pass and re-entered Montana. Here Lewis and Clark separated, the former taking a short-cut to Great Falls, while the latter retraced their outward course to Three Forks, and then descended the Yellowstone River. This gave Lewis an opportunity to explore the Marias River in the vicinity of Shelby, Montana, and Cut Bank Creek. He found elk in the vicinity of Shelby and on the Sun River a few miles above Great Falls; they were scarce, however, on the plains between Great Falls and Shelby.

Clark on the other hand saw elk almost daily while floating down the Yellowstone during July and August, 1806. Herds of 100 to 200 were seen near Livingstone, Montana. They were plentiful in the vicinity of Pompeys Tower, and near Sarpy, Montana.

July 27, 1806 (Vic. of Sarpy, Montana)

"the Buffalow and Elk is astonishingly noumerous on the banks of the river on each side, particularly the Elk which lay on almost every point in large gangs, and are so jentile that we frequently pass within 20 or 30 paces of them without their being the least alarmed."—Clark

After rejoining Lewis below the mouth of the Yellowstone, the party proceeded with much haste. Elk and other species of big game were reported regularly in the Missouri valley throughout North and South Dakota. Probably they were not as abundant, however, in the Dakotas as on the Yellowstone.

Aug. 20, 1806 (Vic. of Cannonball River)

"We have seen great numbers of wolves today, and some buffalo and elk, though these are by no means so abundant as on the Yellowstone."
—Biddle text

The last elk killed on the return journey was taken below the mouth of the Kansas River.

There has been much speculation over the question of whether the elk which were so numerous in the wooded river valleys in primitive times were year-around residents of the plains or whether they migrated to high mountain meadows for the summer months. Olaus J. Murie, an authority on the elk of North America, has given a plausible answer to this question.[6]

"Elk as a genus are tolerant of diverse environments, as shown by their original wide distribution over the American continent and by their varied habitats today.

"It has been assumed that the Rocky Mountain elk were different from the eastern elk, but the exact location of the region of intergradation between these two subspecies cannot be known now.

"Today these elk are primarily mountain dwellers. Practically nowhere do they occur on the plains. Yet records of the early days state that at times elk were noted on the plains in great numbers. Those records so commonly mention elk associating with bison that the thought has developed that elk is primarily a plains animal which in early times did not inhabit the mountains, but has been driven there, to an unnatural home, in comparatively recent years by advancing civilization. To support this contention is the undisputed fact that formerly hordes of elk lived on the plains. Moreover, many early travelers failed to find elk, or at any rate failed to mention them, in certain mountain areas; and some even stated positively that game was scarce.

"Unfortunately, the fact of migration often was overlooked, or at least was not discussed, and it is not always clear whether the plains animals were already on winter range or were in transit to or from it. Now it is known the elk went from the mountains to the plains each winter in great numbers, sometimes on long, well organized migrations. It seems natural that in the early days of great abundance of game an animal so widely distributed as the elk and tolerant of such a diversity of habitats would occupy the plains to some extent even in summer."

Lewis and Clark, in referring to elk habitat, stated "They are common to every part of this country, as well the timbered lands as the plains, but are much more abundant in the former than the latter."

The explorers' comments concerning the food habits, antler development, and behavior of elk are brief but interesting:

April 26, 1805 (Near mouth of Yellowstone River)

"the open bottoms border on the hills, and are covered in many parts by the wild hyssop[7] which rises to a height of two feet. I observe that the Antelope, Buffaloe, Elk and deer feed on this herb; the willow of the sandbars also furnish a favorite winter food of these anamals as well as the growse, the porcupine, hare, and rabbit."—Lewis

May 11, 1805 (Between Milk and Musselshell Rivers)

"the wild Hysop grows here and in all the country through which we have passed for many days past; tho' from big Dry river to this place it has been more abundant than below, and a smaller variety of it grows on the hills, the leaves of which differ considerably being more deeply indented near it's extremity. the buffaloe, deer and Elk feed on this herb in the winter season as they do also on the small willow of the sandbars."—Lewis

Feb. 4, 1806 (Written at Fort Clatsop)

"the Elk are in much better order in the point near the praries than they are in the woody country around us or up the Netul in the praries they feed on grass and rushes, considerable quantities of which are yet green and succulent, in the woods country their food is huckleberry bushes, fern, and an evergreen shrub[8] which resembles the lorel in some measure; the last constitutes the greater part of their food and grows abundantly through all the timbered country, particularly the hillsides and more broken parts of it."—Lewis

April 30, 1805 (Near mouth of Yellowstone River)
"I walked on shore and killed a buck Elk, in tolerable order; it appeared to me to be the largest I had seen, and was therefore induced to measure it; found it five feet three inches from the point of the hoof to the Top of the sholders; the leg and hoof being placed as nearly as possible in the same position they would have been had the anamal been standing."—Lewis

April 21, 1805 (Vic. of White Earth River)
"The Elk now begin to shed their horns."—Lewis

May 3, 1805 (Porcupine River)
"The new horns of the elk begin to appear."—Biddle text

March 12, 1806 (Fort Clatsop)
"The horns of some of the Elk have not yet fallen off and those of others have Grown to a length of six inches, the latter are in the best order, from which it would seem that the pore Elk retain their horns longer."—Clark

Aug. 1, 1806 (Near mouth of Musselshell River)
"The Elk are now in fine order particularly the males. Their horns have obtained their full growth, but not yet shed the velvet or skin which covers them . . . the does are found in large herds with their young and a few young bucks with them. The old bucks yet herd together in parties of two to 7 or 8."—Lewis

Aug. 2, 1806 (Yellowstone River)
"I have noticed a great preportion of Buck Elks on this lower part of the river, and but very fiew above. those above which are emencely numerous are feemales Generally."—Clark

West of the Rocky Mountains the Indians utilized the elk in the same manner, if not to same extent, as those east of the continental divide depended upon the buffalo. Elk meat was an important supplement to a diet which, often for extended periods, consisted of fish and roots; hides furnished clothing and shelter; antlers were useful in making bows and hand-tools; and the tusks were prized as ornaments.

Jan. 15, 1806 (Fort Clatsop)
"The implyments used by the Chinnooks, Clatsops, and Cuthlahmahs,

etc. in hunting are the gun, the bow and arrow, deadfalls, pitts, snares, and spears or gigs; their guns are usually of an inferior quality being oald refuse American and brittish Musquits which have been repared for this trade. there are some very good pieces among them, but they are invariably in bad order . . . they have no rifles. Their guns and ammunition they reserve for the Elk, deer and bear, of the last two however there are but few in their neighborhood . . . when they happen to have no ball or shot, they substitute gravel or potmettal, and are insensible of the damage done thereby to their guns.

"Their pits are employed in taking the Elk and of coarse are large and deep, some of them a cube of 12 or 14 feet. These are usually placed by the side of a large fallen tree which as well as the pit lye across the roads frequented by the Elk—These pits are disguised with the slender boughs of trees and moss; the unwary Elk in passing the tree precipiates himself into the pitt which is sufficiently deep to prevent his escape, and is thus taken."
—Lewis

Feb. 2, 1806 (Fort Clatsop)
"The native of this neighbourhood have a small Dog which they make useful only in hunting the Elk."—Clark

Feb. 16, 1806 (Fort Clatsop)
"The Indian dog is usually small. . . . the natives do not eat them nor appear to make any other use of them but in hunting the Elk, as has been before observed."—Lewis

Aug. 21, 1805 (Shoshone camp on Lemhi River)
"The tusks of the Elk are pierced, strung on a thong and woarn as an orniment[9] for the neck, and is most generally woarn by the women and children."—Lewis.

Aug. 22, 1806 (Vic. of Mandan and Arikara Villages)
"they (Mandan and Arikara Indian dresses) are frequently ornemented with beeds and Shells and Elk tusks of which all Indians are very fond of."—Clark

Aug. 23, 1805 (Shoshone village on Lemhi River)
"They renew the edge (of their flint knives) by flecking off the flint by means of the point of an Elk's or deer's horn—with the point of a deer or Elk's horn they also form their arrow points of the flint, with a quickness and neatness that is really astonishing—we found no axes or hatchets among them; what wood they cut was done either with stone or Elk's horn —the latter they use always to rive or split their wood.

"They sometimes make bows of the Elk's horn and those also of the

137

bighorn—those of the Elk's horn are made of a single piece and covered on the back with glue and sinues like those made of wood, and are frequently ornimented with a strand wrought of porcupine quills and sinues raped around them for some distance at both extremities."—Lewis

If elk had not been plentiful in areas where other game was scarce, the explorers would have suffered for food, clothing, and essential gear.

Sept. 2, 1804 (Vic. Bon Homme Island)
"Newman and Howard killed four fine Elk, we had the meat all jurked and the Skins Dried to cover the Perogue."—Clark

May 13, 1805 (Between Yellowstone and Musselshell Rivers)
"the party killed several deer and some Elk principally for the benefit of their skins which are necessary to them for cloathing, the Elk skins I now begin to reserve for making the leather boat at the falls."—Lewis

June 17, 1805 (Great Falls)
"I found that the Elk skins I had prepared for my boat were insufficient to compleat her, some of them having become dammaged by the weather and being frequently wet."—Lewis

June 21, 1805 (Great Falls)
"Several men employed in shaveing, and graneing Elk hides for the Iron boat as it is called."—Clark

July 7, 1805 (Great Falls)
"we dispatched two hunters to kill Elk or buffaloe for their skins to cover our baggage."—Lewis

Feb. 19, 1806 (Fort Clatsop)
"Sergt. Gass returned with the flesh of eight Elk and seven skins. . . . we had the skins divided among the messes in order that they might be prepared for covering our baggage when we set out in the spring."—Lewis

April 7, 1806 (Mouth of Sandy River, Oregon)
"We had it (dried elk meat) secured in dryed Elk skins and put on board (canoes) in readiness for an early departure."—Lewis

Aug. 26, 1804 (Cedar County, Nebr.)
"After jurking the meat Killed yesterday and preparing the Elk skins for a Toe Roape, we set out. . . ."—Clark

Nov. 24, 1804 (Fort Mandan)
"finished a Cord to draw our boat out on the bank, this is made of 9 strans of Elk skins."—Clark

Feb. 3, 1805 (Fort Mandan)

"we have already prepared a large rope of Elk-skin and a windless by means of which we have no doubt of being able to draw the boat on the bank provided we can free it from the ice."—Lewis

May 28, 1805 (Vic. of Judith River)

"our ropes are but slender, all of them except one being made of Elk's skins, and much woarn, frequently wet and exposed to the heat of the weather are weak and rotten: they have given way several times in the course of the day but happily at such places that the vessel had room to wheel free of the rocks and therefore escaped injury."—Lewis

Nov. 28, 1805 (Tongue Point, Astoria, Ore.)

"we are all wet, bedding and stores, haveing nothing to keep ourselves or stores dry, our Lodge nearly worn out, and the pieces of sales and tents so full of holes & rotten that they will not keep anything dry—aded to this the robes of ourselves and men are all rotten from being continually wet."
—Clark

Nov. 29, 1805 (Tongue Point)

"all the others employed in drying their leather and preparing it for use, as but fiew of them have many other clothes to boste of at this time. . . ."
—Clark

Dec. 1, 1805 (Tongue Point)

"all the men employed today in mending their leather clothes, Shoes & in Dressing leather."—Clark

Jan. 23, 1806 (Fort Clatsop)

"the men of the garrison are still busily employed in dressing Elk's skins for cloathing, they find great difficulty for the want of branes; we have not soap to supply the deficiency, nor can we procure ashes to make the lye; none of the pines which we use for fuel affords any ashes; extrawdinary as it may seem, the greene wood is consoomed without leaving the residium of a particle of ashes."—Lewis

Feb. 23, 1806 (Fort Clatsop)

"the men have provided themselves verry amply with mockersons & leather clothing. . . ."—Lewis

"I had some Elk skins put in the water today to make harness for the pack horses. . . ."—Lewis

THE MOOSE

Neither Lewis nor Clark personally encountered the moose in Montana or Idaho. However, both Ordway and Whitehouse, in their independent diaries, reported that a party of hunters "Saw some mooce Deer which was much larger than the common deer," on May 10, 1805, a few miles above the mouth of the Milk River.

A year later the Indians in the vicinity of Camp Chopunnish on the Clearwater River reported that moose were common in the Salmon River valley.

June 2, 1806 (Camp Chopunnish near Weippe, Idaho)

"The Indians informs us that there are aplenty of moos to the S. E. of them on the East branch of Lewis' River."[10]

Coues' (1893) reaction to the foregoing entry in Lewis' diary is pertinent:

"Here Lewis and Clark lead all naturalists, as usual; for, the American moose, *Alces machlis americanus* or *Alces americanus,* had no scientific standing in their day. Nor has the fact here stated of its inhabiting Idaho been given due weight. I hardly knew where to turn for another Idahoan reference, till 1860, when Dr. Geo. Suckley (Pacific Rail Road Report, No. XII, p. 133) speaks of a pair of moose-horns procured in the most eastern part of Washington Territory, near the St. Mary's valley, i.e., in Idaho, not far from Camp Chopunnish! The U. S. National Museum also has antlers taken by C. Hart Merriam in 1872, in Idaho near the Wyoming border (Fauna No. 5, 1891, p. 79)."

No moose were killed, probably because so few of them were seen by the hunters.

July 7, 1806 (On Lander's Fork in Montana)

"Reuben Fields wounded a moos deer this morning near our camp."— Lewis

THE PRONGHORN ANTELOPE

When Lewis and Clark recorded their observations of the pronghorn antelope in 1804, this species was new to science. It was not technically described and named until 1815. Spanish explorers as early as the 16th century undoubtedly saw antelope in the Southwestern States, but their descriptions are inaccurate and incomplete.

Coronado and his contemporaries called these animals *goats,* and the same term was commonly used by the fur-traders two centuries later. Indeed, Clark frequently used the words *goat* and *cabrie* in preference to antelope in referring to this species.

Coues (1893) points out that the zoologist, George Ord, based his classification of the antelope on specimens furnished by the explorers:

"Lewis and Clark were not its discoverers nor first describers, as the animal had long before been mentioned by the Spaniard, Hernandez . . .

But the first technical name *Antelope americana,* was imposed by George Ord in 1815 (*Gutherie's Geog.* 2nd ed., Vol. II, pp. 292-308); and the second, *Antilocapra americana,* was bestowed by the same naturalist in 1818, in the Bull. de la Societe Philomathique, p. 146, in both cases upon material furnished by Lewis and Clark."

Antelopes were seen for the first time by Clark on Sept. 6, 1804, above the mouth of the Niobrara River. A week later, he killed a male "goat" near the mouth of the White River in South Dakota:

Sept. 14, 1804

"in my walk I Killed a Buck Goat of this Countrey, about the hight of a Grown Deer. its body Shorter the Horns which is not very hard and forks 2/3 up one prong Short the other round and Sharp arched, and is imediately above its eyes the color is a light gray with black behind its ears down its neck. and its face white round its neck, its Sides and its rump round its tail which is short and white: Verry actively made, has only a pair of hoofs to each foot. his brains on the back of his head, his Norstrals large, his eyes like a Sheep he is more like the Antilope or Gazella of Africa than any other species of Goat."—Clark

Sept. 20, 1804 (Vic. of Big Bend of the Missouri, S. Dak.)

"R. Fields killed 1 Deer & 2 Goats, one of them a female. She differs from the Mail as to Size being Smaller, with Small Horns, Streght with a small prong without any black about the Neck. None of those Goats has any beard, they are all keenly made,[11] and is butifull."—Clark

April 28, 1805 (Mouth of Yellowstone River)

"The Antilopes are nearly red, on that part which is subject to change, i.e., the sides and 2/3 of the back from the head, the other part as white as Snow."—Clark

July 16, 1806 (Great Falls, Montana)

"We see a number of goats or antilopes always in passing through the plains of the Missouri above the Mandans. At this season they are thinly scattered over the plains but seem universally distributed in every part."
—Lewis

Feb. 22, 1806 (Fort Clatsop, Oregon)

"The Antelope is found in the great plains of the Columbia and are the same as those on the Missouri found in every part of that untimbered country. they are by no means as plenty on this side of the Rocky Mountains as on the other."—Lewis

Oct. 17, 1804

"Great numbers of Goats are flocking down to the S. Side of the river,

on their way to the Black Mountains where they winter. Those animals return in the Spring in the Same way & scatter in different directions."
—Clark

Dec. 12, 1804 (Fort Mandan, 38° below 0)
"Great numbers of those animals (Antelope) are near our fort (so that they do not all return to rock mountain Goat)."—Clark

April 9, 1805 (Vic. of Souris River)
"Three miles above the mouth of this creek we passed a hunting camp of Minetares who had prepared a park and were wating the return of the Antelope which usually pass the Missouri at this season of the year from the Black hills on the South side, to the open plains on the north side of the river; in like manner the Antelope repasses the Missouri from N. to South in the latter end of Autumn, and Winter in the black hills, where there is considerable bodies of woodland."—Lewis

Sept. 17, 1804 (Vic. of White River, S. Dak.)
"We found the Antelope extreemly shye and watchfull insomuch that we had been unable to get a shot at them; when at rest they generally seelect the most elivated point in the neighbourhood, and as they are watchfull and extreemly quick of sight and their sense of smelling very accute it is almost impossible to approach them within gun-shot; in short they will frequently discover and flee from you at the distance of three miles. I had this day an opportunity of witnessing the agility and the superior fleetness of this anamal which was to me really astonishing. I had pursued and twice surprised a small herd of seven, in the first instance they did not discover me distinctly and therefore did not run at full speed, tho' they took care before they rested to gain an elivated point where it was impossible to approach them under cover, except in one direction and that happened to be in the direction from which the wind blew toward them; bad as the chance to approach them was, I made the best of my way towards them, frequently peeping over the ridge with which I took care to conceal myself from their view the male, of which there but one, frequently incircled the summit of the hill on which the females stood in a group, as if to look out for the approach of danger. I got within about 200 paces of them when they smelt me and fled; I gained the top of the eminence on which they stood, as soon as possible from whence I had an extensive view of the country the antilopes which had disappeared in a steep reveene now appeared at a distance of about three miles on the side of a ridge which passed obliquely across me and extended about four miles, so soon had these antelopes gained the distance at which they had again appeared to my view I doubted at ferst that they

were the same that I had just surprised, but my doubts soon vanished when I beheld the rapidity of their flight along the ridge before me it appeared reather the rappid flight of birds than the motion of quadrupeds. I think I can safely venture the assertion that the speed of this anamel is equal if not superior to that of the finest blooded courser."—Lewis

July 25, 1805 (Vic. of Townsend, Mont.)

"we saw some antelopes of which we killed one. these animals appear now to have collected again in small herds—several females with their young and one or two males compose the herd usually. some males are yet solitary or two perhaps together scattered over the plains which they seem invariably to prefer to the woodlands. if they happen accidentally in the woodlands and are allarmed they run immediately to the plains, seeming to plaise a just confidence in their superior fleetness. . . ."—Lewis

"Buffalo, elk and antelope are so gentle that we pass near them while feeding."—Clark

July 16, 1806 (Great Falls, Mont.)

"they appear very inquisitive usually to learn what we are as we pass, and frequently accompany us at no great distance for miles, frequently halting and giving a loud whistle through their nostrils, they are a very pretty animal and astonishingly fleet and active."—Lewis

April 26, 1805 (Mouth of Yellowstone River)

"The open bottoms border on the hills, and are covered in many parts by the wild hyssop which rises to the height of two feet. I observe that the Antelopes, Buffalow, Elk and deer feed on this herb; the willows of the sandbars also furnish a favorite winter food to these Anamals as well as the grouse, the porcupine, hare, and rabbit."—Lewis

May 12, 1805 (Between Milk & Musselshell Rivers)

"the wild hysop, sage, fleshy leaf thorn, and some other herbs also grow in the plains and hills, particularly the aromatic herb on which the Antelope and large hare feed."—Lewis

May 15, 1805 (Between Milk & Musselshell Rivers)

"We caught two antelopes at our encampment in attempting to swim the river; the anamals are but lean as yet, and of course not very pleasant food."—Clark

April 29, 1805 (Below mouth of Yellowstone River)

"Game is still very abundant—we can scarcely cast our eyes in any direction without perceiving deer, Elk, Buffaloe or Antelope. The quantity of wolves appear to increase in the same proportion; they generally hunt in parties of six, eight or ten; they kill a great number of Antelopes at

143

this season; the Antelopes are yet meagre and the females are big with young; the wolves take them most generally in attempting to swim the river; in this manner my dog caught one, drowned it and brought it on shore; they are but clumsy swimers, tho' on land when in good order, they are extremely fleet and dureable—we have frequently seen the wolves in pursuit of the Antelope in the plains; they appear to decoy a single one from a flock and then pursue it, alternately releiving each other untill they take it."—Lewis

"The wolves destroy great numbers of the Antilopes by decoying those animals singularly out in the plains and pursueing them alternately, those antelopes are curious and will approach anything which appears in motion near them."—Clark

May 5, 1805 (Above Yellowstone)

"The party killed two Elk and a Buffaloe today, and my dog caught a goat, which he over took by superior fleetness, the goat it must be understood was with young and extreemly poor. a great number of these goats are devowered by the wolves and bear at this season when they are poor and passing the river from S.W. to N.E. they are very inactive and easily taken in the water, a man can out swim them with great ease; the Indians take them in great numbers in the river at this season and in autumn when they pass to the S.W.."—Lewis

Oct. 16, 1804 (Vic. of Emmonsburg, N. Dak.)

"Capt. Lewis & the Indian Chief walked on Shore, soon after I discovered great numbers of Goats in the river and Indians on the Shore on each Side, as I approached or got nearer I discovered boys in the water Killing the goats with Sticks and halling them to Shore. Those on the banks Shot them with arrows and as they approached the Shore would turn them back. of this Gangue of Goats I counted 58 of which they had killed on the Shore, one of our hunters out with Capt. Lewis killed three Goats."—Clark

Nov. 5, 1804 (Fort Mandan)

"A camp of the Mandans, a few miles below us Cought within two days 100 Goats, by driving them in a Strong pen, derected by a bush fence widening from the pen, ..."—Clark

April 15, 1805 (Approx. 50 miles above Little Missouri River)

"I saw the remains of several camps of the Assinniboins; near one of which in a small revene, there was a pack which they had formed of timber and brush, for the purpose of taking the cabrie or Antelope. it was constructed in the following manner. a strong pound was first made of timbers, on one side of which there was a small apparture, sufficiently large to admit Antelope; from each side of this apparture, a curtain was extended to a considerable distance, widening as they reached from the pound."—Clark

Aug. 14, 1805 (Shoshone Indian Village on Lemhi River)

"The game which they principally hunt is the Antelope which they pursue on horse-back and shoot with their arrows. This animal is so extreemly fleet and dureable that a single horse has no possible chance to over take them or run them down. The Indians are therefore obliged to have recorse to strategem—when they discover a herd of Antelope they separate and scatter themselves to the distance of five or six miles in different directions arround them—generally scelecting some commanding eminence for a stand; some one or Two now pursue the herd at full speed over the hills and vallies, gullies and the sides of precipices that are tremendous to view. Thus after running them five or six or seven miles the fresh horses that were in waiting head them and drive them back persuing as far or perhaps further quite to the other extreem of the hunters who now in turn pursue on their fresh horses thus worrying the poor animal down and finally killing them with their arrows. Forty or fifty hunters will be engaged for a half day in this manner and perhaps not kill more than two or three Antelopes. . . . I was very much entertained with a view of this Indian chase; it was after a herd of about 10 Antelope, and about 20 hunters. It lasted about 2 hours and considerable part of the chase was in view from my tent. About 1 p.m. the hunters returned—had not killed a single Antelope. My hunters returned soon after and had been equally unsuccessful. . . ."—Lewis

Feb. 22, 1806 (Written at Fort Clatsop, but refers to Indians of the Columbia basin)

"When the salmon begin to decline in the latter end of the summer and Autumn the natives leave the river, at least the majority, and remove to the plains at some distance for the purpose of hunting the Antelope. They pursue them on horseback and shoot them with their arrows."—Lewis

The Indians on both sides of the Rocky Mountains made use of antelope hides for leggings and robes.

Jan. 10, 1805 (Fort Mandan)

"last night was excessively Cold—the Murkery stood at 40° below o. . . . The Indians of the lower Village turned out to hunt for a man & a boy who had not returned from the hunt of yesterday, and borrow'd a Slay to bring them in expecting to find them frosed to death. About 10 o'clock the boy about 13 years of age Came to the fort with his feet frosed and had layed out last night without fire with only a Buffalow Robe to Cover him, the Dress which he wore was a pr. of Cabra (antelope) Legins, which is verry thin and mockersons—we had his feet put in cold water and they are Comeing too. Soon after the arrival of the Boy, a Man Came in who had also Stayed out without fire, and verry thinly Clothed, this man was not the least injured. Customs & habits of those people anured them to bare more Cold than I thought it possible for a man to endure."—Clark

Aug. 20, 1805 (Shoshone Indian Village on Lemhi River)
"their legings are most usually formed of the skins of the Antelope dressed without the hair."—Lewis

"with these people the robe is formed most commonly of the skins of Antelope, Bighorn or deer, dressed with the hair on, tho' they prefer the buffaloe when they can procure them."—Lewis

"the shirt of the men is a commodious and decent garment. . . . these shirts are generally made of deer's, Antelope's, Bighorn's, or Elk's skins dressed without the hair. Elk skin is less used for this purpose than either of the others."—Lewis

Feb. 22, 1806 (Refers to Indians of Columbia basin)
"the natives here make robes of their (Antelope) skins dressed with the hair on them."—Lewis

April 3, 1805 (Fort Mandan)
"we are all day engaged packing up Sundery articles to be sent to the President of the U. S.—
Box No. 1, contains the following articles, i.e.
In package No. 3 & 4 Male & female antelope, with their Skelitons."
—Clark

Aug. 28, 1806 (Vic. of Teton River)
"Sent out Ruebin and Joseph Field to hunt the Mule deer or the Antelope neither of which we have either the skins or scelletins."[12]—Clark

CHAPTER VII
The American Bison

Lewis and Clark's diaries include many entries which clearly indicate their astonishment at finding buffalo, *Bison bison* (Linnaeus), on the plains of the Dakotas and Montana in such numbers that they could only guess at the size of the herds.

Sept. 9, 1804 (Above the Niobrara River)

"I saw at one view near the river at least 500 buffalo, those animals have been in View all day feeding in the Plains . . . every copse of timber appear to have Elk and Deer."

Sept. 17, 1804 (Near mouth of the White River)

"This scenery already rich, pleasing and beautiful was still further hightened by immense herds of Buffaloe, deer, Elk, and Antelopes which we saw in every direction feeding on the hills and plains. I do not think I exagerate when I estimate the number of Buffaloe which could be comprehended at one view to amount to 3,000."

June 3, 1805 (At mouth of Marias River)

"the country in every direction around us was one vast plain in which innumerable herds of Buffalow were seen attended by their shepherds, the wolves; the solitary antelope which now had their young were distributed over its face; some herds of Elk were also seen."

Aug. 29, 1806 (Near Big Bend of the Missouri)

"I ascended to the high Country and from an eminance I had a view of a greater number of buffalow than I had ever seen before at one time. I must have seen near 20,000 of those animals feeding on this plain. . . ."

Buffalo were seen on the western plains for the first time[1] by Lewis and Clark's hunters while the party was camped near the mouth of the Kansas River. None was killed, however, until the expedition reached South Dakota.

Aug. 23, 1804 (Vic. of Elk Point, South Dakota)

"J. Fields Sent out to hunt Came back to the Boat and informed me that he had Killed a Buffalow in the plain ahead. Capt. Lewis took 12 men and had the Buffalo brought to the boat in the next bend."—Clark

Although thousands of buffalo were seen along the Missouri between Bon Homme Island[2] and Mandan villages during September and October of 1804, only 35 of them were killed for meat and hides. Two were killed at Fort Mandan on Oct. 28, but only one was killed during November. Game of all kinds was scarce in the vicinity of the Mandan and Arakara Indian villages, and the Lewis and Clark hunters were obliged to hunt considerable distances from their winter headquarters. On December 6, "Capt. Clark Set out with a hunting party. Killed 8 Buffaloe and returned the next day." During the week which followed a large herd of buffalo moved into the area, and both the Indians and the explorers managed to lay in a supply of meat. Between Dec. 6 and 14, a total of 34 buffalo was killed by the white hunters. Only three other buffalo were killed during the rest of the winter at Fort Mandan. Deer and elk, however, were taken in considerable numbers during January and February.

Buffalo were not reported again until after Lewis and Clark had resumed their journey in the spring.

April 15, 1805 (Approx. 50-60 miles above the Little Missouri River)
"Saw several gangs of buffalow and some elk at a distance."—Clark

April 17, 1805 (Approx. 90 miles above the Little Missouri River)
"we saw immense quantities of game in every direction around us as we passed up the river; consisting of herds of Buffaloe, Elk, and Antelopes with some deer and wolves, ..."—Lewis

April 22, 1805 (Vic. of White Earth River)
"I assended to the top of the cutt bluff this morning, from whence I had a most delightful view of the country, the whole of which except the vally formed by the Missouri is void of timber or underbrush, exposing to the first glance of the spectator immence herds of Buffaloe, Elk, deer, and Antelopes feeding in one common and boundless pasture."—Lewis

Thereafter buffalo were seen and killed regularly from the Yellowstone River to Great Falls, Montana. They were particularly abundant in the vicinity of the Great Falls of the Missouri.

June 17, 1805 (Vic. of Great Falls, Mont.)
"Saw a vast number of buffaloe feeding in every direction arround us in the plains, others coming down in large herds to water at the river, ..."—Lewis

July 11, 1806 (Vic. of Great Falls)
"I arrived in sight of the white bear Islands—the Missouri bottoms on both sides of the river were crouded with buffaloe—I sincerely believe that there were not less than 10 thousand buffaloe within a circle of two miles around that place."—Lewis

July 3, 1805 (Vic. of Great Falls)

"The Indians have informed us that we should shortly leave the buffaloe country after passing the falls; this I much regret for I know when we leave the buffaloe that we shall sometimes be under the necessity of fasting occasionally."—Lewis

The Indians were right; the last buffalo taken on the outward journey was killed in the vicinity of Cascade, Montana. None was seen in the neighborhood of Three Forks or on Jefferson's River. They found evidence that buffalo had formerly frequented the Jefferson River valley, but whether their absence during the summer of 1805 can be attributed to a seasonal migration or some other factor remains a moot question.

Aug. 2, 1805 (Jefferson River near South Boulder Creek)

"The bones of the buffalo and their excrement of an old date are to be met with in every part of the valley, but we have long since lost all hope of meeting with that animal in these mountains."—Lewis

On the return journey Lewis and Clark parted company at Lolo Hot Springs, the former, accompanied by ten men and an Indian guide took a short cut to Great Falls by way of Lewis and Clark Pass and the Sun River. He found buffalo sign on Lander's Fork west of the Pass.

July 7, 1806 (Approaching Lewis & Clark Pass from west)

". . . saw some sighn of buffaloe early this morning . . . from which it appears that the buffaloe do sometimes penetrate these mountains a few miles. We saw no buffaloe this evening, but much old appearance of dung, tracks, etc."—Lewis

July 8, 1806 (Descending mountains east of Lewis & Clark Pass)

"Joseph Fields saw two buffaloe below us at some distance which are the first that have been seen . . . much rejoiced at finding ourselves in the plains of the Missouri which abounds in game."—Lewis

On July 10, 1806, Lewis again reported "vast herds of buffalo" within a few miles of the confluence of the Sun and Missouri Rivers.

While Lewis was charting this new route from Lolo Pass to Great Falls and subsequently exploring the Marias River, Clark was leading his party back to the headwaters of Jefferson's River by way of Gibbon's Pass and thence to Three Forks with Sacajawea serving as guide. Old buffalo trails provided an easy route over the Bitterroot range.

July 6, 1806 (On Camp Creek in the vicinity of Ross' Hole)

"I observe the appearance of old buffalo roads and some heads (of buffalo) on this part of the mountain—proving that formerly Buffs. roved there and also that this is the best route, for Buffs. and Indians always have the best route and here both were joined."—Clark

Clark saw no more buffalo or signs of them until he reached Three Forks.

July 14, 1806 (Gallatin River near Three Forks)
"I saw Elk, deer & Antelopes, and a Great deel of old signs of buffalo. Their roads is in every direction. The Indian woman informs me that a fiew years ago Buffalow was very plenty in those plains and Vallies quite as high as the head of Jefferson's River, but few of them ever came into those vallys of late years, ..."—Clark

On leaving Three Forks, Clark proceeded on horseback to the Yellowstone River following a course roughly paralleling that of highway U.S. 10. He struck the river near Livingston, Montana, on July 15, 1806. Here Clark had hoped to find trees large enough for canoes, but he was obliged to continue down the river by horse for five days before finding any timber that would serve his purpose. On July 23 he started down the river, in two canoes lashed together for stability. The horses were turned over to Serg't. Pryor and two privates with instructions to deliver them to the Mandan Indians.

Elk and antelope were plentiful, but buffalo were scarce in the vicinity of Livingston. They were reported as being more plentiful in the vicinity of Boulder River, and as occurring in great numbers about seventy miles below Clark's Fork. "Emence herds of Buffalo" were seen from the summit of Pompey's Tower, and they were found to be astonishingly "noumerous" near Sarpy, Montana.

Clark was delayed at Glendive, Montana by a herd which was crossing the river.

Aug. 1, 1806 (Vic. of Glendive, Montana)
"at 2 P.M. I was obliged to land to let the Buffalow cross over, notwithstanding an island of a half a mile in width over which this gangue of Buffalow had to pass and the chanel of the river on each side nearly ¼ of a mile in width, this gangue of Buffalow was entirely across and as thick as they could swim. the chanel on the side of the island they went into the river was crouded with those animals for ½ hour. (I was obliged to lay to for one hour) the other side of the island for more than ¾ of an hour. I took 4 of the men and killed 4 fat cows for their fat and what portion of their flesh the small canoes could carry, that which we had killed a few days ago being nearly spoiled from the wet weather."
—Clark

Clark rejoined Lewis below the mouth of the Yellowstone. Because of Lewis' injury, the combined party descended the river with all possible haste.

According to Clark's diary game was quite scarce for many miles above and below the Mandan villages. Buffalo did not appear in great numbers above the Teton River; however, below the Big Bend of the Missouri they were seen in larger herds than ever before.

Lewis and Clark did not remain long enough in any locality to observe the seasonal migrations of the buffalo. They noted areas of abundance and scarcity and attributed this either to localized shifting of the herds in search of food and water, or to harassment by Indian hunting parties. Their interpretation of these local movements cannot be challenged as both factors were operative.

Generally the primitive buffalo had little fear of man. Even though the Indians hunted them regularly, the herds were so vast that thousands of buffalo must have grown old and died without any contact with man and his weapons. The explorers were sufficiently impressed with the tameness of these animals to remark about it on several occasions.

May 4, 1805 (Vic. of Porcupine River)

"I saw immence quantities of buffaloe in every direction . . .; having an abundance of meat on hand I passed them without firing on them; they are extremely gentle—the bull buffaloes particularly will scarcely give way to you. I passed several in the open plain within fifty paces, they viewed me for a moment as something novel and then very unconcernedly continued to feed."—Lewis

May 9, 1805 (Vic. of Milk River)

"We saw a great quantity of game today particularly Elk and buffaloe; the latter are now so gentle that the men frequently throw sticks and stones at them in order to drive them out of their way."—Lewis

April 22, 1805 (Vic. of White Earth River)

"Walking on the shore this evening I met with a buffaloe calf which attached itself to me and continued to follow close at my heels untill I embarked and left it."—Lewis

George Catlin,[3] in 1833, also noted the affectionate disposition of the buffalo calf; he managed to lure several of them to his camp where he fed them milk from a domestic cow.

April 25, 1805 (Near mouth of the Yellowstone River)

"The whol face of the country was covered with herds of Buffaloe, Elk, & Antelopes; deer are also abundant, but keep themselves more concealed in the woodland. the buffaloe, Elk, & Antelope are so gentle that we pass near them while feeding, without apearing to excite any alarm among them; and when we attract their attention, they frequently approach us more nearly to discover what we are, and in some instances pursue us considerable distance apparently with that view."—Lewis

Only in two instances was the party endangered by charging buffalo:

May 29, 1805 (Vic. of Judith River)

"Last night we were all allarmed by a large buffaloe Bull which swam over from the opposite shore and coming along side of the white perogue, climbed over it to land, he then allarmed ran up the bank in full speed directly towards the fires, and was within 18 inches of the heads of some of the men who lay sleeping before the centinel could allarm him or make him change his course; still more allarmed, he now took his direction immediately towards our lodge, passing between 4 fires and within a few inches of the heads of one range of the men as they yet lay sleeping —when he came near the tent, my dog saved us by causing him to change his course a second time, which he did by turning a little to the right, and was quickly out of sight, leaving us by this time all in an uproar with our guns in our hands, enquiring of each other the cause of the alarm, which after a few moments was explained by the centinel: we were happy to find no one hurt. The next morning we found that the buffaloe in passing the perogue had trodden on a rifle which belonged to Capt. Clark's black man, who had negligently left her in the perogue, the rifle was much bent, he had also broken the spindle, pivit, and shattered the stock of one of the blunderbushes on board, with this damage I felt well content, happy indeed, that we had sustained no further injury, it appears that the white perogue which contains our most valuable stores is attended by some evil gennii."—Lewis

This extraordinary tameness of the buffalo either was not universal or was readily lost on contact with hunters. Alexander Henry[4] cites contrary evidence on the basis of his observations in 1800 at the Park River Post of the North West Fur Company.

Nov. 7, 1800 (Park River Post on Red River of the North)

"We saw a great herd of cows (buffalo) going a full speed southward, but on coming to our track which goes to the salt lake they began to smell the ground and, as suddenly as if they had been fired at, turned toward the mountain. It is surprising how sagacious those animals are. When in the least alarmed they will smell the track of even a single person in the grass and run away in a contrary direction. I have seen large herds walking very slowly to pasture and, feeding as they went, come to a place where some person had passed on foot, when they would instantly stop, smell the ground, draw back a few paces, bellow, and tear up the earth with their horns. Sometimes the whole herd would range along the route, keeping up a terrible noise, until one of them was hardy enough to jump over, when they would all follow and run some distance."—Alexander Henry

These instances of extreme wariness may have been due in part to the fact that the French and Indian trappers made a practice of slaughtering buffalo at every opportunity for meat, hides, tallow, and the sport of killing.

John Bradbury,[5] a botanist who accompanied an expedition led by Wilson P. Hunt and Ramsey Crooks as far as the Mandan Indian villages in 1810, likewise made some interesting observations on the abundance and habits of buffalo:

June 22, 1810 (Near mouth of the Heart River)

"I observed the preceding days a sufficient number of buffaloes to induce me to credit the hunters in their reports of the vast numbers they had seen; but this day afforded me ample confirmation. Scarcely had we ascended the bluffs of the Heart River, when we discerned herds in every direction; and had we been disposed to devote the day to hunting, we might have killed a great number, as the country north of the Heart River is not so uniform in its surface as that we had passed. It consists of ridges of small elevation, separated by narrow valleys. This renders it much more favorable for hunting, and although we did not materially deviate from our course, five were killed before noon. Mr. Crooks joined me in remonstrating against this waste; but it was impossible to restrain the hunters, as they scarcely ever loose an opportunity of killing, if it offers, even although not in want of food. About two o'clock we arrived on the summit of a ridge more elevated than any we had yet passed. From thence we saw before us a beautiful plain, as we judged, about four miles across, in the direction of our course, and of a similar dimension from east to west. It was bounded on all sides by long ridges, similar to that which we had ascended. The scene exhibited in this valley was sufficiently interesting to excite even our Canadians a wish to stop a few minutes and contemplate it. The whole of the plain was perfectly level, and, like the rest of the country, without a single shrub. It was covered with the finest verdure, and in every part herds of buffalo were feeding. I counted seventeen herds; but the aggregate number of the animals it was difficult even to guess at; some thought upwards of ten thousand. We descended into the plain, and each having two marrow bones hung to his saddle, we resolved to dine wherever we could first find water. In descending into the plain, we came upon a small herd feeding in a valley. One buffalo was shot by our party before we could possibly restrain them. At about half the distance across the plain we reached a small pond, where we halted, and having collected a sufficient quantity of dry buffaloe's-dung, we made a fire, in which we disposed our bones, and although the water was stagnant, we made free use of it. During our stay here a very large herd of buffalo continued to feed within a quarter of a mile of us. Some of them I observed gazing at us; but as they were to the windward, they had not the power of discovering what we were by the sense of smelling. I found, on inquiry, from some of our party who were well acquainted with the habits of these animals, that they seem to rely chiefly on that sense for their safety. Around this herd we counted fifteen wolves, several of which stood for some minutes looking at us; without exhibiting any signs of fear; and as we did not think them worth shooting, we left them unmolested."—Bradbury

Lewis and Clark's brief comments about the breeding habits of buffalo are of value only because they establish dates for rutting and calving in Montana.

July 11, 1806 (Medicine River, southwest of Great Falls)
"It is now the season at which the buffaloe begin to coppelate and the bulls keep up a tremendous roaring—we could hear them for many miles and there are such numbers of them that there is one continuous roar." —Lewis

July 25, 1806 (Yellowstone River, vicinity of Pompey's Pillar)
"emence herds of Buffalo about our camp as it is now running (rutting) time with those animals—the bulls keep up such a grunting nois which is very loud and disagreeable sound that we are compelled to scear them away before we can sleep—the men fire several shot at them and scear them away."—Clark

April 21, 1805 (Vic. of White Earth River)
"The buffalo is about calving."—Clark

John Bradbury's[6] account of the behavior of bison during the breeding season is much more interesting.

July 20, 18. (Vic. of Niobrara River)
"On my return to the boats, as the wind had in some degree abated, we proceeded, and had not gone more than five or six miles before we were surprised by a dull, hollow sound, the cause of which we could not possibly imagine. It seemed to be one or two miles below us; but as our descent was very rapid, it increased every moment in loudness, and before we had proceeded far, our ears were able to catch some distant tones, like the bellowing of buffaloes. When opposite to the place from whence it proceeded, we landed, ascended the bank, and entered a small skirting of trees and shrubs that separated the river from an extensive plain. On gaining a view of it, such a scene opened to us as will fall to the lot of few travellers to witness. This plain was literally covered with buffaloes

as far as we could see, and we soon discovered that it consisted in part of females. The males were fighting in every direction, with a fury which I have never seen paralleled, each having a single antagonist. We judged that the number must have amounted to some thousands, and that there were many hundreds of these battles going on at the same time, some not eighty yards from us. I shall only observe further that the noise occasioned by the trampling and bellowing was far beyond description."—Bradbury

Lewis and Clark found no direct evidence of starvation among buffalo. Despite the fact that this species is well equipped to withstand severe cold and to forage for grass beneath the snow, Seton (1909) points out that blizzards are known to have wiped out herds which sought shelter in gullies and ravines and were buried in snow. Alexander Henry described a sleet storm which occurred in Saskatchewan in 1810, as a result of which a herd of sixty buffalo died because they could not stand or move about in search of food. George Bird Grinnell reported a similar storm in southeastern Wyoming during which many buffalo and Indian horses were lost.

On the other hand Alexander Henry tells of seeing buffalo graze unconcernedly in a severe blizzard in the Red River valley.

Feb. 1, 1801 (Park River Post on the Red River)

"It is surprising how the cows resist the piercing North wind, which at times blows with such violence over the bleak plains, and raises such drifts that it cannot be faced; still those animals graze in the open field."
—Alexander Henry

Lewis and Clark's diaries include many references to buffalo and elk being killed which were "too poor for uce."

Feb. 12, 1805 (Fort Mandan)

"Capt. Clark arrived with the hunting party. Since they set out they have killed forty Deer, three buffaloe bulls and sixteen Elk, most of them were so meager that they were unfit for use, particularly the Buffaloe and the male Elk."—Lewis

April 17, 1805

"at a place we halted to dine . . . we met with a herd of buffaloe of which I killed the fatest as I conceived among them, however on examining it I found it so poor that I thought it unfit for uce and only took the tongue; the party killed another which was still more lean."—Lewis

April 20, 1805 (Between Little Missouri and White Earth River)

"the Buffaloe, Elk and deer are poor at this season and of cours not very palatable. . . ."—Lewis

155

April 25, 1805 (Approaching the Yellowstone River)

"we met two large herds of buffaloe, of which we killed three cows and a calf, two of the former were so lean we therefore took their tongues and a part of the marrow bones only."—Lewis

This practice of taking only the tongues and marrow bones of the buffalo was common among early explorers and fur traders.

Starvation, however, was only one of the decimating factors in the life of the buffalo. Drowning, prairie fires, predators, and Indian hunters took an annual toll.

April 27, 1805 (Mouth of Yellowstone River)

"For several days past we have observed a great number of buffaloe lying dead on the shore, some of them entire, and others partly devoured by wolves and bear. Those animals either drownded during the winter in attempting to pass the river on the ice . . . , or by swimming across at present to the bluff banks which they are unable to ascend and feeling themselves too weak to return remain and perish for want of food; in this situation we met several little parties of them."—Lewis

May 15, 1805

"We see Buffalow on the banks dead, others floating down dead, and others mired every day, those buffalow either drown in swiming the river or brake thro' the ice."—Clark

June 17, 1805 (Great Falls, Montana)

"The fragments of many carcases of these poor animals daily pass down the river, thus mangled I presume in decending those immence cataracts above us. as the buffaloe generally go in large herds to water and the passages to the river about the falls are narrow and steep the hinder part of the herd press those in front out of their depth and the water instantly takes them over the cataracts where they are instantly crushed to death without the possibility of escaping—in this manner I have seen ten or a dozen disapear in a few minutes—their mangled carcases lie along the shores below the falls in considerable quantities and afford a fine amusement for the bear, wolves and birds of prey; this may be one of the reasons, and I think not a bad one either, that the bear are so tenatious of their right of soil in this neighbourhood."—Lewis

Other early travelers also reported on the number of drowned buffalo that floated down the Missouri and its tributaries. John Bradbury was impressed by the sight of them in the spring of 1810.

April 4, 1810 (Between Fort Osage and the mouth of the Nodaway River —on the Missouri)

"We began to notice . . . the great number of drowned buffalo that were floating on the river; vast numbers of them were also thrown ashore, and upon rafts on the points of the islands. The carcasses had attracted an immence number of turkey buzzards. . . ."—Bradbury

Alexander Henry makes graphic reference to buffalo floating down the Red River in 1801.

March 31, 1801 (Park River Post of Northwest Fur Company)
Rain had broken up the ice on the river on March 30, and it began to move out. "bearing great numbers of dead buffalo from above, which must have drowned in attempting to cross while the ice was weak."

April 1, 1801 (Park River Post)
"River clear of ice, but drown buffalo continue to drift by in entire herds. Several lodged on the banks near the fort. The women cut up some of the fattest for their own use; the flesh appeared to be fresh and good. It is really astonishing what vast numbers have perished; they formed one continuous line in the current for two days and nights."

April 22, 1801 (Park River Post)
"Buffalo still drifting down river, but not in such vast numbers as before."

May 1, 1801 (Park River Post)
"The stench from vast numbers of drowned buffalo along the river was intolerable."

The Indians commonly burned the plains in the early spring as a game management practice. Clark observed this on two occasions.

March 6, 1805 (Fort Mandan)
"A cloudy morning, and Smokey all Day from the burning of the plains, which was set on fire by the Minetarries for an early crop of grass, as an enducement for the Buffalow to feed on, ..."—Clark

March 30, 1805 (Fort Mandan)
"The Plains are on fire in View of the fort on both Sides of the River, it is said to be common for the Indians to burn the Plains near their Villages every Spring for the benefit of their horses, and to induce the Buffalow to come near them."—Clark

Oct. 29, 1804 (Fort Mandan)
"The Prarie was Set on fire (or cought by accident) by a young man of the Mandins, the fire went with such velocity that it burnt to death a man & woman who Could not get to any place of Safety, one man, a

woman & child much burnt and Several narrowly escaped the flame. a boy, half white, was saved unhurt in the midst of the flaim, Those ignerent people say this boy was Saved by the Great Medison Speret because he was white. The couse of his being Saved wase a Green buffalow Skin was thrown over him by his mother who perhaps had more fore Sight for the pertection of her Son, and less for herself, than those who escaped the flame, the Fire did not burn under the Skin leaving the grass around the boy. This fire passed our Camp last night about 8 o'clock P.M.—it went with great rapitidity and looked Tremendious."—Clark

Sometimes these fires which ran out of control spread to such an extent that buffalo and other game species were trapped in the flames and untold numbers were destroyed.

Alexander Henry[7] reported such an incident, though in this case the fire occurred in late fall, and may have been accidental.

Nov. 25, 1804 (Pembina River Post, Red River valley)

"Plains burned in every direction and blind buffalo seen every moment wandering about. The poor beasts have all the hair singed off; even the skin in many places is shriveled up and terribly burned, and their eyes are swollen and closed fast. It was really pitiful to see them staggering about, sometimes running afoul of a large stone, at other times tumbling down hill, and falling into creeks not yet frozen over. In one spot we found a whole herd lying dead. The fire having passed only yesterday these animals were still good and fresh, and many of them exceedingly fat. Our road was on the summit of the Hair Hills where the open ground was uneven—country stony and barren. At sunset we arrived at the Indian camp, having made an extraordinary day's ride, and seen an incredible number of dead and dying, blind, lame, singed, and roasted buffalo. The fire raged all night toward the S.W."—Henry

The prairie wolf, not to be confused with the coyote, was the principal predator of the buffalo. These wolves ran in packs which constantly harassed the herds of big game, and preyed upon such young, old and injured as could not keep pace with the more vigorous members of the gang. They did not hesitate to attack any buffalo which became separated from the herd, and frequently pulled down vigorous bulls or cows after tiring them out in the chase. Despite their abundance, the wolf had no appreciable effect on buffalo populations. Indian and white hunters, storms, fire, and accidents appear to have taken a much greater toll of them under primitive conditions than predation.

Lewis and Clark made frequent reference to the wolf, and cited a few instances of predation.

April 22, 1805 (Above White Earth River)

"Capt. Clark informed me that he saw a large drove of buffaloe pursued by wolves today, that they at length caught a calf which was unable to keep up with the herd. The cows only defend their young so long as they are able to keep up with the herd, and seldom return any distance in surch of them."—Lewis

Oct. 20, 1804 (Vic. of Heart River)

"I observe, near all gangues of Buffalow, wolves and when the buffalow move those animals follow, and feed on those that are too pore or fat to keep up with the gangue."—Clark

The Indians of the Missouri country commonly hunted buffalo on horseback using bows, arrows and spears for weapons. At the time Lewis and Clark visited the Mandans and Arakara tribes, these Indians had few guns, and like the Shoshones and Clatsops, they had little skill in the care and use of them. Their savage recklessness in riding among the frightened, milling herds to loose their arrows at close range has been recounted so often as to have become legendary.

Dec. 7, 1804 (Fort Mandan)

"Capt. Lewis took 15 men & went out joined the Indians, who were at the time . . . Killing the Buffalow on Horseback with arrows which they done with great dexterity, his party killed 10 Buffalow, five of which we got to the fort by the assistance of a horse in addition to what the men Packed on their backs . . . those we did not get in was taken by the indians under a Custom which is established among them . . . any person seeing a buffalow lying without an arrow Sticking in him, or some purticular mark takes possession, ..."—Clark

Other hunting techniques employed by the Indians of the plains are not so well known.

May 29, 1805 (Vic. of Judith River)

"Today we passed on the Star'd side the remains of a vast many mangled carcases of Buffaloe which had been driven over a precipice of 120 feet by the Indians and perished; the water appeared to have washed away a part of this immence pile of slaughter and still there remained the fragments of at least a hundred carcases—they created a most horrid stench. In this manner the Indians of the Missouri destroy vast herds of buffaloe at a stroke; for this purpose one of the most active and fleet young men is selected and disguised in a robe of buffaloe skin, having also the skin of the buffaloe's head with the ears and horns fastened on his head in the form of a cap, thus comparisoned he places himself at a convenient distance between a herd of buffaloe and a precipice proper for the purpose, which happens in many places on this river for miles together. The other Indians now surround the herd on the back and flanks and, at a signal agreed on, all shew themselves at the same time moving forward towards the buffaloe; the disguised Indian or decoy has taken care to place himself sufficiently nigh the buffaloe to be noticed by them when they take to flight and running before them they follow him in full speed to the precipice, the cattle behind driving those in front over and seeing them go do not look or hesitate about following untill the whole are precipitated down the precipice forming one common mass of dead and mangled carcases—the decoy in the meantime has taken care to secure himself in some cranney or crevice of the clift which he had previously prepared for that purpose. The part of the decoy I am told is extreemly dangerous, if they are not very fleet runners the buffaloe tread them underfoot and crush them to death, and sometimes drive them over the precipice also, where they perish in commin with the buffaloe."—Lewis

The Indians as well as the explorers ordinarily dried their meat, if a surplus was on hand, in the sun or over a fire. They also rendered tallow which was eaten as such, or combined with dried, pounded meat to make pemmican.

The northern plains Indians were not averse to salvaging dead buffalo which floated down the rivers during the spring break-up.

Clark reported this practice among the Mandans and the Minitarees; and Alexander Mackenzie corroborated Clark's account (Masson's Bourgeois Nord—Ouest, p. 337)

March 30, 1805 (Fort Mandan)

"The obstickle broke away above and the ice came down in great quantities—the river rose 13 inches the last 24 hours. I observed the extraordinary dexterity of the Indians in jumping from one cake of ice to another for the purpose of catching the buffalo as they floated down."—Clark

"Mackenzie states that the Indians on the Missouri . . . search eagerly for the carcasses of buffaloes and other drowned animals that float down the river in the spring season; these, although rotten and of intolerable stench, are preferred by the Natives to any other kind of food . . . So fond are the Mandanes of putrid meat that they bury animals whole in the winter for the consumption of the spring."[8]

The Indians of the plains were dependent on buffalo hides for making tepees, robes, moccasins, saddle blankets, halters, bull boats, and shields.

Aug. 28, 1804 (Between Virmillion River and Bon Homme Is.)

"The Scioues Camps are handsom, of a conic form, Covered with Buffalow Roabs Painted different colours and all compact and handsomly arranged, Covered all around,—an open part in the Centre for the fire, with Buffalow roabs, each Lodg has a place for Cooking detatched, the lodges contain from 10 to 15 persons."—Clark

April 7, 1805 (A day's journey above Fort Mandan)
"Capt. Clark, myself the two Interpretters and the woman and child sleep in a tent of dressed skins. This tent is in the Indian style, formed of a number of dressed Buffaloe skins sewed together with sinues—it is cut in such a manner that when foalded double it forms the quarter of a circle, and is left open at one side—here it may be attached or loosened at pleasure by strings which are sewed to its sides for the purpose. To erect this tent, a parsel of ten or twelve poles are provided, four or five of which are attached together at one end, they are then elivated and their lower extremities are spread in a circular manner to a width proportionate to the demention of the lodge; in the same manner other poles are leant against those, and the leather is then thrown over them to form a conic figure."—Lewis

Aug. 21, 1806 (Vic. of Mandan Villages)
"The Sun being very hot the Chyenne Chief envited us to his lodge which was pitched in the plain at no great distance from the River. I accepted the invitation and accompanied him to his lodge which was new and much larger than any which I have Seen—it was made of 20 dressed Buffalow Skins in the same form as of the Scioux and the lodges of other nations of this quarter. About this lodge was 20 others, several of them of nearly the same size."—Clark

Sept. 26, 1804 (Vic. of Teton River)
"After the return of Capt. Lewis, I went on Shore—on landing I was receved on a elegent painted Buffalo Robe & taken to the Village[9] by 6 Men & was not permitted to touch the ground untill I was put down in the grand Councill house on a White dressed Robe . . . this house formed a 3/4 Circle of Skins Well Dressed and Sown together—under this Shelter about 70 men Set forming a Circle."—Clark

Jan. 10, 1805 (Fort Mandan)
"The Indians of the lower Villege turned out to hunt for a man & a boy who had not returned from the hunt of yesterday, and borrow'd a Slay to bring them in expecting to find them frosed to death. About 10 o'clock the boy about 13 years of age Came to the fort with his feet frosed and had layed out last night without fire with only a Buffalow Robe to Cover him,

the Dress which he wore was a pr. of Cabra (antelope) Legins, which is verry thin and mockersons—we had his feet put in cold water and they are Comeing too. Soon after the arrival of the Boy, a Man Came in who had also Stayed out without fire, and verry thinly Clothed, this man was not in the least injured. Customs & the habits of those people has anured them to bare more Cold than I thought it possible for man to endure."—Clark

Aug. 20, 1805 (Shoshone village on the Lemhi River)
"the robe woarn by the Shoshonees is the same in both sexes and is loosely thrown over their shoulders, and the sides at pleasure either hanging loose or drawn together with the hands; sometimes if the weather is cold they confine it with a girdel arround the waist; they are generally about the size of a 2½ point blanket for grown persons and reach as low as the middle of the leg. This robe forms a garment in the day and constitutes their only covering at night—with these people the robe is formed most commonly of the skins of Antelope, Bighorn, or deer, dressed with the hair on, *tho' they prefer the buffaloe when they can procure them.* I have also observed some robes among them of beaver, moonox (woodchuck), and small wolves. The summer robes of both sexes are also frequently made of Elk's skin without the hair."—Lewis

Oct. 10, 1805 (Chopunnish village on Clearwater River)
"The Chopunnish or Pierced nose Indians are Stout likely men, handsome women, and verry dressey in their way, the dress of the men are a White Buffalow robe or Elk Skin dressed with Beeds which are generally white, Sea Shells & the Mother of Pirl hung to the hair & on a piece of otter skin about their necks. . . ."—Clark

Aug. 22, 1806 (Vic. of Mandan Villages)
"The Cheyennes are portly Indians . . . their dress in Summer is Simpelly a roab of a light Buffalow Skin with or without the hair, & Breach clout & mockersons—Some wear leagins & Mockersons, ..."—Clark

Aug. 21, 1805 (Vic. of Shoshone village on Lemhi River)
"The mockersons of both sexes are usually the same and are made of deer, Elk or buffalo skin dressed without the hair. Sometimes in winter they make them of buffaloe skin dressed with the hair on and turn the hair inwards as the Mandans, Minetares and most of the nations do who inhabit the buffaloe country."—Lewis

Aug. 24, 1805 (Shoshone village on Lemhi River)
"a piece of buffaloes skin with the hair on is usually put under the saddle, ...

"The most usual caparison of the Shoshone horse is a halter and saddle —the 1st consists either of a round plated or twisted cord of six or seven strands of buffaloe's hair, or a thong of raw hide made pliant by pounding and rubing—these cords of the buffaloe hair are about the size of a man's finger and remarkably strong. This is a kind of halter which is prefered by them.—the halter of whatever it may be composed is always of great length and is never taken from the neck of the horse which they commonly use at any time. It is first attached at one end about the neck of the horse with a knot that will not slip, it is then brought down to his under jaw and being passed through the mouth imbraces the under jaw and tonge in a simple noose formed by crossing the rope underneath the jaw of the horse —this when mounted he draws up on the near side of the horses neck and holds in the left hand, suffering it to trail at a great distance behind him . . . They put their horses to their full speed with these cords trailing on the ground."—Lewis

July 21, 1804 (Mouth of Platte River)
"The Indians pass this river in Skin Boats which is flat and will not turn over."—Clark

Oct. 7, 1804 (Mouth of Moreau River)
"below the mouth of this river is the remains of a Rickorree Village . . . many of their willow and Straw mats, Baskets & Buffalow Skin Canoes remain entire within the Camp."—Clark

Oct. 9, 1804 (Vic. of Rampart Creek; also called Oak Creek)
"I observed Several Canoes made of a Single Buffalow Skin with 3 squars Cross the river today in waves as high as I ever saw them on this river, quite uncompased."—Clark

Nov. 10, 1804 (Fort Mandan)
"a Chief Half Pania came and brought a Side of Buffalow, in return We Gave Some fiew small things to himself & wife & Son, he crossed the river in the Buffalow Skin canoo and the Squar took the Boat (on her back) and proceeded on to the Town, 3 miles. . . ."—Clark

July 11, 1806 (Near mouth of Sun River)
"I directed the hunters to kill some buffaloe as well for the benefit of their skins to enable us to pass the river as for their meat . . . by 3 in the evening we had brought in a large quantity of fine beef and as many hides as we wanted for canoes shelters and gear. I then set all hands to prepare two canoes the one we made after the Mandan fassion with a single skin in the form of a bason and the other we constructed of two skins on a plan of our own."—Lewis

Aug. 8, 1806 (Vic. of Pompey's Pillar on the Yellowstone River)

"Serg't. N. Pryor, Shannon, hall & Windsor came down the river (Yellowstone) in two canoes made of Buffalow Skins. . . . they killed a Buffalow Bull and made a canoe . . . in the form and shape of the mandans and Ricares (the form of a bason) and made in the following manner. Viz: 2 Sticks of 1¼ inch diameter is tied together so as to form a round hoop of the size you wish the canoe, or as large as the Skin will allow to cover, two of those hoops are made one for the top or brim and the other for the bottom—the deabth you wish the canoe, then Sticks of the same size are crossed at right angles and fastened with a thong to each hoop and also where each Stick crosses each other. Then the Skin when green is drawn tight over this fraim and fastened with throngs to the brim or outer hoop so as to form a perfect bason. One of those canoes will carry 6 or 8 Men and their loads. Those two canoes are nearly the same size, 7 feet 3 inches diameter & 16 inches deep, 15 ribs or cross sticks in each. Serg't. Pryor informs me that the cause of his building two Canoes was for fear of one meating with some accident in passing down the Rochejhone, a river entirely unknown to either of them, by which means they might loose their guns and ammunition and be left destitute of the means of procureing food. He informed me that they passed through the worst parts of the rapids and Shoals in the river without taking a drop of water, the waves raised from the hardest winds dose not effect them."—Clark

Aug. 23, 1805 (Shoshone village on the Lemhi River)

"Their (Shoshone Indians) shield is formed of buffaloe hide, perfictly arrow proof, and is a circle of 2 feet 4 inches or 2 F. 6 I., in diameter. This is frequently painted with various figures and ornimented around the edges with feathers and a fringe of dressed leather . . . forming the shield is a cerimony of great importance among them, this implement would in their minds be devested of much of its protecting power were it not inspired with those virtues by their old men and jugglers. Their method of preparing it is thus—an entire skin of a bull buffaloe two years old is first provided; a feast is next prepared, and all the warriors, old men and jugglers invited to partake. A hole is sunk in the ground about the same diameter with the intended shield and about 18 inches deep, a parcel of stones are now made red hot and thrown into the hole—water is next thrown in and the hot stones cause it to emit a very strong, hot steam, over this they spread the green skin which must not have been suffered to dry after taken off the beast. The flesh side is laid next to the ground and as many of the workmen as can reach it take hold on its edges and extend it in every direction. As the skin becomes heated, the hair separates and is taken off with the fingers, and the skin continues to contract until the whole is drawn within the compass designed for the shield. It is then taken off and laid on a parchment hide where they pound it with their heels when barefoot. This operation of pounding continues for several days or as long as the feast lasts—when it is delivered to the propryeter and declared by the jugglers and old men to be sufficient defense against the arrows of their enemies or even bullets if the feast has been a satisfactory one."—Lewis

As long as the expedition remained in the buffalo country east of the Rocky Mountains meat was plentiful. Lewis remarked on one occasion that big game was so abundant and so easily killed that he could have fed a regiment. Yet, his hunters were specifically instructed not to kill more buffalo, or other game species, than needed for food and hides. It is true that during the winter at Fort Mandan there were periods of scarcity because sub-zero weather coupled with the necessity of having to range over many miles in search of game made hunting difficult.

During late winter and spring Lewis and Clark frequently reported that individual buffalo and elk were found to be "too poor for use," and in such cases only the marrow bones and tongues were utilized. Much meat was wasted, too, because of spoilage induced by heat and moisture. The need for making steady progress on their journey precluded taking time ordinarily to cut meat into strips and dry it after the Indian fashion. So, it was necessary to depend upon the hunters to provide fresh meat almost daily.

Space precludes citing many references to the killing and preparation of buffalo meat, except for a few cases of special interest.

April 21, 1805 (Above White Earth River)

"We saw immense herds of buffaloe, Elk, deer and Antelopes. Capt. Clark killed a buffaloe and four deer in the course of his walk today; the party with me killed 3 deer, 2 beaver, and 4 buffaloe calves. The latter we found very delicious. I think it equal to any veal I ever tasted."—Lewis

May 9, 1805 (Near mouth of Milk River)

"Capt. Clark killed two buffaloe, I also killed one buffaloe which proved to be the best meat . . .; we saved the best meat and from the cow I killed we saved the necessary materials for making what our wright hand cook, Charbono, calls boudin blanc, and immediately set him about preparing them for supper; this white pudding we all esteem one of the greatest delacies of the forest, it may not be amiss to give it a place.

"About 6 feet of the lower extremity of the large gut of the buffalo is the first morsel that the cook makes love to, this he holds fast at one end with the right hand, while with the forefinger and thumb of the left he gently compresses it, and discharges what he says is not good to eat, but of which in the sequel we get a moderate portion; the muscle lying underneath the shoulder blade next to the back, and the fillets are next sought, these are needed up very fine with a portion of kidney suet; to this composition is then added a just portion of pepper and salt and a small quantity of flour; thus far advanced our skilfull operator, Charbono, seizes his recepticle, which has never once touched the water for that would entirely destroy the regular order of the whole procedure; you will not forget that the side you now see is that covered with a good coat of fat provided the animal be in good order; the operator seizes the recepticle, I say, and tying it fast at one end, turns it inward and begins now with repeated evolutions of the hand and arm, and a brisk motion of the finger and thumb to put in what he says is *bon pour manger;* thus by stuffing and compressing he soon distends the recepticle to the utmost limits of its powers of expansion, and in the course of its longitudinal progress it drives from the other end of the recepticle a much larger portion of (blank space in ms) than was previously discharged by the finger and thumb of the left hand in the former part of the operation; thus when the sides of the recepticle are skillfully exchanged, the outer for the inner, and all is completely filled with something good to eat, it is tied at the other end, but not any cut off, for that would make the pattern too scant; it is then baptised in the Missouri with two dips and a flirt, and bobbed into the kettle; from whence, after it be well boiled it is taken and fried in bear's oil until it becomes brown, when it is ready to esswage the pangs of a keen appetite, or such as travellers in the wilderness are seldom at a loss for."—Lewis

July 16, 1805 (Vic. of Hardy, Mont.)

"Drewyer killed a buffaloe this morning near the river and we halted and breakfasted on it. Here for the first time I ate of the small guts of the buffaloe cooked over a blazing fire in the Indian style, without any preparation of washing or other clensing, and found them very good."—Lewis

July 11, 1806 (Vic. of Sun River, above Great Falls)

"By 12 o'clock they (hunters) had killed eleven buffaloe, most of them in fine order. The bulls are now generally much fatter than the cows and are fine beef. I sent all hands with the horses to assist in butchering and bringing in the meat. By 3 in the evening we had brought in a large quantity of fine beef and as many hides as we wanted for canoes, shelters, and geer."—Lewis

The explorers, like the Indians, made extensive use of buffalo robes and hides for clothing, blankets, tents, tarpaulins, bull-boats (as described above), saddle blankets, and moccasins for both men and horses.

July 16, 1806 (Yellowstone valley east of Livingston, Mont.)

"Saw a large gangue of about 200 Elk and nearly as many antelope, also two white or grey Bear in the plains, one of them I chased on horseback for about 2 Miles to the rugid part of the plain where I was compelled to give up the chase—two of the horses was so lame owing to their feet being worn quite Smooth, and to the quick, the hind feet was much the worst— I had Mockersons made of green buffalow Skin and put on their feet which seams to relieve them very much in passing over the stoney plains."—Clark

Lewis was impressed with the wool-like qualities of buffalo hair, and speculated on its possibilities as a substitute for sheep's wool.

April 18, 1805 (Between the Little Missouri & White Earth Rivers)

"I also saw several parsels of buffaloe's hair hanging on the rose bushes, which had been bleached by exposure to the weather and become perfectly white. it had every appearance of the wool of the sheep, tho' much finer and more silkey and soft. I am confident that an excellent cloth may be made of the wool of the Buffaloe. the Buffaloe I killed yesterday had cast his long hare, and the poil which remained was very thick, fine, and about 2 inches in length. I think this anamal would have furnished about five pounds of wool."—Lewis

Seton (1909) points out that an attempt was made in 1822 at Fort Garry to commercialize on buffalo wool. A stock company[10] was organized and a limited amount of cloth was produced; but the enterprise failed because of the difficulty of gathering the raw material in quantities, and through general mismanagement. A yard of buffalo wool cloth which cost $12.00 to make, sold at $1.08 in England.

167

CHAPTER VIII
Mountain Goats and Bighorn Sheep

The mountain goat, *Oreamnos americanus* (Blainville), is a native of the northern Rocky and Cascade Mountain ranges. His nearest relatives are the goat-antelopes of Asia and the chamois of Europe. He is a mountaineer in the strictest sense for he makes his home among the rocky crags, chasms, and mountain meadows far above timberline.

The Indian trails which led through mountain passes did not rise high enough to give the explorers an opportunity to see mountain goats in their usual habitats. Clark was fortunate to have seen just one of them in the mountains near The Dalles, Oregon.

On the other hand, the bighorn sheep, *Ovis canadensis* Shaw, was quite at home in the canyons of the upper Missouri River and its tributaries. The explorers discovered them near the mouth of the Yellowstone. They killed their first specimen in Fergus County, Montana, near Armel Creek. It proved to be a female; and, after careful study Lewis described it in detail. Thereafter, bighorns were seen frequently on the cliffs and mountainsides as far west as the Beaverhead Mountains.

MOUNTAIN GOAT

The mountain goat, *Oreamnos americanus* (Blainville), was first described and named as a distinct species by M. H. D. deBlainville in 1816. According to Seton, Blainville based his classification on information provided by Lewis, but we do not know whether, or not, he actually examined the skin, with horns attached, which Lewis purchased from the Indians in the vicinity of the Cascades of the Columbia River.

Although Coues[1] credits Lewis and Clark with the discovery of the mountain goat it is unlikely that they were the first to call attention to its existence. Seton points out that Alexander Mackenzie, in 1789, listed White Buffalo among other quadrupeds inhabiting the Mackenzie River country and that the former was restricted to the Mountains of the Northwest.[2] These "White Buffalo" probably were mountain goats, as this name has been applied to them by other early writers; certainly they were not buffalo.

Von Langsdorff,[3] in 1805, while visiting Kodiak Island, was shown some wool from a wild American sheep which was said to inhabit the mountains of the mainland. Although he did not see a specimen of this animal he noted that the hair differed from that of the wild sheep of Europe *(Ovis ammon)*.

Seton[4] credits Alexander Henry with being the first white man "to see with his own eyes and describe on paper" the mountain goat. At Kootenay Park, on Feb. 9, 1811, Henry wrote:

"Des Jarlaix, my hunter, I left behind to kill a White goat, as it is here they are the most numerous . . . The White Goat is larger than the Gray Sheep, thickly covered with long, pure white wool, and has short, black, erect horns. These animals seldom leave the mountain-tops. Winter and summer, they prefer the highest regions."

Lewis never had the good fortune to see a mountain goat in the flesh, but Clark, on Aug. 24, 1805, was credited with seeing one of them at a distance. In this connection it should be re-emphasized that the term "goat" as used repeatedly by both Lewis and Clark in their diaries refers to the antelope rather than to the white goat of the mountains.

The only diary entries that can be associated with the mountain goat are transcribed below:

Aug. 24, 1805 (Shoshone Indian village on Lemhi River)

"I have seen a few skins among these people which have almost every appearance of the common sheep. they inform me that they finde this animal on high mountains to the West and S.W. of them. it is about the size of the common sheep, the wool is reather shorter and intermixed with long hairs particularly on the upper part of the neck. these skins have been so much woarn that I could not form a just Idea of the animal or it's colour. the Indians however inform me that it is white and that it's horns are lunated comprest twisted and bent backward as those of the common sheep. the texture of the skin appears to be that of the sheep. I am now convinced that the sheep as well as the bighorn exist in these mountains. (Capt. Clark saw one at a distance today.)"—Lewis

Oct. 29, 1805. (Vic. of Celilo Falls, Columbia River)

"I also saw a mountain Sheap[5] skin the wool of which is long, thick, and corse with long corse hare on the top of the neck and back something resembling bristles of a goat, the skin was of white hare, those animals these people inform me by signs live in the mountains among the rocks, their horns are Small and streight, ..."—Clark

Feb. 22, 1806 (Fort Clatsop)

"The sheep is found in various parts of the Rocky mountains, but most commonly in those parts which are timbered and steep. they are also found in greater abundance on the chain of mountains which form the commencement of the woody country on this coast and which pass the Columbia between the great falls and rapids. we have never met with this anamal ourselves but have seen many of their skins in possession of the natives dressed with the wooll on them and also seen the blankets which they manufacture of the wooll of this sheep. from the skin the animal appears to be about the size of the common sheep; of a white colour. the wooll is fine on most parts of the body but not so long as that of our domestic sheep. the wooll is also curled and thick. on the back and more particularly on the top of the neck the wooll is intermixed with a considerable proportion of long streight hairs. there is no wooll on a small part of the body behind the shoulders on each side of the brisquit which is covered with a short fine hairs as in the domestic sheep. from signs which the Indians make in describing this animal they have herect pointed horns, tho' one of our Engages La Page, assures us that he saw them in the black hills where the little Missouri passes them, and that they were in every rispect like the domestic sheep and like them the males had lunated horns bent backwards and twisted. I should be much pleased at meeting with this animal, but have had too many proofs to admit a doubt of it's existing and in considerable numbers in the mountains near this coast."—Lewis

April 10, 1806 (Strawberry Is. near Cascades of Columbia River)
"on entering one of these lodges, the natives offered us a sheepskin for sale, than which nothing could have been more acceptable except the animal itself. the skin of the head of the sheep with the horns remaining was cased in such a manner as to fit the head of a man by which it was woarn and highly prized as an ornament. we obtained this cap in exchange for a knife, and were compelled to give them two Elkskins in exchange for the skin. this appeared to be the skin of a sheep not fully grown; the horns were about four inches long, celindric, smooth, black, erect and pointed; they rise from the middle of the forehead a little above the eyes. they offered us a second skin of a full grown sheep which was quite as large as that of a common deer. they discovered our anxity to purchase and in order to extort a great price declared that they prized it too much to dispose of it. in expectation of finding some others of a similar kind for sale among the natives of this neighbourhood I would not offer him a greater price than had been given for the other which he refused. these people informed us that these sheep were found in great abundance on the hights among the clifts of the adjacent mountains. and that they had lately killed these two from a herd of 36, at no great distance from their village."—Lewis

Coues[6] emphasizes the fact that it was unfortunate that Lewis and Clark called the mountain goat a "sheep," for, in 1815, this led George Ord, who classified many of the animals described by Lewis and Clark, to name the animal, *Ovis montanus*. It was first placed in the goat genus, where it belongs, by Desmarest, who named it *Capra columbiana* (Dict. Class., III, p. 580); then, Dr. R. Harlan changed the name, in 1825, to *Capra montana*. Next, the mountain goat was placed in a new genus, *Aploceros* by Hamilton-Smith in 1827. Following this the name was changed repeatedly before it was finally standardized as *Oreamnos americanus* (Blainville).

BIGHORN SHEEP

Seton has reviewed the taxonomic history of the bighorn sheep:

"In the fall of 1800, Duncan McGillivray, a clerk in the service of the North West Fur Company, was on the headwaters of the Bow River (near where Banff now is) with David Thompson, the famous explorer. While hunting he came on a small herd of bighorn. He recognized them as a new species of animal; and being a man of understanding, he sent a specimen to the Royal Society of London, where it arrived in 1803, and was promptly named and described by nearly everyone in the world of zoology.

"Dr. George Shaw, however, managed to get his name published first; so it stands today *Ovis canadensis* Shaw, Feb. 4, 1804."

The original range of the bighorn involved all of the Rocky Mountain states from southern Alberta and British Columbia to northern Mexico. They also inhabited the Sierra-Nevada range and the peninsula of Lower California. The range of the closely related white sheep, *Ovis dalli* Nelson, included the mountainous regions of Alaska, the Yukon Territory, British Columbia and the State of Washington. During the past fifty years the numbers of bighorn and white sheep have been much reduced, and they are now scarce or absent in many areas which they formerly occupied.

At the time of the Lewis and Clark expedition bighorns probably inhabited the Black Hills of South Dakota. M. Jean Vallé, a Frenchman living at the mouth of the Cheyenne River told the explorers that bighorn sheep inhabited the Black mountains to the west.

Oct. 1, 1804 (Mouth of Cheyenne River)

"No beaver on Dog river, on the Mountains great numbers of goat (antelope) and a kind of anamale with circular horns, this animale is nearly the size of an Small Elk. (Argalia). White bears is also plenty."— Clark

During the winter of 1804-05 at Fort Mandan they obtained additional evidence of the existence of this species from the Indians.

Dec. 22, 1804 (Fort Mandan)

"We precured two horns of the anamals the french Call the rock Mountain Sheep. Those horns are not of the largest kind. The Mandans Call this Sheep, Ar-Sar-ta it is about the Size of a large Deer, or a small Elk, its Horns Come out and wind around the head like the horn of a Ram, and the texture is not unlike it, much larger and thicker, perticelarly that part with which they butt."—Clark

Lewis and Clark saw these animals for the first time at the mouth of the Yellowstone River. One of the Lewis and Clark hunters reported seeing them on returning from a short exploratory trip up the Yellowstone.

April 26, 1805 (Mouth of Yellowstone River)

Joseph Fields, on returning from an eight mile trip up the Yellowstone River, reported that "he saw several of the bighorned anamals in the course of his walk; but they were so shy that he could not get a shot at them; he found a large horn of one of these anamals which he brought with him."—Clark

Thereafter the explorers found bighorns inhabiting the bluffs and cliffs of the Missouri and its tributaries wherever such habitat occurred from the mouth of the Yellowstone to the Beaverhead Mountains.

Aug. 1, 1805 (On Jefferson River near South Boulder Creek)

"Capt. Clark killed a bighorn on these clifts which himself and party dined on."—Lewis

Strangely enough neither Lewis nor Clark mentioned the bighorn sheep while they were crossing the Bitterroot Mountains on their outward journey either in the vicinity of Lost Trail Pass or Lolo Pass west of Missoula, Montana. None was seen in descending the Clearwater, Snake and Columbia Rivers. No reference to the bighorn was made during the winter spent at Fort Clatsop or on the return journey during the spring of 1806 until they had again traversed the Bitterroots and divided their party at Traveler's Rest. Clark headed south toward Three Forks and the Yellowstone River with two thirds of the men while Lewis explored a new and much shorter route to Great Falls with the aid of an Indian guide.

Lewis saw no bighorns in the mountains east and north of Missoula or on the Marias River. His first mention of them while on the return journey occurred after he was back on the Missouri River below the mouth of the Marias.

July 29, 1806 (Below junction of Marias & Missouri Rivers)

"On our way today we killed 9 bighorns of which I preserved the skins and skeletons of 2 females and one male; the flesh of this animal is extremely delicate, tender and well flavoured; they are now in fine order.

Their flesh both in colour and flavor much resembles mutton though it is not so strong as our mutton."—Lewis

Clark, on the other hand, saw bighorns in the Southern Bitterroots in the vicinity of Gibbon's Pass, in the Beaverhead Valley, and at various points on the Yellowstone.

July 4, 1806 (Vic. of Gibbon's Pass)
"On the side of the Hill near the place we dined (we) saw a gangue of Ibex or bighorn Animals I shot at them running and missed."—Clark

July 10, 1806 (Beaverhead Valley)
"I saw also on the sides of the rock in rattlesnake mountain 15 bighorn animals."—Clark

July 25, 1806 (Vic. of Pompey's Pillar on the Yellowstone)
"Saw a gang of about 40 Bighorn animals—fired at them and killed 2 on the sides of the rocks which we did not get."—Clark

July 26, 1806 (Near Mouth of Bighorn River on the Yellowstone)
"I am informed by the Menetarres Indians and others that this river (Bighorn) takes rise in the Rocky mountains . . . there is a variety of wild animals, perticularly the bighorn which is to be found in great numbers on this river."—Clark

July 30, 1806 (On the Yellowstone River near Glendive, Mont.)
"I also saw some of the Bighorn Animals at a distance on the hills."—Clark

Aug. 5, 1806 (Near mouth of the Yellowstone River)
"I had not proceeded far before I saw a ram of the bighorn animal near the top of a Lar'd Bluff. I assended the hill with a view to kill the ram, the Musquetors was so noumerous that I could not keep them off my gun long enough to take sight and by that means Missed."—Clark

Lewis' description of the bighorn sheep was remarkably detailed.

May 25, 1805 (Above the mouth of the Musselshell River)
"As we ascended the river today I saw several gangs of bighorned Anamals on the face of the steep bluffs & clifts on the Star^d side and sent drewyer to kill one which he accomplished; Capt. Clark and Bratton who were on shore each killed one of these anamals this evening. The head and horns of the male which Drewyer killed weighed 27 lbs. it was somewhat larger than the male of the common deer, the boddy reather thicker and deeper and not so long in proportion to it's hight as the common deer; the head and horns are remarkably large compared with the other part of

173

the anamal; the whole form is much more delicate than that of the common goat, and there is a great disparity in the size of the male and female than between those of either deer or goat. the eye is large and prominant, the puple of deep sea green and small, the iris of a silvery colour much like the common sheep; the bone above the eye is remarkably promenant; the head nostrils and division of the upper lip are precisely in form like the sheep. there legs resemble the sheep more than any other anamal with which I am acquainted tho' they are more delicately formed, like the sheep they stand forward in the knee and the lower joint of the foreleg is smallest where it joins the knee, the hoof is black and large in proportion, is divided, very open and roundly pointed at the toe, like the sheep, is much hollowed and sharp on the under edge like the Scotch goat, has two small hoofs behind each foot below the ankle as the goat and sheep and deer have. the belley, inner side of the legs, and extremity of the rump and butocks for about two inches arround the but of the tale, are white, as is also the tale, except just at it's extremity on the upper side which is of a dark brown. the tail is about three inches in length covered with short hair, or at least not longer than that of the boddy; the outher parts of the anamal are of a duskey brown or reather a lead coloured light brown; the anamal is now sheding it's winter coat which is thick not quite as long as that of the deer and appears to be intermixed with a considerable quantity of a fine fur which lyes next to the skin & conceald by the coarser hear; the shape of the hair itself is celindric as that of the antelope is but is smaller, shorter, and not compressed or flattened as that of the deer's winter coat is. I believe this anamel only sheds it's hair once a year. it has eight fore teeth in the under jaw and no canine teeth. The horns are largest at their base, and occupy the crown of the head almost entirely. they are compressed, bent backwards and lunated; the surface swelling into wavey rings which incircleing the horn continue to succeed each other from the base to the extremity and becoming less elivated and more distant as they recede from the head. the horn for about two thirds of it's length is filled with a porus bone which is united with the frontal bone. I obtained the bones of the upper part of the head of this animal at the big bone lick." (in Kentucky) "the horns of the female are small, but are also compressed and bent backwards and incircled with a succession of wavy rings. the horn is of a light brown colour; when dressed it is almost white extreemly transparent and very elastic. this horn is used by the natives in constructing their bows; I have no doubt but it would make eligant and useful hair combs, and might probably answer as many valuable purposes to civilized man, as it does to the savages, who form their water-cups, spoons and platters of it. the females have already brought forth their young.

indeed from the size of the young I suppose that they produce them in March. they have from one to two at birth. they feed on grass but principally on the arromatic herbs which grow on the clifts at inaccessable hights which they usually frequent. the places they generally scelect to lodg is the cranies or crevices of the rocks in the faces of inaccessable precepices, where the wolf nor bear can reach them and where indeed man himself would in many instancies find a similar deficiency; yet these anamals bound from rock to rock and stand apparently in the most careless manner on the sides of precipices of many hundred feet. they are very shye and are quick of both sent and sight."

July 29, 1806 (Below the junction of Marias and Missouri Rivers)
"The eye is large and prominent, the puple of a pale sea green, the iris of a light yellowish brown colour."—Lewis

The explorers were much surprised and entertained by the antics of the bighorns which inhabited the cliffs and bluffs along the river.

April 29, 1805 (Near mouth of Yellowstone)
"Set out this morning at the usual hour, had not proceeded far e'er we Saw a female & her faun of the Bighorn animal on the top of a Bluff lying, the noise we made allarmed them and they came down on the side of the bluff which had but little slope being nearly purpendicular. I directed two men to kill those anamals, one went on top and the other man near the water. they had two shots at the doe while in motion without effect. Those animals run and Skiped about with great ease on this declivity & appeared to prefur it to the leavel bottom or plain."—Clark

July 18, 1805 (Vic. of Cascade, Montana)
"Set out early this morning. previous to our departure saw a large herd of the Bighorned anamals on an immencely high and nearly perpendicular clift opposite to us; on the fase of this clift they walked about and bounded from rock to rock with apparent unconcern where it appeared to me that no quadruped could have stood, and from which had they made one false step they must have been precipitated at least a 500 feet. this anamal appears to frequent such precepices and clifts where in fact they are perfectly secure from the pursuit of the wolf, bear, or even man himself."—Lewis

July 10, 1806 (Beaverhead River valley)
"Those animals feed on the grass which grows on the Sides of this Mountain and in the narrow bottoms on the Water courses near the steep sides of the Mountains on which they can make their escape from pursute of wolves, Bear, etc."—Clark

175

July 29, 1806 (On the Missouri below the Mouth of the Marias River)
"These animals abound in this quarter keeping themselves principally confined to the steep clifts and bluffs of the river."—Lewis

Laminated bows did not originate with modern archers. Lewis and Clark found the Shoshone Indians of the Lemhi River valley using laminated bows made from the horns of mountain sheep and the antlers of elk.

Aug. 23, 1805 (Shoshone Indian village)
"They have spoons made of the Buffaloe's horn and those of the Bighorn.
"They sometimes make bows of the Elk's horn and those of the Bighorn . . . The bows of the bighorn are formed of small peices laid flat and cemented with gleue and rolled with sinews, after which they are covered on the back with sinews and glew, and highly ornimented as they are much prized."—Lewis

July 30, 1806 (On the Missouri below mouth of Marias River)
"We halted several times in the course of the day to kill some bighorns being anxious to procure a few more skins and skeletons of this animal; I was fortunate enough to procure one other male and female for this purpose which I had prepared accordingly."—Lewis

Aug. 3, 1806 (Near the mouth of the Yellowstone River)
"On the side of this bluff I saw some of the Mountain Bighorn animals. I assended the hill below the Bluff. The Musquetors were so noumerous that I could not Shute with any certainty, and therefore soon returned to the Canoes. I had not proceeded far before I saw a large gangue of ewes and yearlins and fawns or lambs of the bighorn, and at a distance alone I saw a ram. Landed and Sent Labiech to kill the ram, which he did kill and brought him on board. This ram is not near as large as many I have seen. However, he is sufficiently large for a Sample. I directed Bratton to Skin him with his head, horns and feet (attached) to the Skin and Save all the bone. I have now the skin and bone of a Ram, a Ewe, & a yearlin ram of those Big Horn animals."—Clark

The two sets of horns purchased from the Indians at Fort Mandan in the winter of 1804 were included in the shipment of skins and Indian goods sent back to President Jefferson in the big batteau in April, 1805.

CHAPTER IX
Diving and Wading Birds

Evidently Lewis and Clark were not acquainted with many of the diving and wading birds. They recognized a loon on the Pacific coast, but concluded that it was the same as the common loon of the eastern states. They identified the grebes merely as large divers and small divers; and, although they appear to have written the first brief description of the western grebe, they designated it as a "second species of loon."

Clark described the tubular nostrils of the Pacific fulmar, and drew a sketch of the bird's head to emphasize this peculiar feature of anatomy, but he classified it as a gull.

On the other hand, Lewis' description of the white pelican and the American egret are remarkably detailed and accurate.

PACIFIC LOON

Coues[1] identified Lewis' "speckled loon" as the western subspecies of the black-throated loon, *Gavia arctica pacifica* (Lawrence).

March 7, 1806 (Written at Fort Clatsop)

"the Speckled loon found on every part of the rivers of this country, they are the same size, colours, and form with those of the Atlantic coast."
—Lewis

HOLBOELL'S GREBE

This bird, *Podiceps grisegena holbollii* Reinhardt, had no scientific status until Bonaparte described and named it, *Podiceps rubricollis*, in 1828. However, Lewis and Clark described it briefly as the larger of two divers seen on the lower Columbia River and in the vicinity of Fort Clatsop.

March 10, 1806 (Written at Fort Clatsop)

"the divers are the same as those of the Atlantic States . . . the larger species are about the size of the teal and can flye a short distance which the small one scarcely ever attempts. they have a short tail. their colour is also an uniform brickredish brown, the beak is streight and pointed. the feet are of the same form of the other species and the legs are remarkably thin and flat, one edge being in front. the food of both species is fish, and the flesh unfit for use."—Lewis

Lewis was correct in saying that Holboell's grebe, and the pied-billed grebe (described below) were common to both the Pacific and the Atlantic coasts. Both species are plentiful on our eastern and western sea coasts during the winter months; and Holboell's grebe has been reported on the Great Lakes, as well, during winter, but Bent[2] points out the wintering records from the interior of the continent are few and unsatisfactory.

The fact that Lewis underrated the grebes' ability to fly can be excused on the basis of his limited observations and short acquaintance with the species.

Coues, in his early commentary[3] on the zoology of the expedition, suggested that the "larger diver" described by Lewis was probably the western grebe rather than Holboell's grebe, but he reversed his decision on this point in his later work.[4]

In any case, if Coues' judgment can be accepted, Lewis probably wrote the first description, despite its lack of diagnostic detail, of Holboell's grebe.

PIED-BILLED GREBE

Coues concluded from Lewis' description that the "small diver" was a pied-billed grebe, *Pedilymbus podiceps* (Linnaeus), and there appears to be little reason to question his determination.

March 10, 1806 (Written at Fort Clatsop)

"the small speceis (of diver) has some white feathers about the rump with no perceptable tail and is very active and quick in its motion; the body is a redish brown. the beak sharp and somewhat curved like that of the pheasant. the toes are not connected, but webed like those described of the black duck (coot)."—Lewis

WESTERN GREBE

The western grebe, *Aechmophorus occidentalis* (Lawrence), is another bird that was first described by Lewis and Clark. It was not technically described until 1858, when Lawrence listed it under the name *Podiceps occidentalis*.

Although it breeds in the northern prairie states and the prairie provinces of Canada, Lewis and Clark did not see it until they reached the Columbia River in the autumn of 1805. They described this grebe as a "second species of loon"; but Coues[5] concluded, on the basis of Lewis' description, that the bird described was the western grebe rather than a loon.

March 7, 1806 (Written at Fort Clatsop)

"The second speceis we first met with at the great falls of the Columbia and from thence down. this bird is not more than half the size of the speckled loon, its neck is long, slender and white in front. the colour of the body and back of the neck and head are of a dun or ash colour, the breast, and belley are white. the beak is like that of the speckled loon and like them it cannot fly but flutters along on the top of the water or dives for security when pursued."—Lewis

This description would seem to be sufficiently detailed for identification; but, of course, Lewis was mistaken in assuming that these birds could not fly.

PACIFIC FULMAR

This is Clark's fourth species of gull. It was identified by Coues[6] as the Pacific fulmar, *Fulmarus glacialis rodgersii* Cassin.

Clark's description:

March 6, 1806 (Written at Fort Clatsop)
"a White Gull about the size of the second with a remarkable beak; adjoining the head and on the base of the upper chap there is an elivated orning of the same substance with the beak which forms the nostriels . . . ; it is somewhat in this form (illustration). the feet are webed and the legs and feet of a yellow colour. The form of the wings, body, etc. are much that of the 2nd species. This bird was seen on Haley's bay."

WHITE PELICAN

The description of this bird, *Pelicanus erythrorhynchos* Gmelin, written by Lewis did not appear in Clark's diary covering this period. It was found by Thwaites in Codex Q[7] which consists of a separate body of notes in Lewis' handwriting.

Lewis' description:

Aug. 8, 1804 (Near mouth of Little Sioux River)
"we had seen but a few aquatic fouls of any kind on the river since we commenced our journey up the Missouri, a few geese accompanied by their young, the wood duck which is common to every part of this country & crains of several kinds which will be discribed in their respective places this day after we had passed the river Souix as called by Mr. Mackay or as is more properly called the stone river, I saw a great number of feathers floating down the river those feathers had a very extraordinary appearance as they appeared in such quantities as to cover prettey generally sixty or seventy yards of the breadth of the river. for three miles after I saw those feathers continue to run in that manner, we did not percieve from whence they came. at length we were surprised by the appearance of a flock of Pillican *(Pelecanus erythrorhynchus)* at rest on

a large sand bar attatched to a small Island the number of which would if estimated appear almost in credible; they apeared to cover several acres of ground, and were no doubt engaged in procuring their ordinary food; which is fish; on our approach they flew and left behind them several small fish of about eight inches in length, none of which I had seen before. the Pellican rested again on a sand bar above the Island which we called after them from the number we saw on it. we now approached them within about three hundred yards before they flew; I then fired at random among the flock with my rifle and brought one down; the discription of this bird is as follows:

Habits

They are a bird of clime remain on the coast of Floriday and the borders of the Gulph of mexico & even the lower portion of the Mississippi during the winter and in the Spring (see for date my *thermometrical observations at the river Dubois*), visit this country and that farther north for the purpose of raising their young. this duty seems now to have been accomplished from the appearance of a young Pilacon which was killed by one of our men this morning, and they are now in large flocks on their return to their winter quarters. they lay usually two eggs only and chuise for a nest a couple of logs of drift wood near the water's edge and with out any other preperation but the thraught formed by the proximity of those two logs which form a trought they set and hatch their young which after (wards they) nurture with fish their common food.

	Measure		
	Ft.		In.
From beak to toe	5.		8
Tip to tip of wing	9	.	4.
Beak Length	I	.	3.
D? Width	from	.	2. to 1½
	F		
Neck Length	I	.	11.
1st Joint of wing	I	.	1.
2ed D?	I	.	4.½
3rd D?	—	.	7.
4th D?	—	.	2¾
Length of leg including foot		.	10.
D? of thy		.	11.

Discription of Colour &c. The beak is a whiteish yellow the under part connected to a bladder like pouch, this pouch is connected to both sides of the lower beak and extends down on the under side of the neck and terminates in the stomach this pouch is uncovered with feathers, and is formed (of) two skins the one on the inner and the other on the outer side a small quantity of flesh and strings of which the anamal has at pleasure the power of moving or drawing in such manner as to contract it at pleasure. in the present subject I measured this pouch and found it's contents 5. gallons of water. The feet are webbed large and of a yellow colour, it has four toes the hinder toe is longer than in most aquatic fouls, the nails are black, not sharp and ½ an inch in length. The plumage generally is white, the feathers are thin compared with the swan goose or most aquatic fouls and has but little or no down on the body. the upper part of the head is covered with black feathers short, as far as the back part of the head. the yellow skin unfeathered extends back from the upper beak and opening of the mouth and comes to a point just behind the eye The large feathers of the wings are of a deep black colour the 1st & 2nd joint of (the wings) from the body above the same is covered with a second layer of white feathers which extend quite half the length of those large feathers of the wing the thye is covered with feathers within a quarter of an inch of the knee.

1st. Joint of wing has feathers		No. 21:Length.	9 Inch
			Black
2ed	D?	No. 17:Length......13 Inch	
3rd	D?	No. 5:Length......18.Inch	
4th	D?	No. 3:Length...... 19.Ich	

it has a curious frothy substance which seems to divide its feathers from the flesh of the body and seems to be composes of Globules of air and perfectly imbraces the part of the feather which extends through the skin. the wind pipe terminates in the center of the lower part of the upper and unfeathered part of the pouch and is secured by an elastic valve commanded at pleasure.

Sept. 11, 1804 (Near Brule City, S. Dak.)
    "the men with me killed . . . a pelican."—Clark

Oct. 18, 1804 (Vic. of Cannonball River)
    "our hunters killed . . . a pelican."—Clark

Oct. 20, 1805 (Near Memaloose Islands in Columbia River)
    "Saw great numbers of Pelicans and black Cormerants."—Clark

July 17, 1806 (Clark on Yellowstone River, near mouth of Boulder Creek)
    "I saw a single Pelican which is the first which I have seen on this river."—Clark

Aug. 5, 1806 (Missouri River near mouth of Milk River)
    "the geese cannot fly a present; I saw a solitary Pellicon the other day

in the same situation. this happens from their sheding or casting the feathers of the wings at this season."—Lewis

Sept. 4, 1806 (Near site of Sioux City, Ia.)

"We see no Species of Game on the river as usial except wild geese and pelicans."—Clark

Sept. 7, 1806 (Above site of Council Bluffs, Ia.)

"two pelicans were killed today."—Clark

FARALLON CORMORANT

Thwaites[8] concluded that the cormorants seen by Lewis and Clark on the Columbia River and its tributaries were the white-crested variety rather than the double-crested cormorants of the Lake and Prairie States. He was evidently influenced by Coues, who had identified them as such in 1893.[9] However, because the southern limit of the winter range of the white-crested cormorant is southern British Columbia, it seems more likely that the birds in question were Farallon cormorants of the sub-species *Phalacrocorax auritus albociliatus* Ridgway.

Feb. 6, 1806 (Fort Clatsop)

"The Cormorant is a large black duck which feeds on fish; I procieve no difference between it and these found in the rivers of the Atlantic Coasts. we met with it as high up as the entrance of the Chopunnish into the Kooskooske (Clearwater) river. they increase in numbers as we decended, and formed much the greatest portion of waterfowls which we saw on the Columbia untill we reached tidewater, where they also abound but do not bear a similar proportion to the fowls found in this quarter. we found this bird fat and tolerably flavoured as we decended the Columbia."

AMERICAN BITTERN

Clark referred to the bittern *Botaurus lentiginosus* (Rackett), as the Indian hen[10] in connection with his discussion of the avocet seen on May 1, 1805. His diary includes no other reference to this species.

AMERICAN EGRET

The following description of the American egret, *Casmerodius albus egretta* (Gmelin), was discovered by Thwaites[11] in some rough notes written by Lewis, who evidently intended to incorporate them in his diary at a later date.

Aug. 2, 1804 (Near mouth of Boyer River, Iowa)

"This day one of our Hunters brought me a *white Heron*. this bird is an inhabitant of ponds and Marasses, and feeds upon tadpoles, frogs, small fish, etc. they are common to the Mississippi and the lower part of the Ohio River, i.e., as high as the falls of that river.

"this bird weighed two lbs. its plumage is perfectly white and very thin, from extremity of beak to the extremity of toe (it measured) 4F. 7¼ I., from tipp to tip of wing on the back 4F. 11 I.

"Its beak is yellow, pointed, flated crosswise and 5 Inches in length, from the upper region of the bill to the eye is one inch in length, covered with a smooth yellow skin, the plumage of the head projecting towards the upper bill and coming to a point at an Inch beyond the eyes on the center of the upper bill. The mouth opens to distance of the eyes. The eye is full and projecting reather, it is 7/10 of half an inch. four joints in the wing.

1st joint from body in length					6	inches
2nd "	"	"	"	"	8¼	"
3rd "	"	"	"	"	3½	"
4th "	"	"	"	"	1	"
1st joint Number of feathers					7	Length of 3 (Inches?)
2nd "	"	"	"		18	
3rd "	"	"	"		6	Length from 10 to 12
4th "	"	"	"		5	" 12

"Its legs are black, the neck and beak occupy ½ its length, it has four toes on a foot, the outer toe on the right foot is from the joining of the leg to extremity of toe nails 4 Inches & ¼, has four joints exclusive of the nail joint, the next is 4¾ inches has three joints exclusive of the nale joints, the next is 3¾ and has two joints, the heel toe has one joint only and is 3 Inches in length. the nails are long, sharp and black. the eye is of a deep seagreen colour, with a circle of pale yellow around the sight forming a border to the outer part of the eye of about half the width of the whole eye. the tale has 12 feathers of six inches in length, the wings when foalded are the same length with the tale.

"has 2 remarkable tufts of long feathers on each side joining the body at the upper joint of the wing. these cover the feathers of the 1st joint of the wings when they are even extended."

GREAT BLUE HERON

Lewis and Clark made only casual reference to the great blue heron, *Ardea herodias* Linnaeus, but the two citations which follow are sufficient to show that they were familiar with this species.

Aug. 11, 1804 (Vic. of Badger Lake, Monona Co., Iowa)
"Great Nos. of Herrons this evening."—Clark

March 6, 1806 (Written at Fort Clatsop)

"The large Blue and brown Herons or crains as they are called in the U' States are found below tide water, they are the same as those of the U' States."—Clark

Obviously Lewis and Clark did not distinguish between the races of blue herons that are recognized today. The bird described at Fort Clatsop probably belonged to the subspecies *hyperonca*, whereas those seen near Badger Lake belonged to the eastern subspecies *herodias*.

WHOOPING CRANE

The whooping crane, *Grus americana* (Linnaeus), is now one of the rarest birds in North America. In spite of the most vigorous efforts on the part of federal and state authorities to give these birds absolute protection throughout their range they have failed to increase in numbers. Today, less than three dozen of these magnificent birds are known to be alive.

The whooping crane is a bird of the wilderness which does not tolerate even casual human associations. They inhabited the prairie provinces of Canada and the northern plains states during the summer months prior to the settlement and cultivation of these areas. They wintered in the Gulf states from Florida to Mexico in primitive times.

Although originally described by Mark Catesby in 1772 and named by Linnaeus in 1776, the whooping crane was generally unknown to the early 19th century naturalists because they were seldom seen in the eastern states.

Lewis and Clark reported them on the Missouri in the spring of 1805, and on the Columbia in the fall of the same year. Since they were unable to collect a specimen their description of this species lacks detail.

April 11, 1805 (Near subsequent site of Fort Berthold)

"Saw some large white cranes pass up the river. these are the largest bird of that genus common to the country through which the Missouri and Mississippi pass. they are perfectly white except the large feathers of the first two joints of the wing which is black."—Lewis

Oct. 26, 1805 (Columbia River near The Dalles, Oregon)

"saw a great number of white crains flying in Different directions very high."—Clark

The whooping crane appears to have started on the down grade more than 75 years ago. Coues[12] in 1874 said of it:

"I have never seen it alive excepting in Northern Dakota, where I observed it in August, September and October, and where, probably, it breeds. Its principal line of migration appears to be the Mississippi Valley at large; accounts of its presence all along this belt from Texas to Minnesota, for a considerable breadth, are unanimous and conclusive. Here it seems to be chiefly migratory, but there is every reason to believe that it breeds in Minnesota and, as just said, in Dakota, as it does further north."

According to Bent[13] a few pairs of whooping cranes were still breeding in central Illinois in 1877; they were found breeding in Hancock County, Iowa, in 1894; five of these cranes were seen in Yellowstone Park in 1914; a few pairs were reported at Quill Lake in Saskatchewan in 1917; and in the spring of 1923, a flock of five adults and one juvenile was reliably reported in the vicinity of Long Lake, south of Steele, North Dakota.

The outlook for the whooping crane is not good; we can only hope that a few of them may survive indefinitely.

SANDHILL CRANE

The sandhill crane, *Grus canadensis tabida* (Peters), population is in no such precarious a condition as that of the whooper. Even though their primitive breeding range has been much reduced by the encroachment of agriculture, small breeding colonies have managed to survive in the Lake States, the Prairie States and the Canadian Provinces. At present, the species does not appear to be in any danger of extinction despite the fact that their numbers have been greatly reduced since the early years of the present century.

Lewis and Clark did not mention the sandhill crane in North Dakota, nor in eastern Montana. Their first recorded observation appears to have been made south of the Great Falls of the Missouri, in the vicinity of the Gates of the Mountains. Thereafter they reported seeing these birds frequently in the Jefferson River valley, in the Clearwater River valley in Idaho, and on the lower Columbia River.

July 21, 1805 (Vic. of the Gates of the Mountains, Montana)

"Saw several of the large brown or Sandhill crain today with their young. the young Crain is as large as a turkey and cannot fly; they are of a bright red bey colour, or that of the common deer at this season. This bird feeds on grass principally and is found in the river bottoms."—Lewis

July 29, 1805 (Near Three Forks, Montana)

"the hunters brought in a living young sandhill crain; it has nearly obtained its growth but cannot fly; they had pursued it and caught it in the meadows. its colour is precisely that of the red deer, we see a number of the old or full grown crains of this species feeding in these meadows. This young animal is very fierce and strikes a severe blow with its beak;

185

after amusing myself with it I had it set at liberty apparently much pleased with being relieved from his capativity."—Lewis

Oct. 31, 1805 (Near the Cascades of the Columbia)
"Jo Fields killed a Sand hill crain."—Clark

March 4, 1806 (Written at Fort Clatsop)
"The large bluish brown or Sandhill Crain are found in the vallys of the Rocky Mountains in summer and autumn when they raise their young, and in the winter and spring on this river below tidewater and on this coast. they are the same as those common to the Southern and Western States where they are most generally known by the name of the Sandhill Crain."—Clark

May 21, 1806 (Near Kamiah, Idaho)
"one of our party brought in a young sandhill crain, it was about the size of a pateridge and of a redish brown colour. it appeared to be about 5 or 6 days old; these crains are abundant in this neighborhood."—Lewis

May 25, 1806 (Near Kamiah, Idaho)
"Gibson and Shields returned this evening haveing killed a Sandhill crain only."—Lewis

CHAPTER X
Ducks, Geese, and Swans

Among the waterfowl, Lewis and Clark made some noteworthy discoveries. Among them are the ring-necked duck, the lesser Canada goose, the white-fronted goose, and the whistling swan.

They wrote descriptions of several other species which were new to them but not new to science.

It is interesting to find that they were the first to report finding Canada geese nesting in trees on the upper Missouri in Montana; and that they coined the term "whistling swan" in describing and comparing this species with the Trumpeter.

BLUE-WINGED TEAL

The explorers merely mentioned seeing this duck, *Anas discors* (Linnaeus), at various points on the Missouri. In their descriptive account of the birds observed west of the Rockies we find the following statement:

March 10, 1806 (Written at Fort Clatsop)

"The blue-winged teal are a very excellent duck, and are the same with those of the Atlantic coast."—Lewis

They may have seen the blue-winged teal in the Astoria area, but it is of rare occurrence west of the Cascade Mountains.

BUFFLEHEAD DUCK

Lewis and Clark consistently referred to the bufflehead as the "black and white duck."

March 9, 1806 (Written at Fort Clatsop)

"The black and white Duck are small about the size of the blue-winged teal, or reather larger. the male is butifully varigated with black and white. the white occupies the side of the head, breast and back. black, the tail, large feathers of the wing, two tufts of feathers which cover the upper part of the wings when folded, the neck and head. the female is darker, or has much less white about her. I take this to be the same species of duck common to the Ohio, as also the Atlantic coast, and some-times called *butter-box*. the back[1] is wide and short, and, as well as the legs, of a dark colour. the flesh of this duck is verry well flavoured. I think superior to the duckinmallard."—Lewis

187

In commenting on the zoology of the expedition, in 1876, Coues identified this "black and white" duck as *Bucephala albeola* (Linnaeus).

CANVAS-BACK DUCK

Despite the fact that the canvas-back duck, *Aythya valisineria* (Wilson), had evidently been known to hunters in the East for an indeterminate number of years prior to the Lewis and Clark expedition, it was not recognized as an established species until Alexander Wilson published his American Ornithology in 1814.[2]

March 9, 1806 (Written at Fort Clatsop)

"A beautifull duck and one of the most delicious in the world is found in considerable quantities in this neighborhood during the Autumn and winter. this is the same with that known in the Delliware, Susquehannah, and Potomac by the name of *Canvisback* and in the James River by that of shell-Drake; in the latter river however I am informed that they have latterly almost entirely disappeared. To the epicure of those parts of the Union where this duck abounds nothing need be added in praise of the exquisite flavor of this duck. I have frequently eaten them in several parts of the Union and think those of the Columbia equally delicious. this duck is never found above tidewater; we did not meet with them untill after we reached the marshey Islands; and I believe that they have already left this neighborhood, but whether they have gone northwardly or Southwardly I am unable to determine; nor do I know in what part of the Continent they raise their young."—Lewis

MALLARD DUCK

The mallard, *Anas platyrhynchos* Linnaeus, was given scientific status by Linnaeus in 1766. Being one of the most widely distributed species in North America, the explorers were thoroughly acquainted with this duck. They mentioned the mallard repeatedly in recording their observations on the occurrence of waterfowl in both the Missouri and Columbia river watersheds. Generally, however, they designated it by its old colloquial name, "duckinmallard."

Although Lewis and Clark's observations on the mallard are not particularly enlightening, perhaps a few of their comments are of sufficient interest to transcribe.

July 29, 1805 (Vic. of Three Forks, Mont.)

"The Duchanmallard were first seen on the 20th inst. and I forget to note it; they are now abundant with their young but do not breed in the Missouri[3] below the mountains."—Lewis

188

Aug. 2, 1805 (Jefferson River, near White Tail Deer Creek)

"many young ducks both of the duckinmallard and red-headed fishing ducks."—Lewis

Nov. 5, 1805 (Vic. of Sauvies Island, near mouth of Willamette River)

"I could not sleep for the noise kept up by Swans, Geese, White and black brants, Ducks, etc. on the opposite base, and sand hill Crane, they were emencely numerous and their noise horrid."—Clark

Although the foregoing does not relate to the mallard specifically, it carries impact with respect to the abundance of waterfowl on the lower Columbia during primitive times.

March 9, 1806 (Written at Fort Clatsop)

"The duckinmallard, or common large duck which resembles the domestic duck, are the same here with those of the U' States. They are abundant and are found on every part of the river below the mountains. they remain here all winter, but I believe they do not continue during winter far above tide water."—Lewis

RED-BREASTED MERGANSER

Authorities now appear to agree that Lewis and Clark's "red-headed fishing duck," first seen by the explorers at the Great Falls of the Missouri, must have been the red-breasted merganser, *Mergus serrator* Linnaeus.

Coues,[4] however, in his earlier commentary on the zoology of the expedition, suggested that the "red-headed duck" might be the redhead, *Aythya americana* (Eyton).

In his later publication (1893), however, Coues[5] identified this "red-headed fishing duck" as the red-breasted merganser, *Mergus serrator*.

As will be seen below, Lewis' description of this duck is too incomplete for positive identification. If the bird was the red-breasted merganser, he described only the female because the head of the male is an iridescent black, except during the autumn moult when the black is replaced by feathers of a brownish-red color.

June 21, 1805 (Vic. of Great Falls, Mont.)

"I have seen for the first time on the Missouri at these falls, a species of fishing ducks with white wings, brown and white body and head and a part of the neck adjoining of a brick red, and the beak narrow; which I take to be the same common to the James river, the Potomic and Susquehanna."
—Lewis

March 9, 1806 (Written at Fort Clatsop)

"The red-headed fishing duck is common to every part of the river and are found as well in the Rocky Mountains as elsewhere; in short this was the only duck we saw on the waters of the Columbia within the mountains. they feed principally on crawfish; and are the same in every rispect as those on the rivers in the mountains of the Atlantic Ocean."—Lewis

RING-NECKED DUCK

The ring-necked duck, *Aythya collaris* (Donovan), was unknown to science when Lewis and Clark discovered and described it in 1806. The first mention of this duck in the technical literature will be found in *Donovan's British Birds, VI,* pl. 147, which was published in 1809.[6]

Lewis' description:

March 28, 1806 (Vic. of Deer Island in the Columbia River)

"we have seen more waterfowl on this island than we have previously seen since we left Fort Clatsop, consisting of geese, ducks, large swan, and Sand hill crains. I saw a few of the Canvis-back duck. the duckinmallard are the most abundant. one of the hunters killed a duck which appeared to be the male, it was a size less than the duckinmallard. the head as low as the croop, the back tail and covert of the wings were of fine black with a small addmixture of perple about the head and neck, the belley and breast were white; some long feathers which lie underneath the wings and cover the thye were of a pale dove colour with fine black specks; the large feathers of the wings are a dove colour, the legs are dark, the feet are composed of 4 toes each of which are three in front connected by a web, the 4th is short flat and placed high on the heel behind the leg. the tail is composed of 14 short pointed feathers. the beak of this duck is remarkably wide, and is 2 inches in length, the upper chap exceeds the under one in both length and width, insomuch that when the beak is closed the under is entirely concealed by the upper chap. the tongue, indenture of the margin of the chaps etc. are like those of the mallard. the nostrils are large longitudinal and connected. a narrow strip of white garnishes the upper part or base of the upper chap—this is succeeded by a pale skye blue colour which occupies about one inch of the chap, is again succeeded by a transverse stripe of white and the extremity is of a pure black. the eye is moderately large the puple black and iris of a fine orrange yellow: the feathers on the crown of the head are longer than those on the upper part of the neck and other parts of the head; these feathers give it the appearance of being crested."

March 29, 1806 (Vic. of Sauvies Island in the Columbia)

"the female of the duck which was described yesterday is of a uniform dark brown with some yellowish brown intermixed in small specks on the back, neck and breast."—Lewis

On the basis of these descriptions Coues[7] identified these ducks as ring-necks, *Nyroca collaris* (Donovan).

SHOVELLER DUCK

The explorers found the shoveller, *Spatula clypeata* (Linnaeus), on the Columbia between The Dalles, Oregon, and the mouth of the Walla Walla River.

April 25, 1806 (Vic. of Arlington, Oregon)

"We killed six ducks in the course of the day; one of them was of a species which I had never before seen. I therefore had the most material parts of it reserved for a specimen, the legs yellow and feet webbed as those of the duckinmallard."

May 8, 1806 (On the Clearwater River)

"Shields killed a duck of an uncommon kind. the head, beak and wing of which I preserved. the beak is remarkably wide and obtusely pointed. on it's edges it is furnished with a sceries of teeth very long and fine not unlike the teeth of a comb. the belley is of a brick red, the lower part of the neck white, the upper part or but of the wing is a sky blue, underneath which a narrow stripe of white succeeds marking the wing transversely, the large feathers are of a dark colour. tail short and pointed and consists of 12 dark brown feathers. the back is black and sides white; legs yellow and feet formed like the Duckinmallard which it also resembles in size and form. the eye is moderately large, puple black, and iris of an orrange colour. the colours and appearance of the female is percisely that of the duckinmallard only reather smaller."

Coues identified the bird described above as a shoveller.[8]

WOOD DUCK

The wood duck, *Aix sponsa* (Linnaeus), as were the mallard, bufflehead, bluewinged teal, and shoveller, was named by Linnaeus in 1766. However, in 1826 Boie reclassified this species, transferring it from *Anas sponsa* Linnaeus to the genus *Aix*. Thus, Lewis and Clark contributed nothing toward the discovery or the original description of this species. They did, however, add to our knowledge of the range of the wood duck at a time when nothing was known about the limits of its range in the interior of the continent.

July 29, 1805 (Vic. of Three Forks, Montana)

"We have not seen the summer duck since we left that place (Great Falls of the Missouri) nor do I believe it is an inhabitant of the Rock Mountains."—Lewis

March 31, 1806 (Vic. of Sandy River, Oregon)

"in the entrance of Seal river I saw a summer duck or wood duck as they are sometimes called, this is the same with those of our country and is the first I have seen since I entered the Rocky Mountains last summer."— Lewis

Lewis was mistaken in assuming that the wood duck did not inhabit the Rocky Mountain region. Bent[9] defines the breeding range of this species in the following words:

"United States and Canada, entirely across the continent. Breeds locally in almost every State and southern Province, where suitable conditions exist."

In this connection we should not be confused by Kortright's range map[10] which shows only the "main ranges" of the wood duck.

AMERICAN BRANT

The explorers mentioned seeing both brant and geese flying southward in large flocks during the fall of 1804, and again in the spring of 1805 after leaving Fort Mandan.

May 5, 1805 (Between Poplar and Milk Rivers on the Missouri)

"Saw great numbers of white brant also the common brown brant, geese of the common kind and a small species of geese which differ considerably from the common Canadian goose; . . . ."—Lewis

It is difficult to segregate Lewis and Clark's comments concerning any single species of brant or goose. In many instances, as in the quotation cited above, they included references to two or more species in a single sentence or paragraph. This, of course, can be accounted for by the fact that geese and brant frequently migrate in mixed flocks, and Lewis and Clark merely recorded the day's events as they saw them. By and large, clear cut accounts of single species only occur in connection with their attempts to write technical descriptions of individual species.

The brown brant, *Branta bernicla hrota* (Müller), was so described during the winter spent at Fort Clatsop:

March 8, 1806 (Fort Clatsop)

"The Brown or pided brant is much the same size and form of the white only that their wings are considerably longer and more pointed. the plumage of the upper part of the body neck head and tail is much the colour of the canadian goose but reather darker in consequence of some dark brown feathers which are distributed and irregularly scattered throughout. they have not the white on the neck and sides of the head as the goose has nor is the neck darker than the body. like the goose there are some white

192

feathers on the rump at the joining of the tail. the beak is dark and the legs and feet also dark with a greenish cast; the breast and belley are of a lighter colour than the back and is also irregularly intermixed with dark brown and black feathers which give it a pided appearance. the flesh of this bird is dark and in my estimation reather better than that of the goose. the habits of this bird are the same nearly with the goose and white brant with this difference that they do not remain in this climate in such numbers during the winter as the others, and that it sets out earlier in the fall season on it's return to the south and arrives later in the spring than the goose. I see no difference between this bird and that called simply *the brant,* common to the lakes the Ohio and Mississippe, etc."

One might question whether Lewis and Clark were not actually describing the black brant, *Branta nigricans* (Lawrence), in this instance because it is much more abundant on the Pacific coast than the brown variety. There appears to have been no question in Coues' mind on this point, however, for he made a positive determination in favor of the brown brant.

The major difference between the two races of brant in North America involves the degree of darkness of the brown areas of the plumage. Bent[11] points out that both *Branta bernicla hrota* and *Branta nigricans* occupy neighboring breeding ranges in Arctic America, and that there is strong evidence of intergradation between them.

The migratory habits of these two subspecies of brant cannot be explained. No one knows why the majority of brown brants winter on the Atlantic coast south of New Jersey, and a small minority of them seek the coastal waters of the Pacific; nor can one explain why black brants habitually winter on the Pacific coast and occur, at best, only as infrequent stragglers on the Atlantic.

It is interesting to note also that the black brant, despite its scarcity on the Atlantic coast, was originally described from a specimen collected at Egg Harbor, New Jersey.[12]

CANADA GOOSE

Probably in view of President Jefferson's admonition about wasting time on familiar species, Lewis and Clark did not attempt to describe the Canada goose, *Branta canadensis* (Linnaeus). However, they frequently referred to its abundance in specific areas during its migratory and breeding seasons. Occasionally they shot geese and other waterfowl for the cooking pot if other game happened to be scarce. In recording daily kill-records, however, they rarely specified the variety of goose or brant that was killed, so we have no way of knowing how many Canada geese were included among the 104 geese and brants accounted for.

Some of their observations, particularly those relating to the nesting habits of the Canada goose on the upper Missouri River, are noteworthy.

April 13, 1805 (Vic. of the Little Missouri River)

"This lake and its discharge we call goos Egg from the circumstances of Capt. Clark shooting a goose while on her nest in the top of a lofty cottonwood tree, from which we afterwards took one egg. The wild gees frequently build their nests in this manner, at least we have already found several in trees, nor have we as yet seen any on the ground or sand bars where I had supposed from previous information that they most commonly deposited their eggs."—Lewis

April 14, 1805 (Little Missouri River)

"Saw many gees feeding on the tender grass in the praries and several of their nests in trees; we have not in a single instance found the nest of this bird on or near the ground."—Lewis

May 3, 1805 (Near the mouth of the Poplar River)

"found the nest of the wild goose among some driftwood in the river from which we took three eggs. this is the only nest we have met with on driftwood, the usual position is the top of a broken tree, sometimes in the forks of a large tree, but almost invariably from 15 to 20 feet or upwards high."—Lewis

Persons familiar with the usual ground nesting habit of the Canada goose may be inclined to doubt the truth of Lewis' report. However, Bent's[13] account of Canada geese nesting in cottonwood trees in Montana cannot be questioned:

"In the Rocky Mountain regions of Colorado and Montana the Canada goose has been known to build its nest, sometimes for successive seasons, on rocky ledges or cliffs at some distance from any water or even at a considerable height. In the northwestern portions of the country it frequently nests in trees, using the old nests of ospreys, hawks, or other large birds; it apparently does not build any such nest for itself, but sometimes repairs the nest by bringing in twigs and lining it with down. John Fannin (1894) says that in the Okanogan district of British Columbia, 'Canada geese are particularly noted for nesting in trees, and as these valleys are subject to sudden inundation during early spring, this fact may have something to do with it.' "

There is nothing in the diaries concerning the life history of the Canada goose other than two entries which refer to its moulting period:

May 23, 1805

"the gees begin to lose the feathers of their wings and are unable to fly."—Lewis

July 21, 1805 (Vic. of Gates of the Mountains, Montana)

"we daily see great numbers of geese with their young which are perfectly feathered except the wings which are deficient in both young and old. My dog caught several today which he frequently does. The young ones are very fine, but the old gees are poor and not fit for use."—Lewis

Goose shooting for sport was not permitted. Waterfowl and other birds were killed only when big game was scarce, or when specimens were wanted for study:

July 25, 1805 (Near Townsend, Montana)

"We killed a couple of young gees which are very abundant and fine; but as they are but small game to subsist a party on, of our strength, I have forbid the men shooting at them as it waists a considerable quantity of ammunition and delays our progress."—Lewis

Lewis did not foresee that a few weeks later he would be obliged to subsist on such items as dog, coyote, owl, half-spoiled, pounded salmon and dried roots.

THE LESSER CANADA GOOSE

Lewis and Clark may be credited with the discovery of the lesser Canada goose, *Branta canadensis leucopareia* (Brandt), but it is doubtful whether they saw Richardson's goose, *Branta canadensis hutchinsii* (Richardson). In any case, the small goose which they described above the mouth of the Musselshell River in Montana on May 26, 1805 was probably the subspecies *leucopareia* rather than *hutchinsii* in as much as migratory flights of Richardson's goose rarely occur as far west as Montana.

May 26, 1805 (On the Missouri River, above the mouth of the Musselshell)

"I saw a number of white brant, also the common brown brant, Geese of the common size & kind, and a small Species of geese, which differs considerably from the common or Canadian Goose; their necks, head and backs are considerably thicker, shorter and larger than the other in proportion to its size they are also more than a third smaller, and their note more like that of the brant or young goose which has not perfectly acquired his note; in all other respects they are the same in colour habits and the number of feathers in the tail, they frequently also ascociate with the large Geese when in flocks, but never saw them pared off with the larger or common goose."—Clark

Lewis again described the lesser Canada goose in somewhat different language in his notes dealing with the birds inhabiting the area west of the Rocky Mountains.

March 8, 1806 (Written at Fort Clatsop)

"The small goose of this country is reather less than the brandt; its head and neck like the brant are reather larger than the goose in proportion; their beak is also thicker and shorter. Their notes are more like those of our tame gees; in all other rispects they are the same with the large goose with which they so frequently associate that it was some time after I first observed this goose before I could determine whether it was a distinct species or not. I have now no hesitation in declaring them a distinct species."—Lewis

Lewis' opinion was upheld by taxonomic authorities for many years; indeed, the lesser Canada goose was considered a separate species until Coues classified it as a subspecies of the Canada goose in 1872.[14]

LESSER SNOW GOOSE

Although the snow goose had been technically described and named, *Anser hyperboreus,* by Pallas in 1767, it was evidently new to the explorers and they described it in detail while on the Missouri River in the spring of 1805 and at Fort Clatsop in 1806.

April 9, 1805 (Between Fort Mandan and the Little Missouri River)

"We saw a great number of brant passing up the river, some of them were white, except the large feathers in the first and second joint of the wing which are black. There is no other difference between them and the common or gray brant but that of their colour. Their note and habits are the same, and they are frequently seen to associate together. I have not yet positively determined whether they are the same or a different species."
—Lewis

April 13, 1805 (Vic. of the Little Missouri River)

"Saw a large flock of white brant or gees with black wings pass up the river; there were a number of gray brant with them; from their flight I presume they proceed much further still N. W. We have never been enabled yet to shoot one of these birds, and cannot therefore determine whether the gray brant found with the white are their brude of last year, or whether they are the same with the grey brant common to the Mississippi and lower part of the Missouri."—Lewis

May 5, 1805 (Vic. of Prairie Elk Creek)

"The white brant associate in very large flocks, they do not appear to be mated or pared off as if they intended to raise their young in this quarter, I therefore doubt whether they reside here during summer for that purpose. This bird is about the size of the common brown brant or two thirds of the common goose, it is not so long by six inches from point to point of the wings when extended as the other; the beak head and neck are also larger and stronger; their beak, legs, and feet are of a redish or flesh coloured white. the eye is of moderate size. the puple of a deep sea green incircled with a ring of yellowish brown. it has sixteen feathers of equal length in the tale; their note differs but little from the common brant, their flesh much the same, and in my opinion preferable to the goose, the flesh is dark. they are entirely of a beautiful pure white except the large feathers of the 1st and second joints of the wings which are jet black, form and habits are the same with the other brants; they sometimes associate and form one common flock."—Lewis

March 8, 1806 (Written at Fort Clatsop)
"The white brant is very common in this country particularly below tidewater where they remain in vast quantities during the winter. They feed like the swan, gees, etc. on the grass, roots and seeds which they find in the marshes. this bird is about the size of the brown brant or a third less than the common Canadian or wild goose. the head is proportionably with the goose, rather large; the beak also thicker shorter and of much the same form, being of a yellowish white colour except the edges of the chaps, which are frequently of a dark brown. the legs and feet are of the same form of the goose and are of a redish white or pale flesh colour. the tail is composed of sixteen feathers of equal length, as those of the geese and brant are, and bears about the same proportion in point of length. the eye is of a dark colour and nothing remarkable as to size. the wings are rether longer compared with those of the goose, but not as much so as in the brown or pided brant. the colour of the plumage of this bird is uniformly a pure white except the large feathers of the extremities of the wings which are black. the large feathers of the 1st joint of the wing next to the body are white. the note of this bird differs essentially from that of the goose; it more resembles that of the brown brant but is somewhat different. it is like the note of a young domestic goose which has not perfectly attained its full note. the flesh of this bird is exceedingly fine, preferable either to the goose or the pided brant."—Lewis

The foregoing descriptions of the lesser snow goose, *Chen hyperborea* (Pallas), are not exact enough to satisfy the demands of modern taxonomy, but they leave no doubt as to the identity of the species described. Coues[15] did not hesitate to print a positive identification based on Lewis' description.

WHITE-FRONTED GOOSE

Lewis and Clark may be given credit for writing the first report of the white-fronted goose, *Anser albifrons* (Scopoli), on the Oregon coast. Moreover, their description of a specimen collected near Fort Clatsop antedated by twenty-two years that of Bonaparte, who assigned this goose to Scopoli's species, *Branta albifrons.*

In 1917, Swarth and Bryant[16] demonstrated that two races of white-fronted geese spend their winters in California. In addition to the more common race, *Anser albifrons frontalis* Baird, a larger and less abundant subspecies, *Anser albifrons gambelli* Hartlaub, is now recognized. Residents of the West coast know the race, *gambelli,* as the tule goose.

March 15, 1806 (Written at Fort Clatsop)

"There is a third species of brant in the neighborhood of this place which is about the size and much the form of the pided brant. they weigh 8½ lbs. the wings are not as long nor so pointed as those of the common pided brant. the following is a likeness of it's head and beak. a little distance around the base of the beak is white and is suddonly succeeded by a narrow line of dark brown. the ballance of the neck, head, back, wings, and tail all except the tips of the feathers are of a bluish brown of the common wild goose, the breast and belley are white with an irregular mixture of black feathers which gave that part a pided appearance from the legs back underneath the tail, and arond the junction of the same with the body above, the feathers are white. the tail is composed of 18 feathers; the longest of which are in the center and measure 6 Inches with the barrel of the quill; those on the sides of the tail are something shorter and bend with their extremities inwards towards the center of the tail. the extremities of these feathers are white. the beak is of a light flesh colour. the legs and feet which do not differ in structure from those of the goose or brant of the other species, are of an orrange yellow colour. the eye is small; the iris is a dark yellowish brown, and pupil black. the note of this brant is much that of the common pided brant from which in fact they are not to be distinguished at a distance, but they certainly are a distinct species of brant. the flesh of this fowl is as good as that of the common pided brant. they do not remain here during the winter in such numbers as the white brant do. tho' they have now returned in considerable quantities. first saw them below tide-water."—Lewis

In the Biddle text of the diaries, the white-fronted goose was referred to as the "pied brant." It was on the basis of the description, contained in this early edition, that Coues determined this "pied brant" to be a specimen of *"Anser albifrons* of American writers."[17] He followed his identification with the statement: "Like the other species of brant, this species is described at length and with accuracy."

Although Lewis and Clark saw the white-fronted goose only on the West coast, its winter range is not confined to the Pacific states. It is not of uncommon occurrence as far east as the Mississippi River, and it may occasionally be seen as a casual visitor on the Atlantic seaboard.

TRUMPETER SWAN

The trumpeter swan, *Olor buccinator* Richardson, has receded before the advance of settlement and agriculture until it is now a vanishing race.

In 1804-05, this swan was common throughout the central and northern areas of the United States and Canada. In 1895 the trumpeter was still common in Montana, but by 1914 they had become scarce in that state.[18]

Lewis and Clark did not write separate descriptions of the two species of American swans, rather they combined their discussion of both in one paragraph. Consequently, we shall transcribe their remarks concerning both under the discussion of the whistling swan.

WHISTLING SWAN

March 9, 1806 (Written at Fort Clatsop)

"The Large Swan is precisely the same common to the Atlantic States. the small swans differs only from the larger one in size and its note. it is about one fourth less and its note entirely different. the latter cannot be justly immetated by the sound of letters nor do I know any sounds with which a comparison would be pertinent. it begins with a kind of whistleing sound and terminates in a round full note which is reather louder than the whistling, or former part; this note is as loud as that of the larger swan. from the peculiar whistleing of the note of this bird I have called it the *whistleing swan*. it's habits colour and contour appear to be percisely those of the large Swan. we first saw them below the great narrows of the Columbia near the Chilluckkittequaw nation. They are very abundant in this neighbourhood and have remained with us all winter. in number they are fully five for one of the large species."—Lewis

It is evident from this description that Lewis and Clark must be awarded the distinction of having coined the popular name, *whistling swan,* for the most abundant and widely distributed swan in America.

Coues[19] in appraising the zoological contributions of Lewis and Clark, is quoted below in reference to the foregoing description which appears both in the Biddle text and in Thwaites', *Original Journals.*

"By their size and the difference in the voice, the two American species are correctly discriminated by Lewis and Clark; unfortunately however, they blunder in the matter of saying that the large species (i.e., the one subsequently called *Cygnus buccinator* by Sir John Richardson) is the same as that common to the Atlantic coast; whereas, it is their other species, here called by them the Whistling Swan, in contradistinction to the Trumpeter, that is found also in the United States. But, this confusion must not be allowed to stand in the light of the main point of this case, which is, that, in 1815, Ord based his *Anas columbianus* exclusively upon the Whistling Swan of Lewis and Clark, i.e., the smaller of the two species, subsequently named *Cygnus americanus* by Sharpless. The blunder of the original authors does not extend to Ord, to whose name *columbianus* should be restored to its rightful priority."

Coues made his point. The accepted name of the whistling swan is *Olor columbianus* (Ord).

CHAPTER XI
Birds of Prey

Vultures, eagles, hawks, and owls are generally regarded as birds of prey. However, the owls, because of their unique structural characteristics, are classified in a separate order in the accepted system of bird classification.

Lewis and Clark were much impressed with the California condor which, although not new to science, was new to them. The two specimens which they collected on the lower Columbia River were described in detail.

Their descriptions of eagles and hawks, however, are not as accurate or complete as one would expect. We were surprised to find that they seemed to regard the "calumet" eagle as a separate species; and that they described the "grey" (golden) eagle as being one fourth larger than the bald eagle. They were wrong in both cases. Hawks were given but scant attention; none was collected. They mentioned having seen the sparrow hawk on the Missouri and in the Columbia valley. Other hawks not specifically identified by Lewis and Clark included "several large hawks that were nearly black," a "hawk of an intermediate size with a long tail and bluish coloured wings," and a "large red-tailed hawk" which was seen at Fort Clatsop. Coues identified these three hawks as (1) the melanistic phase of either the western red-tailed hawk or Swainson's hawk, (2) the marsh hawk, and (3) the western red-tailed hawk.

CALIFORNIA CONDOR

Lewis and Clark first observed the California condor, *Gymnogyps californianus* (Shaw), just above the Cascades of the Columbia River on Oct. 30, 1805; and, about three weeks later, near the river's mouth, they killed and measured a large condor. While at Fort Clatsop Lewis described a second specimen that was wounded and taken alive on Feb. 16, 1806.

Oct. 30, 1805 (Just above the Cascades of the Columbia)
"this day we Saw Some fiew of the large Buzzard. Capt. Lewis shot at one, those Buzzards are much larger than any other of ther Spece, or the largest Eagle, white under part of their wings, etc."—Clark

Nov. 18, 1805 (Vic. of Gray's Point, near mouth of the Columbia River)
"Rubin Fields Killed a Buzzard (Vulture) of the large Kind near the (Meat of the) whale we Saw (wt. 25 lbs.) measured from the tips of the wings across 9½ ft., from the point of the Bill to the end of the tail 3 ft. 10¼ inches, middle toe 5½ inches, toe nale 1 inch & 3½ lines, wing

feathers 2½ feet long & 1 inch & 5 lines diameter, tale feathers 14½ inches, and the head is 6½ inches including the beak."—Clark

Jan. 3, 1806 (Written at Fort Clatsop)
"the butifull Buzzard of the Columbia Still continue with us."—Clark

Feb. 16, 1806 (Written at Fort Clatsop)
"Shannon and Labiesh brought in to us today a Buzzard or Vulture of the Columbia which they had wounded and taken alive. I believe this to be the largest Bird of North America. it was not in good order yet it wayed 25 lbs. had it have been so it might very well have weighed 10 lbs. more or 35 lbs. between the extremities of the wings it measured 9 feet 2 Inches; from the extremity of the beak to that of the toe 3 feet 9 inches and a half. from hip to toe 2 feet, girth of the head 9 inches ¾. Girth of the neck 7½ inches; Girth of the body exclusive of the wings 2 feet 3 inches; girth of the leg 3 inches the diameter of the eye 4½ tenths of an inch, the iris of a pale scarlet red, the puple of a deep sea green or black and occupies about one third of the diameter of the eye the head and part of the neck as low as the figures 1.2. is uncovered with feathers except that portion of it represented by dots foward and under the eye. the tail is composed of twelve feathers of equal length, each 14 inches. the legs are 4¾ inches in length and of a whitish colour uncovered with feathers, they are not entirely smooth but not imbricated; the toes are four in number three of which are forward and that in the center much the longest; the fourth is short and is inserted near the inner of the three other toes and reather projecting forward. the thye is covered with feathers as low as the knee. the top or upper part of the toes are imbricated with broad scales lying transversely, the nails are black and in proportion to the size of the bird comparitively with those of the Hawk or Eagle, short and bluntly pointed. the under side of the wing is covered with white down and feathers. a white stripe of about 2 inches in width, also marks the outer part of the wing, imbracing the lower points of the feathers, which cover the joints of the wing through their whole length or width of that part of the wing. all the other feathers of whatever part are of a Glossy shineing black except the down, which is not glossy, but equally black. the skin of the beak and head to the joining of the neck is of a pale orrange Yellow, the other part uncovered with feathers is of a light flesh colour. the skin is thin and wrinkled except on the beak where it is smooth. This bird flys very clumsily, nor do I know whether it ever seizes its prey alive but am induced to believe it does not. we have seen it feeding on the remains of the whale and other fish which have been thrown up by the waves on the sea coast. these I believe constitute their principal food, but I have no doubt but that they also feed on flesh. we did not meet with this bird untill we had decended the

Columbia below the great falls, and have found them more abundant below the tide water than above. this is the same species of Bird which R. Field killed on the 18th of Nov. last and which is noticed on that day tho' not fully discribed then I thought this of the Buzzard species. I now believe that this bird is reather of the Vulture genus than any other, tho' it wants some of their characteristics particularly the hair on the neck, and the feathers on the legs. this is a handsom bird at a little distance. its neck is proportionably longer than those of the Hawk or Eagle. . . . Shannon and Labiesh informed us that when he approached this Vulture after wounding it, that it made a noise very much like the barking of a Dog. the tongue is long firm and broad, filling the under Chap and partaking of it's transvirs curvature, or its sides forming a longitudinal Groove; obtuse at the point, the Margin armed with firm cartelagenous prickkles pointed and bending inwards."—Clark

March 28, 1806 (Deer Island, in the lower Columbia River)
"the men who had been sent after the deer returned and brought in the remnent which the Vultures and Eagles had left us; these birds had devoured 4 deer in the course of a few hours—the party had killed and brought in three other deer. a goose, some ducks and an Eagle. Drewyer also killed a tiger cat. Joseph Fields informed me that the Vultures had dragged a large buck which he had killed about 30 yards, had skinned it and broken the back bone."—Lewis

April 6, 1806 (Near the mouth of the Sandy River)
"Jos. Field killed a vulture of that species already described."—Clark

It cannot be claimed that the explorers were the first naturalists to write a description of the California condor,[1] but they were the first to collect this species near the Columbia River.

Coues[2] has pointed out that Bonaparte and Nuttall based their conclusion that the Andean condor inhabited the United States on the reports of Lewis and Clark. They, and probably other contemporary ornithologists, evidently had never seen the California condor, and jumped to the conclusion that it was the same as the Andean species.

Although Shaw's description of the California condor preceded that of Lewis and Clark, their contribution should not be minimized; in 1831, David Douglas confirmed their reports of this species on the Columbia, west of the Cascades.

TURKEY VULTURE

Two observations relating to the occurrence of the turkey vulture, *Cathartes aura* (Linnaeus), west of the Rocky Mountains, probably extended the known range of the species at the time they were made:

April 9, 1806 (Below the Cascades of the Columbia River)

"we saw some turkey buzzards this morning of the species common to the United States which are the first we have seen on this side of the rocky mountains."—Lewis

June 13, 1806.

"Labeech and P. Crusatt went out this morning, killed a deer & reported that the buzzards[3] had eate up the deer in their absence after haveing butchered it and hung it up."—Clark

BALD EAGLE

The bald eagle, *Haliaeëtus leucocephalis alascanus* Townsend, was not mentioned by Lewis and Clark until April, 1805, after the expedition left Fort Mandan and resumed its journey up the Missouri. Above the Little Missouri River, and near the mouth of the Yellowstone bald eagles were abundant enough to command attention. From the Yellowstone to Grayling, Montana, they were listed only a few times, along with other birds seen by the explorers. After crossing the Beaverhead Mountains no eagles were reported on the westward journey until the explorers reached the Columbia River; likewise, on the return journey the bald eagle was not mentioned after leaving the Oregon coast until Lewis and Clark were back in area drained by the Missouri River.

April 10, 1805 (Between Fort Mandan and the Little Missouri River)

"we shot a prairie hen and a bald eagle of which latter there are many nests in the tall cottonwood trees." (From Coues edition of the Paul Allen text, p. 265, but not mentioned under this date in Thwaites' *Original Journals*).

April 11, 1805

"The Eagle is now laying their eggs."—Clark

April 13, 1805 (Near mouth of the Little Missouri)

"Observed more bald eagles on this part of the Missouri than we have previously seen."—Lewis

April 26, 1805 (Near the mouth of the Yellowstone River)

"I observe that the Magpie, Goose, duck & Eagle all have their nests in the Same neighbourhood, and it is not uncommon for the Magpie to build in a few rods of the eagle, the nest of this bird (magpie) is built verry strong with sticks covered verry thickly with only one or more places through which they enter or escape, the goose I make no doubt falls pray to those vicious eagles."—Clark

April 27, 1805

"The bald Eagle are more abundant here than I ever observed them in any part of the country."—Lewis

May 7, 1805 (Above the Yellowstone River)

"We continue to see a great number of bald Eagles, I presume they must feed on the carcases of dead animals, for I see no fishing hawks to supply them with their favorite food. the water of the river is so turbid that no bird which feeds exclusively on fish can subsist on it; from its mouth to this place I have neither seen a blue crested fisher or a fishing hawk."—Lewis

Lewis' failure to see the kingfisher and the osprey on the Missouri River below the Yellowstone was obviously due to circumstances other than the turbidity of the water. The known range of the kingfisher extends across the continent from British Columbia to Quebec, and the species is not uncommon in the northern plains states; the American osprey, though never abundant, has a cosmopolitan range in the western hemisphere. Lewis and Clark's observations of this species will be considered in greater detail hereinafter.

May 8, 1805

"The bald Eagle of which there are great numbers now have their young."

Aug. 9, 1805 (Mouth of Prairie Creek, near Grayling, Mont.)

"I saw several bald Eagles, and two large white headed fishing hawks, both of these birds were the same common to our country."—Lewis

GOLDEN EAGLE

The golden eagle, *Aquila chrysaëtos canadensis* (Linnaeus), of North America is a western species. Its range extends from Alaska, and the northern regions of the Prairie Provinces, to Mexico. Occasionally, however, individual golden eagles stray from their normal range, and they have been reliably reported from several eastern states.

The explorers, in referring to this bird, called it either the *grey eagle* or the *calumet eagle*. There is evidence for concluding that they considered the *calumet eagle* a separate species.

While at Fort Clatsop, Clark described the *calumet eagle* as follows:

March 11, 1806 (Fort Clatsop)

"I have some reasons to believe that the Calumet Eagle is sometimes found on this side of the Rocky Mountains from the information of the Indians in whose possession I have seen their plumage. those are the same with those of the Missouri, and are the most butifull of all the family of the Eagle of America it's colours are black and white with which it is butifully varigated. the feathers of the tail which is so highly prized by the Indians is composed of twelve broad feathers of equal length those are white except about two inches at the extremity which is of a jut black. their wings have each a large circular white spot in the Middle when extended. the body is variously marked with white and black. the form is much that of the Common bald Eagle, but they are reather smaller and much more fleet. this Eagle is feared by all carnivarous birds, and on his approach all leave the carcase instantly on which they were feeding. it breeds in the inaccessable parts of the Mountains where it spends the summer, and descends to the plains and low country in the fall and winter when it is usially sought and taken by the nativs. the tails of this bird is esteemed by Mandans, Minnetares, Ricaras, etc. as the full value of a good horse, or gun and accoutrements. With the Osage and Kanzas and those nations enhabiting countrys where this bird is more rare, the price is even double of that mentioned. with these feathers the nativs deckerate the stems of their sacred pipes or calumets; whence the name of Calumet Eagle, which has Generally obtained among the Engages. The Ricaras have domesticated this bird in many instances for the purpose of obtaining its plumage. the nativs in every part of the Continent who can precure those feathers attach them to their own hair and the mains and tail of their favorite horses by way of orniment. they also deckerate their own caps or bonnets with those feathers."—Clark

Coues[4] has pointed out that the *calumet eagle* existed only in the minds of men. His remarks on this subject are noteworthy:

"Under date of Mar. 11, 1806, Clark has this description of the "Callamet" eagle, which has been copied or compiled repeatedly, by various writers, with more or less pertinent comment; and the calumet eagle, thus famed, has often been supposed to be a distinct species. Then, however, the trouble was to find any North American eagle which answered to the description—the fact being that there is none. Just criticism of the passage clears up all doubts. 1st. The description is based primarily upon the common golden eagle of North America, *Aquila chrysaëtos.* 2nd. It is not accurate in all particulars. 3rd. It includes a venerable vague tradition of the king vulture, *Sarcorhamphus papa.* 4th. and especially, any eagle whose tailfeathers suit an Indian for decorative purposes is *ipso facto* a "calumet" eagle; and the bald eagle, *Haliaetus leucocephalis,* when it is changing its tail from black to white, answers the Indian's purpose as well as it does Lewis and Clark's description. I have myself more than once seen forlorn and dilapidated bald eagles cooped in Indian villages, having been taken from the nest to be reared and kept till they should acquire the parti-colored tail-feathers desired for ornamentation. A "calumet" eagle, zoölogically speaking, is as much a myth as the famous "wakon-bird"—though both be great medicine."—Coues

Lewis' first contact with the golden eagle evidently occurred during the winter at Fort Mandan. Under the date of April 8, 1805, he wrote as follows:

"The only birds that I observed during the winter at Fort Mandan was the Missouri magpie, a bird of the Corvus genus, the raven in emmence numbers, the small woodpecker or sapsucker as they are sometimes called, and the beautiful *calumet bird,* so called from the circumstance of the natives decorating their pipe stems with its plumage."

July 11, 1805 (Vic. of Great Falls of the Missouri)

"I saw several very large grey Eagles[5] today they are half as large again as the common bald Eagle of this country.[6] I do not think the bald Eagle here quite so large as those of the U.' States; the grey Eagle is infinitely larger and is no doubt a distinct species."—Lewis

Aug. 21, 1805 (At the Shoshone village on the Lemhi River)

"They (Shoshones) are also fond of the feathers of the tail of the beautiful eagle or callumet bird with which they orniment their own hair and the tails and mains of their horses."—Lewis

Nov. 30, 1805 (Fort Clatsop)

"I observe . . . grey and bald eagles, ..."—Lewis

Feb. 16, 1806 (Fort Clatsop)

"Shannon also brought a Grey Eagle which appeared to be the same kind common to the U.' States. it weighed 15 pds. and measured 7 feet 7 inches between the extremities of the wings."—Clark

March 26, 1806 (Columbia County, Oregon)

"here our hunters joined us having killed three Eagles and a large goose. I had now an opportunity of comparing the bald with the grey Eagle; I found that the grey Eagle was about ¼ larger,[7] its legs and feet were dark while those of the bald Eagle were of a fine orrange yellow; the iris of the eye is also of a dark yellowish brown while that of the other is of a bright silvery colour with a slight admixture of yellow."—Lewis

June 9, 1806 (Vic. of Weippe Prairie, Shoshone Co., Idaho)

"The Cutnose . . . borrowed a horse and rode down the Kooskooske River a few miles this morning in quest of some young eagles which he intends raising for the benefit of their feathers; he returned soon after with a pair of young Eagles of the grey kind; they were nearly grown and prety well feathered."—Lewis

Aug. 3, 1806 (Vic. of mouth of the Musselshell River)

"We saw . . . one Callamet Eagle, and a number of bald Eagles. . . ."—
Lewis

AMERICAN OSPREY

It will be recalled that Lewis mentioned the absence of the osprey, *Pandion
haliaetus carolinensis* (Gmelin), on the Missouri River, below the mouth
of the Yellowstone, in connection with his reference, of May 7, 1805, to
the bald eagle.

It should be emphasized, also, that the "two large white headed fishing-
hawks" reported on Aug. 9, 1805 at Grayling, Montana were American
ospreys.

On Sept. 19, 1805, Clark reported seeing a "Small white headed hawk"
on Collins Creek, west of Lolo Pass in Idaho. This, too, was probably an
osprey.

Then, at Fort Clatsop, Lewis made a more general statement concerning
the distribution of ospreys west of the Rocky Mountains.

March 7, 1806

"The Fishing hawk with the crown of the head White, and back of a
mealy white, and the blue crested or King fisher, are found on every part
of the Columbia and its water along which we passed, and are the same
with those of the U' States. the fishing hawk is not abundant particularly
in the mountains."—Lewis

Coues[8] is our authority for identifying the "fishing hawk with the white
crown" as the American osprey.

OTHER HAWKS

Hawks are treated sketchily in the diaries. They reported seeing them
occasionally; but they did not describe any of them in sufficient detail for
positive identification. Coues, nevertheless, presumed to suggest the probable identity of several hawks reported by the explorers, largely on the
basis of his knowledge of the species that were known to inhabit specific
areas. We may assume that Coues was correct in most of his identifications,
and on this basis we can list the sparrow hawk, the marsh hawk, the western red-tailed hawk, and Swainson's hawk among the birds reported by
Lewis and Clark.

THE MONTANA HORNED OWL

April 14, 1805 (Vic. of the Little Missouri River)

"One of the party killed a large hooting owl; I observed no difference

208

between this bird and those of the same family common to the U.' States except that this appeared to be more booted and more thickly clad with feathers."—Lewis

Bent[9] identified the owl killed on this date as the Montana horned owl, *Bubo virginianus occidentalis* Stone, and he says that this was "probably the first one of this subspecies killed by white man."

On May 20, 1805, near the mouth of the Musselshell River, two other horned owls were seen which, considering that the Montana horned owl is the common subspecies in the area in which they were observed, probably belonged to the same subspecies. Coues, however, merely referred to these owls as *Bubo virginianus*, without assigning them to a subspecies.

The incident referred to is quoted below:

"I saw two large Owls with remarkable long feathers on the sides of the head which resembled ears; I take them to be the large hooting owl tho' their colours brighter than those of the U' States."—Lewis

DUSKY HORNED OWL
March 3, 1806 (Written at Fort Clatsop)

"we also met with a large hooting Owl under the Rocky Mountains on the Kooskooske river. It did not appear to differ materially from those of our country. I think its colours reather deeper and brighter than with us, particularly the redish brown—it is the same size and form."—Lewis

It will be noticed that Lewis' description of the coloring of this owl parallels his characterization of the coloring of the owls seen at the mouth of the Musselshell River. One wonders if the two incidents were not confused in his memory; or, if the owls seen on the Kooskooske in Idaho were possibly of the subspecies, *occidentalis*, in spite of the fact that Coues[10] identified the Idaho specimen, described above, as *Bubo virginianus saturatus* Ridgway.

GREAT GRAY OWL
May 23, 1806 (Vic. of Kamiah, Idaho)

"our hunters brought us a large hooting owl which differ from those of the Atlantic States. The plumage of this owl is an uniform mixture of dark yellowish brown and white, in which the dark brown predominates. Its colour may be properly termed dark Iron gray. The plumage is very long and remarkably silky and soft. those have not the long feathers on the head which give it the appearance of ears or horns. remarkable large eyes."
—Clark

Lewis evidently described the same specimen, in greater detail, a few days later:

May 28, 1806 (Vic. of Kamiah, Idaho)

"our hunters brought us a large hooting Owl. which differs considerably from those of the Atlantic States which are also common here. the plumage of this owl is an uniform mixture of dark yellowish brown and white, in which the dark brown predominates. It's colour may be properly termed a dark iron grey, the plumage is very long and remarkably silky and soft. these have not the long feathers on the head which give it the appearance of ears or horns. the feathers on the head are long narrow and closely set. they rise upwright nearly to the extremity and then are bent back suddenly as iff curled. a kind of ruff of these feathers incircle the throat. The head has a flat appearance being broadest before and behind and is 1 foot 10 Is. in circumference. incircling the eyes and extending from them like rays from the center a tissue of open hairy long feathers are placed of a light grey colour, these conceal the ears which are very large and are placed close to the eyes behind and extending below them. These feathers are remarkably large and prominent, iris of a pale goald colour and iris (sc. pupil) circular and of a deep sea green. the beak is short and wide at its base. the upper chap is much curved at the extremity and comes down over and in front of the under chap. this bird is about the size of the largest hooting Owl. the tail is composed of eleven feathers, of which those in the center are reather the longest. it is booted to the extremity of the toes, of which it has four on each foot, one in the rear one on the outer side and two in front. the toes are short particularly that in the rear, but are all armed with long keen curved nails of a dark brown colour. the beak is white and nostrils circular large and unconnected. the habits and note of this owl is much that of the common large hooting owl."—Lewis

Coues[11] is specific in pointing out that the owl described above was subsequently classified as the great gray owl, *Scotiaptex cinerea* (an accepted name for this species in 1893);[12] and that Lewis and Clark can be credited with its discovery.

Bent did not refer to the taxonomic history of this species; and, consequently, he did not mention Lewis and Clark in his discussion of the great gray owl.

CHAPTER XII
The Gallinaceous Birds

This order of birds includes the turkeys, pheasants, grouse, quail and bobwhites.

Naturally Lewis and Clark were interested in game birds, and their diaries contain much interesting information concerning several kinds of grouse and quail that were entirely unknown to ornithologists of their day. They can be credited with the discovery of the Columbian sharp-tailed grouse, the sage grouse, the dusky grouse, Franklin's grouse, the Oregon ruffed grouse, and the Mountain quail.

They also provided some interesting data on the geographic range of the wild turkey, the prairie chicken and the plains sharptail.

PRAIRIE CHICKEN

There is only one significant entry relating to the prairie chicken, *Tympanuchus cupido pinnatus* (Brewster), in the diaries, and this relates to the northward limit of its range in the Missouri valley.

Sept. 2, 1806 (James River near Yankton, S. Dak.)

"I saw 4 prarie fowls Common to Illinois, those are the highest up[1] which have been seen."—Clark

Actually the range of the greater prairie chicken extended as far north as southern Saskatchewan and southern Manitoba. They were common in North Dakota, South Dakota and Nebraska. According to Bent[2] there was, in 1932, only one authentic record for the species in Montana, which involved a specimen taken in 1917 near Huntley.

PLAINS SHARP-TAILED GROUSE

Lewis and Clark's comments on the sharptail, *Pedioecetus phasianellus jamesi* Lincoln, are not definitive; yet when we compare their remarks about the "prarie fowls Common to Illinois" with those regarding the "pointed tail prairie hens" seen near the mouth of the Musselshell River, and particularly with their description of the grouse that is "perculiarly the inhabitant of the Great Plains of the Columbia," it becomes evident that they did recognize the distinctions between the greater prairie chicken and the sharp-tailed grouse.

They mentioned seeing "Great Number of Grouse" below the mouth of the Grand River in South Dakota on Oct. 7, 1804, and at Fort Mandan in February, 1805.

In view of the fact that Clark stated specifically, on Sept. 2, 1806, that he saw no "prarie fowls Common to Illinois" above Yankton, South Dakota, we may conclude that the grouse referred to above were plains sharptails.

Oct. 7, 1804 (Near mouth of Grand River in S. Dak.)
"this Island is nearly 1¼ ms. Squar, no timber, high and Covered with grass, wild rye, and contains Great Numbers of Grouse."—Clark

Feb. 13, 1805 (Written at Fort Mandan)
"Set out early, Saw great numbers of Grouse feeding on the young Willows on the Sand bars. . . ."—Clark

April 12, 1805 (Near the Little Missouri River, N. Dak.)
"I saw . . . flocks of Grouse."—Clark

April 15, 1805 (Approx. 50 miles above the Little Missouri River)
"I also met with great numbers of Grouse, or prairie hens as they are called by the English traders of the N. W. these birds appear to be mating; the note of the male is *kuck, kuck, kuck, coo, coo, coo.* the first part of the note both male and female use when flying. the male also dubbs (drums with his wings) something like the pheasant, but by no means as loud." —Lewis

Coues[3] concluded, in 1876, that the bird referred to above (April 15, 1805) was a ruffed grouse, probably because of the reference to drumming. However, in his later publication,[4] he inserted the word "sharptailed" before the word "grouse" in the first line of Lewis' entry of April 15 as quoted above.

Dr. George A. Ammann,[5] grouse research specialist with the Michigan Department of Conservation, points out that the male sharp-tailed grouse makes a drumming sound during its characteristic dance which, however, is probably produced by the rapid spreading and closing of the tail feathers rather than with the wings. He agrees, also, that the *kuck* note mentioned by Lewis and Clark is voiced by both the male and female sharptail when they take-off in flight; the *coo* note, however, is made in connection with the "dance," and is quite independent of the *kuck* syllables.

May 21, 1805 (Mouth of the Musselshell River, Montana)
"the growse or prarie hen are now less abundant on the river than they were below; perhaps they betake themselves to the open plains at a distance from the river at this season."—Lewis

May 22, 1805 (A few miles above the Musselshell River)
"Passed the entrance of growse Creek 20 yds. wide, affords but little water. this creek we named from seeing a number of the *pointed tail* prairie hen near its mouth, these are the first we have seen in such numbers for some days."—Lewis

The last quotation is further evidence that Lewis recognized the sharp-tail as distinct from the square-tailed prairie chicken.

COLUMBIAN SHARP-TAILED GROUSE

Bent[6] says that this race of sharp-tailed grouse, *Pedioecetes phasianellus columbianus* (Ord), "inhabits the lowlands of the Great Basin from the Rocky Mountains to the Cascades and Sierra Nevadas"; he also affirms that "it was discovered by Lewis and Clark on the plains of the Columbia River in 1805."

Coues[7] points out that Ord's original description and technical name, *Phasianus columbianus,* as published in 1815, was based directly on Lewis and Clark's description.

Mar. 1, 1806 (Written at Fort Clatsop)

"The Grouse or Prarie hen is peculiarly the inhabitant of the Grait Plains of Columbia they do not differ from those of the upper portion of the Missouri, the tail of which is pointed or the feathers in it's center much longer than those on the sides. this species differs essentially in the construction of this part of their plumage from those of the Illinois which have their tails composed of feathers of equal length. in the winter season this bird is booted even to the first joint of it's toes. the toes are also curiously bordered on their lower edges with narrow hard scales which are placed very close to each other and extend horizontally about ⅛ of an inch on each side of the toes thus adding to the width of the tread which nature seems bountifully to have furnished them at this season for passing over the snow with more ease. in the summer season those scales fall off. they have four toes on each foot. their colour is a mixture of dark brown redish and yellowish brown and white confusedly mixed in which the redish brown prevails most on the upper parts of the body wings and tail and the white underneath the belley and lower parts of the breast and tail. they associate in large flocks in autumn and winter and are frequently found in flocks of from five to six even in summer. They feed on grass, insects, the leaves of various shrubs in the plains and on seeds of several species of spelts and wild rye which grow in the richer parts of the plains. in winter their food is the buds of the willow and cotton wood also the most of the native berries furnish them with food."
—Lewis

SAGE GROUSE

This is the sage hen, *Centrocercus urophasianus* (Bonaparte), of the dry plains of the Northwestern States. It is the largest of the North American grouse.

The sage grouse is one of the few gallinaceous birds for the discovery of which Bent recognizes Lewis and Clark.[8]

"It was discovered by Lewis and Clark about the headwaters of the Missouri River and on the plains of the Columbia; they named it *cock of the plains* and gave the first account of it. The technical description of it and the scientific name, *urophasianus,* were supplied by Bonaparte in 1827."—Bent

In 1874, Coues had called attention to their discovery and description of the sage grouse,[9] and pointed out that it was singular that Ord, who named so many species described by the explorers, should have been "entirely silent respecting this one."[10]

June 5, 1805 (Vic. of the Marias River)

"I saw a flock of the mountain cock, or a large species of heath hen with a long pointed tail which the Indians informed us were common in the Rocky Mountains. I sent Shields to kill one of them, but he was obliged to fire a long distance at them and missed his aim."—Lewis

Aug. 12, 1805 (Lemhi Pass in Beaverhead Mountains)

"we also saw several of the heath cock with a long pointed tail and a uniform dark brown colour but could not kill one of them. they are much larger than the common dung-hill fowls and in their habits and manner of flying resemble the growse or prarie hen."—Lewis

Oct. 17, 1805 (Near mouth of Snake River)

"sent out Hunters to shute the Prarie Cock, a large fowl which I have only seen on this river, several of which I have killed. they are the size of a Small turkey, of the Pheasant kind, one I killed on the waters edge to day measured from Beak to the end of the toe 2 feet 6 and ¾ Inches; from the extremities of its wings 3 feet 6 inches; the tail feathers is 13 inches long. they feed on grasshoppers and Seed of the wild plant which is also peculiar to this river and the upper parts of the Missoury somewhat resembling the whins."—Clark

Mar. 2, 1806 (Written at Fort Clatsop)

"The *cock of the Plains* is found in the plains of Columbia and are in great abundance from the entrance of the S. E. fork of the Columbia to that of Clark's river. this bird is about 2/3^{rds} the size of a turkey. the beak is large short curved and convex. the upper exceeding the lower chap. the nostrils are large and the beak black. the colour is an uniform mixture of dark brown reather bordering on a dove colour, redish and yellowish brown with some small black specks. in this mixture the dark brown prevails and has a slight cast of the dove colour at a little distance. the wider side of the large feathers of the wings are a dark brown only. the tail is composed of 19 feathers of which that in the center is the longest, and the remaining 9 on each side deminish by pairs as they receede from the center; that is only one feather is equal in length to one equadistant from the center of the tail on the opposite side. the tail when foalded comes to a very sharp point. and appears long in proportion to the body. in the act of flying the tail resembles that of a wild pegeon. tho' the motion of the wings is much that of the pheasant and grouse. they have four toes on each foot of which the hinder one is short. the leg is covered with feathers about half the distance between the knee and the foot. when the wing is expanded there are wide openings between it's feathers the plumeage being so narrow that it does not extend from one quill to the other. the wings are also proportionably short, reather more so than those of the pheasant or grouse. the habits of this bird are much the same as those of the grouse. only that the food of this fowl is almost entirely that of the leaf and buds of the pulpy leafed thorn; nor do I ever recollect seeing this bird but in the neighbourhood of that shrub. they sometimes feed on the prickley pear. the gizzard of it is large and much less compressed and muscular than in most fowls; in short it resembles a maw quite as much as a gizzard. when they fly they make a cackling noise something like the dunghill fowl. the following is a likeness of the head and beak. the flesh of the cock of the Plains is dark and only tolerable in point of flavor. I do not think it as good as either the Pheasant or Grouse. it is invariably found in the plains. The feathers about it's head are pointed and stiff. some hairs about the base of the beak. feathers short fine and stif about the ears."—Lewis

March 2, 1806 (Written at Fort Clatsop)
"the first of those fowls which we met with was on the Missouri below and in the neighbourhood of the Rocky Mountains and from there to the Mountain which passes the Columbia between the Great falls and the Rapids. they go in large gangues or singularly and hide remarkably close when pursued, make short flights, etc."—Clark

DUSKY GROUSE

Dusky grouse, *Dendragapus obscurus* (Say), were seen for the first time by the explorers while they were ascending Jefferson's River, west of Three Forks, Montana. They referred to it as the "large black pheasant," the "black pheasant" or the "dark brown pheasant." This was some twenty years before Thomas Say named the species; so the dusky or blue grouse may be added to the list of birds discovered and originally described by Lewis and Clark.

Aug. 1, 1805 (Jefferson River)
"as I passed these mountains I saw a flock of black or dark brown pheasants; the young pheasant is almost grown we killed one of them.

this bird is fully a third larger than the common phesant[11] of the Atlantic states. It's form is much the same. it is booted nearly to the toes and the male has not the tufts of long black feathers on the sides of the neck which are so conspicuous in those of the Atlantic. their colour is a uniform dark brown with a small mixture of yellow or yellowish brown specks on some of the feathers particularly those of the tail, tho the extremities of these are perfectly black for about one inch. the eye is nearly black, the iris has a small dash of yellowish brown. the feathers of the tail are reather longer than that of our phesant or pattridge as they are called in the Eastern States; are the same in number or eighteen and all nearly the same length, those in the intermediate part being somewhat longest. The flesh of this bird is white and agreeably flavored."— Lewis

It is evident that the foregoing description is not sufficiently definitive for positive identification. For example, if the "large black pheasant" is the dusky grouse, Lewis was inaccurate in reporting the number of rectrices. The genus Dendragapus, normally at least, has 16 tail feathers instead of 18 as reported by Lewis. However, other details of the description, especially in view of the locality in which the bird was seen, support Coues' conclusion that the "black pheasant" described by Lewis on Aug. 1, 1805 was a dusky grouse. Coues assigned Lewis' "black pheasant" to the subspecies *richardsoni,* but according to Aldrich and Duvall, Richardson's grouse is restricted in range to the Canadian Rockies whereas the dusky grouse of Montana and Idaho properly belongs to the subspecies *pallidus.*[12]

SOOTY GROUSE

While ascending the Columbia River in the spring of 1806, Lewis described another "black pheasant" which seemed to differ from the "black or brown pheasant" described on Aug. 1, 1805.

April 16, 1806 (Near mouth of the Des Chutes River, Oregon)

"Fields brought me a black pheasant which he had killed; this I found on examination to be the large black or dark brown pheasant I had met with on the upper part of the Missouri, it is as large as a well grown fowl. the iris of the eye is of a dark yellowish brown, the puple black, the legs are booted to the toes, the tail is composed of 18 black feathers tiped with bluish white, of which the two in the center are reather shorter than the others which are all of the same length. over the eye there is a stripe of a ¼ of an inch in width, uncovered with feathers, of a fine orrange yellow. the wide spaces void of feathers on the side of the neck are also of the same colour. I had some parts of this bird preserved."—Lewis

Coues[13] says that this bird probably is the sooty grouse, *Dendragapus obscurus fuliginosus* (Ridgway).

FRANKLIN'S GROUSE

Franklin's grouse, *Canachites canadensis franklinii* (Douglas), has been called the western counterpart of the Canada spruce grouse, or fool-hen, of the boreal forests of eastern Canada and northern United States. Bent[14] suggests that it may intergrade with some of the western races of the Canada spruce grouse.

This is the grouse that Lewis called the "dommanicker or speckled pheasant" in his diary entry of June 26, 1806, and that which he subsequently referred to as the "black and white pheasant."

The explorers saw Franklin's grouse for the first time on the eastern slopes of the Bitterroot Mountains, while ascending Lolo Creek. They were confused, however, by the dissimilarity between the male and female of this species, and regarded the latter as an unrelated bird.[15] Lewis' description of the male bird is followed by a description of the female.

March 3, 1806 (Written at Fort Clatsop)
"The large black and white pheasant is peculiar to that portion of the Rocky Mountain watered by the Columbia river. at least we did not see them in these mountains untill we reached the waters of that river nor since we have left those mountains. they are about the size of a well grown hen. the contour of the bird is much that of the redish brown pheasant common to our country. the tail is proportionably as long and is composed of eighteen feathers of equal length, of an uniform dark brown tiped with black. the feathers of the body are of a dark brown black and white. the black is that which most predominates, and white feathers are irregularly intermixed with those of the black and dark brown on every part, but in greater proportion about the neck breast and belley. this mixture gives it very much the appearance of that kind of dunghill fowl which the hen-wives of our country call *dommanicker* (Dominique). in the brest of some of these birds the white predominates most. they are not[16] furnished with tufts of long feathers on the neck as our pheasants are, but have a space on each side of the neck about 2½ inches long and 1 in. in width on which no feathers grow. tho' this is concealed by the feathers which are inserted on the hinder and front part of the neck; this space seems to serve them to dilate or contract the feathers of the neck with more ease. the eye is dark, the beak black, curved somewhat pointed and the upper exceeds the under chap. they have a narrow stripe of vermillion colour above each eye which consists of a fleshy substance not protuberant but even with a number of minute rounded dots. it has four toes on each

foot of which three are in front. it is booted to the toes, it feeds on wild fruits, particularly the berry of the sac-a-commis,[17] and also much on the seed of the pine fir."—Lewis

March 3, 1806 (Written at Fort Clatsop)

"The small speckled pheasant found in the same country with that above described, differs from it only in point of size and somewhat in colour. it is scarcely half the size of the other; ascociates in much larger flocks and is very gentle. the black is more predominant and the dark brown feathers less frequent in this than the larger species. the mixture of white is also more general on every part of this bird. it is considerably smaller than our pheasant and the body reather more round. in other particulars they differ not at all from the large black and white pheasant. this by way of distinction I have called the speckled pheasant. the flesh of both of these species of party coloured pheasants is of a dark colour and with the means we had of cooking them not very well flavored."—Lewis

Coues[18] determined the identity of the two birds described above as male and female Franklin's grouse, and he regarded Lewis and Clark as the discoverers of this species.

OREGON RUFFED GROUSE

On the basis of the two descriptions which follow, Coues[19] credited Lewis and Clark with the discovery of the Oregon ruffed grouse, *Bonasa umbellus sabini* (Douglas).

Feb. 5, 1806 (Fort Clatsop)

"Fields brought with him a phesant which differed but little from those common to the Atlantic States; its brown is reather brighter and more of a redish tint. It has eighteen feathers in the tale of about six inches in length. This bird is also booted as low as the toes. the two tufts of long black feathers on each side of the neck most conspicuous in the male of those of the Atlantic states is also observable in every particular with this."—Lewis

March 3, 1806 (Written at Fort Clatsop)

"The small brown pheasant is an inhabitant of the same country[20] and it is of the size and shape of the speckled pheasant[21] which it also resembles in its economy and habits. The stripe above the eye in this species is scarcely perceptable, instead of the vermillion of the others. its colour is an uniform mixture of brownish white on the breast, belley and the feathers underneath the tail. the whole compound is not unlike that of the common quail only darker. This is also booted to the toes.

The flesh of this is preferable to each of the others and that of the breast is as white as the pheasant of the Atlantic Coast."—Lewis

Obviously, Lewis' descriptions of this bird are not definitive; particularly in case of his entry on March 3.

Bent points out that the Oregon ruffed grouse is "one of the handsomest races of the ruffed grouse. The ruffed grouse of the southern Alleghenies are quite richly colored, but they will not compare in this respect with these western birds, which Baird, Brewer, and Ridgway (1905) describe as follows:

" 'The upper parts are dark orange chestnut, mottled with black, the cordate light spots very distinct. The feathers of the breast are strongly tinged with redish-yellow; those of the sides marked with broad and conspicuous bars of black, instead of the obsolete brown. The under tail-coverts are orange-chestnut, within distinct bars of black, and an angular terminal blotch of white. All the light brown blotches and edgings of the eastern variety are here dark brown or black. The jugular band between the ruffles is very conspicuously black.' "22

It is difficult to reconcile the foregoing graphic description of the colorful breast and under tail-coverts with Lewis' "brownish white on the breast, belly, and feathers underneath the tail"; and it is equally difficult to accept his statement that the range of the Oregon ruffed grouse, if the bird he described was of that species, coincides with that of Franklin's grouse.

In so far as known, today at least, the ranges of the two species are neither overlapping nor contiguous. According to Bent, Franklin's grouse "occupies a comparatively limited range in the mountainous interior of the Northwestern States and southwestern Canada," whereas that of the Oregon ruffed grouse is confined to the "humid coast belt, west of the Cascades, in Oregon, Washington, and British Columbia."

MOUNTAIN QUAIL

The mountain quail, *Oreortyx picta palmeri* Oberholser, was officially described and named, *Ortyx picta*, by David Douglas in 1829, but Lewis and Clark must be credited with writing the first description of the species. It appears that Lewis based his description on two specimens only; for there is nothing in the diaries to suggest that he encountered the mountain quail on any other occasion.

April 7, 1806 (Vic. of Beacon Rock on the Columbia River)

"last evening Reubin Field killed a bird of the quail kind it is reather larger than the quail, or partridge as they are called in Virginia. (copy for Dr. Barton) it's form is precisely that of our partridge tho' it's plumage differs in every part. the upper part of the head, sides and back of the neck, including the croop and about 1/3 of the under part of the body is of a bright dovecoloured blue, underneath the under beak, as high as the lower edge of the eyes, and back as far as the hinder part of the eyes and thence coming down to a point in front of the neck about two thirds of it's length downwards, is a fine dark brick red. between this brick red and the dove colour there runs a narrow stripe of pure white. the ears are covered with some coarse stiff dark brown feathers. Just at the base of the under chap there is a narrow transverse stripe of pure white. from the crown of the head two long round feathers extend backwards nearly in the direction of the beak and are of a black colour. the longest of these feathers is two inches and a half, it overlays and conceals the other which is somewhat shorter and seems to be raped in the plumage of that in front which folding backwards colapses behind and has a round appearance. the tail is composed of twelve dark brown feathers of nearly equal length. the large feathers of the wings are of a dark brown and are reather short in proportion to the body of the bird in that rispect very similar to our common partridge. the covert of the wings and back are of a dove colour with a slight admixture of redish brown. a wide stripe which extends from side to side of the body and occupyes the lower region of the breast is beautifully varigated with brick red white and black which predominate in the order they are mentioned and the colours mark the feathers transversely. the legs are covered with feathers as low as the knee; these feathers are of a dark brown tiped with dark brick red as are also those between and about the joining of the legs with the body. they have four toes on each foot of which three are in front and that in the center the longest, those on each side nearly of equal length; that behind is also of good length and are all armed with long and strong nails. the legs and feet are white and imbricated with proportionably large broad scales. the upper beak is short wide at it's base, black, convex, curved downwards and reather obtusely pointed. it exceeds the under chap considerably which is of a white colour, also convex underneath and obtusely pointed. the nostrils are remarkably small, placed far back and low down on the sides of the beak. they are covered by a thin protuberant elastic, black leather like substance. the eyes are of a uniform piercing black colour. this is a most beautiful bird. I preserved the skin of this bird retaining the wings feet and head which I hope will give a just idea of the bird. it's loud note is single and consists of a loud squall, entirely different from the whistling of our quales or partridge. it has a cherping note when allarmed something like ours. today there was a second of these birds killed (by Capt. C.) which precisely resembled that just described. I believe these to be the male bird; the female, if so, I have not yet seen."

Coues,[23] on the basis of this description, concluded that this bird was *Oreortyx picta,* the mountain quail of California.

Criswell[24] pointed out that the foregoing description fits the characteristics of *Oreortyx pictus pictus* (Douglas) more closely than it does that of the subspecies, *palmeri.* However, the subspecies, *pictus,* inhabits the dry country west of the Cascades, whereas the specimen collected by Lewis' hunter was taken in the more humid habitat on the western slope of the Cascades, well within the range of *Oreortyx pictus palmeri* Oberholser.

THE EASTERN WILD TURKEY

Before the white man invaded and conquered the North American continent the wild turkey inhabited an area extending from the Atlantic seaboard to the great plains, and southwestward to Mexico. The subspecies, *Meleagris gallopavo silvestris* Vieillot, roamed through the virgin forests of the east from New England to Georgia, and from New York, Michigan, Wisconsin, Minnesota, and South Dakota to the Gulf of Mexico; they occurred in surprising numbers in the wooded river flats of the plains states including the southeastern counties of South Dakota, and eastern sections of Nebraska, Kansas, Oklahoma, and Texas and other subspecies occupied Florida, the upland regions of the Southwest, and the Rio Grande valley. Indeed, the type specimen described and named by Linnaeus in the Eighteenth Century was a native of Mexico rather than the United States.

Lewis and Clark, in 1804, reported wild turkeys in western Missouri, Iowa, Nebraska, and South Dakota. Their notations are of interest because they are among the earliest accurate records dealing with the distribution and abundance of the species in the Missouri valley above the Platte River.

June 21, 1804 (Vic. of Lexington, Missouri)
"Two men Sent out to hunt this evening brought in a Buck & a pore turkey."—Clark

July 1, 1804 (Near Leavenworth, Kansas)
"Deer and turkeys in great quantities on the bank."—Clark

July 25, 1804 (Whitefish camp, about 10 miles above the mouth of the Platte River)
"1 Turkey, Several Grous seen today."—Clark

July 30, 1804 (Vic. of Fort Calhoun, Nebr.)
"Turkeys . . . killed."—Clark

Aug. 5, 1804 (Near mouth of Soldier River)
"I walked on shore this evening in Pursueing Some turkeys."—Clark

Sept. 5, 1804 (Mouth of Niobrara River)
"turkeys seen today."—Clark

Sept. 8, 1804 (Vic. of Fort Randall, South Dakota)
"3 Turkeys" were killed on this date.—Clark

Oct. 3, 1804 (Approx. 20 miles above Cheyenne River, South Dakota)
"an Indian came to the bank (of the river) with a turkey on his back,
. . . ."—Clark

Aug. 27, 1806 (Tylors River above the Big Bend of the Missouri)
"Here we discover the first Signs of the wild turkey."—Clark

The notation of Aug. 27, 1806 was made on the return journey, and
represents the northern limit of range of the wild turkey in the Missouri
valley. Clark reiterated this statement in a separate body of notes, contained in Codex N, pp. 154-155, written at a later date:

"Turkeys first appear at the extrance of Tylors River above the big
bend (1,206) miles up this river (Missouri)."

Sept. 2, 1806 (Below the James River, South Dakota)
"Two turkys killed today of which the Indians[25] very much admired
being the first which they ever Saw."—Clark

Sept. 10, 1806 (Vic. of Big Nemaha River, Nebr.)
"we Saw . . . turkies on the Shores today."—Clark

Sept. 18, 1806 (Vic. of Mine River in Missouri)
"saw one bear at a distance and 3 turkeys only today."—Clark

A few additional comments bearing on the distribution and abundance
of wild turkeys are to be found in Lewis' letter to his mother, written at
Fort Mandan just before resuming his journey in the spring of 1805.
(Appendix.)

"On the lower portion of the Missouri, . . . to the Osage River we met
with some . . . turkeys. From thence to the Kancez river . . . some
turkeys, . . . From thence to the mouth of the great river Platte . . .
some . . . turkeys . . . From thence to the Sioux . . . some turkeys . . .
From thence to the mouth of the White river, . . . a greater quantity of
turkeys than we had before seen, a circumstance which I did not much
expect in a country so destitute of timber."

Maximillian[26] who visited the Mandan Indians almost thirty years
later reported seeing wild turkeys in the Missouri valley as far north as
Wheeler, South Dakota.

April 18, 1833 (Vic. of Fort Osage—Missouri)
"Some of my people, attracted by the crys of the wild turkeys, were
tempted to land, but returned without having met with any success. I
happened to have taken no piece with me, which I much regretted for a

wild turkey cock came out of a bush about ten paces from me, and stood still, looking at me, while its splendid feathers shone in the sun."
—Maximillian

April 20, 1833 (Mouth of Big Blue River near Kansas City)
"He (a half-breed Indian river-boatman) was likewise a sportsman and brought us several turkeys which had been recently shot."—Maximillian

May 16, 1833 (Vic. of Wheeler, S. Dak.)
"This may be considered the limit to which the wild turkey extends on the Missouri. It is true that this bird is now and then found higher up, even on the yellowstone River, but these are exceptions, for beyond this place the woods are too open and exposed."—Maximillian

It will be noted that Maximillian set the northern range boundary of the wild turkey in the Missouri valley some seventy-five miles south of the range limit determined by Lewis and Clark. One might conclude that either Maximillian or Lewis and Clark was mistaken; but both parties based their conclusions on limited observations that were largely conditioned by chance.

CHAPTER XIII
Marsh and Shore Birds

The marsh and shore birds were a confusing group for Lewis and Clark. In most cases their descriptions of curlews and plovers were so brief and generalized that positive identification of the species in question is impossible. On the other hand they wrote adequate descriptions of the coot and the avocet, both of which had been previously described and technically named.

AMERICAN COOT

Coues[1] says: "Not only is the coot extensively and very generally dispersed over North America, but, unlike most birds, its breeding range is almost equally wide."

Bent[2] says: "Except in the Northeastern States and Provinces, where it occurs only as a migrant and not very commonly, everybody who knows birds at all is familiar with the plainly dressed, but exceedingly interesting coot or 'mud hen' or 'blue Peter'."

It is surprising, then, that the explorers, who had spent several years in the Ohio valley prior to their western expedition, should not have been familiar with the coot, *Fulica americana* Gmelin. They did not report this species until they arrived at the mouth of the Columbia River, and, even then, they referred to it as a "black duck."

Clark first reported these birds in the vicinity of Smith's Point, near Astoria, Oregon. His account is as follows:

Nov. 30, 1805 (Tongue Point near Astoria, Ore.)

"The fowlers killed 3 black ducks, with white sharp bills, a brown spot on their forward, some white under the tail which is short, and a fiew of the tips of the wing feathers white. Their toes are long, separated and flaped, no craw, keep in emence flocks in the shallow waters & feed on grass, etc."—Clark

During the winter at Fort Clatsop, Lewis wrote a more detailed description of the coot:

Mar. 10, 1806 (Written at Fort Clatsop)

"The black duck is about the size of the bluewinged teal. their colour is a duskey black the breast and belley somewhat lighter than the other parts, or a dark brown. the legs stand longitudinally with the body, and the bird when on shore stands of cours very erect, the legs and feet are of a dark brown, the toes are four on each foot, a short one at the heel and three long toes in front, which are unconnected with a web. the webs are attached to each sides of the several joints of the toe, and divided by deep sinuses at each joint. the web assuming in the intermediate part an eliptical figure. the beak is about two inches long, streight, flated on the sides, and tapering to a sharp point. the upper chap somewhat longest, and bears on it's base at the joining of the head, a little conical protuber-ance of a cartelagenous substance, being redish brown at the point. the beak is of an ivory white colour. the eye dark. these ducks usually associ-ate in large flocks, and are very noisey; their note being a sharp shrill whistle. they are usually fat and agreeably flavored; and feed principally on moss, and other vegetable productions of the water. we did not meet with them untill we reached tide-water; but I believe them not exclusively confined to that district at all seasons, as I have noticed the same duck on many parts of the Rivers Ohio and Mississippi. the gizzard and liver are also remarkably large in this fowl."

Plovers are mentioned repeatedly by Lewis and Clark. Coues attempted to relate their brief notes to the species which were known to have in-habited the areas in which the observations were made, but his determina-tions can scarcely be regarded as better than educated guesses. Neverthe-less, for the sake of completeness Coues' opinions concerning the plovers mentioned by the explorers are cited below:

THE BLACK-BELLIED PLOVER

Coues[3] identified the "large plover" which the explorers reported seeing in North Dakota as *Squatarola squatarola* (Linnaeus). Reid and Gannon were of the same opinion.[4]

THE GOLDEN PLOVER

Lewis and Clark, in describing the western willet, pointed out that it resembled the "gray or whistling plover." With this as the only evidence at hand, Coues concluded that Lewis' gray, whistling plover was the bird commonly known today as the golden plover, *Pluvialis dominica* (Müller).

THE KILLDEER

Evidently, Lewis and Clark were familiar with the killdeer, *Charadrius vociferus* Linnaeus, but they mentioned the bird on two occasions only.

April 8, 1805 (Vic. of Knife River)

"The *kildee* and the large hawk have returned."—Lewis

April 24, 1806 (Vic. of Arlington, Oregon)
"Saw a kill dee."—Lewis

THE MOUNTAIN PLOVER

Thwaites[5] points out that the small brown plover that Lewis saw on July 22, 1805 near Canyon Ferry, Montana could have been either the mountain plover, *Eupoda montana* (Townsend), or the upland plover, but he gives no evidence in support of either alternative.

The passage in question is transcribed below:

July 22, 1805 (Vic. of Canyon Ferry, Mont.)

"We . . . saw a species of small curlooe or plover of a brown colour which I first met with near the entrance of Smith's river, but they are so shy and watchful there is no possibility of getting a shoot at them. it is a different kind from any heretofore described and is about the size of the yellow leged plover or jack Curloo."[6]—Lewis

Coues' comment concerning the foregoing diary entry is as follows:

"Apparently Bartram's sandpiper,[7] *Bartramia longicauda,* which I found common in various parts of Montana, but the Codex has no more satisfactory description than the text (of the diary). I have been expecting for some weeks to find recognizable mention of the mountain plover, *Charadrius montanus* of Townsend, 1839, now *Podasocys montanus* Coues, 1866. This may be the bird Lewis actually had in view, but I cannot make the identification."[8]

As in the case of the plovers, Lewis' notations on the curlews and other birds in this family are, except in case of the western willet, too incomplete for positive identification.

Nonetheless, Coues suggested specific identifications for a few of the "curloos" which Lewis partially described. These species are here listed along with Lewis' remarks concerning them.

LONG-BILLED CURLEW

June 22, 1805 (Vic. of Great Falls, Mont.)

"Saw . . . quantities of little birds and the large brown curloo; the latter is now setting; it lays its eggs, which are of a pale blue with black specks, on the ground without any preparation of a nest."—Lewis

Since the eggs of the long-billed curlew, *Numenius americanus* Bechstein, are generally described by authorities as olive clay-colored with dark brown spots or blotches, it would appear that Lewis was either careless in his description or that he attributed the eggs of some other species to the long-billed curlew.

March 5, 1806 (Written at Fort Clatsop)

"I have not seen the . . . large brown Curloo so common to the plains of the Missouri, but believe that the latter is an inhabitant of this country during summer from Indian information."—Lewis

UPLAND PLOVER

It seems improbable that Lewis and Clark could have spent the spring and summer of 1805 traveling slowly up the Missouri River from Fort Mandan to the Beaverhead Mountains without becoming acquainted with the upland plover, *Bartramia longicauda* (Bechstein). Yet, their descriptions of this bird are so incomplete as to leave room for doubt that they were referring to it.

We have already quoted, in referring to the Mountain plover, Lewis' recorded observations concerning "a species of small curloo or plover of a brown colour," and pointed out that Coues[9] suggested that this may have related to the upland plover.

THE WESTERN WILLET

According to Coues the bird described below was unquestionably a western willet, *Catoptrophorus semipalmatus inornatus* (Brewster).

May 9, 1805 (Site of Fort Peck)

"I killed four plover this evening of a different species from any I have yet seen; it resembles the grey or whistling plover more than any other of this family of birds; it is about the size of the yellow legged or large grey plover common to the lower part of this river as well as most parts of the Atlantic States where they are sometimes called Jack Curloo; the eye is moderately large, are black with a narrow ring of dark yellowish brown; the head, neck, upper part of the body and coverts of the wings are of a dove coloured brown, which when the bird is at rest is the predominant colour; the breast and belley are of a brownish white; the tail is composed of 12 feathers of 3 Inches being of equal length, of these the two in the center are black, with transverse bars of yellowish brown; the others are brownish white. the large feathers of the wings are white tipped with blacked. the back is black, $2\frac{1}{2}$ inches in length, slightly tapering, streight, of a cilindric form and blontly or roundly pointed; the chaps are of equal length, and nostrils narrow, longitudinal and connected; the feet and legs are smoth and of a greenish brown; has three long toes and a short one on each foot, the long toes are unconnected with a web and the short one is placed very high up the leg behind, insomuch that it dose not touch the ground when the bird stands erect. the notes of this bird are louder and more various than any other of this family that I have seen."—Lewis[10]

THE HUDSONIAN CURLEW

Criswell listed the Hudsonian curlew, *Numenius phaeopus hudsonicus* Latham, among the other birds of this family that were described by Lewis and Clark. It should be noted, however, that the explorers only alluded to this species, which they called the "Jack Curloo," in commenting on mountain plover and the western willet.

THE AVOCET

The avocet, *Recurvirostra americana* Gmelin, had been described and technically named[11] before Lewis and Clark "discovered" and described it in 1805.

May 1, 1805 (About 75 miles above the mouth of the Yellowstone River)

"Shannon killed a bird of the plover kind. weight 1 pound. it measured from the tip of the toe, to the extremity of the beak, 1 foot 10 Inches; from tip to tip of wings when extended 2 F. 5 I.; Beak 3⅝ inches; tale 3⅛ inches; leg and tow 10 Ins. the eye black, piercing, prominent and moderately large. the legs are flat thin, slightly imbricated and of a pale sky blue colour, being covered with feathers as far as the mustle extends down it, which is about half of it's length. it has four toes on each foot, three of which, are connected by a web, the fourth is small and placed at the heel about the ⅛ of an inch up the leg. the nails are black and short, that of the middle tow is extremely singular, consisting of two nails the one laping on or overlaying the other, the upper one somewhat the longest and sharpest. the tale contains eleven feathers of equal length, & of a bluish white color. the boddy and under side of the wings, except the large feathers of the 1st. and 2nd. joints of the same, are white, as are also the feathers of the upper part of the 4th joint of the wing and part of those of the 3rd adjacent thereto. the large feathers of the 1st or pinion and the 2nd joint are black; a part of the larger feathers of the 3rd joint on the upper side and all the small feathers which cover the upper part of the wings are black, as are also the tuft of long feathers on each side of the body above the joining of the wing, leaving however a stripe of white between them on the back. the head and neck are shaped much like the grey plover, and are of a light brick-dust brown; the beak is black and flat, largest where it joins the head, and from thence becoming thiner and tapering to a very sharp point, the upper chap being ⅛ of an inch the longest turns down at the point and forms a little hook. the nostrils which commence near the head are long, narrow, connected and parallel with the beak; the beak is much curved, the curvature being upwards in stead of downwards as is common with most birds; the substance of the beak precisely resembles whalebone at a little distance, and is quite as flexible as is that substance. their note resembles that of the grey plover, tho' is reather louder and more varied, their habits appear also to be the same, with this difference; that it sometimes rests on the water and swims which I do not recollect having seen the plover do. this bird which I shall henceforth stile the *Missouri plover,* generally feeds about the shallow bars of the river, to collect its food which consists of (blank space in MS), it immerces it's beak in the water and throws its head and beak from side to side at every step it takes."—Lewis

Lacking a vernacular name for the avocet, Lewis referred to it either as the "Missouri plover or pleaver," or as the "party coloured plover" in recording its presence in certain areas. The following notation is illustrative:

July 17, 1806 (Vic. of the Teton River, a tributary of the Marias River)
"We saw . . . also the party coloured plover with the brick red head and neck; this bird remains about the little ponds which are distributed over the face of these plains, and here raise their young."—Lewis

CHAPTER XIV
Gulls and Terns

While at Fort Clatsop, Clark described four species of "gulls," one of which was not a gull at all, but the Pacific fulmar.

With the possible exception of the fulmar none of these birds are described in sufficient detail to permit of positive identification. Coues,[1] in 1876, in his "Commentary on the Zoological Results of the Expedition," passed over the gulls with the remarks, "Four kinds are alluded to, none of them described." However, in his later work, Coues[2] attempted to identify all of these gulls as follows:

BONAPARTE'S GULL
March 6, 1806 (Written at Fort Clatsop)

"There are 4 species of *larus* or gull on this coast and river. 1st a small species the size of a Pegion; white except some black spots about the head and a little brown on the butt of the wing."—Clark

Coues concluded that the bird described above was Bonaparte's gull, *Larus philadelphia* (Ord). If his identification is correct it would appear that the bird described must have been a juvenile in its first winter plumage. Otherwise the "black spots about the head" cannot be accounted for. At best, Clark's description is so inadequate that Coues' attempt to classify the bird seems quite unwarranted.

GLAUCOUS-WINGED GULL
March 6, 1806 (Written at Fort Clatsop)

"the 2nd species somewhat larger of a light brown colour, with a mealy coloured back."—Clark.

Coues identified this as the young of *Larus glaucescens* Naumann, though how he arrived at this conclusion is not clear.

WESTERN GULL
March 6, 1806 (Written at Fort Clatsop)

"3rd the large Grey gull, or white larus with a greyish brown back, and the light grey belly and breast, about the size of a well grown pullet, the wings are remarkably long in perportion to the size of the body, and its under chap towards the extremity is more gibbous and protuberant than in either of the other species.

"The large grey gull is found on the Columbian waters as high as the entrance of the Kooskooske (Clearwater River) and in common with the other species on the coast, the others appear confined to the tidewater, and the 4th species not so common as either of the others."—Clark

Coues identified this bird as *Larus occidentalis* Audubon. In this case, too, he pointed out that the gull described by Clark was an immature specimen.

Clark's fourth species of gull, the Pacific fulmar, was discussed under the appropriate family.

LEAST TERN

The least tern, *Sterna albifrons antillarum* (Lesson), is the only member of the family *Laridae* that Lewis or Clark described in detail, and this description was found in a sheaf of rough notes[3] (Codex Q) not incorporated in the body of Lewis' diary.

Aug. 5, 1804 (Near mouth of Soldier River)

"I have frequently observed an aquatic bird in the cours of asscending this river but have never been able to procure one before today, this day I was so fortunate as to kill two of them, they are here more plenty than on the river below. they lay their eggs on the sand bars without shelter or nest, and produce their young from the 15.th to the last of June, the young ones of which we caught several are covered with down of a yellowish white colour and on the back some small specks of a dark brown. they bear a great resemblance to the young quale of ten days oald, and apear like them to be able to runabout and peck their food as soon as they are hatched. this bird, lives on small fish, worms and bugs which it takes on the virge of the water it is seldom seen to light on trees an quite as seldom do they lite in the water and swim tho' the foot would indicate that they did it's being webbed. I believe them to be a native of this country and probably a constant resident. the weight of the male bird is one ounce and a half, its length from beak to toe $7\frac{1}{2}$ inches. from tip to tip of wing across the back one foot seven inches and a half (the beak) is one $\frac{1}{8}$ inch long, large where it joins the head flated on the sides and tapering to a sharp point, a little declining and curvated, a fine yellow, with a shade of black on the extremity of upper beak; the eye is prominent, black and on a angular scale of $\frac{1}{2}$ Inc; occupyse $\overline{3}$. $\frac{7}{3}$. in width. the upper part of the head is black from the beak as low as the middle of the eye and a little below the joining of the neck except however some white which joins the upper part of the beak which forks and passing over the sides of the forehead terminate above each eye. the under part of the bird, that is the throat and cheeks as high as the eye, the neck brest belly and under part of the wings and tail are of a fine white, the upper part of the neck, back, and wings are of a fine, quaker coulour, or bright dove colour with reather more of a bluish tint—except however the three first or larger feathers in the wing which on upper side are of a deep black. the wing has four joints

No.	Joint Length of joint	No. of feathers.	Length of d?
1.......1½	(A Clump of feathers not strong but loosely connected with the flesh of the wing)		1¼
2.......2	16		2
3.......1½	7	from 2½ to	4½
4....... ¾	3		5½

the tail has eleven feathers the outer of which are an inch longer than those in the center gradually tapering inwards which gives the tale a forked appearance like that of the swally the largest or outer feather is 2¾ that of the shortest 1¾. the leg and thye are three inches long the leg occupying one half this length the thye is covered with feathers except about ¼ of an inch above the knee the leg is of a bright yellow and nails, long sharp and black the foot is webbed and has three toes forward; the heel or back toe is fixed to the leg above the palm of the foot, and is unconnected by a web to the other toes, it has no nail. the wings when foalded lap like that of the swallow and extend at least an inch and a half beyond the tale. this bird is very noysey when flying which it dose extreemly swift the motion of the wing is much like that of *Kildee* it has two notes one like the squaking of a small pig only on reather a higher kee, and the other kit'-tee'-kit'-tee' —as near as letters can express the sound. the beak of the female is black and the black and quaker colour of the male in her is yellowish brown mixed with dove colour."—Lewis

CHAPTER XV
Pigeons, Parroquets, Goatsuckers and Hummingbirds

We have grouped these independent Orders and Families of birds together merely for convenience.

Lewis and Clark reported finding passenger pigeons as far west as Great Falls and Lolo Creek in Montana and Lemhi River valley in Idaho; and they saw a flock of Carolina parroquets near the mouth of the Kansas River on June 26, 1804. These would appear to be the earliest records of the occurrence of pigeons and parroquets in the localities indicated.

They also wrote the earliest description of the Pacific nighthawk, but they did not recognize it as being different from the nighthawk of the eastern states. A more notable discovery, however, was made on Oct. 16, 1804, near Emmonsburg, North Dakota. On that date Lewis discovered a small goatsucker which was alive but in a dormant state. The bird was unquestionably Nuttall's poor-will.

PASSENGER PIGEON

Schorger,[1] in his recent book, *The Passenger Pigeon,* has cited Lewis and Clark's observations on the occurrence of passenger pigeons, *Ectopistes migratorius* (Linnaeus), in Montana in 1805 and 1806. He is one of a few authors who have not overlooked their diaries in writing about our western birds. Even so, he has not included all of their statements concerning the distribution of this species, and, for the sake of completeness, we are reiterating, and adding to, Schorger's citations:

Feb. 12, 1804 (Mouth of Du Bois River, opposite mouth of the Missouri)
"Pigeons . . . have returned."—Clark

Sept. 16, 1804 (Near White River in South Dakota)
"Almost every species of game is fond of the acorn . . . pigions feed on them."—Lewis

July 12, 1805 (Near mouth of Sun River, above Great Falls, Mont.)
"a fiew wild pigeons about our camp."—Clark

July 13, 1805 (Near mouth of Sun River in Montana)
"I saw a number of turtle doves and some pigeons today. of the latter I shot one; they are the same common to the United States, or the wild pigeon as they are called."—Lewis

Aug. 26, 1805 (On Lemhi River, near Tendoy, Idaho)
"Some fiew pigions."—Clark

July 5, 1806 (Near Missoula, Montana)

"a great number of pigeons breeding in this part of the mountains."
—Lewis

Schorger points out that it is questionable if these pigeons were breeding; more likely they were post-breeding wanderers.

July 21, 1806 (Yellowstone valley)

"Saw . . . also pigions, doves, ..."—Clark

July 25, 1806 (Cut Bank River, a tributary of the Marias River)

"R. Fields and myself killed nine pigeons which lit in the trees near our camp, on these we dined."—Lewis

MOURNING DOVE

Lewis and Clark were thoroughly familiar with mourning doves, *Zenaidura macroura marginella* (Woodhouse), and mentioned them along with pigeons in the vicinity of the Sun River, on the Marias River, the Big Blackfoot River, on Lolo Creek in Montana, and at Fort Clatsop in Oregon.

Coues identified these "doves" as *Zenaidura carolinensis,* a name in common use in 1893.

CAROLINA PARROQUET

While encamped near the mouth of the Kansas River, Lewis and Clark reported seeing a flock of parroquets, *Conuropsis carolinensis ludoviciana* (Gmelin).

June 26, 1804 (Vic. of Kansas River)

"I observed a great number of Parrot queets (Parroquets) this evening."
—Clark

No other reference to this bird will be found in the Lewis and Clark diaries. However, John K. Townsend[2] reported them in central and western Missouri in 1834.

April 7, 1834 (Near Booneville, Missouri)

"We saw here vast numbers of the beautiful parrot of this country, (*Psittacus carolinensis*). They flew around us in flocks, keeping a constant and loud screaming, as though they would chide us for entering their territory; and the splendid green and red of their plumage glancing in the sunshine, as they whirled and circled within a few feet of us, had a most magnificent appearance. They seem entirely unsuspicious of danger, and after being fired at, only huddle closer together, as if to obtain protection from each other, and as their companions are falling around them, they curve down their necks, and look at them fluttering upon the ground, as though perfectly at a loss to account for so unusual an occurrence. It is a most inglorious sort of shooting; down right, cold-blooded murder." —Townsend

April 20, 1834 (near Independence, Mo.)
"Parroquets are plentiful in the bottom lands. . . ."—Townsend

EASTERN WHIP-POOR-WILL
The explorers were familiar with the whip-poor-will, *Caprimulgus vociferus* Wilson, of the East; they mentioned it occasionally in recording the birds of the lower Missouri valley.

June 11, 1804 (Vic. of mouth of Des Moines River)
"the whip-poor-will (is) setting."—Clark

July 6, 1804 (Vic. of St. Joseph, Mo.)
"The bird called whip-poor-will sat on the boat for some time."[3]—Clark

Sept. 6, 1806 (15 miles above Blair, Nebr.)
"Heard the whip-poor-will common to the U. States at Soldier's River." —Clark

In each of the foregoing instances Coues identified the bird referred to as *Antrostomus vociferus* (Wilson), a bird originally described and named, *Caprimulgus minor* by Forster in 1771.

PACIFIC NIGHTHAWK
On June 30, 1805, Lewis and Clark discussed a nighthawk which they observed in the vicinity of the Great Falls of the Missouri. Although they failed to recognize that it differed from the Eastern subspecies, they must be credited with discovering one of the western races of *Chordeiles minor*.

Coues[4] concluded that the bird they saw, but failed to describe in detail, was *Chordeiles minor henryi* Cassin, but this was before the distribution of the seven subspecies now recognized had been determined. Since, according to Bent,[5] the range of the subspecies, *henryi*, does not extend north of southwestern Colorado, the nighthawks which the explorers saw in Montana could not have belonged to this race; and, we are led to conclude that they were of the subspecies, *Cordeiles minor hesperis* Grinnell, which breeds from central Montana westward to the Pacific coast.

June 30, 1805 (Vic. of Great Falls, Mont.)
"There are a number of . . . goatsucker here. I killed one of them and found that there was no difference between them and those common to the United States; I have not seen the leather-winged bat for some time nor is there any of the small goatsuckers in this quarter of the country. We

have not the whip-poor-will either. This last is by many persons in the U' States confounded with the large goat-sucker or night hawk as it is called in the Eastern States, and are taken for the same bird, it is true that there is a good resemblance, but they are distinct species of goat sucker. here the one exists without the other. The large goatsucker lays its eggs in these open plains without the preparation of a nest we have found their eggs in several instances—they lay only two before they set, nor do I believe that they raise more than one brood in a season; they have now just hatched their young."—Lewis

NUTTALL'S POOR-WILL

Nuttall's poor-will was technically described and named *Caprimulgus nuttallii* by Audubon[6] in 1839. This was thirty years after Lewis and Clark observed "the small whip-poor-will or goatsucker of the Missouri."

The following account by Lewis and Clark, describing their first contact with the bird, is noteworthy in view of Edmond C. Jaeger's recent research on the hibernation of this species.[7] Had zoologists not overlooked this observation by Lewis, the discovery of hibernation of Nuttall's poor-will might not have been delayed for almost 150 years.

Oct. 16, 1804 (Vic. of Emmonsburg, North Dakota)

"This day took a small bird alive of the order of the (blank space in MS) or goatsuckers. It appeared to be passing into the dormant stage. on the morning of the 18th the murcury was at 30ᵃ·ᵒ· (above zero?) the bird could scarcely move. I run my penknife into its body under the wing and completely destroyed its lungs and heart yet it lived upwards of two hours. this fanominon I could not account for unless it proceeded from want of circulation of the blood. the recarees call this bird to'na. its note is at-tah-to'-na at-tah-to'na, to-nak, a nocturnal bird, sings only in the night as dose the whip-per will. its weight (is) 1 oz. 17 grains Troy."—Thwaites, *Original Journals of the Lewis and Clark Expedition*, Vol. VI, p. 132.

The same diary entry is to be found in Coues' *History of the Expedition Under The Command of Lewis and Clark*, Vol. I, p. 171; also in Reed and Gannon's *Birds and Mammals Observed by Lewis and Clark in North Dakota*, North Dakota Historical Quarterly, Vol. I, No. 4, p. 19.

Coues, and Reed and Gannon identified the bird in question as Nuttall's poor-will, *Phalaenoptilus nuttallii* (Audubon).

RUFOUS HUMMINGBIRD

This is one of the two species of hummingbirds seen and reported by Lewis and Clark. Clark concluded that this bird did not differ from the ruby-throated hummingbird, but Coues'[8] comments in this connection are of interest.

The questionable passage in the diaries reads as follows:

March 26, 1806 (Written near Green Point, Oregon)
"The hummingbird has appeared. killed one of them and found it the same with those common to the United States."

Coues amended this to read: "killed one and found it (not to be) the same with those common to the United States." In a footnote Coues justified this change in stating that "the hummingbird of the U. S. (Trochilus colubris) does not occur on the Pacific Coast. The species was probably *Selasphorus rufus*."

BROAD-TAILED HUMMINGBIRD

Coues[9] says: "Credit Lewis and Clark with the discovery of this species, which was unknown to science until described as *Trochilis platycercus* by Swainson, Philos, Mag. I, 1827, p. 441, from Mexico, and was only very recently reported from Idaho again."

The foregoing remarks by Coues referred to Lewis' diary entry of June 15, 1806, written in Idaho, near Weippe prairie:
"found the nest of a hummingbird, it had just begun to lay its eggs."

It is of interest to note that Bent[10] says that the broad-tailed hummingbird, *Selasphorus platycercus* (Swainson), is "the hummingbird of the Rock Mountain region, ranging from southern Idaho, Montana and Wyoming to the valley of Mexico, and it is essentially a mountain bird."

EASTERN BELTED KINGFISHER

The kingfisher, *Megaceryle alcyon* (Linnaeus), was an established species long before Lewis and Clark explored the Missouri and Columbia Rivers. Their observations served only to extend knowledge of its abundance and distribution in 1806.

May 7, 1805 (Nearing mouth of the Milk River)
"from its mouth (Missouri River) to this place I have neither seen the blue crested fisher nor the fishing hawk."

July 12, 1805 (Few miles above the Great Falls of the Missouri)
"The blue crested fisher, or as they are sometimes called the Kingfisher, is an inhabitant of this part of the country; this bird is very rare on the Missouri; I have not seen more than three or four of those birds during my voyage from the entrance of the Missouri to the mouth of Maria's river and those few were reather the inhabitants of streams of clerer water

which discharged themselves into the Missouri than that river, as they were seen about the entrance of such streams."—Lewis

July 29, 1805 (Three Forks, Montana)
"the King fisher is common on the river since we left the falls of the Missouri."—Lewis

March 6, 1806 (Written at Fort Clatsop)
"the blue crested or kingfisher are found on every part of the Columbia and its water along which we passed, and are the same with those of the U. S."—Clark

Coues, in each instance, identified the "blue-crested fisher" as *Ceryle alcyon,* the accepted name of the belted kingfisher in 1893.

CHAPTER XVI
The Woodpeckers

Among all the birds and mammals which the explorers discovered, and described in greater or lesser detail, it seems odd that they are best known for two that are striking in appearance but insignificant in size. They are Clark's nutcracker and Lewis' woodpecker.

Lewis' references and descriptions of other woodpeckers are too brief and incomplete for positive identification. Nevertheless, Elliott Coues has suggested the most plausible conclusion as to their identity in each instance.

LEWIS' WOODPECKER

The fact that Alexander Wilson found a specimen of Lewis' woodpecker, *Asyndesmus lewis* (Gray), among the specimens deposited in Peale's Museum has already been mentioned. Obviously, there is no question concerning Lewis' priority in discovering and describing this species, although credit for its original scientific name, *Picus torguatus,* must go to Wilson.[1]

Lewis and Clark first mentioned seeing this species, which they referred to as a "black woodpecker," in the summer of 1805, near Helena, Montana.

July 20, 1805 (Near site of Helena, Montana)

"I saw a black woodpecker (or crow) today about the size of the lark woodpecker as black as a crow. I indeavored to get a shoot at it but could not. it is a distinct species of woodpecker; it has a long tail and flys a good deal like the jay bird."—Lewis

A much more detailed and accurate description of this bird was written in the spring of 1806, while the expedition was encamped on the Clearwater River in Idaho.

May 27, 1806 (Vic. of Kamiah, Idaho)

"The Black woodpecker which I have frequently mentioned and which is found in most parts of the roky Mountains as well as the Western and S. W. mountains, I had never an opportunity of examining untill a few days since when we killed and preserved several of them. this bird is about the size of the lark woodpecker or the turtle dove, tho' it's wings are longer than either of those birds. the beak is black, one inch long, reather wide at the base, somewhat curved, and sharply pointed; the chaps are of equal length. around the base of the beak including the eye and a small part of the throat is of a firm crimson red. the neck and as low as the croop in front is of an irongrey. the belly and breast is a curious mixture of white and blood reed which has much the appearance of having been artificially painted or stained of that colour. the red reather predominates. the top of the head back, sides, upper surface of the wings and tail are black, with a glossey tint of green in a certain exposure to the light. the under side of the wings and tail are of a sooty black. it has ten feathers in the tail, sharply pointed, and those in the centre reather longest, being 2½ inches in length. the tongue is barbed, pointed, and of an elastic cartelaginous substance. the eye is moderately large, puple black and iris of a dark yellowish brown. this bird in it's actions when flying resembles the small red-headed woodpecker common to the Atlantic states; it's note also somewhat resembles that bird. the pointed tail seems to assist it in seting with more eas or retaining its resting position against the perpendicular side of a tree. the legs and feet are black and covered with wide imbricated scales. it has four toes on each foot of which two are in rear and two in front; the nails are much curved long and remarkably keen or sharply pointed. it feeds on bugs worms and a variety of insects."—Lewis

They also mentioned seeing the "black woodpecker" in the Jefferson River valley on Aug. 2, 1805, and on the Lolo Trail across the Bitterroot Range in Montana on July 1, 1806.

ROCKY MOUNTAIN HAIRY WOODPECKER
While the party was ascending the western slope of the Bitterroot Mountains to Lolo Pass on June 15, 1806, a "small speckled woodpecker" was seen. There is no further mention or description of this bird in the diaries. Nevertheless, Coues identified the speckled woodpecker of this locality as *Dryobates villosus hyloscopus*, Cabanis' woodpecker. However, Coues' identification is untenable because Cabanis' woodpecker does not occur north of California. Therefore, we are obliged to conclude that this bird was the Rocky Mountain hairy woodpecker, *Dendrocopos villosus monticola* (Anthony).

A "speckled woodpecker" was seen again on June 15, 1806, near Collin's Creek, a tributary of the Clearwater River in Idaho.

HARRIS' WOODPECKER
On April 5, 1806, near the mouth of the Willamette River Lewis "saw . . . a small speckled woodpecker with a white back." Coues identified this bird as Harris' woodpecker, *Dendrocopos villosus harrisi* (Audubon), a species unknown to science until Audubon described and named it in 1838.

DOWNY AND HAIRY WOODPECKERS
On May 28, 1805, Lewis and Clark mentioned "a small black and white woodpecker with a red head." This observation was made near the mouth

of Judith River in Montana. The statement here quoted will be found in Thwaites, *Original Journals, op. cit.,* Vol. VI, p. 191.

It seems probable that Lewis and Clark were referring to either the male downy or hairy woodpecker.

On page 187 of the same volume of Thwaites, a "small woodpecker, or sapsucker as they are sometimes called" is mentioned, under the date, April 8, 1805.

Reed and Gannon[2] concluded that the bird referred to as "a small woodpecker or sapsucker" must have been either the hairy or downy woodpecker.

At best, no identification of the woodpeckers referred to in these instances, can be more than conjectures.

NORTHERN RED-BREASTED SAPSUCKER

This sapsucker, *Sphyrapicus varius ruber* (Gmelin), was seen on March 4, 1806, at Fort Clatsop. Lewis referred to it as a "small white woodpecker with a red head."

Again, after visiting a Cathlamet Indian village near Knappa, Oregon on March 24, 1806, he writes:

"Saw a white woodpecker with a red head of the small kind common to the United States; this bird has but lately returned, they do not remain during the winter."

Coues,[3] in referring to these remarks, provides us with the following:

"There is no entirely white woodpecker, but several species are black and white, with a red head. That found east of the Rocky Mountains is *Melanerpes erythrocephalis;* the one mentioned by Lewis, elsewhere (March 24, 1806) said to be migratory, belongs to the Pacific slope, and is identified as Sphyrapicus ruber."

NORTHERN FLICKER

The northern flicker was mentioned occasionally by Lewis and Clark. They invariably referred to it as the "lark-woodpecker."

April 11, 1805 (Fort Mandan)

"The lark-woodpecker, with yellow wings and a black spot on the breast, common to the United States, has appeared. . . ."

Reed and Gannon[4] identified this as the North Dakota race of the northern flicker, *Colaptes auratus luteus* Bangs.

RED-SHAFTED FLICKER

The "lark-wood pecker," which Lewis and Clark mentioned, on March 4, 1806, in the vicinity of Fort Clatsop, was identified by Coues as the red-shafted flicker, *Colaptes mexicanus,* a name which is now obsolete.

241

Probably the "lark woodpeck" seen by Lewis and Clark at Traveler's Rest near the mouth of Lolo Creek, southwest of Missoula, Montana, was also of this species since the range of the red-shafted flicker, *Colaptes cafer collaris* Vigors, extends from the Rocky Mountains to the Pacific coast.

Of course, there is a possibility that the "lark-woodpecker" seen at Fort Clatsop may have been the Northwestern flicker, *Colaptes cafer cafer* (Gmelin) rather than the red-shafted flicker.

Since all of the races of *Colaptes* interbreed freely where their ranges overlap, particularly the Northern and Red-shafted races whose ranges overlap in the Rocky Mountains, it becomes impossible to determine with certainty which of them Lewis and Clark referred to.

RED-HEADED WOODPECKER

The range of the red-headed woodpecker, *Melanerpes erythrocephalis* (Linnaeus), extends westward to the Rocky Mountains. Perhaps, they were not very abundant on the upper Missouri in 1804-06, for Lewis and Clark reported them infrequently.

Sept. 9, 1805 (Bitterroot River valley)

"two of our hunters have arrived, one of them brought with him a red-headed woodpecker of the kind common to the U'. States. This is the first of the kind I have seen since I left the Illinois."—Lewis

July 16, 1806 (Near Great Falls, Montana)

"saw . . . red-headed woodpeckers."—Lewis

Aug. 3, 1806 (Below the mouth of the Musselshell River)

"we saw . . . the red-headed woodpecker."—Lewis

NORTHERN PILEATED WOODPECKER

Lewis and Clark alluded to the pileated woodpecker as the "log-cock." Its occurrence was recorded at Fort Clatsop on March 4, 1806:

"The large woodpecker, or log cock, . . . are the same with those of the Atlantic states and are found exclusively in the timbered country."

Lewis, also, listed it among other species observed in the vicinity of Lolo Creek, southwest of Missoula, Montana, on July 1, 1806.

Coues[5] identified the "log-cock" as the northern pileated woodpecker, *Dryocopus pileatus obieticola* (Bangs). However the specimen seen at Fort Clatsop undoubtedly was the western subspecies *Dryocopus pileatus picinus* (Bangs).

CHAPTER XVII
The Passerine Birds

Lewis and Clark's most notable discoveries among the Passerine birds include the American magpie, the black-headed jay, Clark's nutcracker, the white-rumped shrike, and the western tanager.

Lewis sent both skins and living specimens of the magpie to President Jefferson from Fort Mandan in 1805. There is evidence, cited hereinafter, that at least one of these birds survived the journey and was displayed in Peale's Museum.

Several species of passerine birds were recorded by the explorers but not described at all, or so incompletely described that we cannot be certain of their identity. Among these are the eastern kingbird, the purple martin, northern cliff swallow, northwestern and western crows, northern raven, eastern winter wren, western winter wren, catbird, mockingbird, brown thrasher, eastern robin, cedar waxwing, cowbird, Brewer's blackbird, eastern meadowlark, the lark bunting, eastern cardinal, pale goldfinch, pine siskin, McCown's longspur, and golden-crowned sparrow.

Coues, from his extensive knowledge of western birds, was able to draw conclusions as to the probable identity of many of the species listed above.

On the other hand, several of the strange western species such as the magpie, black-headed jay, pinyon jay, Clark's nutcracker, the northern and Pacific varied thrushes, the white-rumped shrike, the western meadowlark, and the western tanager were described by the explorers accurately enough to warrant positive identifications.

HORNED LARK
In this instance Lewis and Clark mentioned seeing a *prairie lark* in the Bitterroot valley near Traveler's Rest, but they did not describe it.

Coues identified the bird in question as the horned lark, *Eremophila alpestris,* without commenting on his reasoning in this instance.

FLYCATCHER
Coues assigned the second of the "two species of flycatch" which Lewis described at Fort Clatsop to the genus, *Empidonax.*

Lewis' description was not sufficiently complete for determination of the species:

March 4, 1806 (Written at Fort Clatsop)

"the second species has lately returned and dose not remain here all winter. its colours are yellowish brown on the back, head, neck, wings and tail.

the breast and belley of a yellowish white; the tail is in proportion as the wren, but it is a size smaller than that bird. its beak is streight, pointed, convex, reather large at the base and the chaps of equal length. the first species[1] is the smallest. in short it is the smalest bird that I ever seen in America except the hummingbird. both these species are found in the woody country only, or at least I have never seen them elsewhere."

KINGBIRDS

Lewis recorded the kingbird near the mouth of the Marias River in Montana. This may have been the Arkansas kingbird, *Tyrannus verticalis* Say, but the absence of any description whatsoever makes it impossible to ascertain which species was seen. Of course the Arkansas kingbird is more common in the northern plains states than the eastern kingbird, but it seems to us that Lewis would have mentioned the fact if it had differed from the eastern species with which he was familiar. The reference in question follows:

June 10, 1805 (Vic. of the Marias River)

"the bee Martin or Kingbird is common to this country; tho' there are no bees in this country, nor have we met with a honey bee since we passed the entrance of the Osage River (Kansas River)."—Lewis

WOOD PEWEE

On April 16, 1806, Lewis recorded seeing "a species of the peawee" in the vicinity of Celilo Falls of the Columbia River.

CLIFF SWALLOW

The diaries contain only one reference to the cliff swallow, *Petrochelidon pyrrhonota* (Vieillot).

May 31, 1805 (Now Chouteau County, Mont.)

"a number of the small martin which build their nests with clay in a globular form attached to the wall (of cliffs) within those nitches, and which were seen hovering about the tops of the columns did not the less remind us of some of those large stone buildings in the U. States."—Lewis

The identity of the birds mentioned above is unmistakable, and Coues supports this conclusion.

AMERICAN MAGPIE

Lewis and Clark were unquestionably the first observers on the upper Missouri to call attention to the American magpie, *Pica pica hudsonia* (Sabine). They mentioned this species for the first time near the mouth of the Crow Creek, a few miles above the White River, in South Dakota.

Sept. 17, 1804 (Vic. of Crow Creek)

"Capt. Lewis went out with a View to See the Countrey and its productions, he killed a Buffalow and a remarkable Bird (Magpy) of the Corvus Species, long tail and upper part of the feathers and also the wings is of a purplish variated Green, the back and part of the wing feathers are white edged with black, white belly, while from the root of the wings to Center of the back is White, the head nake (neck), breast and other parts are black—the beeke like a Crow. Abt. the Size of a large Pigion, a butifull thing."—Clark

Lewis[2] wrote a more detailed description of this bird on the same day:—

Sept. 17, 1804 (Vic. of Crow Creek)

"one of the hunters killed a bird of the *Corvus genus* and order of the pica & about the size of a jack-daw. with a remarkable long tale. beautifully variagated. it(s) note is not disagreeable though loud—it is twait-twait-twait, twait; twait, twait twait twait.

	Ft.	In.
from tip to tip of wing	1	10
D° beak to extremity of tale	1	8½
of which the tale occupys		11
from extremity of middle toe to hip	5	5½

it's head, beak, and neck are large for a bird of it's size; the beak is black and of a convex and cultrated figure, the chaps nearly equal, and it's base large and beset with hairs. the eyes are black encircled with a narrow ring of yellowish black it's head, neck, brest & back within one inch of the tale are of a fine glossey black, as are also the short feathers of the under part of the wing, the thies and those about the root of the tale. the belly is of a beautiful white which passes above and arround the but of the wing, where the feathers being long reach to a small white spot on the rump one inch in width. the wings have nineteen feathers, of which the ten first have the longer side of their plumage white in the middle of the feather and occupying unequal lengths of the same from one to three inches, and forming when the wing is spread a kind of triangle, the upper and lower part of these party coloured feathers on the under side of the wing being of dark colour but not jut or shining black. the under side of the remaining feathers of the wing are darker. the upper side of the wing, as well as the short side of the plumage of the party-coloured feathers is of a dark blackish or bluish green sonetimes presenting a light orange yellow or bluish tint as it happens to be presented to different exposures of light. the plumage of the tale consists of 12 feathers of equal lengths by pair(s), those in the center are the longest, and the others on each side deminishing about an inch each pair.

the underside of the feathers is a pale black, the upper side is a dark blueish green and which like the outer part of the wings is changable as it reflects different portions of light. towards the extremity of these feathers they become of an orrange green, then shaded pass to a redish indigo blue, and again at the extremity assume the predominant colour of changable green. the tints of these feathers are very similar and equally beatiful and rich as the tints of blue and green of the peacock. it is a most beatifull bird. the legs and toes are black and imbricated. it has four long toes, three in front and one in rear, each terminated with a black sharp tallon of from 3/8ths to ½ an inch in length. these birds are seldom found in parties of more than three or four and most usually at this season single as the halks and other birds of prey usually are. It's usual food is flesh. this bird dose not spread it's tail when it flys and the motion of it's wings when flying is much like that of a Jay-bird."—Lewis

The European magpie had been named by Linnaeus in 1758, and the American species was first assigned to the same species *Corvus pica* by Forster. Sabine, in 1823, must be credited with first describing it as a separate species, *Corvus hudsonius*.

Above Crow Creek, Lewis and Clark mentioned the magpie repeatedly.

Oct. 6, 1804 (Near Swan Creek, Walworth County, S. Dak.)
"The Corvus or Magpie is verry common in this quarter."—Clark

April 12, 1805 (Near mouth of the Little Missouri River)
"I saw the Magpie in pars."—Clark

March 4, 1806 (Written at Fort Clatsop)
"the Magpie is most commonly found in the open country and are the same with those formerly described on the Missouri."—Lewis

Aug. 3, 1806 (Vic. of Musselshell River)
"We saw . . . the party-coloured Corvus. . . ."—Lewis

April 14, 1805 (Mouth of the Little Missouri River)
"We saw a number of Magpies, their nests and eggs—their nests are built in trees and composed of small sticks, leaves and grass, open at the top, and much in the stile of the large blackbird common to the U' States —the egg is of a bluish brown colour, freckled with redish brown spots." —Lewis

Certainly the nest described above is not typical of the magpie, and one is led to surmise that Lewis may have attributed the nest of some other bird to the magpie. However, a few days later, Clark correctly pointed out that the magpies' nests were provided with a canopy with one or more entrance holes.

April 26, 1805 (Near mouth of the Yellowstone River)

"I observe that the Magpie, goose, duck and eagle all have their nests in the same neighbourhood, and it is not uncommon for the Magpie to build in a few rods of the eagle—the nests of this bird is built verry strong with sticks covered verry thickly, with one or more places through which they enter or escape."—Clark

April 17, 1806 (Vic. of the Des Chutes River, Oregon)

"Joseph Fields brought me today three eggs of the party-coloured corvus, they are about the size and shape of those of the pigeon. They are bluish-white, much freckled with reddish brown irregular spots, in short it is reather a mixture of those colours in which the reddish brown predominates, particularly toward the large end."—Lewis

The magpie was mentioned as having been seen at many other locations along the upper Missouri and in the Columbia basin.

A magpie skin, and a cage containing four living magpies, was listed among the items consigned to President Jefferson from Fort Mandan in April, 1805.

Jefferson's letter to Comte de Volney, dated Feb. 11, 1806, clearly states that this shipment, including the magpie skin, had arrived in Washington. Besides, a copy of the invoice on which the items included in the shipment were listed has been preserved among the *Jefferson Papers* (Bureau of Rolls), Codex L., Series 2, Vol. 51, Doc. 105a; and this document bears the notations of a clerk who checked-off the specimens received. The word "came" appears after both the magpie skin and the caged birds.

Alexander Wilson included the magpie in his *American Ornithology*, Vol. II, pp. 73, 77. His remarks concerning it are as follows:

"The drawing was taken from a very beautiful specimen, sent from the Mandan nation, on the Missouri, to Mr. Jefferson, and by that gentleman presented to Mr. Peale of this city, in whose museum it lived for several months, and where I had an opportunity of examining it. On carefully comparing it with the European magpie in the same collection, no material difference could be perceived. The figure on the plate is reduced to exactly half the size of life." And again on page 79: "In 1804, an exploring party under the command of Captains Lewis and Clark, on their route to the Pacific ocean across the continent, first met with the magpie somewhere near the great bend of the Missouri, and found that the number of these birds increased as they advanced. Here also the blue jay disappeared; as if the territorial boundaries and jurisdiction of these two noisy and voracious families of the same tribe had been mutually agreed on, and distinctly settled. But the magpie was found to be far more daring than the jay, dashing into their very tents, and carrying off the meat from the dishes. One of the hunters who accompanied the expedition informed me, that they frequently attended him while he was engaged in skinning and cleaning the carcass of the deer, bear or buffalo he had killed, often seizing the meat that hung within a foot or two of his head."

It is surprising that Henry W. Setzer of the U. S. National Museum claims that no report has been found that any of the living animals included in the shipment from Fort Mandan ever reached St. Louis.[3]

It would appear that he overlooked the references cited above which attest to the fact that the magpies at least were delivered to Jefferson and subsequently displayed in Peale's Museum in Philadelphia.

RAVENS AND CROWS

The explorers reported seeing ravens, *Corvus corax principalis* Ridgway, on the Yellowstone River in southwestern Montana, on the Columbia River below the Cascades, at Fort Clatsop, and on the Marias River in northwestern Montana.

They did not attempt to describe the raven, but simply pointed out that it did not seem to differ from those of the United States.

Crows were seen frequently throughout the course of the journey. Rudolf Bennitt[4] was of the opinion that those seen from the Rocky Mountains to Fort Clatsop were of the race, *Corvis brachyrhynchos hesperis* Ridgway, rather than *Corvus caurinus* Baird as determined by Elliott Coues.

BLACK-HEADED JAY

Lewis and Clark can be credited with the discovery of this bird, which they consistently referred to as the "blue-crested corvus."

They described it briefly on the west slope of the Bitterroot Mountains near Hunger Creek.

Sept. 20, 1805 (On Lochsa River Trail)

"I have also observed two birds of a blue colour, both of which I believe to be of the haulk or vulture kind[5] one of a blue shining colour with a very high tuft of feathers on the head, long tale, it feeds on flesh—the beak and feet black, its note is chă-ăh, chă-chă. it is about the size of a pigeon, and in shape and action resembles the jay bird."—Lewis

Coues[6] has identified the "blue crested corvus" as Steller's jay, but the bird described was not *Cyanocitta stelleri stelleri* (Gmelin), which is restricted to the coniferous forests of the Pacific slope, north from Puget Sound. It was, on the other hand, the black-headed jay, *Cyanocitta stelleri annectens* (Baird).

Lewis described the black-headed jay in much greater detail in a body of zoological notes[7] that were not incorporated in his journals:

"Discription of the blue Crested corvus bird common to the woody and western side of the Rockey Mountains, and all the woody country from thence to the Pacific Ocean. It's beak is black convex, cultrated, wide at its base where it is beset with hairs, and is 1¼ inches from the opening of the chaps to their extremity, and from the joining of the head to the extremity of the upper chap 1⅛ inches, the upper exceeds the under chap a little; the nostrils are small round unconnected and placed near the base of the beak where they lye concealed by the hairs or hairy feathers which cover the base of the upper chap. the eye reather large and full but not prominent and of a deep bluish black, there being no difference in the colour of the puple and the iris. the crest is very full the feathers from 1 to 1½ Inches long and occupye the whole crown of the head. the head neck, the whole of the body including the coverts of the wings, the upper disk of the tail and wings are of a fine glossey bright indigo blue Colour the under disk of the tail and wings are of a dark brown nearly black. the leg and first joint of the thye are 4¼ In. long, the legs and feet are black and the front covered with 6 scales the hinder part smothe, the toes are also imbrecated, four in number long and armed with long sharp black tallons. the upper disk of the first four or five feathers of the wing next to the boddy, are marked with small transverse spripes of black as are also the upper side of the two center feathers of the tail; the tail is five inches long & is composed of twelve feathers of equal length. the tail 1 & ½ as long as the boddy. the whole length from the point of the beak to extremity of the tail 1 Foot 1 Inch; from the tip of one to the tip of the other wing 1 Foot 5½ Inches. the size & the whole Contour of this bird resembles very much the blue jay or jay-bird as they are called in the U'States. like them also they seldom rest in one place long but are in constant motion hoping from spra to spray. what has been said is more immediately applicable to the male, the colours of the female are somewhat different in her the head, crest, neck, half the back downwards and the coverts of the wings are of a dark brown, but sometimes there is a little touch of the Indigo on the short feathers on the head at the base of the upper chap. this bird feeds on flesh when they can procure it, also on bugs flies and buries. I do not know whether they destroy little birds but their tallons indicate their capacity to do so if nature has directed it. their note is loud and frequently repeated chă-ă' chă-ă', &c. also twat twat twat, very quick."—Lewis

Lewis' only remark on the distribution and habitat of this species was written at Fort Clatsop on March 4, 1806. Here he points out that the "blue crested corvus" is a native of "the piney country invariably, being found as well on the rocky mountains as on this coast."

PINYON JAY

Bent[8] says that Maximillian's jay, *Gymnorhinus cyanocephala* Wied, as it was called by some of the earlier writers, "was discovered and first described by that eminent naturalist Maximillian, Prince of Wied, in his book of travels in North America, published in 1841, according to Baird, Brewer, and Ridgway (1874). Mr. Edward Kern, who was connected with Colonel Fremont's expedition in 1846, was the first to bring specimens of this interesting and remarkable bird to the notice of American naturalists, transmitting them to the Philadelphia Academy."

Coues[9] however, maintains that a bird described briefly by Lewis and Clark in the Jefferson River valley was this species. If so, their description antedated that of Maximillian by thirty-six years.

Lewis' description, and Coues' footnote with reference to it, follow:

Aug. 1, 1805 (Jefferson River valley)

"I also saw near the top of the mountain among some scattering pine a blue bird about the size of the common robbin. Its action and form is somewhat that of the jay bird and never rests long in any one position but constantly flying or hoping from sprey to sprey. I shot at one of them but missed it. their note is loud and frequently repeated both flying and when at rest and is a char-âh, char-âh, char-âh, as nearly as letters can express it."—Lewis

"This is the so-called blue crow, or Cassin's or Maximillian's jay, here first discovered and described but not for years afterward scientifically named *Gymnokitta cyanocephala*, first *Gymnorhinus cyanocephalus* Maximillian."—Coues

ROCKY MOUNTAIN JAY

On the same day that Lewis and Clark described the Pinyon jay, they also mentioned seeing "another bird of a very similar genus, the note resembling the mewing of a cat, with a white head and light blue color."

Coues[10] identified this as the Rocky Mountain jay, *Perisoreus canadensis capitalis* Ridgway, a variety of the Canada jay, or "whiskey jack."

This jay is gray with a white crown rather than blue. Evidently the explorers observations or records were faulty.

GRAY JAY

In reviewing the zoology of the region west of the Rocky Mountains, Lewis mentioned a *small white-breasted corvus* that was found both in the Rocky Mountains and on the Pacific coast. Thwaites concluded that it was the gray jay, *Perisoreus canadensis griseus* Ridgway.[11] Coues'[12] footnote concerning the identity of this bird may be quoted:

"The small white breasted corvus might be taken for the California jay, *Aphelocoma californica,* which is blue, with white underparts, and no crest. But this species is not found in the piney country of the northern mountains to which the text refers. Hence, by exclusion, we discover that a species of *Perisoreus* is our "small white-breasted corvus. That one which the explorers found in the mountains of Idaho is *P. canadensis capitalis,*[13] a variety of the familiar Canada jay. That which they found in coast region is *P. obscurus,*[14] technically distinct, but so little different from the other that it has usually been regarded as the same."

CLARK'S NUTCRACKER

Clark's nutcracker, *Nucifraga columbiana* (Wilson), was one of three birds in the Lewis and Clark collection in Peale's Museum in Philadelphia that Alexander Wilson described and named. The other two were Lewis' woodpecker and the Western tanager, both of which will be discussed hereinafter. Wilson included all three of these species in his *American Ornithology, op. cit.*

The explorers first observed this bird in the vicinity of the Lemhi River while encamped with the Shoshone Indians, near Tendoy, Idaho.

Aug. 22, 1805 (Vic. of Shoshone camp site)

"I saw today a species of woodpecker which fed on seeds of pine. its beak and tail were white, its wings were black, and every other part a dark brown. it about the size of a robin."—Lewis

On their return journey, in May, 1806, they succeeded in collecting several specimens near Weippe, Idaho. Here, while waiting for the snow to settle in the passes of the Bitterroot Mountains, they wrote a detailed description of this species:

May 28, 1806 (Camp Chopunnish, near Weippe Prairie)

"Since my arrival here I have killed several birds of the *corvus* genus of a kind found only in the rocky mountains and their neighbourhood. I first met this bird above the three forks of the Missouri and saw them on the hights of the rockey mountains but never before had an opportunity of examining them closely. the small corvus described at Fort Clatsop is a different species, tho' untill now I had taken it to be the same, this is much larger and has a loud squawting note something like the mewing of a cat. the beak of this bird is 1½ inches long, is proportionably large, black and of the form which, characterizes this genus. the upper exceeds the under chap a little. the head and neck are also proportionably large, the eye full and reather prominent, the iris dark brown and puple black, it is about the size and somewhat the form of the Jaybird tho reather rounder or more full in the body. the tail is four and one half inches in length, composed of

12 feathers nearly of the same length. the head neck and body of this bird are of a dove colour. the wings are black except the extremities of six large feathers occupying the middle joint of the wing which are white, the under disk of the wing is not of the shining or glossy black which marks its upper surface. the two feathers in the center of the tail are black as are the two adjacent feathers for half their width the ballance are of a pure white, the feet and legs are black and imbricated with wide scales. the nails are black and remarkably long and sharp, also much curved, it has four toes on each foot of which one is in the rear and three in front. the toes are long particularly that in the rear. This bird feeds on the seed of the pine and also on insects. it resides in the rocky mountains at all seasons of the year, and in many parts is the only bird to be found."—Lewis

WESTERN WINTER WREN
At Fort Clatsop Lewis and Clark observed a small species of bird resembling a wren which they listed as a "species of flycatch."

March 4, 1806 (Written at Fort Clatsop)
"there are two species of fly catch, a small redish brown species with a short tail, round body, short neck and short pointed beak. They have some fine black specks intermixed with the uniform redish brown. This is the same with that which remains all winter in Virginia where it is sometimes called the wren."—Lewis

This description, although brief, was sufficient for Coues[15] to identify the bird as the western winter wren, first classified by Baird as *Troglodytes hiemalis pacificus*, in 1864. The presently accepted name, however, is *Troglodytes troglodytes pacificus* Baird.

The following birds were merely recorded by Lewis and Clark as having been seen in specific localities:

Catbird, *Dumetella carolinensis* (Linnaeus)
  Mentioned on June 10, 1805, in the vicinity of the Marias River.
Mockingbird, *Mimus polyglottos* (Linnaeus)
  On May 17, 1805, Clark recorded seeing this species in Montana two
  days before they arrived at the mouth of the Musselshell River.
Brown thrasher, *Toxostoma rufum* (Linnaeus)
  The "brown thrush" was also mentioned on June 8, 1805.
Eastern robin, *Turdus migratorius* Linnaeus
  On June 8, 1805, Lewis listed the robin among birds seen near the
  Marias River.

PACIFIC VARIED THRUSH
This bird, *Ixoreus naevius* (Gmelin), is known locally in the Pacific Northwest as the "Oregon robin." Lewis and Clark wrote an excellent description

of it, but the specimen intended for Dr. Barton in Philadelphia was evidently damaged or lost. At least, there is no evidence that it was among the specimens turned over to Peale's Museum.

Although the Pacific varied thrush was strange to the explorers, it was not new to science in 1806. Gmelin had named the species *Turdus naevius* in 1788.

Lewis had noticed a bird in the Bitterroot Mountains while descending the Lolo Trail which appeared to be the same as that which he examined and described at Fort Clatsop. However, it probably belonged to a different subspecies.

Sept. 20, 1805 (Written on the Lolo Trail)

"This morning my attention was called to a species of bird which I had never seen before (copy for Dr. Barton). It was reather larger than a robbin, tho' much its form and action. the colours were a bluish brown on the back, the wings, and tale black, as wass a stripe above the croop ¾ of an inch wide in front of the neck, and two others of the same colour passed from its eyes back along the sides of the head. The top of the head, neck brest and belly and butts of the wing were of a fine yellowish brick reed (red). it was feeding on the buries of a species of shoemake or ash which grows common in (this) country."—Lewis

Then, during the winter at Fort Clatsop he described another specimen in greater detail.

Jan. 31, 1806 (Written at Fort Clatsop)

"Charbono found a bird dead lying near the fort this morning and brought it to me. I immediately recognized it to be of the same kind of that which I had seen in the Rocky Mountains on the morning of the 20th of September last. this bird is about the size as near as may be of the robbin. it's colour also is precisely the same with that bird. it measures one foot 3¼ Inches from tip to tip of the wings when extended. 9¼ inches from the extremith of the beak to that of the tail. the tail is 3¾ inches in length, and composed of eleven feathers of the same length. The beak is smoth, black, convex, and cultrated; one and ⅛ inches from the point to the opening of the chaps and ¾ only uncovered with feathers; the upper chap exceeds the other a little in length. a few small black hairs garnish the (sides of the) base of the upper chap. the eye is of a uniform deep sea green or black, moderately large, it's legs and tallons are white; the legs are an inch and ¼ in length and smoth; four toes on each foot, of which that in front is the same length with the leg including the length of the tallon, which is 4 lines; the three remaining toes are ¾ of an inch, each armed with proportionably long tallons, the toes are slightly imbricated. the tallons are curved and sharply pointed. The crown of the head from the beak back to the neck, the back of the head imbracing reather more than

253

half the circumphrence of the neck, the back and tale, are of bluish dark brown; the two outer feathers of the tale have a little dash of white near their tips not perceptible when the tail is foalded. a fine black forms the ground of the wings; two stripes of the same colour pass on either side of the head from the base of the beak along the side of the head to it's junction with the neck, and imbraces the eye to it's upper edge; a third stripe of the same colour ¾ of an inch in width passes from the sides of the neck just above the butts of the wings across the croop in the form of a garget. the throat or under part of the neck brest and belly is of a fine yellowish brick red. a narrow strip of this colour also commences just above the center of each eye, and extends backwards to the neck as far as the back stripe reaches before discribed, to which, it appears to answer as a border. the feathers which form the 1st and second ranges of the coverts of the two joints of the wing next the body, are beautifully tiped with this brick red; as is also each large feather of the wing on the short side of its plumage for ½ an inch in length commensing at the extremity of the feathers which form the first or main covert of the wing. this is a beautiful little bird. I have never heard it's note it appears to be silent. it feeds on berries, and I believe is a rare bird even in this country, or at least this is the second time only that I have seen it. between the legs of this bird the feathers are white, and those which form the tuft underneath the tail are a mixture of white and a brick red."—Lewis

Perhaps it should be emphasized that, even though Lewis considered the two birds described above to be identical, the bird collected in the Bitterroot Mountains may have been the northern varied thrush, *Ixoreus naevius meruloides* (Swainson).

CEDAR WAXWING

The cedar waxwing, *Bombycilla cedrorum* Vieillot, had no scientific status when Lewis recorded its occurrence in the Missouri valley and wrote a brief description of it. It was not technically named until 1807, when Vieillot published an account of it in *Historie Naturelle des Oiseaux de l'Amérique Septentrionale* (Paris: Desray), Vol. I, p. 88.

Lewis' notations are as follows:

Nov. 10, 1804 (At Fort Mandan)

"Saw a flock of the crested Cherry birds passing to the South."

April 6, 1805 (At Fort Mandan)

"This day a flock of cherry or cedar birds were seen, one of the men killed several of them which gave me an opportunity of examining them. They are common in the United States; usually asociate in large flocks and are frequently destructive of the chery orchards, and in winter in the lower parts of the state of Virginia and Maryland feed on the buries of Cedar. They are a small bluish brown bird crested with a tuft of dark brown feathers with a narrow black stripe passing on each side of the head underneath the eye from the base of the upper beak to the back of the head. it is distinguished more particularly by some of the shorter feathers of the wing, which are tiped with a red spots that have much the appearance at a little distance of sealing wax."

WHITE-RUMPED SHRIKE

We can credit Lewis and Clark with the discovery of this bird, *Lanius ludovicianus excubitorides* Swainson, and with writing the first description of it.

Swainson's technical description, whereby the species was given scientific status, was not published until 1831.

Lewis' description is sufficiently detailed to permit positive identification of the bird he described, and Coues[16] did not hesitate to assign it to *Lanius excubitorides*.

June 10, 1805 (Near mouth of Marias River)

"I saw a small bird today which I do not recollect ever having seen before. it is about the size of the blue thrush or catbird, and it's colour not unlike that bird. the beak is convex, moderately curved, black, smoth, and large in proportion to its size. the legs were black, it had four toes of the same colour on each foot, and the nails appeared long and somewhat in form like the tallons of the haulk, the eye black and proportionately large. a bluish brown colour occupied the head, neck, and back, the belly was white; the tail was reather long in proportion and appeared to be composed of feathers of equal length of which a part of those in the center were white the others black, on each side of the head from the beak back to the neck a small black stripe extended imbrasing the eye. it appeared to be very busy in catching insects which I presume is it's usual food; I found the nest of this little bird, the female which differed but little from the male was seting on four eggs of a pale blue colour with small black freckles or dots."— Lewis

BREWER'S BLACKBIRD

Brewer's blackbird, *Euphagus cyanocephalus* (Wagler), is closely related to the rusty blackbird of the East. Coues,[17] in his edited version of the Biddle Text of the diaries, quotes Lewis as saying that "the large blackbird (blue-headed grackle, *Scolecophagus cyanocephalis*) is (not) the same with those of our country"; whereas, the Thwaites text reads as follows:

"The Crow, Ravine and large Blackbird are the same as those of our country, only that the crow is much smaller, yet its note is the same."

Lewis was writing his review of the fauna of the area west of the Bitterroot Mountains. Obviously Coues inserted the word "not" to emphasize the fact that Lewis was mistaken in saying that the large blackbird of the Oregon coast was the same as the large eastern blackbird.

COWBIRD

In the Biddle text of the diaries the cowbird is referred to as "the buffalo-pecker."

July 11, 1805 (At Great Falls, Montana)

"Among the smaller game are the brown thrush, pigeons, doves, and a beautiful bird called the buffalo-pecker."

In a footnote to this entry, Coues points out that the cowbird, or cow blackbird, *Molothrus ater* (Boddaert), has the habit of alighting on the backs of cattle to pick the ticks or other insects which infest their hides.

WESTERN MEADOWLARK

Lewis noted the distinction between the meadowlarks of the western plains and those of the east. Nevertheless, the western meadowlark, *Sturnella neglecta*, remained unknown to science until 1843, when Audubon described and named it.

June 22, 1805 (Vic. of the Great Falls of the Missouri)

"There is a kind of larke here that much resembles the bird called the old field lark, with a yellow brest and a black spot on the croop; tho' this differs from ours in the form of the tail which is pointed being formed of feathers of unequal length; the beak is somewhat longer and more curved, and the note differs considerably; however, in size, action and colours there is no perceptable difference; or at least none that strikes my eye."—Lewis

March 4, 1806 (Written at Fort Clatsop)

"the lark is found in the plains only and are the same with those before mentioned on the Missouri, and not very unlike what is called in Virginia the old field lark."[18]

WESTERN TANAGER

Coues[19] points out that Lewis and Clark wrote the earliest description of the western tanager, *Piranga ludoviciana* (Wilson). Moreover, the specimen which they procured, one of the few that they succeeded in bringing out of the wilderness, was subsequently made available to Alexander Wilson by Peale's Museum in Philadelphia. Wilson included this bird in his *American Ornithology,* published in 1811.

Lewis' description is remarkably accurate:

June 6, 1806 (Written at Camp Chopunnish on the Clearwater River, a few miles east of Kamiah, Idaho)

"we meet with a beautifull little bird in this neighbourhood about the size and somewhat the shape of the large sparrow. it is reather longer in proportion to its bulk than the sparrow. it measures 7 inches from the extremity of the beak to that of the tail, the latter occupying 2½ inches. the beak is reather more than half an inch in length, and is formed much like the virginia nitingale; it is thick and large for a bird of it's size; wide at the base, both chaps convex, and pointed, the upper exceeds the under chap a little is somewhat curved and of a brown colour; the lower chap of a greenish yellow. the eye full reather large and of a black colour both puple and iris. the plumage is remarkably delicate; that of the neck and head is of a fine orrange yellow and red, the latter predominates on the top of the head and arround the base of the beak from whence it graduly deminishes and towards the lower part of the neck, the orrange yellow prevails most; the red has the appearance of being laid over a ground of yellow. the breast, the sides, rump and some long feathers which lie between the legs and extend underneath the tail are of a fine orrange yellow. the tail, back and wings are black, except a small stripe of yellow on the outer part of the middle joint of the wing. ¼ of an inch wide and an inch in length. the tail is composed of twelve feathers of which those in the center are reather shortest, and the plumage of all the feathers of the tail is longest on that side of the quill next the center of the tail. the legs and feet are black, nails long and sharp; it has four toes on each foot, of which three are forward and one behind; that behind is as long as the two outer of the three toes in front."

EASTERN CARDINAL

The Eastern cardinal, *Richmondena cardinalis cardinalis* (Linnaeus), has been listed by Criswell[20] and by Coues[21] among the birds seen by the explorers in the Missouri valley. There is only one entry in their diaries that may or may not have referred to this species. In this instance Clark called the bird *a nightingale.*

The entry in question reads as follows:

June 4, 1804

"passed a Small Creek at 1 mile, 15 yds. Wide which we named Nightingale Creek from a Bird of that discription which sang for us all last night, and is the first of the Kind I ever heard."

In reference to this entry Coues[22] may be quoted:

"No species of the true nightingale (Daulias luscinia) is found in North America; the so-called 'Virginia nightingale' is the cardinal or redbird (Cardinalis virginianus)."

It seems doubtful that Coues' statement can be interpreted as an identification.

Cardinals commonly whistle at dawn and at dusk, but it would be most unusual to hear one "singing" all night.

It would be more plausible to assume that the bird in question was a mockingbird, except that Clark evidently knew the mockingbird because he identified one of them positively at a later date.

GOLDEN-CROWNED SPARROW

While at Fort Clatsop Lewis and Clark mentioned "a large brown sparrow" along with other birds seen on the Oregon coast. This bird was not described in detail, and there is nothing in the diaries to suggest that a specimen was collected for examination.

Coues suggested that it may have been the golden-crowned sparrow, *Zonotrichia atricapilla* (Gmelin), but he gives no basis for his identification.

GOLDFINCH

On June 8, 1805, Lewis listed the goldfinch, *Spinus tristis pallidus* Mearns, with other small birds seen at the mouth of the Marias River. He evidently did not distinguish this western subspecies from the familiar wild canary of the East.

Although the American Goldfinch was described by Linnaeus in 1758, the western subspecies was not given scientific status until 1890.

LARK-BUNTING

The second of two species of prairie birds that Clark mentioned on June 23, 1805, near Great Falls, Montana, was possibly a lark-bunting, *Calamospiza melanocorys* Stejneger, but his description is inconclusive. He referred to it as an abundant species of prairie bird that was "now setting." It was described only as being "larger than a Sparrow," and having a "white tail." However, the white wing patches which are characteristic of the lark-bunting are not mentioned.

Criswell[23] cited this reference as evidence for including the lark-bunting among the birds discovered by Lewis and Clark, but on whose authority he does not state.

Coues did not attempt to identify either of the "prairie birds" mentioned by Clark on this date.

MC COWN'S LONGSPUR

McCown's longspur, *Rhynchophanes mccownii* (Lawrence), was unknown to zoologists in 1805, when Lewis and Clark wrote the following description of its habits. Evidently they did not examine a specimen in hand; for, had they done so, they would undoubtedly have described its appearance as well as its behavior.

June 4, 1805 (Near mouth of the Marias River)

"I observed also a small bird which in action resembles the lark. it is about the size of a large sparrow of a dark brown colour with some white feathers in the tail; this bird, or that which I take to be the male, rises in the air about 60 feet and supporting itself in the air with a brisk motion of the wings, sings very sweetly, has several shrill soft notes reather of the plaintive order which it frequently repeats and varies, after remaining stationary for about a minute in his aireal station he descends obliquely occasionally pausing and accomnying his decension with a note something like twit twit twit; on the ground he is silent. thirty or forty of these birds will be stationed in the air at a time in view. those larks as I shall call them add much gayety and cheerfullness to the scene. All of those birds are now seting, and laying their eggs in the plains; their little nests are to be seen in great abundance as we pass. there are meriads of small grasshoppers in these plains which no doubt furnish the principal aliment of this numerous progeny of the feathered creation."—Lewis

Coues[24] writes, in reference to the foregoing citation as follows:

"This is the black-breasted lark-bunting or longspur, *Centrophanes maccowni,* which abounds in Montana in the breeding season, together with the chestnut-collored lark-bunting, *C. ornatus.*"

PINE SISKIN

In listing the small birds seen in the vicinity of the Marias River on June 8, 1805, Lewis included the "linnet."

Criswell[25] identified this bird as the pine siskin, *Spinus pinus* (Wilson), but he cites no authority for his conclusion. At best, his identification can be regarded as a conjecture.

Coues did not hazard a guess as to its identity.

CHAPTER XVIII
Fishes

Thirty-one species of fish are mentioned in the explorers' diaries, but more than half of this number were merely listed as being taken in seining or by hook and line. These included the bass, sturgeon, red horse, buffalo, catfish, white bass, and the "silver fish of the Ohio," which according to Coues, may have been the golden shiner. A few others, such as the hickory shad and fallfish were mentioned incidentally in comparing strange specimens with familiar species.

Lewis and Clark, however, can be credited with the discovery of several species of fishes which are characteristic of the Northwest. They wrote detailed descriptions of the silver salmon, king salmon, and the eulachon; and they included sufficient descriptive information about the blue-backed salmon, the silver salmon, the steelhead trout to leave little, if any doubt as to the identity of the species to which they referred.

In other instances, they provided so little information concerning the specimens which they caught by seine, gig, or hook and line that identification cannot be made with certainty. Thus, it appears that some of the thirty-one species mentioned in the diaries may or may not be valid. Nevertheless, Coues[1] did not hesitate, except in a few cases, to identify them. His classifications, however, are obviously conjectures based on his knowledge of the geographic distribution and relative abundance of different species.

For want of an alternative method of presenting Lewis and Clark's observations relating to fishes we have followed Coues' classification whether the data is conclusive or otherwise.

SKATES

Coues concluded that the "skait" listed by Lewis among the fishes of the Oregon coast was either the big skate, *Raja binoculata* Girard, or the California skate, *Raja inornata* Jordan and Gilbert.

Lewis' brief reference, written at Fort Clatsop on March 13, 1806, is as follows:

"the Skait is also common to the salt water—we have seen several of them that had perished and were thrown out on the beach by the tide."

NORTHERN MOONEYE

Coues concluded that the fish described as follows was the mooneye, *Hiodon alosoides* (Rafinesque). Now classified *Hiodon tergisus* Le Sueur.

June 11, 1805 (Vicinity of the Marias River)

"Goodrich who is remarkably fond of fishing caught several douzen fish of two species,—one about 9 inches long of a white colour, round and in form and fins resembling the white chub common to the Patomic; this fish has a smaller head than the chubb and the mouth is beset both above and below with a rim of fine sharp teeth; the eye moderately large, the pupil dark and the iris which is narrow is of a yellowish brown colour, they bite on meat and grasshoppers. this is a soft fish, not very good, tho' the flesh is of a fine white colour. . . . we had caught some few before our arrival at the entrance of Maria's river."

SALMON AND TROUT

Lewis and Clark described five species of salmonoid fishes which were, at the time, new to science. Their descriptive names for these fishes may be confusing unless clarified at once:

Silver salmon (Coho)	— "white salmon trout"
King salmon (Chinook)	— "common salmon"
Blue-backed salmon (Sockeye)	— "red char"
Steelhead trout	— "salmon-trout"
Yellowstone cutthroat trout	— "trout resembling our mountain or speckled trout"

March 16, 1806 (Fort Clatsop)

"The white Salmon Trout [*Oncorhynchus kisutch* (Walbaum)] which we had previously seen only at the great falls of the Columbia has now made it's appearance in the creeks near this place, one of them was brought us today by an Indian who had just taken it with his gig. this is a likeness of it; it was 2 feet 8 Inches long, and weighed 10 lbs. the eye is moderately large, the puple black and iris of a silvery white with a small addmixture of yellow, and is a little terbid near it's border with a yellowish brown. the position of the fins may be seen from the drawing, they are small in proportion to the fish, the fins are boney but not pointed except the tail and back fins which are a little so, the prime back fin and ventral ones, contain each ten rays; those of the gills thirteen, that of the tail twelve, and the small fins placed near the tail above has no bony rays, but is a tough flexable substance covered with smooth skin. it is thicker in proportion to it's width than the salmon. the tongue is thick and firm beset on each border with small subulate teeth in a single series. the teeth of the mouth are as before discribed. neither this fish nor the salmon are caught with a hook, nor do I know on what they feed."

March 13, 1806 (Fort Clatsop)

"the common Salmon [*Oncorhynchus tshawytscha* (Walbaum)] and red

261

charr are the inhabitants of both the sea and rivers. the former is usually largest and weighs from 5 to 15 lbs. it is this species that extends itself into all the rivers and little creeks on this side of the Continent, and to which the natives are so much indebted for their subsistence. the body of this fish is from 2½ to 3 feet long and proportionably broad. it is covered with imbricated scales of a moderate size and is variagated with irregular black spots on it's sides and gills. the eye is large and the iris of a silvery colour the pupil black. the nostrum (rostrum) or nose extends beyond the under jaw, and both the upper and lower jaws are armed with a single series of long teeth which are subulate and inflected near the extremities of the jaws where they are also more closely arranged. they have some sharp teeth of smaller size and same shape placed on the tongue which is thick and fleshey. the fins of the back are two; the first is plaised nearer the head than the ventral fins and has rays, the second is placed far back near the tail is small and has no rays. the flesh of this fish is when in order of a deep flesh coloured red and every shade from that to an orrange yellow, and when very meager almost white. the roes of this fish are much esteemed by the natives who dry them in the sun and preserve them for a great length of time. they are about the size of a small pea nearly transparent and of a redish yellow colour. they resemble very much at a little distance the common currents of our gardens but are more yellowish. this fish is sometimes red along the sides and belley near the gills; particularly the male."—Lewis

Coues concluded that Lewis' description of a white species of trout [*Oncorhynchus nerka* (Walbaum)] with a bluish cast on the back and head probably related to the blue-backed salmon despite the fact that Lewis' reference to the "red char," written at Fort Clatsop on March 13, 1806, specifically states that the red char was not seen above Celilo Falls. It seems to us that the white species of trout taken on the Lemhi River on Aug. 22, 1805, may have been the steelhead trout. The questionable passage is quoted below.

Aug. 22, 1805 (Lemhi River)
"late in the evening I made the men form a bush drag, and with it in about 2 hours they caught 528 very good fish, most of them large trout. among them I now for the first time saw ten or a dozen of the white species of trout. they are silvery colour except on the back and head, where they are of a bluish cast. the scales are much larger than the speckled trout, but in their form, position of their fins, teeth, mouth, etc. they are precisely like them. they are not generally quite as large but equally well flavoured."

March 13, 1806 (Written at Fort Clatsop)
"The red charr are reather broader in proportion to their length than the

262

common salmon, the skales are also imbricated but reather large. the nostrum (rostrum) exceeds the lower jaw more and the teeth are neither as large nor so numerous as those of the salmon and none of them are varigated with dark spots which make the body of the other. their flesh, roes and every other particular with rispect to their form is that of the Salmon. this fish we did not see untill we decended below the great falls of the Columbia, but whether they are exclusively confined to this portion of the river or not at all seasons I am unable to determine."

March 13, 1806 (Written at Fort Clatsop)

"The Salmon Trout [*Salmo gairdneri* (Richardson)] are seldom more than two feet in length they are narrow in proportion to their length, at least much more so than the Salmon or red charr. the jaws are nearly of the same length, and are furnished with a single series of small subulate streight teeth, not so long or as large as those of the Salmon. the mouth is wide, and the tongue is also furnished with some teeth. the fins are placed much like those of the salmon. at the great falls we met with this fish of a silvery white colour on the belly and sides, and a bluish light brown on the back and head. in this neighbourhood we have met with another species which dose not differ from the other in any particular except in point of colour. this last is of a dark colour on the back, and it's sides and belly are yellow with transverse stripes of dark brown. sometimes a little red is intermixed with these colours on the belly and sides toward the head. the eye flesh and roes are like those described of the Salmon. the white species which we found below the falls was in excellent order when the salmon were entirely out of season and not fit for uce. the species which we found here on our arrival early in November has declined considerably reather more so inded than the red charr with which we found them ascociated in the little rivulets and creeks. I think it may be safely asserted that the red Charr and both species of the salmon trout remain in season longer in the fall of the year than the common Salmon; but I have my doubts whether either of them ever pass the great falls of the Columbia. The Indians tell us that the Salmon begin to run early in the next month; it will be unfortunate for us if they do not, for they must form our principal dependence for food in ascending the Columbia, above the falls and it's S. E. branch to the Mountains."

June 13, 1805 (Great Falls, Montana)

"Goodrich had caught half a dozen very fine trout and a number of both species of the white fish. These trout [*Salmo lewisi* (Girard)] (caught in the falls) are from sixteen to twenty-three inches in length, precisely resemble our mountain or speckled trout in form and the position of their fins, but the specks on these are of a deep black instead of the red or gould colour of those common to the U'. States. these are furnished long sharp teeth on the pallet and tongue and have generally a small dash of red on each side behind the front ventral fins; the flesh is of a pale yellowish red or when in good order of a rose red."

The cutthroat trout is now classified *Salmo Clarki* Richardson.

March 14, 1806 (Written at Fort Clatsop)
"The mountain or speckled trout are found in the waters of the Columbia within the mountains. they are the same as those found in the upper part of the Missouri; but are not so aboundant in the Columbia as in that river. we never saw this fish below the mountains but from the transparency and coldness of the Kooskooske[2] I should not doubt it's existing in that stream as low as it's junction with the S. E. branch of the Columbia."

SUCKERS

This fish [Northern sucker, *Catostomus catostomus* (Forster)] was first taken by Lewis and Clark on the upper Missouri southeast of Helena, Montana.

Aug. 3, 1805 (Vic. of Madison County, Montana)
"The fish of this part of the river are trout and a species of scale fish of a white colour and a remarkable long mouth which one of our men inform us are the same with the species called in the Eastern states *bottlenose.*"

Aug. 19, 1805 (Vic. of Grayling, Montana)
"this evening I made a few of the men construct a sein of willow brush which we hawled and caught a large number of fine trout and a kind of mullet about 16 Inches long which I had not seen before. the scales are small, the nose is long and obtusely pointed and exceeds the under jaw. the mouth is not large but opens with foalds at the sides, the colour of it's back and sides of a bluish brown and belley white; it has the faggot bones, from which I suppose it to be of the mullet kind. The tongue and pallate are smooth and it has no teeth."

Mullet are the fish properly called suckers, belonging to the family Catostomidae. This, according to Forster, was probably *Catostomus catostomus.*—Thwaites' footnote.

March 13, 1806 (Written at Fort Clatsop)
"The bottlenose is the same with that before mentioned on the Missouri and is found exclusively within the mountains."

This fish, the Mountain sucker, *Pantosteus platyrhynchus* (Cope), is mentioned on only one occasion by Clark while descending the Yellowstone River. Coues concluded that the specimen referred to was a mountain sucker, *Pantosteus jordani,* the accepted name in 1893.

FISHES

July 16, 1806 (Vicinity of Livingston, Montana)

"one of the men brought me a fish of a species I am unacquainted with; it was 8 inches long, formed like a trout. its mouth was placed like that of a Sturgeon—a red streak passed down each side from the gills to the tail."

Other species in this family which were merely mentioned as being taken in seining on the lower Missouri included the buffalo fish and the red horse.

THE CHUB

April 26, 1806 (On the Umatilla River)

"after we encamped a little Indian boy caught several chubbs [Columbia chub, *Mylocheilus caurinus* (Richardson)] with a bone in this form which he substituted for a hook. these fish were about 9 inches long small head large abdomen, small where the tail joined the body, the tail wide, long in proportion and forked. the back and ventral fins were equadistant from the head and had each 10 bony rays, the fins next the gills nine each and that near the tail 12. the upper exceeded the lower jaw, the latter is truncate at the extremity and the tonge and pallet are smooth. the colour is white on the sides and belley and a blewish brown on the back."

CATFISH

While ascending the Missouri, Clark frequently referred to the abundance of catfish, but there is little to indicate whether these notations refer to the blue cat, the channel cat, or the bullhead. Probably all species inhabiting the Missouri River were taken at one time or another.

July 24, 1804 (Above the mouth of the Platte River)

"This evening Guthrege caught a White catfish, its eyes small and tale much like that of a Dolfin."

July 29, 1804 (Few miles below site of Omaha)

"in a fiew minits caught three verry large catfish, one nearly white, those fish are in great plenty on the Sides of the river and verry fat, a quart of Oile came out of the surpolous fat of one of those fish."

Sept. 1, 1804 (Near Yankton, S. Dak.)

"numbers of Catfish caught, those fish is so plenty that we catch them at any time and place in the river."

SAUGER

Lewis characterized this fish which was first taken on the Missouri above the mouth of the Marias River, as a species which resembled the hickory

265

shad, or oldwife. Coues identified it as *Stizostedion canadense* (Smith) on the basis of the description which follows:

June 11, 1805

"the other species (caught by Goodrich) is precisely the form and about the size of the well known hickory shad or oldwife, with the exception of the teeth, a rim of which garnish the outer edge of both upper and lower jaw; the tonge and pallet are also beset with long sharp teeth bending inwards, the eye of this fish is very large, and the iris a silvery colour and wide.——we had seen none untill we reached that place and took them in the Missouri above its junction with that river."

STARRY FLOUNDER

Coues concluded that the flounder discussed below probably belonged to this species, *Platichthys stellatus* (Pallas).

March 13, 1806 (Written at Fort Clatsop)

"The flounder is also an inhabitant of the salt water. we have seen them also on the beach where they had been left by the tide. The Indians eat the latter (flounder) and esteem it very fine."

EULACHON

The eulachon or candle fish,[3] was one of the most interesting species discovered by Lewis and Clark. David Starr Jordan's comments concerning the taxonomic history of this species, *Thaleichthys pacificus* (Richardson), is included with Lewis and Clark's description of the fish, since it appears as a footnote in Thwaites' *Original Journals*.

Feb. 24, 1806 (Written at Fort Clatsop)

"The chief and his party had brought for sail a Sea Otter skin some hats, stergeon and a species of small fish which now begin to run, and are taken in great quantities in the Columbia River about 40 miles above us by means of skinning or scooping nets. on this page I have drawn the likeness of them as large as life; it is as perfect as I can make it with my pen and will serve to give a general idea of the fish. the rays of the fins are boney but not sharp tho somewhat pointed. the small fin on the back next to the tail has no rays of bone being a thin membranous pellicle. the fins next to the gills have eleven rays each. those of the abdomen have eight each; those of the pinna-ani are 20, and 2 half formed in front. that of the back has eleven rays. all the fins are of a white colour. the back is of a bluish dusky colour and that of the lower part of the sides and belly is of a silvery white. no spots on any part. the first bone of the gills next behind the eye is of a bluish cast, and the second of a light goald colour nearly white. the pupil of the eye is black and the iris of a silver white. the under jaw exceeds the upper; and the mouth opens to great extent, folding like that of the herring. it has no teeth, the abdomen is obtuse and smooth; in this differing from the herring, shad, anchovey, etc. of the Malacopterygious Order & Class Clupea, to which however I think it more nearly allyed than to any other altho' it has not their accute and sereate abdomen and the under jaw exceeding the upper. the scales of the little fish are so small and thin that without minute inspection you would suppose they had none. they are filled with roes of a pure white colour and have scarcely any perceptable alimentary duct. I find them best when cooked in Indian stile, which is by roasting a number of them together on a wooden spit without any previous preparation whatever. they are so fat they require no additional sauce, and I think them superior to any fish I ever tasted, even more delicate and lussious than the white fish of the lakes which have heretofore formed my standart of excellence among the fishes. I have heard the fresh anchovey much extolled but I hope I shall be pardoned for believing this quite as good. the bones are so soft and fine that they form no obstruction in eating this fish."[4]

March 4, 1806 (Written at Fort Clatsop)

"the Anchovey is so delicate that they soon become tainted unless pickled or smoked. the natives run a small stick through their gills and hang them in the smoke of their lodges, or kindle small fires under them for the purpose of drying them. They need no previous preparation of gutting etc and will cure in 24 hours. The natives do not appear to be very scrupelous about eating them a little feated."

March 29, 1806 (Sauvies Island)

"They had large quantities of dryed Anchovies strung on small sticks by the gills and others which had first been dryed in this manner, were now arranged in large sheets with strings of bark and hung suspended by poles in the roofs of their houses."

Lewis and Clark were much interested in Indian methods of taking fish, and their descriptions of the devices used by some of the western tribes were similar in design to certain items of modern fishing gear.

The Shoshones encamped on the Lemhi River employed a unique gig in spearing salmon and trout. It was a forerunner of the modern arrow developed recently by bowmen in shooting carp and other rough fish.

Aug. 21, 1805 (Mouth of Prairie Creek, near Armstead, Montana)

"Their method of taking fish with a *gig* or bone is with a long pole, about a foot from one End is a Strong String attached to the pole, this String is a little more than a foot long and is tied to the middle of a bone from 4 to 6 inches long, one end Sharp the other with a whole to fasten on the end of the pole with a beard (i.e. barb) to the large end, they fasten this bone on one end (of the pole) and with the other, feel for the fish and turn and Strike them so hard that the bone passes through and catches on the opposite Side, and Slips off the End of the pole and holds the Center of the bone."

The Shoshone fish weir which Clark found in the Lemhi River and described in detail shows how ingenious the primitive Indians were in making effective use of native materials.

Aug. 21, 1805 (Lemhi River)

"after smoking with them he (Clark) visited their fish wear which was abut 200 yds. distant. he found the wear extended across four channels of the river which was here divided by three small islands. Three of these channels were narrow, and were stopped by means of trees fallen across, supported by which stakes of willow were driven down sufficiently near each other to prevent the salmon from passing. about the center of each a cilindric basket of eighteen or twenty feet in length terminating in a conic shape at it's lower extremity, formed of willows, was opposed to a small apperture in the wear with it's mouth up stream to receive the fish. the main channel of the water was conducted to this basket, which was so narrow at it's lower extremity that the fish when once in could not turn itself about, and were taken out by untying the small ends of the longetudinal willows which form the hull of the basket. the wear in the main channel was somewhat differently contrived. There were two distinct wears formed of poles and willow sticks, quite across the river, at no great distance from each other. each of these, were furnished with two baskets; the one wear to take them ascending and the other in decending. in constructing these wears, poles were first tyed together in parcels of three near the smaller extremity; these were set on end, and spread in a triangular form at the base, in such manner, that two of the three poles ranged in the direction of the intended work, and the third down the stream. two ranges of horizontal poles were next lashed with willow bark and wythes to the ranging poles, and on these willow sticks were placed perpendicularly, reaching from the bottom of the river to about 3 or four feet above its surface; and placed so near each other, as not to permit the passage of the fish, and even so thick in some parts, as with help of gravel and stone to give a direction to the water which they wished. the baskets were the same in form of the others. this is the form of the work, and disposition of the baskets."

Other weirs of different construction were found in use by the Wallawalla Indians and the Chopunnish tribes on the Clearwater River in Idaho.

April 29, 1806 (Near mouth of Walla Walla River)

"we therefore though it best to remain on the Wallahwallah river about a mile from the Columbia untill the morning, accordingly we encamped on the river near a fish wear, this weare consists of two curtains of small willows wattled together with four lines of withes of the same materials extending quite accross the river parralal with each other and about 6 feet asunder. Those are supported by several parrelals of poles placed in this manner (sketch) those curtains of willows is either roled at one end for a few feet to permit the fish to pass or are let down at pleasure. They take their fish which at present are a mullet only of from one to 5 pounds wt. with small seines of 15 or 18 feet long drawn by two persons; these they drag down to the wear and rase the bottom of the seine against the willow curtain. they have also a small seine managed by one person, it bags in the manner of the scooping nets; the one side of the net is confined to a semicircular bow of half the size of a mans arm, and about 5 feet long, the other side is confined to a strong string which being attached to the extremities of the bow forms the cord line to the semicurcle."—Clark

May 8, 1806 (On the Clearwater River, near mouth of Big Canyon River)

"on the creek near our camp I abserved a kind of trap which was made with great panes to catch the small fish which pass down with the stream. This was a dam formed of stone so as to collect the water in a narrow part not exceeding 3 feet wide from which place the water shot with great force and scattered through some small willows closely connected and fastened with bark, this mat of willow switches was about 4 feet wide and 6 long lying in a horizontal position, fastened at the extremity. the small fish which fell on those willows was washed on the willows where they lie untill taken off and I cought or took off those willows 9 small trout from 3 to 7 Inches in length. Soon after I returned from the fishery an Indian came from a fishery of a similar kind a little above with 12 small fish which he offered me which I declined axcepting as I found from his signs that his house was a short distance above, and that those fisheries afforded the principal part of the food for his children."—Clark

Jan. 16, 1806 (Fort Clatsop)

"The Catsops Chinnooks etc. in fishing employ the common streight net, the scooping or diping net with a long handle, the gig, and the hook and line. the common net is of different lengths and depths usually employed in taking sammon, Charr and trout in the inlets among the marshey grounds and the mouths of deep creeks. the skiming or scooping net to take small fish in the spring and summer season; the gig and hook are employed indiscriminately at all seasons in taking such fish as they can procure by their means. their nets and fishing lines are made of the silk-grass or white-cedar

269

bark; and their hooks are generally of European manufactory tho' before the whites visited them they made hooks of bone and other substance.

    A

C   B formed in the following manner A C and C B are two small

    D

pieces of bone about the size of a strong twine, these are flattened and leveled off of their extremities near C where they are firmly attached together with sinues and covered with rosin. C A is reduced to a sharp point at A where it is also bent in a little; C B is attached to the line, for about half its length at the upper extremity B. the whole forming two sides of an accute angled triangle, the line has a loop at D by which it is anexed to a longer line and taken off at pleasure."—Lewis

May 11, 1806 (Clearwater River)

"These nativs take their fish in the following manner towit. a stand small stage or warf consisting of sticks and projecting about 10 feet into the river and about 3 feet above the water on the extremity of this the fisherman stands with his guig or a skooping net which differ but little in their form from those commonly used in our country . . . with those nets they take the Suckers and also the salmon trout and I am told the salmon also."—Clark

Fish was important in the diet of the Indians of the Columbia River system and the Northwest coast. Their methods of taking, drying, and cooking fish were of much interest to the explorers.

Oct. 16, 1805 (Columbia River above mouth of Snake River)

"I took 2 men and set out in a small canoe with a view to go as high up the Columbia river as the 1st fork which the Indians made signs was but a short distance. . . . The west 4 miles to the Lower point of an Island on the Star'd side 2 lodges of Indians large and built of mats, passed 3 verry large mat lodges at 2 miles on the Star'd Side large scaffoes of fish drying at every lodge, and piles of salmon lying, the squars engaged preparing them for the scaffol. a squar gave me a dried salmon. from those lodges on the Island an Indian woman showed me the mouth of the river which falls in below a high hill on the Lar'd N. 80° W. 8 miles from the Island. The river bending Lar'd. This river is remarkably clear and crouded with salmon in many places, I observe in assending great numbers of salmon *dead* on the shores, floating on the water and in the Bottom which can be seen at the debth of 20 feet, the cause of the emence numbers of dead salmon I can't account for so it is I must have seen 3 or 400 dead and many living the Indians, I believe made use of the fish which is not long dead as, I struck one nearly dead and left him floating, some Indians in a canoe behind took the fish on board his canoe."—Clark

Oct. 17, 1805 (Above mouth of Snake River)

"passed three large lodges on the Star'd Side near which great number of Salmon was drying on scaffolds one of those mat lodges I entered found it crouded with men women and children and the entrance of those houses I saw many squars engaged in splitting and drying Salmon. I was furnished with a mat to set on, and one man set about preparing me something to eate, first he brought in a piece of Drift log of pine and with a wedge of the elks horn, and a malet of Stone curioesly carved he Slpit the log into small pieces and lay'd it open on the fire on which he put round stones, a woman handed him a basket of water and a large Salmon about half Dried, when the Stones were hot he put them into the basket of water with the fish which was soon sufficiently boiled for use. it was then taken out put on a platter of rushes neetly made, and set before me they boiled a salmon for each of the men with me, . . . after eating the boiled fish which was delicious, I set out. . . ."—Clark

Oct. 24, 1805 (Vic. of Celilo Falls)

"the mode of burying those fish is in holes of various Sizes, lined with straw on which they lay fish Skins in which then inclose the fish which is layed very close, and then covered with earth of about 12 or 15 inches thick. . . . on those rocks I Saw Several large scaffols on which the Indians dry fish, as this is out of Season the poles on which they dry those fish are tied up verry Securely in large bundles and put upon the scaffolds, I counted 107 stocks of dried pounded fish in different places on those rocks which must have contained 10,000 lbs. of neet fish, . . ."—Clark

Jan. 14, 1806 (Fort Clatsop)

"From the best estimate we were able to make as we descended the Columbia we conceived that the natives inhabiting that noble stream, for some miles above the great falls to the Grand rapids inclusive annually prepare about 30,000 lbs. of pounded salmon for market. but whether this fish is an article of commerce with the whites or is exclusively sold to and consumed by the natives of the sea Coast, we are at a loss to determine."
—Lewis

CHAPTER XIX

Reptiles and Amphibians

We cannot explain why Lewis and Clark encountered so few reptiles, other than rattlesnakes, considering that either one or the other of them, and several of their companions, spent all or a part of each day in hunting or exploring the countryside. The only species of snakes concerning which they recorded sufficient data for identification were the prairie rattler, the bull snake, the hog-nosed snake, and two species of western garter snakes.

In case of lizards, they can be credited with writing an excellent description of *Phrynosoma douglassi,* but the only other species which they mentioned was a "black or dark-brown lizzard" seen in the Clearwater River country and in Columbia gorge below The Dalles.

Evidently the only turtle which excited their interest was the soft-shelled species.

Writing at Fort Clatsop on March 11, 1806, Lewis summarized his observations relating to the reptiles west of the Rocky Mountains:

"The reptiles of this country are the rattlesnake, garter snake, and the common brown lizzard. The season was so far advanced when we arrived on this side of the Rocky Mountains that but few rattlesnakes were seen. I did not remark one particularly myself, nor do I know whether they are of either of the four species found in the different parts of the United States, or of that species before mentioned peculiar to the upper parts of the Missouri and its branches. The garter snake so called in the United States is very common in this country; they are found in great numbers on the open and sometimes marshey grounds in this neighbourhood. They differ not at all from those of the U'. States. The black or dark brown lizzard we saw at the rock fort camp at the commencement of the woody country below the great narrows and falls of the Columbia; they are also the same with those of the United States."

Later, while encamped on the Clearwater River in the neighborhood of Weippe Prairie in May 1806, Lewis amplified the foregoing statement:

"The reptiles which I have observed in this quarter are the Rattlesnakes of the species described on the Missouri; they are abundant in every part of the country and are the only poisonous snake which we have yet met with since we left St. Louis. The 2 species of snakes of an inosent kind already described, common black lizzard and the horned lizzard . . . the mockerson snake, coperhead, a number of vipers, a variety of lizzard, the toad, bullfrog, etc. common to the U' States are not to be found in this country."

REPTILES AND AMPHIBIANS

Lewis and Clark's recorded observations relative to several species of reptiles and amphibia are transcribed below:

PRAIRIE RATTLER

May 17, 1805 (Missouri valley above mouth of Yellowstone River)

"Capt. Clark narrowly escaped being bitten by a rattlesnake in the course of his walk. the party killed one this evening at our encampment which he informs me was similar to that he had seen. this snake is smaller than those common to the middle Atlantic States, being about 2 feet 6 inches long; it is of a yellowish brown colour on the back and sides, variagated with one row of oval spots of a dark brown colour lying transversely over the back from neck to the tail, and two other rows of small circular spots of the same colour which garnis(h) the sides along the edge of the scuta. Its belly contains 176 scutae . . . and 17 on the tale."

This was evidently the party's first encounter with *Crotalus viridis* Rafinesque. Clark's version of this incident is succinct:

"I was nearly treading on a small fierce rattlesnake different from any I had ever seen, and one man of the party killed another of the same kind."

This, of course, was not the first rattlesnake encountered by the expedition, but those seen below the mouth of the Platte probably were timber rattlers.

It must be kept in mind that the following quotations probably relate to two species of rattlesnakes; and that Lewis and Clark's failure to notice the prairie rattlesnake below the mouth of the Yellowstone River does not mean that the western species did not occur along the Missouri River in both North and South Dakota.

June 7, 1804 (Limestone Cliffs near mouth of Manitou River in Missouri)

"We landed at the inscription and found it a Den of Rattle Snakes, we had not landed 3 Minutes before three verry large Snakes was observed in the Crevises of the Rocks and killed."—Clark

June 25, 1804 (Approaching mouth of Kansas River)

"We killed a large rattle Snake Sunning himself on the bank."—Clark

July 4, 1804 (Independence Creek, Mo.)

"Jos. Fields got bit by a Snake which was quickly doctored with Bark[1] by Capt. Lewis."—Clark

Aug. 8, 1804 (Washington County, Nebr.)

"worthie of remark that Snakes are not plenty in this part of the Missourie."—Clark

Sept. 17, 1804 (Near White River in S. Dak.)

"Capt. Lewis saw a hare and killed a Rattle snake in the village of Barking Squarels."—Clark

May 26, 1805 (Approaching Judith River in Mont.)

"it was after Dark before we finished butchering the buffaloe, and on my return to camp I trod within a few inches of a rattle snake, but being in motion I passed before he could probably put himself in a striking attitude and fortunately escaped his bite, I struck about with my espontoon being directed in some measure by his nois(e) until I killed him."—Lewis

June 12, 1805 (Above mouth of Marias River, Mont.)

"Several Rattle Snakes has been Seen by the party today. one man took hold of one with his hand, which was in a bunch of bushes, but luckily he escaped being bit."—Whitehouse

Clark's version of the same incident:

"one of the men cought one by the head in catching hold of a bush on which his head lay."

June 15, 1805 (Approaching Great Falls, Mont.)

"the current excessively rapid and dificuelt to assend—great numbers of dangerous places, and the fatigue which we have to encounter is incretiatable. the men in the water from morning untill night hauling the cord and boats, walking on sharp rocks and round sliperey stones which alternately cut their feet and throw them down, not with standing all this dificuelty they go with great cheerfulness, aded to those dificuelties the rattle snakes are inumerable & require great caution to prevent being bitten."—Clark

June 15, 1805 (Vic. of Great Falls, Mont.)

"when I awoke from my sleep today I found a large rattlesnake coiled on the leaning trunk of a tree under the shade of which I had been lying at the distance of about ten feet from him. I killed the snake and found that he had 176 scuta on the abdomen and 17 half formed scuta on the tale; it was of the same kind which I had frequently seen before; but they do not differ in colours from the rattlesnakes common to the middle Attlantic states, but considerably in the form and figures of those colours."—Lewis

June 20, 1805 (Great Falls, Mont.)

"I saw a rattle snake in an open plain 2 miles from any creek or woods." —Clark

July 8, 1805 (Vic. of Sun River above Great Falls)

"in the afternoon the hunters returned from the falls and plains had killed Several buffalow, 1 antelope, and a yellow fox, also 2 rattlesnakes." —Whitehouse

July 10, 1805 (Great Falls—Sun River Area)

"We killed a large rattle Snake."—Whitehouse

July 11, 1805

"I walked a Short distance in the plains to day when we were waiting for the wind to abate, and trod on a verry large rattle snake. it bit my leggin on my legg, I shot it, it was 4 feet 2 Inches long, and 5 Inches and a half round."—Whitehouse

Aug. 15, 1805 (Vic. of the Gates of the Mountains, Mont.)

"Capt. Clark was near being bit by a rattle snake which was between his legs as he was Standing on Shore a fishing—he killed it and Shot Several others this afternoon."—Whitehouse

Aug. 2, 1805 (Vic. of White Tail Deer Creek in the Beaverhead valley)

"I walked out this morning on Shore and Saw Several rattle Snakes in the plain."—Clark

Aug. 10, 1805 (Vic. of Grayling, Mont.)

"from the number of rattlesnakes about the Clifts at which we halted we called them rattlesnake clifts.—this serpent is the same before described with oval spots of yellowish brown."—Lewis

Aug. 15, 1805 (Near Gallagher's Creek in Beaverhead valley)

"Capt. Clark was very near being bitten twice today by rattlesnakes, the Indian woman (Sacajawea) also narrowly escaped."—Lewis

April 25, 1806 (Vic. of Walla Walla, Wash.)

"Saw many common lizzards, several rattlesnakes killed by the party, they are the same common to the U. States. The horned lizzard is also common."—Lewis

July 10, 1806 (Beaverhead valley)

"I saw several large rattle snakes in passing rattle Snake Mountain[2]— they were fierce."—Clark

July 27, 1806 (Yellowstone valley between Billings and Miles City, Mont.)

"was near being bit by a rattle snake."—Clark

Aug. 4, 1806 (Missouri valley above Yellowstone River)

"during our halt we killed a very large rattlesnake of the species common to our country. it had 176 scutae on the abdomen and 25 on the tail, its length 5 feet, the scutae on the tail fully formed."—Lewis

BULL SNAKE

All of the following observations and descriptions appear to refer to the bull snake, *Pituophis melanoleucus sayi* Schlegel.

Aug. 5, 1804 (Vic. of Blair, Nebraska)

"Killed a serpent[3] on the bank of the river adjoining a large prarie. Length from nose to tail 5 F. 2 In.; circumpherence in largest part 4½ In.; number of scuta on belly 221; number of scuta on tail 53. No pison teeth therefore think him perfectly inocent, eyes—center black with a border of pole brown-yellow-colour of skin on head yellowish green with black specks on the extremity of the scuta which are pointed or triangular—colour of back, transverse strips of black and dark brown, of an inch in width, succeeded by a yellowish brown of half that width, the end of the tale hard and pointed like a cock's spur. the sides are speckled with yellowish brown and black. two roes (rows) of black spots on a lite yellow ground pass through out his whole length on the upper points of the scuta of the belly and tale, ½ inch apart. This snake is vulgarly called the cow or bull snake from a bellowing nois which it is said sometimes to make resembling that amamal, tho' as to this fact I am unable to attest it, never having heard them make that or any other nois myself."—Lewis

Aug. 5, 1804 (Clark's notation relating to same specimen)

"Snakes are not plenty, one was killed today, large and resembling the rattlesnake, only something lighter."

Aug. 6, 1804 (Whitehouse, although writing a day later, may have been referring to the snake mentioned by Clark on Aug. 5)

"A verry Large Snake was Killed to day Called the Bull Snake, his colure Somethink like a Rattel Snake."—Whitehouse

Sept. 5, 1804 (Western Bonhomme County, S. Dak.)

"This day one of our hunters brought us a Serpent beautifully varigated with small black spots of a romboydal form on a light yellow-white ground. The black predominates most on the back, the whitish yellow on the sides, and it is nearly white on the belly with a few partly coloured scuta on which the black shews but imperfectly and the colouring matter seems to be underneath the scuta. it is not poisonous—it hisses remarkably loud; it has 221 Scuta on the belly and 51 on the tale. the eyes are of a dark black colour, the tale terminates in a sharp point like the substance of a cock's spur. Length 4 F. 6 I."—Lewis

WESTERN HOG-NOSED SNAKE

Although brief, the following description of a snake with a black belly cannot be confused with any species other than the hog-nosed snake, *Heterodon nasicus* Baird and Girard. In this instance Coues identified the specimen on the basis of Lewis' description as "the dark variety of the so-called spreading adder or blowing viper, a species of Heterodon."

July 23, 1805 (Vic. of Townsend, Mont.)

"I saw a black snake today about two feet long—the belly of which was as black as any other part, or as jet itself. it had 128 scuta on the belley, 63 on the tail."—Lewis

Strangely enough, Lewis did not mention the characteristic behavior of this species.

GARTER SNAKES

On July 24, 1805, Lewis and Clark mentioned seeing some snakes which cannot be identified positively. However, Coues concluded that the striped snakes mentioned in the quotation were of the species *Eutaenia vagrans,* and that the brown snakes were *Pituophis sayi.*

July 24, 1805 (Missouri River, few miles north of Three Forks, Mont.)

"we observed a great number of snakes about the water of a brown uniform colour, some black, and others speckled on the abdomen and striped with black and brownish yellow on the back and sides. The first of these is the largest being about 4 feet long, the second is of that kind mentioned yesterday, and the last is much like the garter snake of our country and about its size—none of these species are poisonous—I examined their teeth and found them innocent. They all appear to be fond of water, to which they fly for shelter immediately on being pursued."—Lewis

Another possibility is that the brown snakes mentioned in this instance may have belonged to the subspecies *Thamnophis ordinoides vagrans* Baird and Girard, the great basin garter snake.

On the other hand Lewis' description of the garter snakes seen on Deer Island below the mouth of the Willamette River in the spring of 1806 were undoubtedly the Pacific red-sided variety, *Thamnophis sirtalis concinnus* Hallowell.

March 28, 1806 (Lower Columbia River on Deer Island)

"we saw a great number of snakes on this island; they were about the size and much the form of the common garter snake of the Atlantic coast and like that snake are not poisonous—they have 160 scuta on the abdomen and 71 on the tail—the abdomen near the head and jaws as high as the eyes are a bluish white, which as it receeds from the head becomes a dark brown—the field of the back and sides is black—a narrow stripe of a light yellow runs along the center of the back, on each side of this stripe there is a range of small transverse oblong spots of a pale brick red which gradually diminish as they receede from the head and disappear at the commencement of the tail. the puple of the eye is black, with a narrow ring of white bordering its edge; the ballance of the iris is of a dark yellowish brown."—Lewis

Coues suggested that the garter snakes seen "in bundles" on March 29, 1806 were Pacific red-sided garter snakes, now classified as *Thamnophis sirtalis concinnus* Hollowell.

March 29, 1806 (Sauvies Island in the Columbia R.)
"the garter snakes are innumerable and are seen entwined arround each other in large bundles of forty or fifty lying about in different directions through the praries."—Lewis

The diaries also contain some of the superstitions which are commonly attached to the subject of snakes.

June 14, 1804 (Vic. of Grand River, Mo.)
"George Drewyer gives the following account of a Pond. . . . he heard in this Pond a Snake making goubleing noises like a turkey, he fired his gun and the noise increased, he heard the Indians mention this Species of Snake, one Frenchman gives a similar account."—Clark

June 24, 1804 (Clay County, Mo.)
"I will only remark that dureing the time I lay on the sand waiting for the boat, a large Snake Swam to the bank imediately under the Deer which was hanging over the water and no great distance from it. I threw chunks and drove this snake off Several times. I found that he was determined on getting to the meat. I was compelled to kill him—the part of the Deer which attracted this Snake I think was the Milk from the bag of the Doe."—Clark

Sept. 7, 1804 (Near The Tower, Boyd County, Nebr.)
"It is Said that a kind of Lizard also a Snake reside with those amimals (prairie dogs), did not find this correct."—Clark

Feb. 28, 1805 (Fort Mandan)
"Two men of the N. W. Company arrive with letters on Sackacomah, also a Root and top of a plant, presented by Mr. Haney, for the Cure of Mad Dogs, Snakes, etc., and to be found & used as follows; viz., this root is found on the highlands and asent of hills, the way of useing it is to scarify the part when bitten, to chu or pound an inch, or more if the root is small, and applying it to the bitten part, renewing it twice a Day. The bitten person is not to chaw nor Swallow any of the Root for it might have contrary effect."—Clark

March 18, 1805 (Included in Thwaites' *Original Journals*, Vol. 6, Meterology Section, p. 184.)
"collected Some roots, herbs and plants in order to send by the boat, particularly the root said to cure the bites of a mad dog and rattlesnake."
—Lewis

Included in the list of plant specimens sent to President Jefferson from Fort Mandan when the keel-boat was sent down the Missouri in the spring of 1805 we find the following reference to this plant which was supposed to cure snake bite.

April 3, 1805 (Included in box #4, shipped to Jefferson from Fort Mandan)

"a specimen of a plant and a parcel of its roots highly prized by the natives as an efficatious remidy in cases of the bite of the rattle Snake or Mad dog."[4]

Feb. 11, 1805 (Fort Mandan)

"about five o'clock this evening one of the wives of Charbono[5] was delivered of a fine boy. it is worthy of remark that this was the first child which this woman had boarn, and as is commin in such cases her labour was tedious and the pain violent; M. Jessome informed me that he had frequently administered a small portion of the rattle of the rattlesnake which he assured me had never failed to produce the desired effect, that of hastening the birth of the child; having the rattle of a snake by me I gave it to him, and he administered two rings of it to the woman, broken in small pieces with the fingers, and added a small quantity of water. Whether his medicine was truly the cause or not I shall not undertake to determine, but I was informed that she had not taken it more than ten minutes before she brought forth. Perhaps this remedy may be worthy of future experiments, but I must confess that I want faith as to its efficacy."—Lewis

HORNED LIZARD

In so far as we have been able to determine Lewis and Clark can be credited with writing the earliest, detailed description of the horned lizard, *Phrynosoma douglassi* (Bell). Other lizards, referred to as the "common black" or "brown" lizards, were seen west of the Rocky Mountains, but they were not described.

May 29, 1806 (Clearwater River area)

"a Species of Lizzard called by the French engages, Prarie buffaloe are nativs of these plains as well as those of the Missouri. I have called them the horned Lizzard. they are about the size and a good deal the figure of the common black lizzard, but their bellies are broader, the tail shorter and their action much slower; they crawl much like the toad. they are of a brown colour with yellowish and yellowish brown spots. it is covered with minute scales intermixed with little horney-like blunt prickkles on the upper serface of the body. the belly and throat is more like the frog, and are of a light yellowish brown colour, around the edge of the belly is regularly set with little horney prejections which give to those edges a serrate figure, the eye is small and of a dark colour. above and behind the eyes there are several projections of the bone which being armed at their extremities with a firm black substance has the appearance of horns sprouting out from the head. this part has induced me to distinguish it by the appellation of the *Horned Lizzard.* I cannot conceive how the engages ever assimilated this animal with the Buffalow for there is not grater anology than between the Horse and the frog. this Animal is found in greatest numbers in the sandy open parts of the plains, and appear in great abundance after a rain; they are sometimes found basking in the sunshine but conceal themselves in little holes under the tufts of grass or herbs much the greater proportion of their time. they are noumerous about the Falls of Missouri, and in the plains through which we passed lately above the Falls of the Columbia."—Lewis

SOFT-SHELLED TURTLE

The only turtle mentioned in the Lewis and Clark diaries was the soft-shelled species. It would appear that other turtles must have been seen, but, if so, they were probably regarded as familiar species that were of too little interest to be noteworthy.

May 26, 1805 (Above mouth of Musselshell River)

"in this creek l saw several soft shelled turtles which were the first that have been seen this season; this I believe proceeded reather from the season than from their non-existence in this portion of the river from the Mandans hither."—Lewis

June 25, 1805 (Vic. of Great Falls, Mont.)

"See a number of water terripens."—Lewis. Thwaites' footnote to this entry: "The water terrepin is doubtless *Emys elegans* of Maximillian."

July 29, 1806 (Yellowstone River, near mouth of Tongue River)

"Cought . . . a Soft Shell turtle."—Clark

WARTY SALAMANDER

The warty salamander, *Diemyctylus torosus,* was first described by Lewis and Clark in 1806. Although they called the specimen a "water lizzard," there is little or no question about the true identity of the subject of their description.

March 11, 1806 (Written at Fort Clatsop)

"There is a species of water lizzard of which I saw one only just above the grand rapids of the Columbia. it is about 9 inches long and the body is reather flat and about the size of a mans finger covered with a soft skin of a dark brown colour with an uneven surface covered with little pimples. the neck and head are short, the latter terminating in an accute angular point and flat. the fore feet each four toes, the hinder ones five unconnected with a web and destitute of tallons. it's tail was reather longer than the body and in form like that of the Musk-rat, first rising in an arch higher than the back and decending lower than the body at the extremity, and flated perpendicularly. the belley and under part of the neck and head were of a brick red, every other part of the colour of the upper part of the body a dark brown. the mouth was smooth, without teeth."

FROGS AND TOADS

Lewis and Clark's principal reference to frogs and toads was written while the explorers were encamped on the Clearwater River in the spring of 1806. While on the outward journey they mentioned hearing frogs singing above Fort Mandan, but they did not describe any of them.

May 30, 1806 (Near Kamiah, Idaho)

"a small green tree-frog,[6] the small frog[7] which is common to our country which sings in the spring of the year, a large species of frog[8] which resorts to the water, considerably larger than our bull frog, its shape seems to be a medium between the delicate and lengthy form of our bull frog and that of our land frog or toad as they are sometimes called in the U' States. like the latter their bodies are covered with little pustles or lumps, elevated above the ordinary surface of the body; I never heard them make any sound or noise."—Lewis

CHAPTER XX

Quantity and Distribution of Game Killed

The Lewis and Clark diaries contain the first reliable record of game populations during primitive times in the Missouri valley, in the mountains and the intermountain plateaus of the northern Rockies, and in the Columbia River basin. Both Lewis and Clark, as well as a few of their followers, kept daily records relating to the abundance of wildlife observed and to hunting success. There is no valid reason for questioning the accuracy of their observations, or the veracity of their records. Both men were competent naturalists, thoroughly familiar with life in the wilderness, meticulous in every detail that might mean the difference between death and survival.

One of the major problems with which Lewis and Clark were concerned was the health and welfare of the men whom they commanded. It was apparent to them that a party which numbered forty-five at the outset, and thirty-three from Fort Mandan westward, could not subsist on the quantity of food that could be transported. Even though they packed upwards of seven tons of nonperishable food items—dried soup, parched corn, meal, flour, lard, salt and spices—into a keelboat at St. Louis, fresh meat had to be provided daily by hunters. Since the strong current of the Missouri made it necessary to drag the keelboat and two pirogues upstream by towline, the hunters generally had the easier task, and were often out in front of the boatmen.

The capacity of these men to consume meat is astonishing; even when we take into account the magnitude of their labor, Clark's statement relative to the quantity of meat consumed by these men in a day, if it was available, is extraordinary:

> "It requires 4 deer, or an elk and a deer, or one buffalow to supply us for 24 hours."

Actually, the expedition alternated between periods of feasting and starvation, depending on the abundance of big game within hunting distance from the rivers and Indian trails which they followed.

The table below presents this editor's compilation of the total kill of the principal big game species and the major groups of birds.

Game Killed by the Lewis and Clark Expedition
May 14, 1804 to Sept. 24, 1806

Deer (all species combined).................1,001
Elk 375
Bison 227
Antelope 62
Bighorned Sheep.............................. 35
Bears, grizzly 43
Bears, black 23
Beaver (shot or trapped).................... 113
Otter 16
Geese and Brant............................. 104
Ducks and Coots............................. 45
Grouse (all species)........................ 46
Turkeys 9
Plovers 48
Wolves (only one eaten)..................... 18
Indian dogs (purchased and consumed)........ 190
Horses 12

These totals, in most instances, represent a minimum kill for, occasionally, Lewis and Clark failed to record a specific figure; for example, sometimes they reported taking "a few" grouse, or "several" ducks and geese, and even in case of deer, they were equally vague in a few cases.

Kill records, no matter how impressive in total, can be misleading unless they are interpreted in terms of the distribution and seasonal abundance of the species involved.

DEER

The distribution of the deer kill, with a few exceptions, was quite uniform from central Missouri to the Beaverhead and Bitterroot mountain ranges. There were, of course, concentrations at points where the expedition encamped for weeks or months before proceeding.

Deer were scarce in the Lemhi River valley west of the Beaverhead Mountains where only 21 were killed during 9 days of hunting in late August, 1805. No deer were seen during a week spent in going over Lost Trail Pass, but 2 were killed on the headwaters of the Bitterroot River, and several were killed in the vicinity of Lolo Creek. Game was very scarce on the western slope of the Bitterroots. After going over Lolo Pass only one deer, 9 grouse and a coyote were taken between Sept. 12 and Sept. 22, and it became necessary to kill 3 colts and 2 horses for food. On the evening before the party finally escaped from the maze of mountains and canyons which characterized the Lolo Trail, Lewis wrote in his diary:

Sept. 21, 1805 (Vic. of Lochsa River, Idaho)

"We killed a few pheasants, and I killed a prairie wolf, which together with the balance of the horse beef and some crawfish which I obtained in the creek enabled us to make one more hearty meal, not knowing where the next was to be found."—Lewis

During the next eight days while encamped with a band of Chopunnish Indians on the Clearwater River, only 14 deer were killed. It was necessary to supplement them with dried pounded salmon and roots purchased from the Indians.

No deer were seen or killed while descending the Clearwater, Snake and Columbia Rivers until the party arrived at the mouth of the Sandy River, west of the Cascades.

Deer may have been plentiful on the lower Columbia, but few were killed. Only 17 were taken between late November 1805 and March 23, 1806, at Fort Clatsop. Three factors—climate, topography, and cover—made deer hunting extraordinarily difficult on the lower Columbia. Nonetheless on the return journey, 10 deer were killed in one day (March 28, 1806) on Deer Island below the mouth of the Willamette, and 12 deer were taken in 4 days at the mouth of the Sandy. Back on the Clearwater between May 14 and June 23, 1806, 72 deer were killed. This does not sound like starvation, but a deer per day was inadequate for thirty-three persons even though supplemented by a few bear and two horses. It was during this period that Lewis and Clark, entirely out of trade goods, cut the buttons from their carefully preserved army uniforms and exchanged them (the buttons) for a few bushels of dried roots. It was here that Clark worked up a considerable medical practice among the Chopunnish for fees consisting of dried roots, Indian dogs and horses.

It was impossible to determine how many of the deer killed were whitetails, Columbian blacktails, or mule deer. Sometimes Lewis and Clark indicated the kind of deer taken, but frequently they failed to do so.

It is of interest to note, however, that Lewis and Clark can be definitely credited with writing the first detailed descriptions of both the Columbian black-tailed deer, and of the mule deer. Indeed, the evidence is conclusive that Lewis coined the name "mule deer," for the latter species.

ELK

No elk were seen on the outward journey below the mouth of the Kansas River. A few were seen between the Kansas and the mouth of the Platte, but none was killed below the Platte. On the return trip, however, one elk was killed a few miles below the Kansas River. Above Council Bluffs elk were plentiful as far west as the Beaverhead River valley. Two were taken on Lolo Creek, east of Lolo Pass. None was reported between Lolo Pass and the estuary of the Columbia River. Elk sign was observed in the vicinity of Gray's Bay in southwestern Washington, but none was killed.

It was the Chinook Indians' report that elk were plentiful south of the Columbia that led Lewis and Clark to move across the river and set up winter headquarters at Fort Clatsop. The reports were true; the hunters killed 129 elk between Dec. 1, 1805 and March 23, 1806 when they abandoned the Fort and started home. Fifteen more were taken between Fort Clatsop and Celilo Falls on the Columbia, but none was reported thereafter until the expedition arrived at Traveler's Rest, east of Lolo Pass.

BISON

Lewis and Clark reported finding buffalo sign near Split Rock Creek about one hundred miles west of St. Louis, but they did not see any of them until they arrived at the Kansas River on June 28, 1804. Buffalo were not mentioned again until the expedition reached the mouth of the Big Sioux River, and it may be concluded that the Kansas and Nebraska herds were feeding on the plains at some distance from the Missouri. Large herds were seen between the James and White Rivers in South Dakota, and in even larger herds between the Big Bend of the Missouri and Fort Mandan.

The explorers were much impressed with the quantity of big game seen almost daily above the Niobrara River:

"I saw at one view near the river at least 500 buffalo, those animals have been in view all day feeding in the plains—every copse of timber appear to have elk and deer."—Clark

Near the mouth of the White River, Clark wrote:

"This scenery already rich, pleasing and beautiful was still further heightened by emmence herds of buffalo, deer, elk and antelopes which we saw in every direction feeding on the hills and plains. I do not think I exaggerate when I estimate the number of buffalo which could be comprehended at one view to amount to 3,000."—Clark

Between the Niobrara River and Fort Mandan, only 18 bison were killed, and some of these were so poor that only the tongues and marrow bones were taken for food. During the same period (Sept. 6—Oct. 31, 1804), however, the hunters killed 83 deer, 17 elk, and 17 antelope.

Game was scarce in the vicinity of Fort Mandan during the winter of 1804-5, and the hunters were obliged to travel 20 to 40 miles from camp in sub-zero weather to procure deer, elk, and buffalo. However, 38 bison, 120 deer, and 46 elk were killed between Nov. 1, 1804 and Apr. 6, 1805.

Between Fort Mandan and Great Falls bison were seen almost daily in vast herds, but above Great Falls none was seen beyond the Gates of the Mountains on the Westward journey. Old signs of buffalo were observed in the Beaverhead valley west of Three Forks, but the herds in that area had evidently departed. The expedition was now definitely beyond the buffalo country. None was seen thereafter until, on the return journey,

Lewis encountered them again on the headwaters of the Sun River east of the Rockies; and Clark, in pursuit of the Yellowstone, found them in the vicinity of Bozeman, Montana.

ANTELOPE

The explorers saw the antelope for the first time on Sept. 6, 1804, in the vicinity of Bon Homme Island below the mouth of the Niobrara River. They were seen in small herds almost daily between the Niobrara and Fort Mandan; and, in favorable habitat, from Fort Mandan to Three Forks. A few were taken in the Beaverhead valley, and three were taken in the Lemhi River valley. None was taken west of Lolo Pass. Writing at Fort Clatsop on Feb. 27, 1806, Lewis says:

"The antelope is found in the great plains of the Columbia and are the same as those on the Missouri, found in every part of the untimbered country. They are by no means as plenty on this side of the Rocky Mountains as on the other."

BIGHORN SHEEP

At the time of the Lewis and Clark expedition bighorns probably inhabited the Black Hills of South Dakota. M. Jean Vallé, a Frenchman living at the mouth of the Cheyenne River, told the explorers that bighorns inhabited the "Black Mountains" to the west.

Lewis and Clark saw the animals for the first time on the river bluffs at the mouth of the Yellowstone. Thereafter they found bighorns inhabiting the bluffs and cliffs of the Missouri as far west as the Beaverhead Mountains.

Clark killed a bighorn a few miles west of Three Forks. He watched a herd of 15 of them on the Rattlesnake Cliffs which towered above the Beaverhead River; he killed two, out of a herd of 40, at Pompey's Pillar on the Yellowstone River; he was advised by the Indians that they were plentiful on the Bighorn River, tributary to the Yellowstone. Lewis hunted them on the bluffs bordering the Missouri below the mouth of the Marias River, and concerning this experience he wrote:

July 29, 1806 (Below mouth of Marias River)

"On our way today we killed 9 bighorns of which I preserved the skins and skeletons of 2 females and one male."—Lewis

Oddly enough neither Lewis nor Clark mentioned seeing this species in the vicinity of Lolo Pass, or at any place west of the Bitterroot Mountains.

BLACK BEAR

Lewis and Clark's hunters killed their first black bear in the vicinity of Good Woman's River in Missouri on June 7, 1804. Several bear were taken thereafter as far westward as the Little Blue River in Jackson County, Missouri. None was killed above the Kansas River, but in a letter sent back from Fort Mandan to his mother, Lewis indicated that "some bear" inhabited the Missouri valley between the Kansas and Big Sioux rivers. On April 15, 1805 a black bear was seen near the mouth of the Little Missouri. Black bear were not mentioned again east of the Bitterroot Mountains.

However, on the return journey several cinnamon bear were killed in the Clearwater River country, and a black bear was taken in the foothills of the Cascades near the Sandy River.

GRIZZLY BEAR

The explorers first encountered the grizzly at the mouth of the Heart River, near the present site of Bismarck, North Dakota. Of this experience, Clark wrote:

"Our hunters killed 10 deer and a goat today and wounded a white (grizzly) bear, I saw several fresh tracks of those animals which is 3 times as large as a man's track."—Clark

They saw another grizzly swim the Missouri below the mouth of the Milk River on May 6, but they did not succeed in killing one of them until they reached the mouth of the Yellowstone River. Thereafter they saw them frequently between the Yellowstone and Great Falls, Montana. Lewis and a few of his hunters had narrow escapes from these bears in the vicinity of Great Falls and at White Bear Island near the mouth of the Sun River; ten were killed in that locality, and two near Three Forks. West of the Bitterroot Mountains six grizzlies were killed in the vicinity of Kamiah, Idaho, while the party was encamped in the Clearwater valley during May, 1806.

Concerning the distribution and abundance of this species, Lewis wrote as follows:

Feb. 16, 1806 (Written at Fort Clatsop)

"The brown, white or grizzly bear are found in the rocky mountains in the timbered parts of it, or westerly side, but rarely; they are more common below the Rocky Mountains on the border of the plains where there are copses of brush and underwood near the water courses. They are by no means as plenty on this side of the rocky mountains as on the other, nor do I believe they are found at all in the woody country, which borders this coast as far in the interior as the range of mountains (Cascades) which pass the Columbia between the Great Falls (Celilo Falls) and rapids of that river."—Lewis

In conclusion, it is evident that hunting success in 1804-6, even as now, was conditioned by the seasonal distribution and local abundance of game, as well as by the over-all range limits of species. Of course, weather, terrain, and cover conditions influenced their success in local areas. Wherever bison, elk, and deer were abundant they could have killed many more than they did, but Lewis ordered his men to shoot only as many bison and elk as they could consume; and, whenever big game was available, he forbade them to waste ammunition on waterfowl and upland game birds.

APPENDIX

JEFFERSON'S INSTRUCTIONS TO LEWIS[1]

[From the *Jefferson Papers* (Bureau of Rolls), Series 1, Vol. 9, Doc. 269.]

To Meriwether Lewis, esquire, Captain of the 1st regiment of infantry of the United States of America: Your situation as Secretary of the President of the United States has made you acquainted with the objects of my confidential message of Jan. 18, 1803, to the legislature. You have seen the act they passed, which, tho' expressed in general terms, was meant to sanction those objects, and you are appointed to carry them into execution.

Instruments for ascertaining by celestial observations the geography of the country thro' which you will pass, have already been provided. Light articles for barter, & presents among the Indians, arms for your attendants, say for from 10 to 12 men, boats, tents, & other travelling apparatus, with ammunition, medicine, surgical instruments & provisions you will have prepared with such aids as the Secretary of War can yield in his department; & from him also you will receive authority to engage among our troops, by voluntary agreement, the number of attendants above mentioned, over whom you, as their commanding officer are invested with all the powers the laws give in such a case.

As your movements while within the limits of the U. S. will be better directed by occasional communications, adapted to circumstances as they arise, they will not be noticed here. What follows will respect your proceedings after your departure from the U. S.

Your mission has been communicated to the Ministers here from France, Spain & Great Britain, and through them to their governments; and such assurances given them as to it's objects as we trust will satisfy them. The country of Louisiana having been ceded by Spain to France, the passport you have from the Minister of France, the representative of the present soverign of the country, will be a protection with all it's subjects; And that from the Minister of England will entitle you to the friendly aid of any traders of that allegiance with whom you may happen to meet.

The object of your mission is to explore the Missouri river, & such principal stream of it, as, by it's course & communication with the waters of the Pacific Ocean, may offer the most direct & practicable water communication across this continent, for the purposes of commerce.

Beginning at the mouth of the Missouri, you will take observations of latitude & longitude, at all remarkable points on the rivers, & especially at the mouths of rivers, at rapids, at islands & other places & objects distinguished by such natural marks & characters of a durable kind, as that they may with certainty be recognized hereafter. The courses of the river between these points of observation may be supplied by the compass, the log-line & by time, corrected by the observations themselves. The variations of the compass too, in different places, should be noticed.

The interesting points of the portage between the heads of the Missouri & the water offering the best communication with the Pacific Ocean should also be fixed by observations, & the course of that water to the ocean, in the same manner as that of the Missouri.

Your observations are to be taken with great pains & accuracy, to be entered distinctly, & intelligly for others as well as yourself, to comprehend all the elements necessary, with the aid of the usual tables, to fix the latitude and longitude of the places at which they were taken, & are to be rendered to the war office, for the purpose of having the calculations made concurrently by proper persons within the U. S. Several copies of these, as well as your other notes, should be made at leisure times & put into the care of the most trustworthy of your attendants, to guard by multiplying them, against the accidental losses to which they will be exposed. A further guard would be that one of these copies be written on the paper of the birch, as less liable to injury from damp than common paper.

The commerce which may be carried on with the people inhabiting the line you will pursue, renders a knolege of these people important. You will therefore endeavor to make yourself acquainted, as far as a diligent pursuit of your journey shall admit,

with the names of the nations & their numbers;

the extent & limits of their possessions;

their relations with other tribes or nations;

their language, traditions, monuments;

their ordinary occupations in agriculture, fishing, hunting, war, arts, & the implements for these;

their food, clothing, & domestic accomodations;

the diseases prevalent among them, & the remedies they use;

moral & physical circumstances which distinguish them from the tribes we know;

peculiarities in their laws, customs & dispositions;

and articles of commerce they may need or furnish, & to what extent.

And considering the interest which every nation has in extending & strengthening the authority of reason & justice among the people around them, it will be useful to acquire what knolege you can of the state of morality, religion & information among them, as it may better enable those who endeavor to civilize & instruct them, to adapt their measures to the existing notions & practices of those on whom they are to operate.

Other objects worthy of notice will be

the soil & face of the country, it's growth & vegetable productions; especially those not of the U. S.

the animals of the country generally, & especially those not known in the U. S.

the remains and accounts of any which may be deemed rare or extinct;

the mineral productions of every kind; but more particularly metals, limestone, pit coal & saltpetre; salines & mineral waters, noting the temperature of the last, & such circumstances as may indicate their character.

Volcanic appearances.

Climate as characterized by the thermometer, by the proportion of rainy, cloudy & clear days, by lightening, hail, snow, ice, by the access & recess of frost, by the winds prevailing at different seasons, the dates at which particular plants put forth or lose their flowers, or leaf, times of appearance of particular birds, reptiles or insects.

Altho' your route will be along the channel of the Missouri, yet you will endeavor to inform yourself, by inquiry, of the character & extent of the country watered by it's branches, & especially on it's southern side. The North river or Rio Bravo which runs into the gulph of Mexico, and the North river, or Rio colorado, which runs into the Gulf of California, are understood to be the principal streams heading opposite to the waters of the Missouri, and running Southwardly. Whether the dividing grounds between the Missouri & them are mountains or flatlands, what are their distance from the Missouri, the character of the intermediate country, & the people inhabiting it, are worthy of particular enquiry. The Northern waters of the Missouri are less to be enquired after, because they have been ascertained to a considerable degree, and are still in a course of ascertainment by English traders & travellers. But if you can learn anything certain of the most Northern source of the Mississippi, & of it's position relative to the lake of the woods, it will be interesting to us. Some account too of the path of the Canadian traders from the Mississippi, at the mouth of the Ouisconsin river, to where it strikes the Missouri and of the soil & rivers in it's course, is desirable.

In all your intercourse with the natives treat them in the most friendly & conciliatory manner which their own conduct will admit; allay all jealousies as to the object of your journey, satisfy them of it's innocence, make them acquainted with the position, extent, character, peaceable and commercial dispositions of the U. S. of our wish to be neighborly, friendly and useful to them, and of our dispositions to a commercial intercourse with them; confer with them on the points most convenient as mutual emporiums, and the articles of most desirable interchange for them and us. If a few of their influential chiefs, within practicable distance, wish to visit us, arrange such a visit with them, and furnish them with authority to call on our officers, on their entering the U. S. to have them conveyed to this place at public expense. If any of them should wish to have some of their young people brought up with us, and taught such arts as may be useful to them, we will receive, instruct and take care of them. Such a mission, whether of influential chiefs, or of young people, would give some security to your own party. Carry with you some matter of the kine-pox, inform those of them with whom you may be of it's efficacy as a preservative from the small-pox; and instruct and incourage them in the use of it. This may be especially done wherever you winter.

As it is impossible for us to foresee in what manner you will be received by those people, whether with hospitality or hostility, so is it impossible to prescribe the exact degree of perseverance with which you are to pursue your journey. We value too much the lives of citizens to offer them to probable destruction. Your numbers will be sufficient to secure you against the unauthorized opposition of individuals, or of small parties; but if a superior force, authorized or not authorized, by a nation, should be arrayed against your further passage, and inflexibly determined to arrest it, you must decline it's further pursuit, and return. In the loss of yourselves, we should lose also the information you will have acquired. By returning safely with that, you may enable us to renew the essay with better calculated means. To your own discretion therefore must be left the degree of danger you may risk, and the point at which you should decline, only saying we wish you to err on the side of your safety, and bring back your party safe, even if it be with less information.

As far up the Missouri as the white settlements extend, an intercourse will probably be found to exist between them and the Spanish posts at St. Louis, opposite Cahokia, or Ste. Genevieve opposite Kaskaskia. From still farther up the river, the traders may furnish a conveyance for letters. Beyond that you may perhaps be able to engage Indians to bring letters for the government to Cahokia or Kaskaskia, on promising that they shall there receive special compensation as you shall have stipulated with them. Avail yourself of these means to communicate to us, at seasonable intervals, a copy of your journal, notes and observations of every kind, putting into cypher whatever might do injury if betrayed.

Should you reach the Pacific ocean (One full line scratched out, indecipherable.—Ed.) inform yourself of the circumstances which may decide whether the furs of those parts may not be collected as advantageously at the head of the Missouri (convenient as is supposed to the waters of the Colorado and Oregon or Columbia) as at Nootka sound or any other point of that coast; and that trade be consequently conducted through the Missouri & U. S. more beneficially than by the circumnavigation now practised.

On your arrival on that coast endeavor to learn if there be any port within your reach frequented by the sea-vessels of any nation, and to send two of your trusty people back by sea, in such way as shall appear practicable, with a copy of your notes. And should you be of opinion that the return of your party by the way they went will be eminently dangerous, then ship the whole, and return by sea by way of Cape Horn or the Cape of good Hope, as you shall be able. As you will be without money, clothes or provisions, you must endeavor to use the credit of the U. S. to obtain them; for which purpose open letters of credit shall be furnished you authorizing you to draw on the Executive of the U. S. or any of its officers in any part of the world, on which drafts can be disposed of, and to apply with our recommendations to the Consuls, agents, merchants or citizens of any nation with which we have intercourse, assuring them in our name that any aids they may furnish you, shall be honorably repaid, and on demand. Our consuls Thomas Howes at Batavia in Java, William Buchanan of the isle of France and Bourbon, and John Elmslie at the Cape of good hope will be able to supply your necessities by draughts on us.

Should you find it safe to return by the way you go, after sending two of your party round by sea, or with your whole party, if no conveyance by sea can be found, do so; making such observations on your return as may serve to supply, correct or confirm those made on your outward journey.

In re-entering the U. S. and reaching a place of safety, discharge any of your attendants who may desire and deserve it, procuring for them immediate paiment of all arrears of pay and cloathing which may have incurred since their departure; and assure them that they shall be recommended to the liberality of the legislature for the grant of a soldier's portion of land each, as proposed in my message to Congress and repair yourself with your papers to the seat of government.

To provide, on the accident of your death, against anarchy, dispersion and the consequent danger to your party, and total failure of the enterprise, you are hereby authorized, by any instrument signed and written in your hand, to name the person among them who shall succeed to the command on your decease, and by like instruments to change the nomination from time to time, as further experience of the characters accompanying you shall point out superior fitness; and all the powers and authorities given to yourself are, in the event of your death, transferred to and vested in the successor so named, with further power to him, and his successors in like manner to name each his successor, who, on the death of his predecessor, shall be invested with all the powers and authorities given to yourself.

Given under my hand at the city of Washington, this 20th day of June 1803.

Th. Jefferson
Pr. U. S. of America

SUPPLIES AND EQUIPMENT [2]

Articles Purchased by Israel Whalen, Purveyor of Public Supplies, for the Lewis and Clark Expedition.

INDIAN PRESENTS

12 Pipe Tomahawks
6½ lbs. Strips of Sheet Iron
1 Ps. red flannel, 47½ yds.
11 Ps. Handkercheiffs, assorted
1 doz. Ivory combs
½ Catty India S. Silk
21 bbls. T(h)read, assorted
1 Ps. Scarlet cloth 22 yds.
5½ doz. fan: Floss
6 Gross Binding
2 Cards Beads
4 doz. Butcher Knives
12 doz. Pocket Looking Glasses
15 " Pewter " "
8 " Burning Glasses
2 " Nonesopretty
2 " Red striped tapes
72 ps. Striped Silk Ribbon
3 lbs. Beads
6 Papers Small Bells
1 Box with 100 Larger Bells
73 bunches Beads, assorted
3½ doz. Tinsel Bands, assorted
1 doz. Needle Cans
2¾ doz. Lockets

8½ lbs. Red Beads
2 doz. Earrings
8 Brass Kettles
12 lbs. Brass strips
500 Broaches
72 Rings
2 Corn Mills
15 doz. Scissors
12 lbs. Brass Wire
14 lbs. Knitting Pins
4600 Needles, assorted
2800 Fish Hooks, assorted
1 gross Iron Combs
3 gross Curtain Rings
2 gross Thimbles, assorted
11 doz. Knives
10 lbs. Brads
8 lbs. Red Lead
2 lbs. Vermillion
130 rolls of Tobacco (pig tail)
48 Calico Ruffled Shirts
15 Blankets (from Public Store)
1 Trunk to Pack Sundry Indian Presents
8 Gross Seat or Mocassin Awls
Total cost of Indian Presents $669.50

CAMP EQUIPAGE

4 Tin Horns
2 " Lanthorns
2 " Lamps
1 box Sq'r. of Small ast'd.
3 doz. Pint Tumblers
125 Large Fishing Hooks
Fishing Lines Assorted
1 Strand Fishing Lines with Hooks
Complete

1 Sportsman's Flaske
8 pc. Cat Gut for Mosquito Cart
6 Brass Kettles and Porterage 25 ft.
1 Block Tin Sauce Pan
1 Corn Mill

From Public Store:

8 Receipt Books
48 P's. Tape
6 Brass Inkstands
6 Papers Ink Powder
1 Common Tent
1 lb. Sealing Wax
100 Quils
1 Packing Hogshead

Brought by the Purveyor of

Richard Wevill:

8 Tents, Oil Treated

1 Set Gold Scales and Wts.
1 Rule
1 Set Iron Weights
2 pr. Large Shears
4 doz. Pack'g Needles & Large Awls
2 doz. Table Spoons
4 Drawing Knives
3 doz. Gimblets
17 " Files & Rasps & 1 Shoe float
1¼ " Small Cord
2 Small Vices
2 pr. Plyers
1 Saw Sett
9 Chisels
2 Adzes
2 Hand Saws
6 Augers
2 Hatchets
1 Whetstone
2 Pocket Steel yards
12 lb. Pkg. Castile Soap
Total Cost................$117.67

45 Bags, " "
10 Yds. Country Linen, Oil Treated
20 " Brown " " "

MATHEMATICAL INSTRUMENTS

		Cost
1	Spirit level	$ 4.00
1	Case platting Instruments	14.00
1	Two pole chain	2.00
1	Pocket Compas plated	5.00
1	Brass Boat Compass	1.50
3	" Pocket Compasses	7.50
1	Magnet	1.00
1	Hadleys Quadrat with Tang't Screw	22.00
1	Metal Sextant	90.00
1	Microscope to index of d.	7.00
1	Sett of Slates in a case	4.00
4	oz. of Talc	1.25
1	Surveying Compass with extra needles	23.50
1	Circular protractor and index	8.00
1	Six In. Pocket Telescope	7.00
1	Nautical Ephmeris	1.50
1	Requisite Tables	2.50
	Kirwan's Mineralogy	5.00
1	Chronometer & Keys (watch)	250.75
1	Copy of Barton's Botany	6.00
	Kelley's Spherics	3.00
2	Nautical Ephemeris	4.00
	Log line reel and log ship	1.95
	Parallel Glass for a Horison	1.00
2	Mercury Thermometers (Hand made by Dr. Antoine Sangrain of St. Louis)	

ARMS & ACCOUTREMENTS & AMMUNITION

1 Pair Pocket pistols		10.00
176 lbs. Gun powder		155.75
52 Leaden Canisters for Gun Powder		26.33
15 Powder Horns and Pouches		26.25
15 Powder Horns	From Public Store	
18 Tomahaws	" " "	
15 Scalping Knives & belts	" " "	
15 Gun Slings	" " "	
30 Brushes & Wires	" " "	
15 Cartouch Boxes	" " "	
15 Painted Knapsacks	" " "	
500 Rifle Flints	" " "	
125 Musket Flints	" " "	
50 lbs. best rifle Powder	" " "	
1 pr. Horsemans Pistols	" " "	
420 lbs. Sheet Lead	" " "	

Box of *Friction Matches* produced by Dr. Antoine Sangrain for the expedition twenty years before they were generally known.

1 Air-gun—Valued show piece of the expedition; developed in Great Britain in 18th century, but little known in America. (Good accuracy and killing powder sufficient for small game at close range.)

15 Flint-lock rifles, also obtained from public stores; presumably the Kentucky volunteers provided their own rifles.

PROVISIONS (ACQUIRED BY WHALEN)

193 lbs. Portable Soup		$289.50
30 gals. Spr. of Wine in 6 kegs		77.20
2 lbs. Tea & cannister		3.80
15 Blankets	From Public Store	
15 Match Coats	" " "	
15 Priv. Blue Wool Overalls	" " "	
36 Pairs Stockings	" " "	
20 Frocks	" " "	
30 Priv. lin. Shirts	" " "	
20 Priv. Shoes	" " "	
1 pk. Hhd.	" " "	

MEDICAL AND SURGICAL SUPPLIES

15 lbs. powdered Bark (Peru)	1 lb. Ung. Epispastric (ointment)
½ lb. powdered Jalap	1 lb. " Mercuriale (ointment)
½ " " Rhubard	1 Emplast. Diach. S.
4 oz. " Ipecacuana	1 Set Pocket Instruments—small
2 lbs. " Crem. Tart.	1 Set Teeth " "
2 oz. Gum Camphor	1 Clyster Syringe

1 lb. Assofoetida

½ lb. Gum Opii Turk. opt. (opium)

¼ lb. Gum Tragacanth

6 lbs. Sal Glauber (Epsom salts)

2 lbs. " Nitri

2 lbs. " Copperos

6 oz. Sacchar. Saturni

4 oz. Calomel

1 oz. Tartar Emetic

4 oz. White Vitriol

½ lb. Columbo Rad.

¼ lb. Elix. Vitriol

¼ lb. Ess. Menth. pip.

¼ lb. Bals. Copaiboe

¼ lb. " Traumat

2 oz. Magnesia

4 oz. Laudanum

2 lbs. Ung. Basilic Fla. (ointment)

1 lb. Ung. e lap Calimin (ointment)

4 Penis Syringe

3 Best Lancets

1 Tourniquet

2 oz. Patent Lint

50 doz. Bilious Pills (Dr. Rush's)

6 Tin Canisters

3—8 oz. Glass Stoppered Bottles

5—4 oz. Tinctures "

6—4 oz. Salt

1 Walnut Chest

1 Pine Chest

¼ lb. Indian Ink

2 oz. Gum Elastic

2 oz. Nutmegs

2 oz. Cloves

4 oz. Cinnamon

Total cost of Medical Supplies—$90.69

Additional Provisions Listed in Clark's "Memorandum of Articles in Readiness for the Voyage":

14 bags of Parchment of 2 bu.	1,200 lbs. weight	
9 " " Common Meal of 2 bu.	800 " "	
11 " " Corn-hulled of 2 bu.	1,000 " "	
30 half barrels of Flour ⎫ 2 bags " " ⎬ (gross 3,900)	3,400 " "	
7 " " Bisquit ⎫ 4 bbls " " ⎬ (gross 650)	560 " "	
7 " " Salt (gross 870)	750 " "	
50 kegs " Pork (gross 4,500)	3,705 " "	
2 boxes of candles ⎫ 50 lbs. " soap ⎬	170 " "	
1 bag " candle-wick	8 " "	
1 " " coffee	50 " "	
1 " " beans & 1 of peas	100 " "	
2 " " sugar	112 " "	
1 keg " hogs lard	100 " "	
4 bbls. " Corn—hulled (gross 650)	600 " "	
1 " " Meal (" 170)	150 " "	
600 lbs. " Grees	600 " "	
50 bu. " Meal		
21 bales " Indian Goods (described above)		
Tools of Every Description (described above)		
24 bu. of Natchies Corn—hulled		

LEWIS TO HIS MOTHER[3]

Fort Mandan, 1609 Miles
above the entrance of the Missouri—
March 31st, 1805

Dear Mother:—I arrived at this place on the 27th. of Oct. last, with party under my command destined to the Pacific Ocean, by way of the Missouri and Columbia rivers. The near approach of winter, the low state of the water and the known scarcity of timber which exists on the Missouri for many hundred miles above the Mandans, together with many other considerations equally important, determined my friend and companion Capt. Clark and myself to fortify ourselves and remain for the winter in the neighborhood of the Mandans, Minetares and Ahwaharways, who are the most friendly and well disposed savages that we have yet met with. Accordingly we sought and found a convenient situation for our purposes a few miles below the villages of these people on the north side of the river in an extensive and well timbered bottom, where we commenced the erection of our houses on the 2d. of Nov. and completed them so far as to put ourselves under shelter on the 21st. of the same month, by which time the season wore the aspect of winter. Having completed our fortify (cation) early in Dec. 23 called it Fort Mandan, in honor of our friendly neighbors. So far we have experienced more difficulties from the navigation of the Missouri than danger from the savages. The difficulties which oppose themselves to the navigation of this immense river arise from the rapidity of its currents, its falling banks, sand bars and timber which remains wholly or partially concealed in its bed, usually called by the navigators of the Missouri, and the Mississippi "sawyer" or "planter," one of these difficulties the navigator never ceases to contend with from the entrance of the Missouri to this place; and in innumerable instances most of these obstructions are at the same instant combined to oppose his progress or threaten his destruction. To these we may also add a fifth, and not much less inconsiderable difficulty—the turbed quality of the water—which renders it impracticable to discover any obstruction, even to the depth of a single inch. Such is the velocity of the current at all seasons of the year, from the entrance of the Missouri to the mouth of the great river Platte, that it is impossible to resist its force by means of oars or poles in the main channel of the river; the eddies which therefore generally exist on one side or the other of the river, are sought by the navigators, but these are almost universally encumbered with concealed timber, or within reach of the falling banks, but notwithstanding, are usually preferable to that of passing along the edges of the sand bars, over which the water, tho' shallow, runs with such violence that if your vessel happens to touch the sand, or is by any accident turned sidewise to the current, it is driven on the bar and overset in an instant, generally destroyed, and always attended with the loss of the cargo. The base of the river banks being composed of a fine light sand, is easily removed by the water. It happens when this capricious and violent current sets against its banks, which are usually covered with heavy timber, it quickly undermines them, sometimes to the depth of 40 or 50 paces, and several miles in length. The banks being unable to support themselves longer tumble into the river with tremendous force, destroying everything within their reach. The timber thus precipitated into the water with large masses of earth about their roots are seen drifting with the stream, their points above the water, while the roots, more heavy, are dragged along the bottom until they become firmly fixed in the quick sand, which forms the bed of the river, where they remain for many years, forming an irregular tho' dangerous chevaux-de-frise to oppose the navigator. This immense river, so far as we have yet ascended, waters one of the fairest portions of the globe, nor do I believe there is in the universe a similar extent of country equally fertile, well watered, and intersected by such a number of navigable streams. The country as high up the river as the mouth of the river Platte, a distance of 630 miles, is generally well timbered. At some little distance above this river the open or prairie country commences. With respect to this open country, I have been agreeably disappointed. From previous information I had been led to believe that it was barren, sterile and sandy; but, on the contrary, I found it fertile in the extreme, the soil being from one to twenty feet in depth, consisting of a fine black loam, intermixed with a sufficient quantity of sand only to induce a luxuriant growth of grass and other vegetable productions, particularly such as are not liable to be much injured, or wholly destroyed by the ravages of the fire. It is also generally level, yet well watered, in short, there can exist no other objection to it, except that of the want of timber, which is truly a very serious one. This want of timber is by no means attributable to a deficiency in the soil to produce it, but owes its origin to the ravages of the fires, which the natives kindle in these plains at all seasons of the year. The country on both sides of the river, except some of its bottom lands, for an immense distance is one continued open plain, in which no timber is to be seen except a few detatched and scattered copses, and clumps of trees, which, from their moist situation, or the steep declivities of hills, are sheltered from the effects of fire. The general aspect of the country is level so far as the perception of the spectator will enable him to determine, but from the rapidity of the Missouri, it must be considerably elevated, as it passes to the N. West; it is broken only on the borders of the water courses. Game is very abundant, and seems to increase as we progress— our prospect of starving is therefore consequently small. On the lower portion of the Missouri, from its junction with the Mississippi to the entrance of the Osage river we met with some deer, bear and turkeys. From thence to the Kancez river the deer were more abundant. A great number of black bear, some turkeys, geese, swans and ducks. From thence to the mouth of the great river Platte an immense quantity of deer, some bear, elk, turkeys, geese, swans and ducks. From thence to the river S(ioux) some bear, a great number of elks, the bear disappeared almost entirely, some turkeys, geese, swan and ducks. From thence to the mouth of the White river vast herds of buffalo, elk and some deer, and a greater quantity of turkeys than we had before seen, a circumstance which I did not much expect in a country so destitute of timber. Hence to Fort Mandan the buffalo, elk and deer increase in quantity, with the addition of the cabie (cabra), as they are generally called by the French engages, which is a creature about the size of a small deer. Its flesh is deliciously flavored. The ice in the Missouri has now nearly disappeared. I shall set out on my voyage in the course of a few days. I can foresee no material obstruction to our progress and feel the most perfect confidence that we shall reach the Pacific ocean this summer. For myself, individually, I enjoy better health than I have since I commenced my voyage. The party are now in fine health and excellent spirits, are attached to the enterprise and anxious to proceed. Not a whisper of discontent or murmur is to be heard among them. With such men I feel every confidence necessary to insure success. The party, with Capt. Clark and myself, consists of thirty-one white persons, one negro man, and two Indians. The Indians in this neighborhood (assert) that the Missouri is navigable nearly to its source, and that from a navigable part of the river, at a distance not exceeding a half a days march, there is a large river running from south to north along the western base of the Rocky Mountains, but as their war excursions have not extended far beyond this point, they can give no account of the discharge or source of this river. We believe this stream to be the principal South Fork of the Columbia river, and if so, we shall probably find but little difficulty in passing to the ocean. We have subsisted this winter on meat principally, with which our guns have furnished us an ample supply, and have, by that means, reserved a sufficient stock of the provisions we brought with us from the Illinois to guard us against accidental want during the voyage of the present year. You may expect me in Albemarle about the last of next Sept.—twelve months. I request that you will give yourself no uneasiness with respect to my fate, for I assure you that I feel myself perfectly as safe as I should do in Albemarle, and the only difference between three or four thousand miles and 130 is that I can not have the pleasure of seeing you as often as I did while at Washington.

I must request of you before I conclude this letter, to send John Marks to the college of Williamsburgh as soon as it shall be thought that his education has been sufficiently advanced to fit him for that seminary; for you may rest assured that as you regard his future prosperity you had better make any sacrifice of his property than suffer his education to remain neglected or incomplete. Give my love to my brothers and sisters and all my neighbors and friends, and rest assured yourself of the most devoted and filial affection of yours,

Meriwether Lewis.

TABLE I

List of Articles sent to President Jefferson from Fort Mandan on the big bateau which left for St. Louis on Apr. 7, 1805.[4]

Box No. 1, contains the following articles, i.e.

In package No. 3 and 4 Male and female antilope with their skiletons.

No. 7 & 9, the horns of two mule or Black tailed deer, a Mandan bow and quiver of arrows—with some Recarra's tobacco seed.

No. 11, a Martin Skin, Containing the tail of a Mule Deer, a weasel and three squirrels from the Rocky Mountains.

No. 12, the bones and skeliton of a Small burrowing wolf of the Praries the skin being lost by accident.

No. 99, The Skeliton of the white and Gray hare.
Box No. 2
Contains 4 Buffalo Robes, and a ear of Mandan Corn.
Box No. 3

Nos. 1 & 2, the Skin of the Male and female Antelope with their Skelitons, & the Skin of a Yellow Bear which I obtained from the Sioux.
Box No. 4
Specimens of plants numbered from 1 to 67.

Specimens of plants numbered 1 to 60.
1 Earthen pot Such as the Mandans manufacture and use for culinary purposes.

1 Tin box containing insects, mice, etc.

a Specimine of the fur of the antilope.

a Specimon of a plant, and a parcel of its roots highly prized by the natives as a efficatious remidy in cases of the bite of the rattle snake or Mad Dog.

In a large Trunk. No. 5

Skins⁣ of a male & female Braro, or burrowing Dog of the Prarie, with skeliton of the female.

1 Skin of the red fox containing a Magpie.

2 Cased Skins of the white hare.

1 Minitarra Buffalo robe Containing some articles of Indian Dress.

1 Mandan Buffalo robe Containing a dressed Louserva (Lynx) Skin, and 2 cased Skins of the Burrowing Squirrel of the Praries.

13 red fox Skins

4 Horns of the Mountain Ram, or big horn

1 Buffalo robe painted by a mandan man representing a battle fought 8 years Since by the Sioux & Ricaras against the mandans, menitarras & Ah wah har ways. (Mandans, etc. on horseback)

Cage No. 6

Contains a liveing burrowing squirrel of the praries

Cage No. 7

Contains 4 liveing Magpies

Cage No. 8

Contains a liveing hen of the Prarie

a large par of Elks horns contained (held together) by the frontal bone.

Note: These specimens were delivered safely to President Jefferson, who sequently consigned them to Peale's Museum in Philadelphia.

LEWIS TO JEFFERSON [5]

[From the original *Jefferson Papers* (Bureau of Rolls), Series 2, Vol. 51, Doc. 107.]

Fort Mandan, April 7th, 1805

Dear Sir: Herewith inclosed you will receive an invoice of certain articles, which I have forwarded to you from this place. among other articles, you will observe by reference to the invoice, 67 specimens of earths, salts and minerals; and 60 specimens of plants: these are accompanyed by their rispective labels expressing the days on which obtained, places where found, and also their virtues and properties when known. by means of these labels, reference may be made to the Chart of the Missouri forwarded to the Secretary at War, on which, the encampment of each day has been carefully marked; thus the places at which these specimens have been obtained may be easily pointed out, or again found, should any of them prove valuable to the community on further investigation. (these have been forwarded with a view of their being presented to the Philosophical society of Philadelphia, in order that they may under their direction be examined or analyzed. after examining these specimens yourself, I would thank you to have a copy of their labels made out, and retained until my return. the other articles are intended particularly for yourself, to be retained, or disposed off as you may think proper.)

You will also receive herewith inclosed a part of Capt. Clark's private journal, the other part you will find inclosed in a separate tin box. this journal (is in it's original state, and of course incorrect, but it) will serve to give you the daily detales of our progress, and transactions. (Capt. Clark does not wish this journal exposed in it's present state, but has no objection, that one or more copies of it be made by some confidential person under your direction, correcting it's gramatical errors &c. indeed it is the wish of both of us, that two of those copies should be made, if convenient, and retained untill our return; in this state there is no objection to your submitting them to the perusal of the heads of the departments, or such others as you may think proper. a copy of this journal will assist me in compiling my own for publication after my return.) I shall dispatch a canoe with three, perhaps four persons, from the extreem navigable point of the Missouri, or the portage between this river, and the Columbia river, as either may first happen; by the return of this canoe, I shal send you my journal, and some one or two of the best of those kept by my men. I have sent a journal kept by one of the Sergeants,[6] to Capt. Stoddard, my agent at St. Louis, in order as much as possible to multiply the chances of saving something. we have encouraged our men to keep journals, and seven of them do so, to whom in this respect we give every assistance in our power.

I have transmitted to the Secretary at War, every information relative to the geography of the country which we possess, together with a view of the Indian nations, containing information relative to them, on those points with which I, conceived it important that the government should be informed. (If it could be done with propriety and convenience, I should feel myself much obliged by your having a copy taken of my dispatches to the Secretary at War, on those subjects, retaining them for me untill my return.) By reference to the Muster-rolls forwarded to the War Department, you will see the state of the party; in addition to which, we have two Interpretors, one negro man, servant to Capt. Clark, one Indian woman, wife to one of the interpreters, and a Mandan man, whom we take with a view to restore peace between the Snake Indians, and those in this neighborhood amounting in total with ourselves to 33 persons. by means of the Interpreters and Indians, we shall be enabled to converse with all the Indians that we shall probably meet with on the Missouri.

I have forwarded to the Secretary at War, my public Accounts rendered up to the present day. they have been much longer delayed than I had any idea that they would have been, when we departed from the Illinois, but this delay, under the circumstances which I was compelled to act, has been unavoidable. The provision peraque and her crew, could not have been dismissed in time to have returned to St. Louis last fall without evedently in my opinion, hazarding the fate of the enterprise in which I am engaged, and I therefore did not hesitate to prefer the sensure that I may have incurred by the detention of these papers, to that of risking in any degree the success of the expedition. to me, the detention of those papers has formed a serious source of disquiet and anxiety; and the recollection of your particular charge to me on this subject, has made it still more poignant. I am fully aware of the inconvenience which must have arisen to the War Department, from the want of these vouchers previous to the last session of Congress, but how to diver it was out of my power to devise.—

From this plase we shall send the barge and crew early tomorrow morning with orders to proceed as expeditiously as possible to St. Louis, by her we send our dispatches, which I trust will get safe to hand. Her crew consists of ten able-bodied men well armed and provided with a sufficient stock of provision to last them to St. Louis. I have but little doubt but they will be fired on by the Siouxs: but they have pledged themselves to us that they will not yeald while there is a man of them living.

Our baggage is all embarked on board six small canoes and two perogues; we shall set out at the same moment that we dispatch the barge. one or perhaps both of these perogues we shall leave at the falls of the Missouri, from whence we intend continuing our voyage in the canoes and a perogue of skins, the frame of which was prepared at Harper's ferry. this perogue is now in a situation which will enable us to prepare it in the course of a few hours. as our vessels are now small and the current of the river much more moderate, we calculate on traveling at the rate of 20 or 25 miles pr. day as far as the falls of the Missouri. beyond this point, or the first range of rocky Mountains situated about 100 miles further, any calculation with rispect to our daily progress, can be little more than bare conjecture. the circumstance of the Snake Indians possessing large quantities of horses, is much in our favour, as by means of horses, the transportation of our baggage will be rendered easy and expeditious over land, from the Missouri, to the Columbia river. should this river not prove navigable where we first meet with it, our present intention is, to continue our march by land down the river untill it becomes so, or to the Pacific Ocean. The map, which has been forwarded to the Secretary at War, will give you the idea we entertain of the connection of these rivers, which has been formed from the corresponding testimony of a number of Indians who have visited that

306

country, and who have been separately and carefully examined on that subject, and we therefore think it entitled to some degree of confidence.

Since our arrival at this place we have subsisted principally on meat, with which our guns have supplyed us amply, and have thus been enabled to reserve the parched meal, portable Soup, and a considerable proportion of pork and flour, which we had intended for the more difficult parts of our voyage. if Indian information can be credited, the vast quantity of game with which the country abounds through which we are to pass leaves us but little to apprehend from the want of food.

We do not calculate on completeing our voyage within the present year, but expect to reach the Pacific Ocean, and return, as far as the head of the Missouri, or perhaps to this place before winter. you may therefore expect me to meet you at Montochello in September 1806.

On our return we shal probably pass down the yellow stone river, which from Indian informations, waters one of the fairest portions of this continent.

I can foresee no material or probable obstruction to our progress, and entertain therefore the most sanguine hopes of complete success. As to myself individually I never enjoyed a more perfect state of good health than I have since we commenced our voyage. my inestimable friend and companion Capt. Clark has also enjoyed good health generally. At this moment, every individual of the party are in good health, and excellent sperits; zealously attached to the enterprise, and anxious to proceed; not a whisper of discontent or murmur is to be heard among them; but all in unison, act with the most perfect harmoney. with such men I have every thing to hope, and but little to fear.

Be so good as to present my most affectionate regard to all my friends, and be assured of the sincere and unalterable attachment of

Your most Obt. Servt.
Meriwether Lewis
Capt. 1st U' S. Regt. Infty.

JEFFERSON TO CONSTANTIN FRANCOIS DECHASSE-BOEUF COMTE DE VOLNEY[7]

Feb. 11, 1806

Our last news of Captn Lewis was that he had reached the upper part of the Missouri, & had taken horses to cross the Highlands to the Columbia river.[8] He passed the last winter among the Mandans 1610 miles above the mouth of the river. So far he had delineated it with as great accuracy as will probably be ever applied to it, as his courses & distances by mensuration were corrected by almost daily observations of latitude and longitude. With his map he sent us specimens or information of the following animals not before known to the northern continent of America. 1. The horns of what is perhaps a species of Ovis Ammon. 2. A new variety of the deer having a black tail. 3. An antelope. 4. The badger, not before known out of Europe. 5. A new species of marmotte. 6. A white weasel. 7. The magpie. 8. The Prairie hen, said to resemble the Guinea hen (peintade). 9. A prickly lizard. To these are added a considerable collection of minerals, not yet analyzed. He wintered in Lat. 47° 20′ and found the maximum of cold, 43° below the zero of Fahrenheit. We expect he has reached the Pacific, and is now wintering on the head of the Missouri, and will be here next autumn. [Extract, Paul Leicester Ford, *The Writings of Thomas Jefferson* (New York: P. G. Putnam's Sons, 1892), Vol. VIII, p. 419.]

PART OF JEFFERSON'S MESSAGE TO CONGRESS, 1806[9]

Feb. 19, 1806

To the Senate and House of Representatives of the United States:

In pursuance of a measure proposed to Congress by a message of January 18, 1803, and sanctioned by their approbation for carrying it into execution, Captain Meriwether Lewis, of the First Regiment of infantry, was appointed, with a party of men, to explore the river Missouri from its mouth to its source, and, crossing the highlands by the shortest portage, to seek the best water communication thence to the Pacific Ocean; and Lieutenant Clarke was appointed second in command. They were to enter into conference with the Indian nations on their route with a view to the establishment of commerce with them. They entered the Missouri May 14, 1804, and on the 1st of November took up their winter quarters near the Mandan towns, 1,609 miles above the mouth of the river, in latitude 47° 21′ 47″ north and longitude 99° 24′ 45″ west from Greenwich. On the 8th of April, 1805, they proceeded up the river in pursuance of the objects prescribed to them. A letter of the preceding day, April 7th, from Captain Lewis is herewith communicated. During his stay among the Mandans he had been able to lay down the Missouri according to courses and distances taken on his passage up it, corrected by frequent observations of longitude and latitude, and to add to the actual survey of this portion of the river a general map of the country between the Mississippi and Pacific from the thirty-fourth to the fifty-fourth degree of latitude. These additions are from information collected from Indians with whom he had opportunities of communicating during his journey and residence with them. Copies of this map are now presented to both Houses of Congress. With these I communicate also a statistical view, procured and forwarded by him, of the Indian nations inhabiting the Territory of Louisiana and the countries adjacent to its northern and western borders, of their commerce, and of other interesting circumstances respecting them. [From James D. Richardson, *A Compilation of the Messages and Papers of the Presidents, 1789-1817* (53rd Congress, 2nd Session, House of Representatives, Misc. Doc. No. 210, 1896), Vol. I, p. 398.]

LEWIS TO JEFFERSON[10]

[*Jefferson Papers* (Bureau of Rolls), Codex S., Series 6. Vol. II, Doc. 103. Apparently the first draft of the document is found here. The original MS. is in the *Lewis and Clark Journals*.]

St. Louis September 23rd., 1806

Sir: It is with pleasure that I announce to you the safe arrival of myself and party at this place on the (blank space in MS.) inst. with our papers and baggage. no accedent has deprived us of a single member of our party since I last wrote you from the Mandans in April 1805. In obedience to your orders we have penetrated the Continent of North America to the Pacific Ocean and suficiently explored the interior of the country to affirm that we have discovered the most practicable communication which dose exist across the continent by means of the navigable branches of the Missouri and Columbia Rivers; this is by way of the Missouri to the foot of the rapids five miles below the great falls of that river a distance of 2575 Miles, thence by land passing the Rocky mountains to the Kooskooske 340 and from thence by way of the Kooskooske, the S. E. branch of the Columbia and the latter river to the Ocean of 640 Miles making a total of 3555 Miles. the Missouri possesses sufficient debth of water as far as is specifyed for boats of 15 tons burthen, but those of smaller capacity are to be prefered, the navigation may be deemed safe and good. of 340 Miles land carriage 200 Miles is along a good road and 140 over tremendious mountains which for 60 Miles are covered with eternal snows. notwithstanding the Rocky Mountains thus present a most formidable barrier to this tract across the continent a passage is practicable from the last of June to the last of September, and the expense of transportation over land may be reduced to a mere trifle by means of horses which can be procured in immence numbers and for the most trivial considerations from the natives inhabiting the rocky Mountains and Plains of Columbia West of those Mountains. the Navigation of the Columbia and it's branches is good from the 1st. of April to the middle of August when their waters subside and leave their beds obstructed by a great number of difficult and dangerous shoals and rapids. the Columbia in every stage of it's water has three portages. the first in decending is a portage of 1200 paces at the great falls, a pitch of 37 feet 8 inches being 261 Miles from it's mouth, the second of 2 Miles at the long narrows 6 miles below the falls, and the third of 2 miles at the great rapids 65 miles still lower down. the tides flow within

7 miles of these rapids or 183 miles up the Columbia. thus far large sloops might ascent the river with safety and ships of 300 tons burthen might ascend 125 miles to the entrance of Multnomah river a large Southen branch of the Columbia which takes its rise on the confines of Mexico with the Collorado and Apostles R. from the head of tidewater to the foot of the long narrows the river would be most advantageously navigated in large batteaux, and from thence upwards in light perogues we vew this passage across the continent as affording immence advantages to the fir trade but fear that advantages wich it offers is a communication for the productions of the East Indias to the United States and thence to Europe will never be found equal on an extensive scale to that by the way of the Cape of good hope. still we believe that many articles not bulky brittle nor of a perishable nature may be conveyed to the U'. States by this rout with more facility and less expence than by that at present practiced. That portion of the Continent watered by the Missouri and all it's branches from the Cheyenne upwards is richer in beaver and Otter than any country on earth particularly that proportion of it's subsiduary streams lying within the Rocky mountains; the furs of all this immence tract of country including such as may be collected on the upper portion of the river St. Peters, the Assinniboin & Red rivers may be conveyed to the mouth of the Columbia by the 1st of August in each year and from thence be shiped to and arrive at Canton earlier than the furs which are annually shiped from Montreal arrive in England. The N West Company of Canada were they permitted by the U. S. might also convey their furs collected in the Athebaske on the Saskashawan and South and West of lake Winnipicque by that rout within the same period. in the infancy of this trade across the Continent or during the period that the trading establishments shall be confined to the branches of the Missouri the men employed in this trade will be compelled to convey the furs collected in that quarter as low on the Columbia as tide water in which case they could not return to the falls of the Missouri untill about the 1st. of October which would be so late in the season that there would be considerable danger of the river being obstructed by ice before they could reach St. Louis and the comodities of the East Indias thus detained untill the following spring. but this dificulty will vanish when establishments are made on the Columbia and a sufficient number of men employed at them to convey the East India commodities to the upper establishment on the Kooskooske and there exchanging them with the men of the Missouri for their furs in the beginning of July. by these means the furs not only of the Missouri but those of the Columbia may be shiped to Canton by the season before mentioned and the comodit(i)es of the East Indias arrive at St. Louis by the last of September in each Year. altho' the Columbia dose not as much as the Missouri

abound in beaver and Otter yet it is by no means despicable in this respect and would furnish a profitable fur trade, in addition to the otter and beaver considerable quantities of the finest bear of three species affording a great variety of colours, the Tyger catt, several species of fox, the Martin and Sea Otter might be procured beside the rackoon and some other animals of an inferior class of furs. If the government will only aid even on a limited scale the enterprize of her Citizens I am convinced that we shall soon derive the benefits of a most lucrative trade from this source. and in the course of 10 or 12 Years a tour across the Continent by this rout will be undertaken with as little concern as a voyage across the Atlantic is at present.

The British N. West company of Canaday have for several years past carried on a partial trade with the Mandans Minnetares and Avahaways on the Missouri from their establishments on the Assinniboin near the entrance of Mouse R. at present I have every reason to believe that they intend forming an establishment very shortly on the Missouri near those nations with a view to ingroce the fir trade of that River. the known enterprize and resou(r)ces of this Company latterly stre(n)ghtened by an union with its powerfull rival the X. Y. Company have rendered them formidable in that distant part of the continent to all other traders, and if we are to regard the trade of the missouri as an object of importance to the U. States the strides of this company towards that river cannot be too vigelently watched nor too firmly and spedily opposed by our government. the imbarrasment under which the navigation of the Missouri at present labours from the unfriendly dispositions of the Cancezs the several bands of Tetons, Assiniboins and those tribes that resort the British establishments on the Suskashawan is also a subject which requires the earliest attention of our government. as I shall shortly be with you I have deemed it unnecessary here to detail the several ideas which present themselves to my mind on those subjects more especially when I consider that a thorough knoledge of the geography of the country will be absolutely necessary to their being understood, and leasure has not yet permited us to make but one general Map of the country which I am unwilling to wrisk by the Mail. As a sketch of the Most prominent features of our perigrinations since we left the Mandans may not be uninteresting I shall indeavour to give it to you by way of letter from this place, where I shall necessarily be detained for some days in order to settle with and discharge the men who accompanied me on the voige as well as to prepare for my rout to Washington. (not sending a party from the falls) We left fort Clatsop where we wintered on the Pacific Ocean the 27th of (Mar)ch last and arrived at the foot of the Rocky Mts. on the 10th of May here we were detained untill the 24th of June in consequence of the snow rendering those mountains im-

311

passable, had it not been for this detention I should have joined you at Montechello in this month agreeably to the promise made you previous to our departure from the Mandans. I have brought with me several skins of the Sea Otter 2 skins of the native Sheep of N. America. 5 skins and skelitons complete of the Bighorn or mountain ram, and a skin of the mule deer besides the skins of several other quadrupeds and birds natives of the country through which we have passed; I have also preserved a pretty extensive collection of pla(n)ts in Horteo have obtained 10 vocabularies. have also prevailed on the principal Chief of the Mandans to accompany me to washington, he is now with my worthy friend and Colleague Capt. C. and myself at this place, in good health and spirits. With rispect to the exertions and services rendered by this estimable man Capt. Wm. Clark on this expedicion I cannot say too much, if sir, any credit be due to the success of the arduous enterprise in which we have been engaged he is equally with myself entitled to the consideration of yourself and that of our common Country. The anxiety which I feel to return once more to the bosom of my friends is a sufficient guarantee that no time will be expended unnecessarily in this quarter. the rout by which I purpose traveling is from hence by Cahokia Vincennes LouisVill Kty. the Craborchard Abington Fincastle, Stanton and Charlotsville to Washington. any letters directed to me at Louisvill 10 days after the receipt of this will most proba(b)ly meet me at that place. I am very anxious to learn the state of my friends in Albemarle particular(l)y whether my mother is yet alive. I am with every sentiment of esteem your most Obt. Servt.

Meriwether Lewis

Capt. 1st U' S Regt Infty

BIBLIOGRAPHY

John W. Aldrich, and Allen J. Duvall, *Distribution of American Gallinaceous Game Birds* (U.S. Fish and Wildlife Service, Circular No. 34, 1955).

Joel A. Allen, *North American Rodentia* (U.S. Geological Survey of the Territories, Report No. 11, 1877).

Paul Allen, *A History of the Expedition Under the Command of Lewis and Clark to the Source of the Missouri, Thence Across the Rocky Mountains, and Down the Columbia River to the Pacific Ocean* (Philadelphia: Bradford and Inskeep, 1814), 2 Volumes.

Geo. A. Amman, *The Prairie Grouse of Michigan* (Lansing, Mich.: Michigan Department of Conservation, Game Division, 1957).

N. E. Anthony, *Fieldbook of North American Mammals* (New York: G. P. Putnam's Sons, 1928).

John J. Audubon, *Ornithological Biography* (Philadelphia: J. Dobson, 1831-1839). 5 Volumes.

Audubon and Bachman, *The Quadrupeds of North America* (New York: V. G. Audubon, 1851-1855), 6 Volumes.

John Bachman, *Proceedings of the Zoological Society of London* (1838).

Vernon Bailey, *The Mammals and Life Zones of Oregon* (Washington, D.C.: U.S. Department of Agriculture Publication, North American Fauna No. 55, 1936).

Spencer F. Baird, *Catalog of North American Mammals* (Smithsonian Institution Publication No. 105, 1857).

Baird, Brewer, and Ridgway, *History of North American Birds* (Boston: Little Brown & Co., 1874), Vol. II.

John Bakeless, *Lewis and Clark: Partners in Discovery* (New York: William Morrow and Company, 1947).

Arthur C. Bent, *Life Histories of North American Diving Birds* (U.S. National Museum Bulletin No. 107, 1919; reprinted New York: Dodd, Mead & Co., 1946).

Arthur C. Bent, *Life Histories of North American Gulls & Terns* (U.S. National Museum Bulletin No. 113, 1921).

Arthur C. Bent, *Life Histories of North American Petrels, Pelicans and Their Allies* (U.S. National Museum Bulletin No. 121, 1922).

Arthur C. Bent, *Life Histories of North American Wild Fowl* (U.S. National Museum Bulletin No. 126, 1923).

Arthur C. Bent, *Life Histories of North American Wild Fowl* (U.S. National Museum Bulletin No. 130, 1925).

Arthur C. Bent, *Life Histories of North American Marsh Birds* (U.S. National Museum Bulletin No. 135, 1927).

Arthur C. Bent, *Life Histories of North American Gallinaceous Birds* (U.S. National Museum Bulletin No. 162, 1932).

Arthur C. Bent, *Life Histories of North American Birds of Prey* (U.S. National Museum Bulletin No. 170, 1938), Part II.

Arthur C. Bent, *Life Histories of North American Cuckoos, Goatsuckers, Hummingbirds and Their Allies* (U.S. National Museum Bulletin No. 176, 1940).

Arthur C. Bent, *Life Histories of North American Jays, Crows, and Titmice* (U.S. National Museum Bulletin No. 191, 1946).

George Catlin, *North American Indians* (2nd Ed., New York, 1842; 5th Ed., London: H. G. Bohn, 1845; Philadelphia, 1913).

Elliott Coues, *Key to North American Birds* (Salem: Naturalist's Agency, 1872; New York: Dodd, Mead & Co., 1872; Boston: Estes & Lauriat, 1884, 1887, 1903).

Elliott Coues, *Birds of the Northwest* (U.S. Geological Survey of the Territories, Miscellaneous Publication No. 3, 1874).

Elliott Coues, *An Account of the Various Publications Relating to the Travels of Lewis and Clark, with a Commentary on the Zoological Results of the Expedition* (U.S. Geological and Geographical Survey of the Territories, 1874-1875), Vol. I.

Elliott Coues, *History of the Expedition Under the Command of Lewis and Clark* (New York: Francis P. Harper, 1893), 4 Volumes.

Elliott Coues, *Manuscript Journals of Alexander Henry and David Thompson, 1799-1814* (New York: Francis P. Harper, 1897), 3 Volumes. (This is a copy of George Coventry's edition of 1824).

I. McT. Cowan, "Distribution and Variation in Deer (Genus *Odocoileus*) of the Pacific Coast Region of North America," *California Fish and Game* (July 1936), Vol. XXII, No. 3, pp. 155-246.

Elijah H. Criswell, *Lewis and Clark: Linguistic Pioneers* (University of Missouri Studies, 1940), Vol. IV, No. 2.

Bernard DeVoto, *Across the Wide Missouri* (Boston: Houghton-Mifflin Company, 1947).

Bernard DeVoto, *Journals of Lewis and Clark* (Boston: Houghton-Mifflin Company, 1953).

Walter Faxon, *Relics of Peale's Museum* (Museum of Comparative Zoology, 1915), Vol. LIX.

Paul Leicester Ford, *The Writings of Thomas Jefferson* (New York: G. P. Putnam's Sons, 1892).

Capt. John Franklin, *Narrative of a Journey to the Shores of the Polar Sea, 1819-22* (1823; reprinted by Dutton, Every Man's Library Series, 1910).

Patrick Gass, *Gass' Journal of the Lewis and Clark Expedition* (Philadelphia, 1807; London, 1808; and Chicago: A. C. McClurg & Co., 1904).

Richard E. Griffith, *What Is The Future of the Sea Otter?* (Washington 5, D.C.: Wildlife Management Institute, Transactions of the Eighteenth North American Wildlife Conference, 1953).

E. Raymond Hall and Keith R. Kelson, *The Mammals of North America* (New York: The Ronald Press, 1959), 2 Volumes.

Samuel Hearne, *A Journey From Prince Wale's Fort on Hudson's Bay to the Northern Ocean* (London: A. Strahan and T. Cadell, 1795; reprinted Toronto: Champlain Society, 1911), Vol. I.

Charles K. Hosmer, *History of the Expedition of Captains Lewis and Clark* (Chicago: A. C. McClurg & Co., 1st Ed., 1902; 5th Ed., 1924), 2 Volumes.

Arthur H. Howell, *Revision of the North American Ground Squirrels* (Washington, D.C.: U.S.D.A. Publication, North American Fauna No. 56, 1938).

Edmond C. Jaeger, "Does the Poor-will Hibernate?" *The Condor* (Jan.-Feb. 1948).

Edmond C. Jaeger, "Further Observations on the Poor-will," *The Condor* (May-June 1949).

Johnson's Natural History (New York: A. J. Johnson & Co., 1889), Vol. II.

David Starr Jordan and Barton W. Everman, *American Food and Game Fishes* (New York: Doubleday, Page & Co., 1902).

F. H. Kortright, *Ducks, Geese, and Swans of North America* (Harrisburg, Pa.: The Stackpole Company, and The Wildlife Management Institute, 1953).

Louis-Armand LaHontan, *New Voyages to North America* (London, 1703; reprinted Chicago: A. C. McClurg & Co., 1905), 2 Volumes.

Georg Heinrich von Langsdorff, *Voyages and Travels in Various Parts of the World, 1803-1807* (London: 1813-1814; Carlisle, Pa.: George Phillips, 1817).

Carolus Linnaeus, *Systema Naturae* (10th Ed., 1785), Vol. I.

Alexander MacKenzie, *Voyages from Montreal on the River St. Laurence Through the Continent of North America to the Frozen and Pacific Oceans in the Years 1789-1793* (London: T. Cadell, & W. Davies, 1801), 2 Volumes.

W. L. McAtee, "Birds Do Hibernate," *Audubon Magazine* (Nov.-Dec. 1950).

Gerrit S. Miller, Jr., *List of North American Recent Mammals* (U.S. National Museum Bulletin No. 128, 1924).

Gerrit S. Miller, Jr. and Remington Kellogg, *List of North American Recent Mammals* (U.S. National Museum Bulletin No. 205, 1955).

John Muir, "Among the Animals of the Yosemite," *The Atlantic Monthly* (Nov. 1898).

Olaus J. Murie, *The Elk of North America* (Harrisburg, Pa.: The Stackpole Company, and The Wildlife Management Institute, 1951).

George Ord, in *Guthrie's Geography, A New Geographical, Historical, and Commercial Grammar and the Present State of Several Kingdoms of the World* (2nd American Ed., Philadelphia: Johnson and Warner, 1815), Vol. II, pp. 290-361.

Milo M. Quaife, *The Journals of Captain Meriwether Lewis and Sergeant John Ordway* (Madison: Wisconsin Historical Society Collections, 1916), Vol. XXII.

Russell Reid and Clell G. Gannon, "Birds and Mammals Observed by Lewis and Clark in North Dakota," *North Dakota Historical Quarterly* (1927), Vol. I, No. 4.

James D. Richardson, *A Compilation of the Messages and Papers of the*

Presidents, 1789-1817 (53rd Congress, 2nd Session, House of Representatives, Misc. Doc. No. 210, 1896), Vol. I, p. 398.

Robert Ridgway, *Revisions of Nomenclature of Certain North American Birds* (Washington, D.C.: Proc. U.S. National Museum, 1880), Vol. III.

Robert Ridgway, *The Auk* (1899), Vol. XVI.

A. W. Schroger, *The Passenger Pigeon* (Madison: University of Wisconsin Press, 1955).

E. T. Seton, *Lives of Game Animals* (Garden City, New York: ed., Doubleday Doran & Co., 1925), 4 Volumes.

Henry W. Setzer, "Zoological Contributions of the Lewis and Clark Expedition," *Journal of the Washington Academy of Sciences* (Nov. 1954), Vol. XLIV, No. 11.

K. A. Spaulding, *On The Oregon Trail: Robert Stuart's Journey of Discovery* (Norman, Oklahoma: University of Oklahoma Press, 1953).

Harry S. Swarth and Harold C. Bryant, *A Study of the Races of the White-fronted Goose (Ancer albifrons) Occurring in California* (The University of California Publications in Zoology, 1917), Vol. XVII.

Reuben G. Thwaites, *The Original Journals of the Lewis and Clark Expedition* (New York: Dodd, Mead and Company, 1904), 8 Volumes.

Reuben G. Thwaites, *Early Western Travels,* Vol. V, *Bradbury's Travels in the Interior of North America, 1809-1810* (Cleveland: A. H. Clark and Company, 1904).

Reuben G. Thwaites, *Early Western Travels,* Vol. XIV-XVII, *Account of An Expedition from Pittsburgh to the Rocky Mountains, Performed in the Years 1819-1820* (Cleveland: A. H. Clark and Company, 1905; originally edited by Edwin James, 1823).

Reuben G. Thwaites, *Early Western Travels,* Vol. XXI, *Narrative of a Journey Across the Rocky Mountains* (Cleveland: A. H. Clark and Company, 1905; originally published, 1839).

Reuben G. Thwaites, *Early Western Travels,* Vol. XXII-XXIV, *Maximillian's Travels in the Interior of North America* (Cleveland: A. H. Clark and Company, 1905).

Edward Umfreville, *Present State of Hudson's Bay* (London: Printed for Charles Stalker, Stationer of the Court, 1790).

Louis Jean Pierre Vieillot, *Histoire Naturelle des Oiseaux de l'Amérique Septentrionale* (Paris: Desray, 1807), Vol. I.

Count Volney, *Tableau du Climat et du Sol des Etats-Unis d'Amerique* (Paris: Courcier, 1803), 2 Volumes.

Alexander Wilson, *American Ornithology* (Philadelphia: Bradford and Inskeep, 1801-1814), Vols. I, III, V.

Stanley P. Young and E. A. Goldman, *The Wolves of North America* (American Wildlife Institute, 1944).

1. Elliott Coues, *Account of the Various Publications Relating to the Travels of Lewis and Clark, with a Commentary on the Zoological Results of the Expedition* (Washington, D.C.: U.S. Geological and Geographical Survey of the Territories, 1874-75), Vol. I, p. 430. (Although dated Feb. 8, 1876, this paper is included in Vol. I.)

2. Alexander Wilson, *American Ornithology* (Philadelphia, Pa.: Bradford and Inskeep, 1811), Vol. III, pl. 20, p. 31.

3. Reuben G. Thwaites, *The Original Journals of the Lewis and Clark Expedition* 1804-1806 (New York: Dodd, Mead, and Company, 1904), 8 Volumes.

4. Walter Faxon, *Relics of Peale's Museum* (Bulletin of the Museum of Comparative Zoology, 1915), Vol. 59, pp. 119-148.

5. Henry W. Setzer, "Zoological Contributions of the Lewis and Clark Expedition," *Journal of the Washington Academy of Sciences* (Nov. 1954), Vol. XLIV, No. 11, p. 357.

6. Biddle did not edit Sergeant Ordway's journal or include it with the Lewis and Clark manuscripts which, on Clark's orders, were deposited with the American Philosophical Society for safekeeping. In 1913, a grandson of Nicholas Biddle discovered Ordway's manuscript among family papers which he was sorting preparatory to offering them to the Library of Congress. This treasure, hidden for so many years, was published by Milo M. Quaife, ed., *The Journals of Captain Meriwether Lewis and Sergeant John Ordway* (Madison: Wisconsin Historical Society Collections, 1916), Vol. XXII.

7. Thwaites evaluated, in *The Original Journals, op. cit.* Vol. I, all of the books published prior to 1904 which were purported to be authentic versions of the diaries. For example, he cited Charles K. Hosmer, *History of the Expedition of Captains Lewis and Clark* (Chicago: A. C. McClurg & Co., 1st ed., 1902; 5th ed., 1924) 2 Volumes, as an accurate reprint of the Biddle text.

8. Patrick Gass, *Gass' Journal of the Lewis and Clark Expedition* (Philadelphia, 1807; London, 1808; Paris, 1810; reprinted Chicago: A. C. McClurg & Co., 1904).

9. Elliott Coues, *History of the Expedition Under the Command of Lewis and Clark* (New York: Francis P. Harper, 1893), 4 Volumes.

NOTES TO CHAPTER I

1. *History of the Expedition under the Command of Captains Lewis and Clark, to the Sources of the Missouri, thence across the Rocky Mountains, and down the Columbia River to the Pacific Ocean.* Prepared for the press by Paul Allen, Esq. (Philadelphia: Bradford and Inskeep, 1814), Vol. I, pp. xi-xii.

2. See Appendix.

3. See Appendix.

4. Although Lewis, with President Jefferson's approval, invited Clark to participate in the expedition on the basis of "equal rank and authority," the Army refused to raise Clark's rank above that which he already held in the Corps of Engineers. Nevertheless, Lewis always referred to him as Captain

Clark, and it is improbable that any member of the expedition, other than Lewis, knew that Clark did not hold a captain's commission.

5. Richard Warvington and John Robertson, soldiers whose periods of enlistment were due to expire in a few months, remained with the expedition until April 7, 1805. Warvington was placed in command of the keelboat which was sent back to St. Louis on this date.

6. Court-martialed for mutinous expression, October 13, 1804.

7. Punished for desertion and discharged from duty. Both Newman and Reed were permitted to travel with the expedition as far as Fort Mandan but were sent back to St. Louis on April 7, 1805.

8. Reuben G. Thwaites, *The Original Journals of the Lewis and Clark Expedition* (New York: Dodd Mead & Co., 1904), Vol. I, p. 98.

9. *Ibid.,* p. 280.

10. See Appendix.

11. Thwaites, *op. cit.,* pp. 284-285.

12. Now called the Poplar River.

13. Thwaites, *op. cit.,* pp. 362-363.

14. *Ibid.,* p. 364.

15. *Ibid.,* Vol. II, p. 37.

16. *Ibid.,* p. 142.

17. *Ibid.,* p. 144.

18. *Ibid.,* pp. 144-145.

19. *Ibid.,* pp. 149-150.

20. *Ibid.,* p. 158.

21. *Ibid.,* p. 181.

22. *Ibid.,* pp. 182-183.

23. *Ibid.,* p. 198.

24. *Ibid.,* p. 266.

25. *Ibid.,* p. 283.

26. *Ibid.,* pp. 329-330.

27. *Ibid.,* p. 331.

28. *Ibid.,* p. 335.

29. *Ibid.,* p. 340.

30. *Ibid.,* p. 347.

31. *Ibid.,* pp. 355-356.

32. *Ibid.,* p. 361.

33. *Ibid.,* p. 370.

34. *Ibid.,* Vol. III, pp. 213-214.

35. *Ibid.,* p. 254.

36. *Ibid.,* pp. 290-291.

37. *Ibid.,* Vol. IV, pp. 193-194.

38. It is interesting to note that Nicholas Biddle, who edited the first printed edition of the Lewis and Clark journals, tells us that one of these documents was delivered to Captain Hill of the "Lydia." On arriving in China, Hill gave it to a friend in Canton, who enclosed a copy of it in a letter, dated January, 1807, to a friend in Philadelphia.

39. Thwaites, *op. cit.,* Vol. IV, pp. 197-198.

40. *Ibid.,* p. 239.

41. *Ibid.,* p. 237.

42. *Ibid.,* p. 269.

43. *Ibid.,* p. 358.
44. Nearly opposite town of Kamiah, Idaho.
45. Thwaites, *op. cit.,* Vol. V, p. 98.
46. For the Indian tradition of the encounter here described, see Wheeler, *Trail of Lewis and Clark,* Vol. II, pp. 311-314. The name of the first man killed was Side Hill Calf. The long-continued hostility of the Blackfeet to the Whites has often been attributed to this incident. But Chittenden (*History of American Fur Trade,* p. 714) declares that Manuel Lisa found that the Indians of that tribe justified the action of Lewis, and were inclined to be friendly to the Whites. The real cause of the Blackfeet enmity was the appearance of white trappers in the ranks of their enemies, the Crows, in a battle which occurred in 1807. It is noteworthy that Drouillard (Drewyer) finally lost his life in a contest with the Blackfeet.
47. Now Birch Creek, the largest southern tributary of the Big Medicine.
48. The bivouac for this night was not far from the site of Fort Benton.
49. Thwaites, *op. cit.,* pp. 223-227.
50. The rendezvous at the mouth of Maria's River.
51. Thwaites, *op. cit.,* pp. 227-229.
52. *Ibid.,* pp. 240-242.
53. The Indian trail over which they rode from Three Forks to Livingston, Montana, followed about the same route as U.S. No. 10 Highway does now.
54. Clark's inscription is still legible on Pompey's Pillar due to the efforts of the Montana Historical Society.
55. History indicates that Big White would have been wise to have remained at home. He was treated well in Washington, but when he got back to St. Louis he had difficulty in getting passage back to Mandan. During months of delay both his squaw and his son died.
56. Hosmer, *op. cit.,* Vol. II, pp. 435-436.

NOTES TO CHAPTER II

1. Reuben G. Thwaites, *Early Western Travels,* Vol. V, *Bradbury's Travels in the Interior of North America, 1809-10* (Cleveland: A. H. Clark and Company, 1904), p. 59. Bradbury traveled as far as Fort Mandan with an expedition headed for Astoria under the leadership of Wilson P. Hunt and Ramsey Crooks.
2. *Ibid.,* Vol. XXII, *Maximillian's Travels in the Interior of North America,* p. 282.
3. Alexander Henry, the younger, served the North West Fur Company as factor in charge of the Red River Department from 1800 to 1808.
4. Elliott Coues, *The Manuscript Journals of Alexander Henry and David Thompson, 1799-1814* (New York: Francis P. Harper, 1897), Vol. I, pp. 1-446.
5. Brown, *Forest and Stream* (Dec. 16, 1893), Vol. XLI, p. 519 (Part).
6. G. S. Miller, *List of North American Recent Mammals* (U.S. National Museum Bulletin No. 128, 1924).
7. H. E. Anthony, *Field Book of North American Mammals* (New York: G. P. Putnam's Sons, 1928).

8. G. S. Miller and Remington Kellogg, *List of North American Recent Mammals* (U.S. National Museum Bulletin No. 205, 1955), p. 694.
9. E. Raymond Hall and Keith R. Kelson, *The Mammals of North America* (New York: The Ronald Press, 1959).
10. Edward Umfreville, *Present State of Hudson's Bay* (London: Printed for Charles Stalker, Stationer of the Court, 1790).
11. Samuel Hearne, *A Journey from Prince Wale's Fort on Hudson's Bay to the Northern Ocean* (London: A. Strahan and T. Cadell, 1795; reprinted Toronto, Ontario: The Champlain Society, 1911).
12. Alexander MacKenzie, *Voyages from Montreal on the River St. Laurence through the Continent of North America to the Frozen and Pacific Oceans in the Years 1789-1793* (London: T. Cadell, Jun., & W. Davies, 1801).
13. George Ord, in *Gutherie's Geography* (2nd American Edition, Philadelphia: Johnson and Warner, 1815), Vol. II, p. 299.
14. About twenty-five miles below the mouth of the Niobrara River.
15. It will be noted that Lewis and Clark used the terms "white," "brown," "yellow," and "grizzly" interchangeably in referring to the grizzly bear in this and other entries in their diaries. Their choice of term used generally depended upon the color phase of the animal they happened to have encountered.
16. K. A. Spaulding, *On the Oregon Trail; Robt. Stuart's Journey of Discovery* (Norman: University of Oklahoma Press, 1953).
17. Coues, *Manuscript Journals of Alexander Henry, op. cit.,* Vol. I, p. 121.
18. Thwaites, *Early Western Travels,* Vol. XXII, *op. cit.,* p. 369.
19. Coues identifies the Goat-pen River as the Upper Knife River (now called Little Knife River) not the present White Earth River.
20. Lewis was mistaken.
21. "Pomme de terre" of the French, *Psoralia esculenta.*
22. John Muir, "Among the Animals of the Yosemite," *Atlantic Monthly* (Nov. 1898), Vol. LXXXII, p. 617.

NOTES TO CHAPTER III

1. A French scientist and writer who had visited the United States in 1797-1798.
2. Joseph Whitehouse, a private in the ranks of the Lewis and Clark Expedition, kept an independent diary which is included in Thwaites' *Original Journals of the Lewis and Clark Expedition,* Vol. VII.
3. Minitaree Tribe of the Arapaho Indians, called Gros Ventres (meaning Big-bellies) by the French.
4. Elliott Coues, *Manuscript Journals of Alexander Henry, op. cit.;* Data compiled from tables on pp. 184, 198, 221, 245, 259, 281, 422, 440.
5. Thus gaining a trade advantage over the British companies which, at that time, were shipping furs to China from Montreal.
6. Carolus Linnaeus, *Systema Naturae,* 10th ed. (1785), Vol. I, p. 45; *Mustela lutris* was the accepted name of the sea-otter until 1843, when Gray transferred it to the genus, *Enhydra.*
7. Richard E. Griffith, *What Is The Future of the Sea Otter?* (Washington,

D.C.: Wildlife Management Institute, Transactions of the Eighteenth North American Wildlife Conference, 1953), pp. 472-478.
8. British, American and Russian vessels were competing for furs at the mouth of the Columbia River in 1805-06.

NOTES TO CHAPTER IV

1. Lewis was mistaken; the wolf of the Northwest Coast belongs to the subspecies, *gigas,* and that of the Atlantic States, to the subspecies *lycaon.*
2. Hugh Heeney, who represented the Hudson's Bay Company on the Assiniboin, and M. Larocque, a clerk of the North West Company, visited the Mandans and Minnitares while Lewis and Clark were at Fort Mandan, ostensibly to trade; but actually to determine the objectives of the United States in sending out an expedition.
3. Reuben G. Thwaites, *Early Western Travels,* Vol. XIV, *Account of an Expedition from Pittsburg to the Rocky Mountains, Performed in the Years 1819-1820* (Cleveland, Ohio: A. H. Clark Co., 1905; originally edited by Edwin James, 1823. Major Stephen H. Long's Expedition), p. 251.
4. *Ibid.,* Vol. XV, pp. 261-262.
5. Lewis was in error; Elliott Coues concluded that the specimen here described was a kit fox; besides, no similar species of fox is known to have inhabited the area.
6. Elliott Coues, *Journals of Alexander Henry, op. cit.,* Vol. I, pp. 184, 198, 221, 245, 259.
7. Elliott Coues identified this as the cross-fox a color phase of the red fox.
8. According to Seton the Canada lynx has been taken on the Little Missouri River in North Dakota, and at Norfolk, Nebraska, but these animals probably had strayed from their normal range.
9. Elliott Coues, *History of the Expedition under the Command of Lewis and Clark* (New York: Francis P. Harper, 1893), Vol. III, p. 847.
10. Vernon Bailey, *The Mammals and Life Zones of Oregon* (Washington, D.C.: U.S.D.A. Publication, North American Fauna No. 55, 1936), p. 269.

NOTES TO CHAPTER V

1. Elliott Coues, *History of the Expedition, op. cit.,* Vol. I, p. 271; Vol. III, p. 859.
2. Fox squirrel, *Sciurus niger* Linnaeus, and the gray squirrel, *Sciurus carolinensis* Gmelin.
3. The fate of these specimens is unknown; and no one, Coues included, has been willing to hazard a guess (in print) as to the identity of the two small, gray squirrels that Lewis skinned.
4. John Bachman, *Proceedings of the Zoological Society of London* (1838), p. 99.
5. Elliott Coues, *History of the Expedition, op. cit.,* Vol. III, p. 855.
6. Arthur H. Howell, *Revision of the North American Ground Squirrels*

(Washington, D.C.: U.S.D.A. Publication, North American Fauna No. 56, 1938), p. 55.

7. George Ord, *Gutherie's Geography*, *op. cit.*

8. Howell indicates that the range of the Columbian ground squirrel extends "east to the Cutbank and Townsend, Montana."

9. Elliott Coues, *History of the Expedition*, *op. cit.*, Vol. II, p. 405.

10. Joel A. Allen, *North American Rodentia* (U.S. Geological Survey of the Territories, Report No. 11, 1877).

11. Russell Reid, and Clell G. Gannon, "Birds and Mammals Observed by Lewis and Clark in North Dakota," *North Dakota Historical Quarterly* (1927), Vol. I, No. 4, p. 23.

12. Thus the myth that snakes (usually specified as rattle snakes) and prairie dogs inhabited the same dens would seem to have originated with the French, British and American fur traders who preceded Lewis and Clark on the Missouri River. However, Lewis and Clark did not mention seeing the small burrowing owl which, in truth and fiction, is the third member of the prairie dog-rattlesnake-owl triumvirate.

13. Coues, *History of the Expedition*, *op. cit.*, Vol. I, p. 111.

14. Probably the Richardson ground squirrel is referred to in this instance.

15. Colloquial name for a rodent; not an amphibian in this instance.

16. Reid, "Birds and Mammals," *op. cit.*, p. 24.

17. Lewis' Newfoundland dog, *Scammon*, survived this, as well as encounters with bison, wolves, bears, rattlesnakes and Indians, to make the entire trip with the Explorers.

18. Spaulding, *op. cit.*

19. Coues, *Manuscript Journals of Alexander Henry*, *op. cit.*, pp. 184, 198, 221, 245, 259, 281, 422, 440.

20. Bernard DeVoto, *Across the Wide Missouri* (Boston: Houghton-Mifflin Company, 1947), pp. 1-483.

21. Coues, *History of the Expedition*, *op. cit.*, Vol. II, p. 400.

22. Ord, *Gutherie's Geography*, *op. cit.*, p. 292.

23. Coues, *History of the Expedition*, *op. cit.*, Vol. I, p. 40.

24. Gass, *op. cit.*

25. Sacajawea.

26. Thwaites, on the basis of Coues' interpretation, suggests that gophers instead of mice were involved but Reid and Gannon concluded that "they were mice as Lewis & Clark called them."

27. Reid, *op. cit.*, p. 24.

28. Now called the Poplar River.

29. Sagebrush, *Artemisia tridentata*.

30. Unidentified.

31. George Shannon, the youngest member of the expedition, was only 17 years old in 1804.

NOTES TO CHAPTER VI

1 Recently it has been established that Zimmerman named the white-tailed deer in 1780, four years prior to Boddaert's publication. See Miller and

Kellogg, *List of North American Recent Mammals* (U.S. National Museum Bulletin No. 205, 1955).
2. Bailey, *op. cit.,* p. 90.
3. Now Clearwater River.
4. Cascade Range.
5. Serg't. Gass, in his diary, reported 131 elk and 20 deer for the period Dec. 1, 1805 to March 20, 1806. This discrepancy cannot be explained.
6. Olaus J. Murie, *The Elk of North America* (Harrisburg, Pa.: The Stackpole Company, and the Wildlife Management Institute, 1951), p. 47-48.
7. Sagebrush, *Artemisia tridentata.*
8. Identified by C. V. Piper as Salal, *Gaultheria shallon.*
9. An illustrated article in the Chicago Record-Herald of Aug. 25, 1901, states that the writer visited an Indian village in southern Montana where it was estimated that 20,000 elk-teeth were in the possession of its inhabitants. On a mother and child were counted 600 of these ornaments, and another woman had the estimated number of 1,500 on her garments. They were highly valued by the Indians, who would seldom part with them. Three photographs of persons thus adorned were used to illustrate the article; the negatives are in the possession of L. E. Cavalier of St. Paul—Thwaites' footnote in the *Original Journals of the Lewis and Clark Expedition.*
10. Now the Snake River, the east branch of which is the Salmon River.
11. Delicately formed—Biddle text.
12. The explorers had no knowledge of the fate of the shipment from Fort Mandan.

NOTES TO CHAPTER VII

1. Clark had reported seeing "some buffalo sign" near Split Rock Creek in Missouri, about one hundred miles above St. Louis.
2. Situated in the Missouri River, near the eastern boundary of Bonhomme County, South Dakota.
3. George Catlin, *North American Indians* (London: Henry G. Bohn, 5th Edition, 1845), Vol. I, p. 255-256.
4. Coues, *Journals of Alexander Henry, op. cit.,* Vol. I, p. 136.
5. Thwaites, *Early Western Travels,* Vol. V, *op. cit.,* pp. 148-149.
6. *Ibid,* pp. 188-189.
7. Coues, *Journals of Alexander Henry, op. cit.,* Vol. I, p. 253.
8. Thwaites, *Original Journals,* Vol. I, p. 279.
9. Teton Indians—Sioux Nation.
10. Buffalo Wool Company.

NOTES ON CHAPTER VIII

1. Coues, *History of the Expedition, op. cit.,* Vol. III, pp. 850-851.
2. MacKenzie, *op. cit.,* pp. 169, 201, 210.
3. G. H. von Langsdorff, *Voyages and Travels in Various Parts of the World During the Years 1803-1807* (Carlisle, Pa.: George Phillips, 1817).

4. E. T. Seton, *Lives of Game Animals* (Garden City, New York: ed., Double-day Doran & Co., 1925), Vol. III, p. 477.
5. Not a sheep, but the mountain goat (*Haplocerus montanus*). Thwaites' footnote.
6. Coues, *History of the Expedition, op. cit.,* Vol. III, p. 851.

NOTES TO CHAPTER IX

1. Coues, *History of the Expedition, op. cit.,* Vol. III, p. 881.
2. Arthur C. Bent, *Life Histories of North American Diving Birds* (Reprinted New York: Dodd, Mead & Co., 1946), p. 19.
3. Coues, *Account of the Various Publications, op. cit.*
4. Coues, *History of the Expedition, op. cit.,* Vol. III, p. 888.
5. *Ibid.,* pp. 882, 888.
6. *Ibid.,* p. 881.
7. Thwaites, *Original Journals, op. cit.,* Vol. VI. pp. 125-127.
8. *Ibid.,* Vol. IV. p. 140.
9. Coues classified this cormorant as *Phalacrocorax dilophus cincinatus,* the accepted name of the white-crested cormorant in 1893.
10. Indian Hen is one of the colloquial names of the American Bittern, *Johnson's Natural History* (New York: A. J. Johnson & Co., 1889), Vol. II, p. 291.
11. Thwaites, *Original Journals, op. cit.,* Vol. VI, pp. 122-123.
12. Elliott Coues, *Birds of the Northwest* (U.S. Geological Survey of the Territories, Miscellaneous Publication No. 3, 1874), p. 531.
13. Arthur C. Bent, *Life Histories of North American Marsh Birds* (U.S. National Museum Bulletin No. 135, 1927), p. 220.

NOTES TO CHAPTER X

1. According to Clark's description the *beak* rather than the "back" is "wide and short."
2. Coues, *Birds of the Northwest, op. cit.,* p. 575.
3. Lewis could not have been more wrong about the breeding range of the mallard.
4. Coues, *An Account of the Various Publications, op. cit.,* p. 444.
5. Coues, *History of the Expedition, op. cit.,* Vol. II, pp. 386-456.
6. Donovan based his description on a specimen found in Leadenhall Market in London even though the species is considered to be of rare occurrence in England.
7. Coues, *History of the Expedition, op. cit.,* Vol. III, pp. 888-889.
8. *Ibid.,* p. 968.
9. Arthur C. Bent, *Life Histories of North American Wild Fowl* (U.S. National Museum Bulletin No. 126, 1923), pp. 158-159.
10. F. H. Kortright, *Ducks, Geese, and Swans of North America* (Harrisburg, Pa.: The Stackpole Company, and The Wildlife Management Institute, 1953), p. 228.

11. Arthur C. Bent, *Life Histories of North American Wild Fowl* (U.S. National Museum Bulletin No. 130, 1925), pp. 237-238.
12. *Ibid.*, p. 249.
13. *Ibid.*, p. 208.
14. Elliott Coues, *Key to North American Birds* (Salem: Naturalist's Agency, 1872), p. 284.
15. Coues, *Account of the Various Publications, op. cit.*, p. 443.
16. Harry S. Swarth and Harold C. Bryant, *A Study of the Races of the White-Fronted Goose* (*Anser albifrons*) Occurring in California (University of California Publications in Zoology, 1917), Vol. XVII, pp. 209-222.
17. Coues, *Account of the Various Publications, op. cit.*, p. 443.
18. Bent, *Life Histories of North American Wild Fowl, op. cit.*, Bulletin No. 130, p. 294.
19. Coues, *Account of the Various Publications, op. cit.*, p. 444.

NOTES TO CHAPTER XI

1. The California condor has been described and named *Vultur californianus*, by Shaw, *Naturalist's Misc.*, Vol. IX, text to pl. 301.
2. Coues, *Birds of the Northwest, op. cit.*, p. 376.
3. Coues says the buzzards mentioned here are turkey vultures; *History of the Expedition, op. cit.*, Vol. III, p. 1042.
4. *Ibid.*, p. 878.
5. *Ibid.*, pp. 878-879; Coues identified the "grey eagle" of Lewis and Clark as *Aquila chrysaëtos.*
6. Lewis was mistaken. The average bald eagle is larger than the average golden eagle.
7. Lewis may have been comparing a female golden eagle with a male bald eagle.
8. Coues, *History of the Expedition, op. cit.*, Vol. III, p. 880.
9. Arthur C. Bent, *Life Histories of North American Birds of Prey* (U.S. National Museum Bulletin No. 170, 1938), Part II, p. 348.
10. Coues, *History of the Expedition, op. cit.*, Vol. III, p. 875.
11. *Ibid.*, p. 1028.

NOTES TO CHAPTER XII

1. Clark means to say that prairie chickens were not seen further northward in the Missouri valley.
2. Arthur C. Bent, *Life Histories of North American Gallinaceous Birds* (U.S. National Museum Bulletin No. 162, 1932), p. 262.
3. Coues, *Account of the Various Publications, op. cit.*, p. 439.
4. Coues, *History of the Expedition, op. cit.*, Vol. III, p. 867.
5. Geo. A. Ammann, *The Prairie Grouse of Michigan* (Lansing, Mich.: Michigan Department of Conservation, Game Division, 1957), p. 143.
6. Bent, *Gallinaceous Birds, op. cit.*, p. 288.
7. Coues, *Account of the Various Publications, op. cit.*, p. 439.

8. Bent, *Gallinaceous Birds, op. cit.*, p. 300.
9. Coues, *Birds of the Northwest, op. cit.*, p. 401.
10. Coues, *Account of the Various Publications, op. cit.*, p. 439.
11. Lewis is referring to the ruffed grouse.
12. John W. Aldrich, and Allen J. Duval, *Distribution of American Gallinaceous Game Birds* (U. S. Fish and Wildlife Service, Circular No. 34, 1955), p. 4.
13. Coues, *History of the Expedition, op. cit.*, Vol. III, p. 953.
14. Bent, *Gallinaceous Birds, op. cit.*, p. 136.
15. Thwaites, *Original Journals, op. cit.*, Vol. III, p. 76.
16. The original Paul Allen text of the Lewis and Clark diaries omitted the word "not" from this entry. This ommission inevitably led to confusion concerning the identity of the bird.
17. Bear berry, *Arctostaphylos uva-ursi.*
18. Coues, *History of the Expedition, op. cit.*, Vol. III, pp. 870-871.
19. Coues, *Account of the Various Publications, op. cit.*, p. 440.
20. Here Lewis refers to his comments on the range of Franklin's grouse.
21. Franklin's grouse, female.
22. Bent, *Gallinaceous Birds, op. cit.*, p. 174.
23. Coues, *History of the Expedition, op. cit.*, Vol. III, p. 936.
24. Elijah H. Criswell, *Lewis and Clark; Linguistic Pioneers* (University of Missouri Studies, 1940), Vol. XV, No. 2, p. 91.
25. These were Mandan Indians (Chief Big White, his squaw and child) whom Lewis and Clark had invited to accompany them to St. Louis and Washington for an interview with President Jefferson.
26. Thwaites, *Early Western Travels, op. cit.*, Vol. XXII, p. 297.

NOTES TO CHAPTER XIII

1. Coues, *Birds of the Northwest, op. cit.*, p. 541.
2. Bent, *North American Marsh Birds, op. cit.*, p. 358.
3. Coues, *History of the Expedition, op. cit.*, Vol. III, p. 1287.
4. Reid, *op. cit.*, p. 17.
5. Thwaites, *Original Journals, op. cit.*, Vol. II, p. 260.
6. "Jack curloo" was a vernacular name for the Hudsonian curlew.
7. Another name for the upland plover.
8. Coues, *History of the Expedition, op. cit.*, Vol. II, p. 433.
9. *Ibid.*
10. This description is repeated in Thwaites, *Original Journals, op. cit.*, Vol. VI, pp. 133-134.
11. Linnaeus, *Systema Naturae* (1789), Vol. I, p. 693.

NOTES TO CHAPTER XIV

1. Coues, *An Account of the Various Publications, op. cit.*, p. 443.
2. Coues, *History of the Expedition, op. cit.*, Vol. III, p. 881; also see footnote in Thwaites, *Original Journals, op. cit.*, Vol. IV, p. 141.
3. Thwaites, *Original Journals, op. cit.*, Vol. VI, p. 124-125.

NOTES

NOTES TO CHAPTER XV

1. A. W. Schroger, *The Passenger Pigeon* (University of Wisconsin Press, 1955), pp. 258, 265.
2. Thwaites, *Early Western Travels*, Vol. XXI, Narrative of a Journey Across the Rocky Mountains (Cleveland: A. H. Clark and Company, 1905; originally published, 1839), p. 134.
3. From the Biddle Text.
4. Coues, *History of the Expedition, op. cit.*, Vol. II, p. 398.
5. Arthur C. Bent, *Life History of North American Cuckoos, Goatsuckers, Hummingbirds and their Allies* (U. S. National Museum Bulletin No. 176, (1940), p. 240.
6. John J. Audubon, *Ornithological Biography* (Philadelphia: J. Dobson, 1839), Vol. V, p. 335.
7. Edmond C. Jaeger, "Does the Poor-will Hibernate?", *The Condor* (Jan.-Feb. 1948); Jaeger, "Further Observations on the Poor-will," *The Condor* (May-June 1949); W. L. McAtee, "Birds Do Hibernate," *Audubon Magazine* (Nov.-Dec. 1950).
8. Coues, *History of the Expedition, op. cit.*, Vol. III, p. 1294.
9. *Ibid.*, p. 1044.
10. Bent, *Cuckoos, Goatsuckers, Hummingbirds, op. cit.*, p. 387.

NOTES TO CHAPTER XVI

1. Wilson, *American Ornithology, op. cit.*
2. Reid, *op. cit.*, p. 19.
3. Coues, *History of the Expedition, op. cit.*, Vol. III, p. 877.
4. Reid, *op. cit.*, p. 19.
5. Coues, *History of the Expedition, op. cit.*, Vol. III, p. 877.

NOTES TO CHAPTER XVII

1. Western winter wren.
2. Thwaites, *Original Journals, op. cit.*, Vol. VI, pp. 130-131.
3. Setzer, *op. cit.*, p. 357.
4. Criswell, *op. cit.*, p. 84.
5. In this, Lewis was mistaken.
6. Coues, *History of the Expedition, op. cit.*, Vol. III, p. 876.
7. Thwaites, *Original Journals, op. cit.*, Vol. VI, pp. 134-135.
8. Arthur C. Bent, *Life Histories of North American Jays, Crows and Titmice* (U. S. National Museum Bulletin No. 191), p. 302.
9. Coues, *History of the Expedition, op. cit.*, Vol. II, p. 454.
10. *Ibid.*, Vol. III, p. 876.
11. Thwaites, *Original Journals, op. cit.*, Vol. III, p. 309.

12. Coues, *History of the Expedition, op. cit.*, Vol. III, p. 876.
13. Rocky Mountain jay.
14. Oregon jay.
15. Coues, *History of the Expedition, op. cit.*, Vol. II, p. 724; Vol. III, p. 876.
16. *Ibid.*, Vol. II, p. 361.
17. *Ibid.*, Vol. III, p. 875.
18. Coues, *History of the Expedition, op. cit.*, Vol. II, p. 388; Coues identified these meadowlarks, respectively, as *Sturnella neglecta*, and *Sturnella magna*.
19. *Ibid.*, Vol. III, p. 1035.
20. Criswell, *op. cit.*, p. 94.
21. Coues, *History of the Expedition, op. cit.*, Vol. I, p. 14.
22. *Ibid.*
23. Criswell, *op cit.*, p. 82.
24. Coues, *History of the Expedition, op. cit.*, Vol. I, p. 349.
25. Criswell, *op. cit.*, p. 95.

NOTES TO CHAPTER XVIII

1. Coues, *History of the Expedition, op. cit.*, Vol. II, pp. 362, 545; Vol. III, pp. 875, 891, 892, 893, 970, 1138.
2. Clearwater River.
3. Called the anchovey by Lewis and Clark.
4. This is the Eulachon, which Clark is quite correct in saying is the most delicate in flavor of any fish in the world—a statement almost identical with something I had once written myself. Clark's description was written thirty-one years before Sir John Richardson's (1836); but Richardson called it *Salmo pacificus,* wrongly taking it for a trout, as Clark did. It belongs to the smelt family, and is related to the Capelin, and is far more delicate than any trout. It was next noticed by the Pacific Railroad survey in 1858, and named by Girard *Thaleichtys stevensi.* Its present name is *T. pacificus*—David Starr Jordan and B. W. Everman, *American Food and Game Fishes* (New York: Doubleday, Page & Co., 1902), p. 227.

NOTES TO CHAPTER XIX

1. According to the Allen-Biddle text a poultice of bark and gunpowder was sufficient to cure the wound.
2. Called "rattlesnake cliffs" on outward journey.
3. Coues for unexplained reasons identified this as *Pituophis melanoleuca.*
4. The identity of this plant has not been determined. The records relating to this specimen appear to have been lost.
5. Sacajawea.
6. *Hyla regilla,* according to Coues.
7. "*Rana pretiosa,* the only frog of this region, not the spring peeper of eastern United States."—C. V. Piper.
8. *Bufo columbiensis,* according to Coues.

NOTES

NOTES TO APPENDIX

1. Thwaites, *Original Journals, op. cit.,* Vol. VII, pp. 247-252.
2. *Ibid.,* pp. 238-244.
3. *Ibid.,* pp. 309-312. From the original MS. which in 1904 was in possession of the oldest living relative of Meriwether Lewis' family, C. Harper Anderson, of Ivy Depot, Vr. This letter was subsequently deposited with the Missouri Historical Society and has been reprinted with their permission.
4. *Ibid.,* Vol. I, pp. 280-282.
5. *Ibid.,* Vol. VII, pp. 318-321.
6. Doubtless Floyd's Journals.
7. Count Volney was an illustrious French savant and writer, who visited the United States in 1797 and 1798, and was expelled from the country under the alien and sedition laws. His book, *Tableau du Climat et du Sol des Etats-Unis d'Amerique* (Paris: Courcier), on the climate and soil of the United States was published in 1803.
8. Thwaites, *Original Journals, op. cit.,* Vol. III, p. 327. Nowhere in the journals are there any indications of messages having been sent to Washington from the expedition, between leaving the Mandans in the spring of 1805 and the arrival at St. Louis in September, 1806; nor was it practicable to send such messages. Moreover, in doc. lviii, below, Jefferson practically states, on February 19, that he had heard nothing from Lewis since April 8, 1805.
9. *Ibid.,* Vol. VII, p. 328.
10. *Ibid.,* pp. 334-337.

Aechmophorus occidentalis (Lawrence), 178-179.
Aix sponsa (Linnaeus), 191-192.
Alces alces americana (Clinton), 139-140.
American Fur Company, 116.
American Philosophical Society, 2, 4, 70.
Amphibians: discovered and described by Lewis and Clark, x.
Anas discors (Linnaeus), 187.
Anas platyrhynchos Linnaeus, 188-189.
Anchovy. *See* Eulachon, 267.
Anser albifrons (Scopoli), 197.
Anser albifrons frontalis Baird, 197-198.
Anser albifrons gambelli Hartlaub, 198.
Antelope, pronghorn: abundance and distribution of, 141-146; discovery and description of, 140-142; easily killed in water, 144; habits, 142-143; hunted on horses, 145; killed for food, 283, 286; prey of wolves, 143-144; specimens collected, 146; trapped in pens, 144-145; uses of hides, 145-146.
Antilocarpa americana (Ord), 140-146.
Aplodontia rufa (Rafinesque), 118-119.
Aquila chrysaëtos canadensis (Linnaeus), 205-207.
Arctomys columbianus Ord, 99-101.
Ardea herodias Linnaeus, 183.
Ardea herodias hyperonca Oberholser, 184.
Arikara Indians, 50, 76.
Ashley, William H., 116.
Assiniboin Indians, 74, 108.
Assiniboin Post of North West Company: mentioned, 74.
Astor, John Jacob, 116.
Asyndesmus lewis (Gray), 239-240.
Avocet: detailed description of, 228-229.
Aythya collaris (Donovan), 190-191.
Aythya valisineria (Wilson), 188.

Badger: collected, 70; description of, 71-72; distribution of, 72; first reported, 70.
Baird, Brewer and Ridgway: quoted, 219.
Barnum, P. T.: museum destroyed by fire, xi; purchased part of Lewis and Clark collection, xi; specimens lost, xii.
Barton, Dr. Benjamin S., xiii, 3.
Bartramia longicauda (Bechstein), 227.
Beads: blue, white and red, 78.
Bear, black: abundance and scarcity, 52; Bradbury's reports of, 53; color phases, 54-56; hides in fur trade, 53; killed for food, 283, 286-287; Maximillian's reports of, 53; taxonomy, 56-57.
Bear, cinnamon: described, 55-56; mentioned, 57.
Bear, grizzly: abundance of, 58-59; color phases, 55, 61-62; encounters with and escapes from, 63-67; feed on buffalo carcasses, 58; feeding habits, 67-68; ferocity, 58, 63-65; first description of, 60-61; kill records, 283, 287; mentioned, ix, 54; reported by Samuel Hearne, Edward Umfreville, and Alexander Mackenzie, 57.
Bear, white. *See* Bear, grizzly.
Bee, honey, 244.
Bent, Arthur C.: quoted, 192, 194, 209, 213, 214, 224, 237, 250.
Bering, Vitus, 76.
Bighorn sheep: abundance and distribution of, 171-172; detailed description, 173-175; discovered by Duncan McGillivary, 171; laminated horn bows, 176; mentioned, 25, 168; specimens collected, 176.
Big White; subchief of Mandans, 48.
Birds: discovered and described by Lewis and Clark, x.
Bison, American: areas of abundance and scarcity, 147-151; bellowing and fighting, 154-155; bullboats and shields, 164-165; carcasses, 67; carcasses salvaged by Indians, 160;